A Guide to Rehabilitation Testimony: The Expert's Role as an Educator

About the Author

Paul M. Deutsch is a Certified Rehabilitation Counselor and a licensed Mental Health Counselor in the State of Florida. He has practiced in the fields of rehabilitation counseling and rehabilitation psychology for eighteen years. For the past twelve years of practice, Dr. Deutsch has specialized in catastrophic case management, life care planning, and rehabilitation research and writing. He has extensive experience in personal injury consultation and testimony. His research interests have focused on brain injury, spinal cord injury, and multiple amputations.

Dr. Deutsch has written and lectured extensively on the expanding role of the rehabilitation professional and on the application of rehabilitation techniques to a broader range of age groups and client needs. He has travelled extensively in the Soviet Union, where he has been participating in a research project, and where two of his books are being translated into Russian. Dr. Deutsch is also responsible for organizing and implementing the translation into English of numerous important Soviet scientific works, and several of these will be published under the imprint of Paul M. Deutsch Press in 1990.

Dr. Deutsch is co-author of Volumes 8 and 9 in the series entitled *Damages in Tort Actions*; *A Guide to Rehabilitation*, and *Innovations in Head Injury Rehabilitation*, and has authored numerous monographs and journal articles.

About the Contributors

Dennis A. Vandenberg is a defense attorney certified by The Florida Bar and the American Bar Association (Member, Tort and Insurance Practice Section) and the Palm Beach County Bar Association, practicing in the area of professional liability, including legal and medical accounting; insurance coverage; and products liability, with the law firm of Peterson & Bernard, Attorneys at Law, in West Palm Beach, Florida.

Paul E. Godlewski is a personal injury trial specialist certified by the Minnesota State Bar Association, practicing in the areas of plaintiffs personal injury, product liability, and wrongful death with the law firm of Schwebel, Goetz and Sieben, P.A. in Minneapolis, Minnesota.

Dr. Frederick A. Raffa holds the position of Professor of Economics at the University of Central Florida in Orlando, having served as Chairman of the UCF Department of Economics there from 1977 to 1980. He has published numerous monographs and professional articles, as well as three books. He has performed extensive contract research work in the field of labor economics and acts as a consultant to government, business, and financial institutions in matters of economic evaluation. In addition, Dr. Raffa has an active consulting practice providing litigation support in matters involving personal injury and wrongful death. He earned his MBA in Finance in 1966 and Ph.D. in Economics in 1969 from Florida State University. He maintains professional memberships in the American Economics Association, the Southern Economics Association, and the Western Economics Association.

Mr. Richard C. Raffa is a graduate of Florida State University and the University of Central Florida, receiving a Bachelor of Business Administration degree in Accountancy in 1975. He is president of Liberty Financial Group, a structured settlement company located in Orlando, Florida, which specializes in structured settlements involving catastrophic personal injury and wrongful death litigation.

A Guide to Rehabilitation Testimony: The Expert's Role as an Educator

Paul M. Deutsch, Ph.D.

With contributions from:

Dennis A. Vandenberg
Paul E. Godlewski
Frederick A. Raffa, Ph.D.
Richard C. Raffa

Copyright © 1990 by Paul M. Deutsch Press, Inc.

All rights reserved.

No part of this book may be reproduced, stored in a retrieval system, or transmitted in any form or by any means, electronic, mechanical, photocopying, microfilming, recorded, or otherwise, without written permission from the Publisher.

Printed in the United States of America.

Copies may be ordered from:

Order Department
Paul M. Deutsch Press, Inc.
2208 Hillcrest Street
Orlando, Florida 32803

Telephone: 1-800-999-8773

ISBN: 1-878205-02-1
Library of Congress Card Catalog Number: 90-93269

Keystroking, coding, and typesetting by Stephanie Murphy
Printing by Arcata Graphics Company, Brentwood, Tennessee

KF
8961
.D48
1990

The following works have been reprinted with the permission of Matthew Bender & Co.:

1. *Damages in Tort Actions* (1990) Vol. 8: pages 112-9 to 112-11; pages 112-3 to 112-6; pages 112-7 to 112-8; pages 112A-4 to 112A-18.

2. *Rehabilitation Testimony* (1985): pages 4-5.

Table of Contents

About the Author v

About the Contributors vi

Acknowledgement xiii

Foreword xv

1   The Dual Role of the Rehabilitation Expert 1

2   Utilizing the Rehabilitation Expert:
    A Defense Attorney's Perspective 9
      by Dennis A. Vandenberg

3   Utilizing the Rehabilitation Expert:
    A Plaintiff Attorney's Perspective 25
      by Paul E. Godlewski

4   Qualifying the Expert and Defining the
    Role of the Rehabilitation Professional 43

5   The Presentation of the Evaluation, Data
    Gathering, and Test Procedures 73

6   Presenting the Non-Catastrophic Case 97

7   Presenting the Catastrophic Injury
    Case and Life Care Plan 183

8   The Role of the Economist: Coordinating
    with the Rehabilitation Expert 305
      by Frederick A. Raffa, Ph.D.

9   Understanding Structured Settlements:
    The Role of the Rehabilitation
    Professional in Working with the
    Annuity Broker 323
      by Richard C. Raffa

10 Glossary of Legal Terms 333

Appendix A	Philosophical Focus for the Rehabilitation Professional: Nine Steps to Reducing Stress in Testimony	373
Appendix B	Questions for Qualifying the Rehabilitation Expert	377
Appendix C	Questions for Educating the Judge or Jury on Evaluation Procedures	383
Appendix D	Questions for the Non-Catastrophic Rehabilitation Case	387
Appendix E	Questions for Presentation of the Catastrophic Injury	389
Appendix F-1	Questions for Attorneys to Use in Deposing the Injured Party	393
Appendix F-2	Clinical Interview and History for Chronic Pain/Chronic Disability	403
Appendix F-3	Clinical Interview and History for Head and Spinal Cord Injury	417
Appendix F-4	Clinical Interview and History for Pediatrics	437
Appendix G	File Check List for Testimony Preparation	453
Appendix H	Life Care Plan Shell	457

Acknowledgement

It is typical on such pages to express thanks to family, friends, and colleagues who have in some way provided support (moral or through contributions) to the development of a text.

In this case, I feel the need to break with tradition. It is my wish to thank the practitioners in rehabilitation counseling, rehabilitation nursing, and rehabilitation psychology who have lent such strong support to my work in rehabilitation, life care planning and catastrophic case management over the years. Your encouraging words, attendance at seminars, and purchase of my texts have given a large, extra measure of satisfaction and a sense of accomplishment to my career. Your willingness to network, respond to questions, and interact professionally has been a reflection of the strong sense of professionalism our rehabilitation field has developed. I'm proud to be a part of this group and proud to have been able to contribute to its development.

Foreword

The advent of litigation is a major force in shaping public policy in private industry and has accelerated at a geometric pace over the past ten to fifteen years. The impact on a broad range of industries is apparent in the policies, procedures and processes implemented in day-to-day business. This has effected hiring policies, equipment and manufacturing design, product design, and packaging and certainly, not least, pricing policies. Public policy has been equally impacted and shaped. Certainly, this has had both a good and a bad result. Although, for example, many companies have decried product liability laws as an unfair windfall for attorneys and a major cost factor in pricing, there appears little doubt that it has forced greater product safety. This has occurred in an environment where concern for worker and public safety is often not a major factor in shaping corporate responsibility.

Overall, the legal community has had a far-reaching impact on many areas of our life today and rehabilitation is by no means left untouched. Even in this arena, the legal and insurance industries have played a significant role in broadening and reshaping the professions of rehabilitation counseling, rehabilitation nursing, and rehabilitation psychology. The effect has been largely positive, but it has created a health-related profession that of necessity must be involved in the legal or forensic arena. Whether Social Security, Workers' Compensation, Supplemental Security Income, long-term disability, personal injury (civil tort), federal tort claims, medical malpractice, Longshoremen's Act workers, or even handicapped children under the federal mainstreaming laws (PL 94-142) almost all disabled clients are somehow involved with the legal community. From this environment comes the need for "expert testimony". A role created not by our profession but by the lawyers, and despite their attempts (in some instances) to decry our involvement or to "put down" the expert witness, this is clearly a necessity created by lawyers that is here to stay.

Whether called into a case as a treating professional or as a consultant in litigation, every rehabilitation professional must be prepared to confront the forensic arena in a professional, open and honest fashion with a clear understanding of the correct role. It is the understanding of the legal process insofar as it involves rehabilitation professionals and a clear view of the role which must be assumed by the expert that forms the purpose and basis for this text.

1

The Dual Role of the Rehabilitation Expert

Initiating the counseling or consulting relationship with a disabled client is a significant responsibility for the rehabilitation professional. It is important to begin by establishing an effective rapport and helping the client develop a clear understanding of the role of the rehabilitation professional, the steps that are going to be taken in the evaluation process, the responsibility involved in implementing rehabilitation recommendations and what the client or family can expect from the involvement of this professional. The need for rapport-building in orientation is no less great and in fact may even be greater in those instances in which the rehabilitation expert is called upon for consultation in litigation. Because the rehabilitation professional may have only one or two opportunities to meet with, evaluate, and counsel with the disabled client and family members, it is particularly important that time be set aside to orient the client to the process and build an effective rapport that will allow for a meaningful relationship.

The focus of this chapter is to explore the dual role of the rehabilitation professional who is consulting in the litigation process and to provide a clear and concise orientation statement which can be utilized as an effective introduction for the client.

Introduction of the Rehabilitation Professional

An effective approach is first to introduce your own professional training, background, and expertise in a clear but brief statement to the rehabilitation client and family. It is important to keep in mind that the client is an equal member of the rehabilitation team and must be treated, regardless of the nature of the disability, with respect as a participating, decision-making adult. Obviously, parameters must be set, based on the limitations involved in each disability case but to underestimate the client is a poor way to begin building rapport. Of necessity, the rehabilitation professional should remember that a patient is someone typically involved in acute care treatment that lies back passively and allows the physician to perform necessary services. The assumption is that what the physician is doing will result in an effective treatment and healing process. When the acute care stage has been completed and the disabled individual is moving into post-acute rehabilitation, it is necessary to understand that this entire concept of "the patient" must be left behind. It is not possible to passively participate in rehabilitation. Instead, each client must be a fully participating team member and this has to be reinforced by the rehabilitation professional through interaction with the client. Verbalizing this belief without backing it through appropriate behavioral interaction will represent the first backward step in the effort to achieve appropriate rehabilitation goals.

The first step in this process is making sure that the consumer, the disabled client, fully understands who this professional is: educational background, work background, and expertise in this particular disability must be understood. It is clear that this is far different from the way we typically approach the physician. There is a tendency on all our parts to go into a doctor's office almost as if we felt that all M.D.'s are created equal and rarely do they take the time to explain their background and even more rarely does the patient take the time to question their abilities, training, or expertise. By taking time to educate the client in this fashion we are showing a degree of respect which is necessary for us to gain the confidence for both the client and the family.

The Dual Role of the Rehabilitation Professional

In the instance the rehabilitation client is referred because of the need for consultation in this area of expertise in the litigation process it is extremely important that the dual role of the rehabilitation professional be understood. Each client should be told in a straightforward and forthright fashion the primary and secondary purposes of their referral for the rehabilitation evaluation. A suggested approach follows:

> You have been referred for a two-fold purpose to complete a rehabilitation evaluation. The primary purpose of this evaluation is to allow me to act as a consultant in the litigation process. In that role, I have the responsibility of working within the damages portion of the case and in that regard, I must learn the functional implications of your disability and how it effects you in your day-to-day life.
>
> My secondary purpose in completing this evaluation, although it has equal importance, is to be available to you and your family to make rehabilitation recommendations and to act as a resource person in solving problems or difficulties which might arise during the rehabilitation process. I will be taking time over the next few minutes to explain each of these roles to you in more detail.

Role in Litigation

It is at this point that the rehabilitation professional should provide more detailed information on the primary reason for the attorney's referral of this patient. Although this information is being provided assuming that the plaintiff attorney has referred the patient for a full evaluation, the orientation is only modestly changed and no less important if you are evaluating a disabled client having been referred by a defense attorney for an independent exam. The primary difference in orientation is that there is no expectation on the part of the rehabilitation professional to interact with the client to implement the rehabilitation plan or act as a resource person subsequent to litigation. For that reason, no unnecessary modification to the orientation process should be made.

A suggested framework for this portion of the client introduction process follows:

> In my role as a consultant in litigation, my primary purpose is to educate all parties concerned as to the nature of your disability and how it may effect you in your independent living activities, your ability to demonstrate independent living skills, your vocational development, and your educational development. I am concerned with not only how this disability effects you but also how it impacts your family. So my role as an educator will extend to helping all parties involved understand the full impact of the injury as it relates to you the client, as well as each of your family members.
>
> In this role, I will be working primarily in the damages portion of the case. As each doctor may have given you an anatomical rating, it is my responsibility to focus on functional impairment. The anatomical rating or percentage of your body that is involved in the injury cannot be related directly to day-to-day activities. This is something we will be accomplishing through our evaluation today.
>
> In fulfilling this role, I will be completing two primary analyses. The first is a life care plan which is designed to outline all of your needs as dictated by the onset of the disability through the end of your life expectancy. Not only will I be outlining all of these necessities, but I will also be evaluating the cost of each of these needs so that it can be effectively communicated to those interested.
>
> The second step in my report is the completion of a Vocational Worksheet. Here, I will be exploring the vocational handicaps which have resulted from your injury and how it impacts your ability to be placed in the labor market and the range of jobs for which you can still compete. I will look at strictly vocational rehabilitation recommendations including their cost and duration and I will be evaluating the loss or diminution of your capacity to earn a living after the accident as compared to before the accident.

Obviously, the rehabilitation professional must adjust the above example if the client has a non-catastrophic injury and does not require a life care plan. If the client is catastrophic, but so severely impaired that no consideration of post-accident earning capacity would be given, it is still appropriate to discuss the Vocational Worksheet insofar as it involves demonstrating the loss of capacity to earn.

It is particularly important for you (the client) to understand what our relationship must be and what my role within the courtroom setting will be.

It is essential that we have the type of rapport and relationship in which you can openly and honestly point out your differences of opinion or feelings from my opinions and recommendations. My role is to make sure as you are making decisions regarding your future that you have considered all of the options as well as the consequences and we must be able, behind the closed doors of my office, to argue while still maintaining a good relationship. It is important, if you are reading my report or my deposition, to carefully write down any questions you have and don't waste time by becoming upset or angry. If you disagree or if you feel I have missed some important information or failed to make an important recommendation, you must contact me and communicate this information. It is impossible for me to make the necessary changes and/or compromises if this communication does not take place. You must keep in mind that rehabilitation and rehabilitation planning is a series of compromises. The best alternative, and perhaps the only ideal alternative, would be for an injury not to have occurred in the first place. Once it has, everything we are doing is a compromise to balance your interests, your values, your motivators, and your goals against your limitations and the needs that your disability creates. It is quite possible that we won't agree in every instance and that I will feel the need to make recommendations which you would prefer not to pursue. Nevertheless, wherever possible, it is important for you to keep an open mind and for us to be able to enter the courtroom with my life care plan and Vocational Worksheet, reflecting to the extent possible, those recommendations and services of which you are willing to partake.

Role in Courtroom

The next step in the orientation process is to make sure the client fully understands your role once you have entered the courtroom setting. I find that by communicating openly to the client about the process and about your opinions, you will solve many of the problems which often develop to cause disagreement, anger, or loss of respect. A suggested discussion follows:

Once I have entered the courtroom, it is important for you to understand that I do not work for you (the client), your attorney (the plaintiff's attorney), or the insurance company and their attorney. My sole responsibility in the courtroom is to act as an educator with the jury as my class. If I act as an advocate for you, a role which is really fulfilled by your attorney, then the jury may appreciate my support of my client but will fail to give credibility to my testimony. I am there to teach the jury and the judge about the disability, its functional impact, and the long-term needs it creates. It is important that they have sufficient information to be able to evaluate the damages portion of the case effectively. Although I certainly would want them to understand and accept my opinions, I believe the opinions of the professional are icing on the cake. Each step in the life care plan and each step of the Vocational Worksheet should be solidly based on fact and be able to stand alone demonstrating to the jury why I have reached the conclusions I have reached. For this reason, it is important for you to listen carefully to both the questions that are being asked and the answers that are being given. I am not there to defend my position, an opinion, or the client. I am there to answer questions in my role as an educator in rehabilitation. The opposing counsel has the right to ask what is known as hypothetical questions. They may or may not directly relate to my findings in the evaluation process. Regardless, I am going to be asked to assume certain facts under an hypothesis and I will answer in a straightforward and truthful fashion. If the hypothesis is inaccurate, your attorney has the right to object but if the judge allows the question, I will respond. I view this as an important process of helping the jury understand the nature of the disability and its impact.

Your responsibility is to write down any of concern or questions and come to me after the litigation so that I can help you understand fully what I was trying to communicate or how our recommendations might be implemented. There is no cost to any of our clients post-litigation to come back for such explanations or instructions.

The Role of the Rehabilitation Professional Outside the Courtroom

Now that time has been taken to help each disabled client understand the courtroom role of the rehabilitation consultant, the effort should also be made to help them understand how they can utilize what is being done even in the instance in which this rehabilitation professional is not necessarily going to be used for the implementation of the life care plan or the rehabilitation recommendations. A suggested format follows:

> Outside the courtroom setting, my role as a rehabilitation professional is to be a client advocate. This includes helping both the family and the client obtain appropriate benefits, contact appropriate durable or replenishable medical supply companies, and organize the rehabilitation team which will implement the plan in the home area.
>
> My primary role to the rehabilitation client who has been referred first for litigation consultation, is to act as a resource person. This has been an effective program for myself and my staff since we developed it early in my practice. We encourage any client who has been through a rehabilitation evaluation with our office to feel free to call us to ask questions regarding any aspect of their disability. This may include asking questions regarding a new facility which has opened, new techniques which have developed, resolutions to problems which are occurring, equipment recommendations or any other aspects that arise. This is done at no charge to the client as long as it can be handled through telephone conferencing. Although it may seem magnanimous, in truth, it is not. It is a helpful service to us as well as to the client. Clients and their families are particularly interested in their disability and are often finding important articles in the popular newspapers and magazines which raise issues that have not yet appeared in the professional journals. By contacting us, they are keeping us informed. If the information already exists in our database, we are happy to share it and it costs us little to take the time to do so. If it does not exist, then we have been shown an area that must be researched and added to our database and in return for your assistance, we are happy to share that information.
>
> It is important for you as a rehabilitation client and for your family members to recognize that you are evaluating me as a rehabilitation professional at the same time I am evaluating you as a

rehabilitation client. Keep in mind that you are an equal and active participating member of the rehabilitation team and it is necessary for us, whether it be in the consultation process or in the rehabilitation process, to have the kind of rapport that will allow us to work together effectively. This is important particularly when we are attempting to answer questions or make decisions involving the disability and the aging process. Since age and disability tend to create greater dependency over a period of time, we must be able to make decisions when developing a life care plan, as to how we will approach those problems many years into the future. It is only through an effective working relationship that we are going to be able to answer these questions and help you meet these needs.

Summary

It is clear from the recommended format presented in this chapter that great importance is being placed on the initial orienttation. The client must have an opportunity to ask questions and must feel comfortable prior to proceeding with the evaluation. The final step in the orientation is to explain the evaluation process itself including the review of the medical, psychological and vocational information, the clinical history and interview through which you will be taking the client, and the appropriate vocational or psychological testing which you will be completing and/or ordering as a part of your process. It is common to expect to spend as much as 30 to 40 minutes in this initial process of orientation and rapport-building and it is critical that it does not appear to be rushed. In the instance in which the team approach is used to complete the evaluation, a very common practice in my office, then you should also take the time to introduce the other participating members and explain their role and purpose, as well as give a brief summary of their background.

Having completed the orientation and feeling comfortable with the rapport that has been built, the evaluation process can begin.

2

Utilizing the Rehabilitation Expert: A Defense Attorney's Perspective

Purpose

The general theory in the aggressive defense of a personal injury action is to minimize the various elements of damage. Specifically, the defense wishes to demonstrate that the functional impairment is less than depicted by the plaintiff's Rehabilitation/Habilitation Expert (RHE). To convince a jury that the reduction in earning capacity is less than that advocated by plaintiff's counsel is the other position taken.

To envision it as a matrix of elements, the defense expert seeks to establish that employability of the plaintiff is high and that the enjoyment of his life is not hampered in any realistic manner. And, of course, that future medical or rehabilitation therapies are less extensive than shown by others. Another side of the matrix would be to establish that the pre-morbid condition of the plaintiff was less favorable than projected by the plaintiff.

Another avenue is for the defense RHE to serve solely as a weapon of attack against the plaintiff's RHE. Primarily, that is a situation in which the defense expert is used for consultation. The plaintiff's plan may be more subject to attack, but an alternative plan or option would not be presented to the jury (i.e., there is no need for rehabilitation).

Possibly the last facet of the matrix exists where the plaintiff is truly disabled or impaired to an extreme degree. The emphasis shifts to establishing that the pre-morbid status and prospects for that individual were far less than projected by plaintiff's counsel or his experts.

Rehabilitation/habilitation is one of the more flexible areas of expert testimony, as it incorporates several overlapping elements of damages: (1) past and future, (2) physical injury, (3) functional impairment, (4) employment, (5) earning capacity, (6) enjoyment of life, (7) emotional/psychological injury, and (8) intellectual impairment.

With this flexibility, defense counsel has the means at his disposal for not only an attack on the plaintiff's proposals, but a creative means by which to offer to the jury a reasonable alternative. This does require a sense of direction dictated by counsel, insightful analysis by both counsel and his experts, and the communication of their conclusions in an effective manner to a jury.

Investigation

Investigation is the process of obtaining information in a lawsuit without the structure or formality of court-governed discovery, i.e. depositions, requests for production, interrogatories. It can commence immediately after the accident, and continue up to the time of judgment, and run concurrent with the more formalized discovery tools. Plaintiff's counsel need not be advised of the investigative efforts to the same degree as those efforts undertaken under the rules of discovery.

Aggressive counsel, both on the plaintiff and defense side, lay a considerable amount of the groundwork in this phase for the successful prosecution or defense of a lawsuit. Generally, plaintiff's counsel will have entered the picture well in advance of the insurance carrier or defense counsel, and accordingly, there can be much catch-up work required of the defense.

At some point along this time-line, defense counsel may decide to retain an investigative RHE, in addition to the RHE intended to be called as a witness in the trial. Possibly the former expert has no inclination to become involved as a direct participant in litigation, lacks all of the proper credentials, or simply doesn't have the special aptitude for communication with a jury. Nonetheless, that individual can be most helpful and is frequently the most accessible to defense counsel in terms of communicating ideas or analyzing the information as it is generated.

The obvious first point to be examined by the RHE is the true extent of the plaintiff's injury, both in current terms and the future. This can set the pace and direction for future handling of the matter. The records should be analyzed in detail by this RHE, with appropriate communication, either by face-to-face conference or by reports on a timely basis. The reports (either verbal or written) are generally not subject to discovery by plaintiff's counsel, and therefore, may be less formal or structured. The form and content of reports should be discussed with retaining defense counsel before their issuance.

At this stage, the RHE can give a thumbnail sketch on the "likely" future scenarios of the plaintiff and how they will be portrayed to the jury. It is unlikely that much in the way of background information has been generated at this point. Nonetheless, the expert has the experience to advise as to potential sources of investigation and future areas for discovery, particularly those requiring considerable lead time, i.e., requests for tax records, military records or social security documents. Consideration of other experts for retention is also important.

Evaluation of the investigative material is necessary for analysis and planning. The material may include general background information on the plaintiff, items gained from other court actions brought by the plaintiff, his worker's compensation file, and all other sources accessible as public record or obtained through investigative technique. Hopefully, the RHE is astute enough to determine what records and sources are missing from material which may have been voluntarily provided by plaintiff's counsel; and the probable course and timing of the continuing evaluations by other experts, such as the social security or worker's compensation people.

At this point, the RHE may be able to identify, based upon past experience with plaintiff's counsel, who will be retained by plaintiff's counsel to serve as the trial RHE. This provides the opportunity for an early accumulation of information on that expert by defense counsel, including prior depositions, transcripts, and trial testimony. Reports and material presented by that expert at seminars or conferences should be accumulated by the investigative RHE, as it is not normally available to defense counsel.

Occasionally, the source of documents to be obtained later by discovery is also not as obvious to defense counsel as it is to the RHE. For example, some corporations separate their personnel departments and their medical benefit plans to the extent that separate subpoenas must be issued to obtain both sets of records. The same would hold true to state agencies and the myriad of bureaucracies involved therein.

Very high on the list of benefits to early contact with an RHE are those special contacts an experienced professional should have and the access to his ability to obtain information without invading the privacy of the plaintiff.

As information is developed, the RHE should construct a timeline for the health, medical, and work history of the plaintiff. This will be helpful in preparing the discovery and the presentation at trial as to the inconsistency and variability of the plaintiff's background. It may also provide leads as to missing periods of time in the plaintiff's life as a result of causes as variant as military service, prison time, or the use of drugs.

Though most injuries with claims for worker's compensation benefits or social security are obvious, nonetheless some are not as clear. There may be other less obvious programs or expanded coverages under the familiar programs of which the plaintiff or his attorney may well be unaware. This raises an interesting ethical situation. If the defense notifies plaintiff's counsel of such program he would presumably be bound to advise the plaintiff of the availability of such benefits, though it may be admissible in court before a jury as a "collateral source". This is a two-edged sword in that it shows the availability of public programs to the jury for this type of injury; therefore, the unlikely change that the plaintiff will go untreated.

This should act to prevent double payment to the plaintiff and a larger verdict. On the other hand, it does provide the financial means for the plaintiff to continue the litigation with a lightened financial burden. It also finances some of the plaintiff's expert preparation, such as social security evaluations or medical treatment through worker's compensation.

Depending upon the rule of evidence or statute, the collateral source may not be admissible unless there has actually been payment, rather than a prospect for such payment. Accordingly, enrollment of the plaintiff into a program may insure the admissibility of that evidence at time of trial; again, a point for planning.

In evaluating the local programs, information should be generated as to the availability of the necessary rehabilitation specialists. This information will be utilized at a later time to generate a realistic and reasonable program for the plaintiff, in light of available resources. That is, a program formulated in a lower cost area closer to the plaintiff's roots would be inappropriate if there were not sufficient programs or specialists within a reasonable distance to that locale. In addition, when dealing with cluster homes or institutions, the expert must be able to advise defense counsel of their true nature and their reputation in the venue of trial, but also where those institutions are located. Not many things can be more devastating for defense counsel than to rely upon an institution as a viable alternative, and then to have it disclosed as the subject of a grand jury inquiry for patient abuse or sexual molestation. This information is also necessary for later presentation to the jury, in terms of statistics, videotape, or other demonstrative aids concretely depicting this facility to the jury.

As an adjunct to the evaluation of local programs, the RHE should be able to provide insight into the local programs. This should extend not only to the obvious price discrepancies between institutional settings versus the homebound one-on-one programs, but the geographical differences and quality information. This is particularly important in our transient society. Many people migrate to the high cost of living areas (Southeast Florida, Southern California) for work, but once totally disabled, they may well return to their roots, where costs for such services are considerably down-scale.

The essence of this phase of the litigation and the relationship between the defense counsel and the investigative RHE is one of communication and responsiveness. That is, the lead time required for much of the discovery and the foundations which are laid in this phase of litigation cannot wait for a leisurely approach, but rather are served effectively only by aggressive tackling of the problem. Procrastination and failure to attend to detail is unacceptable to the defendant and the attorney. The true purpose of the RHE at this point, is to analyze information and to provide a synthesis of it to defense counsel on a real-time basis.

Discovery

This describes the aspect of litigation, or the procedural machinery for discovering the factual basis of a party's claim or defense. There are court rules, statutes, codes of evidence, and case law which not only enable the parties to accomplish this, but also define the parameters within which they must work. Not only are the methods defined, but also the timing and the sanctions for failure to comply with discovery.

It is in the stage of litigation that the RHE investigator may be transformed into the expert to be presented at trial. In addition, that person may help defense counsel in the attack on plaintiff's position by aiding in the discovery process, and also by his contribution to establishing the credibility of the defense's view of the damages.

For the RHE to be credible before the jury, it is almost always necessary for that expert to have conducted some type of examination or evaluation of the plaintiff on a first-hand, face-to-face basis. This may be accomplished by stipulation with plaintiff's counsel, or pursuant to one of the discovery tools, such as the rule for physical and mental examinations of persons (Florida Rule of Civil Procedure 1.360; Federal Rule of Civil Procedure 35). The circumstances of the appointment may range from the expert serving as one reporting to the court as truly an independent expert witness to the situation, wherein he is essentially hand-picked by defense counsel, and so referred to at time of trial.

In many situations, defense counsel will review the case with the RHE in advance of such an order being obtained, particularly if that expert was not the investigative RHE, to be relatively certain that opinions eventually obtained will probably not be more damaging than the plaintiff's RHE and to ascertain if the expert has previously been contacted concerning the matter, so as to avoid a conflict of interest. Again, this is the phase calling upon the judgment and experience of both the rehabilitation/habilitation expert and defense counsel. If the RHE is new to the case, this is the appropriate time for the first of many face-to-face conferences or in-depth discussions between the two. Both individuals should be totally conversant with the file material. From this understanding, the goals should be determined and the direction and tactical decisions formulated. By that, the RHE should begin providing much of the information detailed above in the investigative section to defense counsel so that discovery can be initiated on a timely basis. The RHE should begin thinking in terms of the nature and parameters of any testing to be conducted upon the plaintiff and the necessary logistics, such as travel and time requirements for the expert or the plaintiff. Specifically, the RHE can have input in terms of the appropriateness of the plaintiff entering local or distant programs or institutions. Input should be forthcoming as to advisability of discovery to be undertaken by defense counsel, such as depositions or videotaping of current facilities where plaintiff is receiving care.

The plaintiff's RHE will, at some time, be disclosed, either by the investigative material, answers to interrogatory questions, by filing of his report, and eventually his deposition and disclosure on the witness list. Information should be forthcoming on that witness's reputation, prior testimony or opinions, and an in-depth analysis of that material.

Both RHE and defense counsel should be very cognizant of the time parameters. Most discovery provides for a mailing period, and then 30 days within which to respond or object. If an objection is made, or if it is necessary to obtain a court order requiring the opposition to comply with a request for discovery, this imposes a delay in the litigation. Discovery is not obtained overnight and is frequently delayed more than what would seem to be reasonable or to be in good faith.

The material obtained by investigation or voluntarily provided by plaintiff's counsel will, in most cases, be repeated in responses to requests for that material as part of the discovery process. It should be repeatedly examined to determine if something is missing which, particularly on its face, would not be obvious to defense counsel. For example, the underlying test data input for an MMPI might not be provided, but it is probably retained by a testing psychologist. The same would also hold true of a day-in-the-life videotape of the plaintiff. The film may show some aspect of rehabilitation or habilitation therapy which is particularly damaging, but the experienced observer may be able to conclude there is missing information or a grossly edited videotape.

The examination should be appropriate, depending upon the circumstances. It should contemplate referral to other appropriate experts, such as psychologists or additional medical experts, another point for planning. Timing can be important if there is a learning aspect to the testing process. Repetition of the same test might not be appropriate if it has just been conducted by plaintiff's examining or treating RHE. It should also be noted that, depending upon the governing rules and the persons, such as plaintiff's paralegal and other experts, a court reporter, or it may even be videotaped. Objectivity and professionalism can be effective in defeating anything to be accomplished by those tactics.

Occasionally, the plaintiff will, of his own volition or by prompting from counsel, seek to become the patient or client of an examining expert, whether it be a physician or rehabilitation expert. Before undertaking that course, the expert should contact the defense counsel. Though that could add to the credibility of the witness by a display of confidence, it has other implications which must be explored with defense counsel on a case-by-case basis. Specifically, that may shift the confidential or protected relationship from the defense attorney to the patient and the plaintiff's attorney. This impairment of the protected and free-flow of communication may not be acceptable.

A report will probably be the end result of this examination. Defense counsel may request a conference to discuss the opinions prior to it being reduced to written form. Suffice it to say that there are factors of which the defense counsel is highly sensitive governing the content of the report, which are beyond the purview of the RHE's knowledge and understanding. That is not to say that the opinions or their truthfulness should be subject to manipulation by defense counsel. Rather, the report may not be desired, as it may be discoverable, or perhaps the content may need clarification as to its assumptions. The format of the report should cover the information reviewed, the nature of the testing, the results of the testing, and any conclusions or opinions arrived at. The detail is governed by the particular circumstance.

It should be kept in mind that the report will be analyzed by many people to include defense counsel, plaintiff's counsel, the other RHE, the insurance carrier, the court, and potentially the jury. It will, in many cases, also serve as the basis for other expert opinions, such as the annuitist, accountant, or economist who will take certain opinions and project them within their expertise. This is particularly true of the life care plan opinions of the RHE. This imposes a high degree of care upon the RHE in the preparation of the report, not only as to accuracy and completeness, but also just plain common sense, structuring, and grammar. The report is prepared by a professional and should project that.

The last practical note is that the report should be addressed and sent to defense counsel, unless directed otherwise. Depending upon the rules and law in the particular jurisdiction, continued work by the RHE may or may not be permissible. Consultation should be obtained with the defense attorney as to that aspect. That is a scheduling matter that must be accounted for in the preparation for the examination.

The RHE will, at some point in time, probably be deposed by plaintiff's counsel. Preparation and conduct at a deposition is beyond the scope of this chapter. Suffice it to say that the expert should have an ample conference with defense counsel to again concentrate on the facts and details of the case. The scheduling of the examination, conferences, depositions, and appearance at trial must be accommodated. The expert can be challenged on each and every aspect of his review of the material, familiarity with it, the course and conduct of the examination and the opinions. The plaintiff's attorney is there to test the knowledge of the witness and also to judge the relative effectiveness of the defense RHE's presentation versus his own. That obviously affects his thinking as to the strengths and weaknesses of his case.

As the witness is an expert, plaintiff's counsel is entitled to ask hypothetical questions. By that, the witness is asked to assume, just for the sake of the question, and then to provide his opinion from those facts. Primarily, those will be facts from the viewpoint of the plaintiff, or what they think they will establish before the jury at time of trial. This is a serious area for discussion with defense counsel. This is frequently the method by which a defense expert is rotated or turned into the plaintiff's expert, given those assumed facts, which are then established before the jury at trial. Hence, the plaintiff now has two experts supporting his position, but he had to pay for only one.

Evaluation / Settlement

The RHE can be of great benefit to defense counsel during the evaluation and settlement process, drawing upon his general experience and his specific analysis of the case at hand. By keeping in touch with both plaintiff and defense counsel, he is able to accumulate a base of knowledge as to relative value in several cases. This knowledge may become specific enough to advise defense counsel as to the trial or settlement posturing usually employed by plaintiff's counsel.

Insightful analysis can also provide an educated estimation as to the "true" nature of the injury and probable settlement postures of the plaintiff, apart from his attorney. Is it the plaintiff who will continue to medically improve and re-enter the mainstream work force? Are there anticipated points of financial or psychological vulnerability which can be exploited? The parameters of public programs, resources of the plaintiff, and the "street-wise" reality of the case are some of the factors to be considered. The RHE with a good base of information and insight into the particular case at hand can be of real benefit to defense counsel during the somewhat ephemeral process of evaluation and settlement of a lawsuit.

As part of that early investigation analysis of the record and testimony, the RHE may also provide information on the life expectancy of the plaintiff. That information may be used to hire an epidemiologist or medical expert to testify on the reduction of life expectancy, in addition to providing that information to an annuitist. If a reduced life expectancy is accepted by the underwriter or annuity company, the structured settlement package can be improved to a dramatic degree.

Inherent in the evaluation/settlement process is a desire by defense counsel to know how the plaintiff is approaching settlement and how offers are being evaluated. Specifically, does the plaintiff truly believe that the proceeds must be sufficient to satisfy the requirements of the inflated plaintiff's RHE's life care plan? Or, in the alternative, is the plaintiff giving full consideration to the public programs and other collateral sources in determining exactly what is required as to the amount of net settlement proceeds? Aiding defense counsel in the presentation of his settlement offer or package should include documentation to support the availability and appropriateness of public programs. Input from the RHE on these same points serves as a guide to the defendant in structuring its offer. That is, the offer may be more appropriately matched to the needs of the plaintiff, given a more accurate analysis, i.e., a deferred compensation plan to a financially sophisticated plaintiff.

Presentation

The end product of the foregoing is the presentation to the jury. This requires the ongoing organization and preparation by both the RHE and defense counsel. It draws upon the expert's general knowledge of the field and his detailed and accurate understanding of the case at hand. Combine the foregoing with polished verbal skills, the appropriate appearance for the local courtroom; and this will with most important factor, <u>credibility</u>, provide an effective communication of the ideas and be persuasive to the jury.

Credibility is a combination of honesty and professionalism. As a practical matter, this means that opposing counsel is unable to impeach the witness's credentials, hands-on experience, or knowledge of a particular case. The tools of impeachment include misrepresentations in credentials and the use of prior reports of sworn testimony, wherein a differing opinion was given.

The standard questions on credibility concern the fees charged for the service, the split of the expert's work between plaintiff and defense, and prior associations with defense counsel on cases. The witness must not appear to be a hired gun who will say anything for his favorite defense lawyer for a price. Confrontation of the witness with his own advertisements placed in trial attorney publications is also effective to show the "paid for and packaged" approach of a witness. Fees should be fair but reasonable. The appearance of impeachment may also be achieved if the witness becomes flustered during examination, even if the witness was not impeached on the factual content of his testimony. Preparation should diminish this risk.

The organizational aspect of the presentation revolves around the adherence to time constraints and file control. The expert must learn from defense counsel, as soon as possible, the expected trial date, actual trial date, and its docket duration. The docket may be for a very limited period of time, such as one week, or maybe for practical purposes ongoing for a considerable period of time. These dates, along with the court's trial order, give the participants a framework for scheduling not only the court appearance, but the identification and listing of experts, lay witnesses, and documents. That framework can impose limitations upon defense counsel and his expert as to the commitment to be deposed, completion of work on the matter, and identification and production or inspection of demonstrative aids, such as charts, videotapes, photographs, or other items to be submitted to the jury. This requires planning to prevent forgotten witnesses or documents which should have been timely disclosed and listed and are therefore, inadmissible and of no use when later discovered. These frameworks or time parameters can vary from jurisdiction to jurisdiction and from court to court. A well organized and trained staff at both ends of the relationship will go far to minimize last minute preparation and undue stress.

The material and resources should be continually updated on almost a real-time basis. As additional witnesses are deposed, including opposing experts, that material will be forwarded to the expert at a pace which continues to accelerate. This will require ongoing contact as the opposition may shift theories. The actual trial testimony of the opposition experts may or may not be available for study, depending upon court procedures. If not, a summary review with the defense team most certainly would be appropriate, including review of documents or demonstrative aids admitted into evidence. This last review may only be accomplished just prior to testimony by the RHE. Part of his review should include the interpretation by the defense team of the juror response to the respective points presented by plaintiff's RHE. Weaknesses or obvious unrealistic positions may be further exploited during the defense presentation. There may be appropriate breaks in the plaintiff's RHE's testimony, which provide an opportunity for further consultation and preparation of defense counsel by his own expert. Again, it is at this point that much of the investigative background and research undertaken by the defense expert helps with the cross-examination and hopeful impeachment of the plaintiff's expert.

On the forefront of the presentation, it should be kept in mind that the expert is the advocate for the defense. He must be assertive and emotive. The expert must be able to communicate a compassionate and reasonable program devised to be accepted by the jury, rather than a sympathy-engendering, inflated approach submitted by the plaintiff. The "Chevrolet" approach must be presented with a certain emotional element to effectively counter the plaintiff's "Mercedes Benz" approach.

This covers all aspects of the plan, including the reasonableness of congregate living or institutionalization versus the intensive, ad infinitum and redundant plaintiff's program. The presentation must defuse the plaintiff's express or implicit argument that the plaintiff, having lost a significant aspect of his life, should be overcompensated in some other facet of his life. Part of the analysis will include an attack on the plaintiff's type and frequency of rehabilitation.

It should be kept in mind by the expert that _he_ is the expert, not the plaintiff's attorney, nor the plaintiff's treating physicians. Many physicians merely plug in the type of rehabilitation program without a true consultation with the experts in the field. Many rehabilitation experts see and treat far more injured people than the treating physician. The RHE should have a much better understanding of the appropriate parameters and limitations of the various modalities of therapy. The expert does have in his experience the realistic benefits of those therapies versus the attitude that more money and therapies will achieve continued improvement or results.

Just as preparation for the deposition is beyond the scope of this chapter, so is in-depth preparation for examination at time of trial. Suffice it to say, preparation of the direct testimony also contemplates anticipation of the cross-examination questions. Practice sessions covering that aspect of presentation must be undertaken to avoid embarrassment and loss of credibility at time of trial.

In preparation for actual testimony, there should be a detailed dress rehearsal of the testimony. This should extend not only to a general outline of the presentation, but also a step-by-step analysis with a word-for-word phrasing of important questions. This is not only to be certain that the word choice is appropriate to the setting, but to establish certain predicates necessary for the conclusions or opinions of that expert. Appropriate cueing is also necessary for reference to demonstrative aids and for interruptions for explanations. The foregoing should not constitute scripting to the point of a dry lecture-like presentation.

Drafting of questions can also be particularly important when they directly invade the personal experience of the jurors. For example, it would be difficult to convince a juror who is in the construction trades that the plaintiff who has sustained a lumbar fusion will be a viable competitor in the labor market, or that institutionalization of a brain injured child is appropriate if the local institutions have been the subject of notoriety.

In preparation of the questions and presentation, there should be anticipated interruptions for explanation of terms, such as the difference between impairment and disability. The explanation can be aided with the appropriate use of examples planned in advance, i.e., the effect of a below-the-knee amputation on a laborer versus an attorney.

The presentation of the defense analysis of the life care plan should draw upon concrete examples of where such programs have been implemented by the defense expert, in litigation or otherwise. Planning must also anticipate the protection of the privacy of the participants of those other programs.

Some opinions or testimony may be inadmissible at first blush, but questions and answers can be appropriately crafted to establish their admissibility. For example, the RHE may be able to testify as to the plaintiff's prior criminal history and possible drug usage, because they are part of the predicate for future employability.

Another area for objection to be anticipated is when the testimony calls for a legal opinion from a non-lawyer. This can be encountered when testifying concerning the availability of collateral sources and other entitlement programs. Adequate knowledge and preparation is necessary when testifying concerning local programs which are available, and of such programs as the Individual Education Program 20 USC, Section 140 (19) or Education for All Handicapped Children Act, 20 USC, Section 1400, or The Rehabilitation Act, 29 USC, Section 794. A detailed knowledge of the programs and their practical application will help in overcoming the objection.

As part of the last minute preparation for testimony, defense counsel must advise the witness as to court rulings on motions in limine. Such motions are brought usually even before the jury is questioned to prevent the mention of certain testimony or documents, due to their prejudicial nature. If the court grants such a request or motion, reference to that forbidden material in the presence of the jury risks having the case declared a mistrial and potential sanctions being imposed upon that witness, or party or counsel, a situation to be avoided.

Verbal skills are also important. The witness should neither speak down to nor pander to the jury. The witness's appearance should also be discussed with defense counselor before testimony. Overuse of professional lingo or vocabulary may sound impressive, but won't do very much to communicate the concepts. At the other end of the spectrum, needless repetition of terms or concepts which have been repeated ad nauseum by plaintiff's expert or counsel would probably only serve to tune out the jury.

Demeanor and personal appearance are important. Just as counsel dresses in appropriate manner, as affected by the locale, so should the expert. Demeanor encompasses not only respect for the court, but the appropriate rapport with the jury and counsel. The ground rules must be discussed. As a component of the emotional presentation, the witness may wish to avoid the cold detached analytical approach in favor of a humanistic one.

There are many who view a trial as a high stakes version of the performing arts. As such, it certainly combines the elements of organization, preparation, emotional outpourings, and practice, practice, practice. This demands that both defense counsel and the RHE work as a team and share a common approach and goal with respect to the litigation. This cannot be accomplished by merely forwarding the material to the witness and then to simply put him on the stand. Reliance upon each person's individual talent, which has not been coordinated with the other, does not work. Just as in the theater, there are many hours spent in preparation and dress rehearsal before the relatively few moments of appearance. Unlike the theater, there are no understudies or continuing runs of the play.

In summary, effective communication of the defense position in a case involving a catastrophic injury requires of counsel and the RHE coordination of their efforts, communication of their ideas on an ongoing basis, attention to detail, responsiveness to the demands of the case, and preparation of the final product for consumption by the audience. As in the performing arts, the critics may not like it, but if the audience does, it will still be judged a success.

3

Utilizing the Rehabilitation Expert: A Plaintiff Attorney's Perspective

Introduction

A personal injury trial lawyer represents clients who are victims of sudden and unforeseen traumatic events that result in disabling injuries. Although some clients suffer permanent injuries from exposure to environmental hazards over time, it is the onset of disability and its impact on employability which leads clients into law offices.

Often, a personal injury trial lawyer is the first professional the injured victim or family seeks out when faced with the economic consequences of disabling injuries.

There are cases where the injuries are obviously significant, however the physicians, therapists, and other health care providers are not coordinated in their efforts for long-term planning and rehabilitation. This leaves the patient and family confused as to the long-term recovery process and the economic consequences of injury.

In each of these instances, the personal injury lawyer must analyze the rehabilitation posture of the case when it comes into his or her office. This includes the selection of a rehabilitation expert or experts to assist the injured victim and his or her family during the short- and long-term recovery process.

Criteria for Selection of Rehabilitation Experts

There are many consultants claiming expertise as rehabilitation specialists with diversified backgrounds in nursing, psychology, and counseling. Other disciplines and experience factors in the field of rehabilitation include education and training in family counseling, individual counseling, and psychosocial adaptation to disability. It is preferable that the expert have a Ph.D. demonstrating concentrated study in these or related fields.

A rehabilitation expert, then, is a person educated and trained in the process of evaluating individuals who have incurred a disability. This evaluation includes an assessment of the handicaps which may impact on vocational and educational development, as well as considering the individual's ability to demonstrate independent living skills and to perform basic activities of daily living. In many cases, this evaluation includes family members and others who are close to the patient and who may become involved as support persons or disability managers.

The rehabilitation expert determines the extent to which a handicap exists, and develops a rehabilitation plan designed to bring about a maximum level of recovery following injury. This analysis may include a study of economic loss, a prognosis on future unemployment and underemployment, together with the financial requirements of implementing a rehabilitation plan.

When selecting the rehabilitation expert, counsel should keep in mind a broad perspective of the case. The rehabilitation expert will be providing services to the injured victim and family. The expert will also provide the lawyer with the necessary foundation to determine economic loss, as well as important information to present a proper analysis of injury, disability, and financial loss to a third party insurer, opposing counsel, and jury. The expert should have a local or national reputation for fairness without obvious bias for either the plaintiff or the defense. The rehabilitation expert's analysis should be exact and accurate, based on local economic data. The expert should have experience in the particular area of disability confronting the client.

The most reliable rehabilitation experts will be thorough in their analysis, including the gathering of complete and accurate historical information about the client so that the premises and assumptions that form the expert's opinions will be based on solid, confirmed factual information.

The trial lawyer should not overlook the present health care providers who are working with the client when the case comes into the office. Depending upon the stage of the rehabilitation process when the file is opened, it often happens that the present health care providers and the facility providing therapies are well-qualified and in the best position to serve as consultants to the attorney and work with the client during the short- and long-term rehabilitation process.

Timing of Selection of the Rehabilitation Expert Witness

As a general rule, a personal injury attorney should select or have in mind the rehabilitation expert as soon as the file is opened in the office. It is widely recognized that the rehabilitation process should begin as soon as possible. This is particularly so in catastrophic injury cases where there should be some formulation of a goal-oriented rehabilitation program instituted immediately. The rehabilitation plan should be reviewed on a regular basis by the rehabilitation expert. The consulting rehabilitation expert should be able to work with the attorney providing him or her with reports, updates and, when needed, assistance to obtain insurance coverage benefits.

If the injury is minor and of recent origin when a file is opened at the attorney's office, there may be less urgency to consult with a rehabilitation expert until the nature of the disability can be accurately assessed. There are, however, factors that arise during the course of representing clients with minor injuries which indicate the potential for rehabilitation consultation early in the recovery process.

For a client who is particularly discouraged with the injury or is susceptible to a chronic pain syndrome, an early rehabilitation consultation can be utilized in the case to support the client and direct the appropriate therapies. There may be a psychological reaction to a traumatic event which must be addressed early in the recovery process, particularly if the treating physician is not sympathetic or empathetic to the client's individual reaction to pain.

Some of the most difficult cases that a personal injury attorney is confronted with involve clients who have apparently relatively minor physical disabilities, but face greater disabilities in light of the psychological residuals of trauma and the pain component of injury.

The experience of a traumatic event and the lingering pain can be as great a factor in disability than the actual anatomic injury. Physicians are not always the most sensitive or in the best position to analyze this development. Here, a rehabilitation consultant experienced with the individual and psychological aspects of pain would be an appropriate referral to the client as soon as possible. A qualified expert can assist the client in the recovery process, as well as document the genuine nature of psychological injury and pain.

In catastrophic injury cases, the selection of a rehabilitation expert can occur as early as the acute recovery phase is completed following injury. This is the point when the injured victim is stabilized medically. The client will still be in a health care facility that may have resources available from many disciplines to begin the rehabilitation process.

If a major injury case comes into the attorney's office while the client is at a health care facility that is not in a position to provide immediate rehabilitation support services, then the attorney must consult with a rehabilitation expert to participate in discussions with health care providers and arrange for admission to an appropriate facility as soon as possible.

If the case comes into the attorney's office after the acute recovery stage is completed, then it is necessary to gather all of the medical records available to determine whether there is an individual or individuals who are coordinating the rehabilitation and medical treatment of the client. Often, a thorough review of all the medical and rehabilitation records will not identify any one person or persons who are coordinating the health care and other therapy requirements. This compels immediate action by the attorney to consult with a rehabilitation expert outside the present health care providers for thorough review and analysis in order that appropriate recommendations can be made to the client and family.

If the attorney can identify a person who is coordinating and managing the rehabilitation requirements of the client, then an assessment has to be made as to whether this plan is in the best interests of the client. A consultation with a rehabilitation expert is indicated, here too.

It may be that the person identified as coordinating the health care requirements is employed by an insurer who is providing benefits. In this instance, it would not be acceptable for the attorney to consult with an independent expert to review the injury, the recovery process, and current rehabilitation program. An outside consultant can, however, provide an objective assessment as to whether this plan is in the best interests of the client. The independent rehabilitation expert can be extremely helpful to the client and plaintiff's counsel by working with the insurance company's rehabilitation consultant to coordinate a mutually agreeable rehabilitation plan.

The Purpose of Utilizing the Rehabilitation Expert in Both the Catastrophic and Non-Catastrophic Cases

A rehabilitation expert can be utilized in minor and major injury cases. In the non-catastrophic injury case, the rehabilitation consultant can provide an assessment of vocational alternatives and evaluate the long-term consequences of the injury.

The expert, with sufficient educational background and training, should be able to identify the potential for future chronic underemployment. This can result in significant economic loss of future wages in a case where an injured person is not educationally or vocationally qualified to do other than manual labor.

A minor back or neck injury may result in significant periods of underemployment over the person's lifetime if he or she is unable to sustain optimum working capacity on an eight-hour-a-day, five-day-a-week, twelve-month-a-year basis. Absences from work that result in unfavorable reviews and ultimate discharge will begin to accumulate, thereby making future employment difficult and eventually impossible.

A rehabilitation expert experienced in working with clients presenting this injury profile will be able to minimize the impact of injury on the client, as well as identify and prepare the client for realistic expectations of periods of unemployment and underemployment.

In the catastrophic injury case, the purpose of utilizing the rehabilitation expert depends in large part on when they are consulted on the case. If it is during the acute rehabilitation process, while the client is still recovering from the injuries medically, there may be little that an outside rehabilitation expert can do. This is so, primarily because the client is still an in-patient at a facility that presumably provides therapy modalities as part of its acute care treatment.

However, once the client is discharged into a longer term facility and has been weaned from primary acute medical care, then a rehabilitation expert will be in the best position to provide an analysis as to the type of care that should be provided, with a view toward long-term medical, rehabilitation, and financial recovery.

Once the client has been stabilized medically and is able to participate in rehabilitation therapy modalities, there are several decisions which the client-patient, family and rehabilitation consultant must consider. Hospitals and rehabilitation facilities actively compete for patients to enter their rehabilitation programs. If a rehabilitation facility is affiliated with an acute care-trauma hospital, it is not axiomatic that this facility is in the best position to provide the specific rehabilitation needs of the client.

There are specialized rehabilitation programs available for specific injuries such as spinal cord injuries, burn injuries, and head trauma. The rehabilitation expert selected by plaintiff's counsel must review all of the client's records and be thoroughly familiar with the rehabilitation program offered at the facility where the client is a patient in order to make appropriate recommendations, redirect therapies, or consider alternative placement in other facilities with the long-term picture in mind.

It is at this time that the rehabilitation experts selected by the lawyer and family may be in the best position to impose their influence and redirect and organize long-term rehabilitation. A reputable rehabilitation consultant will be able to persuade the present health care providers to participate in a coordinated long-term rehabilitation plan. This persuasiveness upon health care providers carries over to the insurers who provide benefits. The process involves delicate negotiations that directly depend upon an astute and knowledgeable rehabilitation expert.

If there is no additional source of insurance funds to provide for a costly rehabilitation program, a knowledgeable expert will be in a position to assist the client in the application process for various federal, state, and local grants. There are many rehabilitation facilities that will reduce costs or provide waivers of fees or scholarships in appropriate instances of financial need allowing the client to receive the best possible specialized care for the particular injury and disability.

The knowledgeable rehabilitation expert will also be able to identify the appropriate facilities to treat the specific disability. For example, therapeutic modalities in rehabilitation centers for spinal cord injuries are very different from the rehabilitation modalities and requirements for a victim of head trauma. In the case of spinal cord injuries, therapies include problems with bowel, bladder, sexual, and other dysfunctions that relate to disabilities that are 90% in the physical realm. There certainly is a strong psychological component to spinal cord injuries, but in many instances there is very little or no disability in the cognitive areas.

Rehabilitation therapies involving a head injured patient must be designed to address the major concern, which is 90% in the cognitive-behavioral-social areas. Consequently, a facility designed to treat all injuries, whether they are burn, spinal cord, or brain injuries, may not treat any one thoroughly, or may favor one type of injury over another.

With recent advances in brain injury rehabilitation research, there has been a significant increase in the fund of knowledge generated to direct therapy modalities for optimal recovery of the patient. This has inspired the development of specialized inpatient rehabilitation centers that address the particular needs of the head injured patient.

An example of inappropriate placement can illustrate the adverse consequences upon the patient's recovery as well as an enormous waste of financial resources. In an actual case, a brain injured patient was placed in a facility well-recognized for its expertise in treating spinal cord injuries.

The facility had recently expanded its rehabilitation program to include victims of head trauma. However, it did not adapt its internal management of patients. The rehabilitation facility intermixed its patient population with head trauma patients residing in the same rooms as spinal cord injury patients. All patients were treated the same within the facility.

Each patient, whether spinal cord or brain injured, signed a contract whereby they agreed to be present at their specific assigned therapies. This was designed in the first instance to provide a method of motivating spinal cord injured patients to get themselves out of bed, get dressed, get into their wheelchairs, and to their therapies on time.

The program worked well for spinal cord injured patients. It did not work well for patients who were the victims of head trauma. One head injured patient had problems with memory, lacked motivation, and initiative which was typical for his particular injury. The patient really never did understand or appreciate the contractual agreement to attend his therapies on time. As a result, this patient missed therapies, did not get up on time, stayed up late, often slept throughout the afternoon, and overall never did fit within the rehabilitation program.

After nine months of frustration and an expenditure of significant financial resources, the final decision to withdraw the patient resulted from an incident when he was placed on a public transportation bus to travel to a downtown metropolitan area. He was accompanied on two occasions by a therapist, and then sent out on his own to see if he could remember how to return to the institution.

To make matters worse, it was also expected that he attend a course at a local community college in the downtown metropolitan area. Needless to say, the patient was not able to return to the facility. It was fortunate that he carried the telephone number of the facility in his pocket and was able to call the facility and give his location in order to be picked up and returned.

This is a good example why a rehabilitation expert must be able to identify the appropriate facility so as to provide a positive rehabilitation experience for the patient. An improper placement in the wrong facility that does not provide proper therapy modalities will result in failure. This experience makes it far less likely that the patient will succeed in the next placement attempt, even if it is a much better facility. The patient begins to see himself or herself as disabled, not functional, and as a failure. This has unfortunate consequences which carry beyond rehabilitation and follow the patient after community re-entry.

The rehabilitation expert should also be knowledgeable in the areas of transitional living requirements and long-term follow-up care after discharge from all treatment facilities. After a long-term inpatient program, a most important component is proper supervision during the transitional living experience. This includes proper supervision in the practical applications of everyday living including shopping, budgeting, and meal planning. Arrangements should be made for regular follow-up contact with the patient once community entry is achieved. The long-term cost of the rehabilitation consultant must be included in any analysis of settlement and in the economic loss that will be proven at trial.

Techniques for Working With the Rehabilitation Expert in Reviewing the File and Preparing for Trial

The role of the rehabilitation expert serving as a consultant in coordinating and implementing the rehabilitation plan for the client, and assisting the personal injury trial attorney in preparation for trial merges with the development and implementation of a life care plan. Depending on the nature of the injury and the needs of the client, the life care plan can be simple or complex.

The purpose of the plan is to provide for the long-term medical, therapeutic, rehabilitation, occupational and other needs of the client in order to obtain optimal recovery. This plan must be based upon the expert's assessment after a thorough review of all medical information and summarizing it; meeting with the client and family; reviewing employment and educational history (both of the injured victim and of the family); selecting appropriate tests for vocational, psychological, and neuropsychological testing; in-home observation of the patient and family; and evaluating any information that may be applicable and relevant in the case. The rehabilitation consultant then pulls all of the data together, and develops an initial set of recommendations regarding rehabilitation for both short- and long-term services.

The data-gathering is an important component of the expert's analysis. The plaintiff's attorney must participate in the gathering of this historical data in order to be as thoroughly familiar with the foundation to support reasonable inferences and opinions of the expert that are based upon a reasonable degree of rehabilitation certainty.

It is also incumbent upon the attorney to keep the consulting rehabilitation expert appraised of any developments on the file or with the client during the course of the case, whether the information be adverse or advantageous.

School work, achievement tests, family background, role models within the family and environment, and test results (pre- and post-accident) are all important to the expert's information. This will allow the expert to make assumptions regarding alternative rehabilitation, vocational, and educational development, and to provide the basis for the expert's opinion at trial regarding the future health care and other rehabilitation-related expenses that meet the legal standard within the generally-accepted reasonable degree of rehabilitation certainty.

The attorney must be sure that the rehabilitation expert renders opinions that are directly related to the specific occupation and characteristics of the client. This includes the client's physical skills, the skills required for a particular job, the mental skills that are necessary to perform different kinds of jobs, and a complete evaluation as to how the disability affects the client in terms of occupational and vocational requirements.

The rehabilitation expert must also provide the attorney with insight into the presentation of evidence at trial, making sure that all testimony preceding the expert's testimony sets forth the proper foundation to support the inferences and opinions of the expert.

This does not in any way excuse proper preparation for trial by the attorney. There is no substitute for a thorough knowledge of the client and the client's disabilities. In catastrophic injury cases, day-in-the-life films will be prepared for use at trial. Prior to the documentary videotape or film, it is good practice for the attorney to spend two or three days living with the client in his or her present environment. If they are in-patient at a rehabilitation facility, the attorney should spend at least two days from early morning until bedtime going through the daily routine at the facility.

This will allow for proper arrangements with the professional videotape or camera crew, and will give the attorney knowledge by experience in presenting the client's circumstance to the jury.

At trial, the rehabilitation expert is one of the best witnesses to present objective testimony regarding the non-economic damages of the client's case. This includes mental anguish, pain, and learning to live with a disability. The struggles that a catastrophically injured client must go through during both the acute and long-term rehabilitation process can be explained in compelling testimony by the rehabilitation expert.

In order to be able to work and communicate effectively with the rehabilitation expert and especially in preparing for trial, the attorney must make sure that he or she possesses the same documentation that is in the expert's file. This includes all employment and school records, test data, as well as a complete medical portfolio. All psychological and neuropsychological test scores, including raw test score data which allow for interpretation and application of the test results by the expert must be understood. If there is an adverse or independent rehabilitation expert's report, the plaintiff's attorney should request all test score data, including the notes of the adverse examining expert as well as the raw test score data for review by plaintiff's expert.

It is also helpful if the attorney participates in the obtaining of the medical and other historical documents, paginating them sequentially and organizing the records by tabs in a notebook categorized by health care provider and institution. This insures that the attorney has an exact duplicate of all records in the possession of the rehabilitation expert, and allows for effective communication between the attorney and the expert as the case proceeds. It is also helpful for quick reference during depositions or trial when opposing counsel begins to examine the expert on the basis of a single document in the records. It can be quickly located by page number, and put in context for proper explanation by plaintiff's expert.

In preparing for trial or pretrial depositions, there is no substitute for a person-to-person conference with the expert, reviewing the entire chart, including personal notes taken by the expert or the expert's staff. If there is any difficulty in interpreting the notes of the consulting expert, it should be reviewed thoroughly and explained so that the plaintiff's attorney is in a position to know of any potentially objectionable matter prior to the deposition or trial testimony.

If there is information that the expert has requested but not received, this should be provided before the deposition or trial testimony. If there are weaknesses in the case generally, or as part of the foundation to support the expert witness' testimony, plaintiff's counsel should assist in the obtaining of the required information. In all cases, the expert should not voluntarily or otherwise be pressured to render opinions based upon weak or unsupportable assumptions.

In terms of trial strategy, the likely order of calling the rehabilitation expert would be near the end of plaintiff's case, just prior to the economist's testimony as to the present value calculations. This will include the life care plan of the rehabilitation expert and the costs associated with implementing the plan for the lifetime of the plaintiff.

An unprepared rehabilitation expert, or an expert who renders opinions that can be attacked on cross-examination could jeopardize the client's legitimate recovery for economic loss because the entire testimony will be called into question. Likewise, lawyers should not press experts to render weak opinions under the guise of attempting recovery, because it is trial.

In preparing for trial, counsel should review with the rehabilitation experts the appropriate charts, graphs, and other demonstrative exhibits that will help present the expert's testimony at trial. This should include a discussion as to how to go about filming the day-in-the-life of the client as part of trial preparation.

The day-in-the-life film can be run intermittently throughout the trial very effectively, with different therapists and physicians testifying while the film is presented to the jury. Some of the film documentation may be explained by the rehabilitation expert as part of the basis to support the opinions and costs associated with the implementation of the life care plan.

The life care plan in a catastrophic injury case can be lengthy and complex. The purpose of the plan is to identify each specific future therapy or other assistance that the client will require for the rest of his or her life. This multiple-page plan can be easily followed by the jury if, during the course of the expert's testimony, permission is requested and granted by the judge to give each juror a copy. The jurors can then page through the plan as the expert is testifying and identify each specific recommendation in the plan and associate the cost on an individual catastrophic injury case.

Although overhead projectors and large exhibits can also serve this purpose, experience has shown that each juror holding a copy of the life care plan while the expert testifies seems to make the process of following the testimony easier.

The rehabilitation expert usually has many ideas to offer the attorney in presenting trial testimony. The expert can review with counsel the weaknesses in the case, as well as emphasizing the strengths and how best to present the testimony based upon the historical data, and injuries as they relate to the client on an individual basis.

Pros and Cons Involved in Bringing a Rehabilitation Expert Into a Case -- Avoiding Pitfalls

There is nothing to lose by bringing a rehabilitation expert into a case for evaluation and consultation. Of course, this is an expense item that will have to be discussed with the attorney's client, and then fully understood between the rehabilitation expert and the attorney. Most rehabilitation experts bill on an hourly basis, with certain minimums, depending on the nature of the assignment.

All rehabilitation consultants include in their billings travel expenses and other out-of-pocket expenses. Many have set schedules of fees for testifying at depositions and at trial.

These fees and expenses should be fully understood between the client and the attorney and the rehabilitation expert. There should be a clear understanding at the outset as to who is responsible to pay for the professional fee, and when the payment is due after billing. This will avoid misunderstandings which could result in the expert's withdrawal from the case thereby harming the client's case.

It is highly advisable that the rehabilitation expert provide a written description of the costs for services and billing practices. If there are any changes in the expert's fee schedule, the client and lawyer should be advised immediately.

In many cases, there are insurance benefits to pay for some of the early rehabilitation analysis. An attorney representing a plaintiff can generally negotiate payment for part of the analysis and expert's time from available insurance sources. This includes worker's compensation insurers as well as negligence and automobile no-fault carriers.

In most states, it is the obligation of the attorney to pay for the rehabilitation expert's costs as they are billed. Some rehabilitation experts bill at the completion of certain tasks along the way in their analysis. This should be fully understood between the attorney, client, and rehabilitation expert, especially as to when billings can be expected to be presented and paid. This can help alleviate unpleasant surprises when long periods of time elapse between the initial consultation and first billing with a very substantial fee due on a 30-day basis.

The attorney should index the file to make sure that all expenses are paid prior to disbursing any sums received in settlement or in payment of a judgment. A bill arriving late from the consulting expert after the monies are disbursed can result in an unpleasant dispute if the attorney is obligated to pay the expert and then must bill the client for this incurred, but unexpected expense.

There are some experts who base their fee contingent on the outcome of the case. This is an undesirable and potentially unethical practice. Experts who arrange for fee payment under this method avoid ethical problems with the attorney by contracting directly with the client. These types of fee arrangements are not in the best interests of the client and can compromise the credibility of the witness to the point where such a fee arrangement could jeopardize an otherwise meritorious claim.

It is proper grounds on cross-examination for opposing counsel to inquire into the nature of the fee arrangement of the expert together with ascertaining the amount paid and to be paid for the expert's services. Trial lawyers know that the expert witness must be fully prepared to face cross-examination on this issue at trial. The jury must understand that the expert's fees are fair and reasonable for the same services offered by other professionals.

Another pitfall to avoid is the surprise cross-examination of plaintiff's expert if he or she has previously testified under oath or has published opinions which are inconsistent with those rendered in the present case. The plaintiff's attorney must review with the rehabilitation expert all previous cases which the expert has rendered written opinions, or has testified by deposition or at trial. The rehabilitation expert should be very candid to the referring attorney in reviewing previous written reports and prior sworn testimony as well as disclosing all books and articles published in periodicals that are circulated to the public because they are available for impeachment at trial by opposing counsel.

The expert should have available a bibliography of publications that the attorney or the attorney's staff can review in order to determine whether there have been any previous inconsistencies in opinions, interpretation of test data, or statements in articles published by the expert. Inconsistent opinions by the expert on the same or similar subject matter can be used at trial to impeach the credibility of the rehabilitation expert. Unexplained impeachment of the expert at trial can be devastating to the plaintiff's case.

There are some rehabilitation experts who testify either entirely for the defense in opposition to claims, or for the plaintiffs in support of claims. These experts are well-known, and both the defense and plaintiff's lawyers develop a portfolio on the expert that can be used effectively at trial. This portfolio includes articles, trial transcript, or deposition testimony where the expert has taken inconsistent positions. It is important therefore, that the plaintiff's lawyer become familiar with the expert and the expert's previous consulting experience together with a list of clients so as to avoid or minimize any potentially impeaching testimony at trial.

If the expert recognizes, or has in the past recognized certain periodicals or other treatises as reliable authority in the field of rehabilitation, this should also be made known to plaintiff's counsel. Treatises or other reference sources that are recognized by an expert can be used for impeachment purposes at trial. On the other hand, treatises and other authoritative articles and publications can be used affirmatively by plaintiff's counsel once they have been recognized by the expert.

Plaintiff's rehabilitation expert should be utilized in preparing for cross-examination of the defense expert. This preparation can be very helpful in defining the areas of weakness in the defense expert's position as well as outlining a proposed course of cross-examination.

This chapter would not be complete without a discussion of the obligation to identify the need for a rehabilitation expert or the right to representation by counsel.

There will be instances where clients may be unaware that the long-term rehabilitation plan is not being implemented, or not addressed at all by present health care providers. These patients may not know they have legal rights as it relates to their economic recovery and ability to pay for future rehabilitation costs.

Frequently, it is family members, parents, or significant others in relationship to the injured victim who first begin to get concerned about long-term rehabilitation and legal rights to economic benefits. If a lawyer is consulted by the family members and injured victim, the lawyer may well have an obligation to review and identify whether the present rehabilitation plan is proper for the client given the nature of the injuries, the potential for recovery based upon liability and applicable insurance policy limits.

On the other hand, if health care providers or rehabilitation experts working at a particular facility consult with the patient or the patient's family and identify rehabilitation needs for which there are no apparent financial resource, it would be most appropriate to advise the patient and the patient's family that they should consult with an attorney to review the liability, damages, and potential application of insurance benefits in order to pay for a rehabilitation program.

An inappropriate rehabilitation plan which is not in the best interests of the patient could lead to a professional negligence claim against the rehabilitation expert for any shortcomings in a long-term rehabilitation plan. A rehabilitation expert has a duty to his client/patient to provide a proper rehabilitation plan that is developed according to recognized standards for the same or similar services in the community. Any departures from a recognized standard of care could result in liability by the rehabilitation expert to the patient/client.

Rehabilitation experts who are employed by insurance carriers providing and developing a plan for a victim who is not represented by counsel must make every effort to be fair and reasonable in light of the client's disability and available insurance resources without compromising their opinion and evaluation.

Conclusion

Rehabilitation consultants and personal injury trial lawyers are professionals who must work together and coordinate the injured victim's long-term optimum rehabilitation in light of available financial resources.

The common goal of the two professions is for the ultimate well-being of the client, both physically and emotionally, and to provide for the best possible quality of life.

4

Qualifying the Expert and Defining the Role of the Rehabilitation Professional

The Goals of *Voir Dire*

The presentation of the rehabilitation testimony in the courtroom setting is broken down into four basic areas. The first is the qualifying of the expert; the second is defining the roles and goals of the rehabilitation professional; the third is reviewing the evaluation procedures used by the rehabilitation professional; and the fourth is presenting the conclusions developed as a result of the evaluation. This chapter will focus on the first two of these four primary purposes. I have chosen to present the qualifying of the expert witness together with defining the roles and goals of the rehabilitation professional primarily because the two are so interrelated in the early stages of trial or hearing testimony.

There are five primary goals to achieve during the qualifications process. These include:

1. Establishing the basic credentials of the rehabilitation professional who will be presenting the testimony at trial.

2. Establishing in a fashion clearly understood by the jury, the general knowledge base held by this rehabilitation professional by virtue of his background, training during degree programs, and training as well as expertise obtained post-graduation from his degree programs.

3. Setting the parameters of the professional's expertise in a clear fashion that can be understood by the judge as well as the jury. This can be particularly important when the judge is asked to

make rulings on whether or not the rehabilitation expert will be allowed to testify in specific areas. It is important, during the questioning, to be very specific in setting these parameters to include not only the areas in which the individual holds expertise but also setting the precedent that establishes this expertise. Once having set these parameters, it is equally important for the expert and the attorneys involved not to cross the line outside that area of expertise.

4. Defining the profession of rehabilitation counseling, rehabilitation nursing, or rehabilitation psychology (obviously depending upon the specific expert being utilized). It is extremely important that the jury understand not only the qualifications of the particular expert being utilized but also understand the nature of that profession, the goals involved, and the manner in which this treating professional is working with the patient population concerned.

5. Finally, an important goal of *Voir Dire* is to deal in a very straightforward fashion with any potential problem areas which might be brought up by opposing counsel in cross-examination of qualifications. Examples may include inquiry into the reason for this particular referral, who made the referral, the frequency of the professional's participation in consultation on litigation matters, the percentage of defense versus plaintiff referrals for litigation consultation, and the fees charged for services. By dealing in a very relaxed and straightforward fashion with areas such as this, it is difficult for the opposing counsel to then come back and ask these questions in an effort to paint the witness as a "hired gun" or as being limited to working as a professional witness.

Opposing Counsel's Goals in *Voir Dire*: The Cross-Examination

Just as there are specific goals to be established by the attorney who has brought the expert witness to trial, there are also specific goals that the opposing counsel will try to reach in cross-examination of issues of qualification. These include the following:

1. Establishing the expert as a "hired gun".

2. Establishing the expert as being one-sided, (testifying almost solely for either the plaintiff and/or for the defense, rather than demonstrating a healthy balance of referrals).

3. Establishing the expert as having a practice limited to forensics or expert testimony with no participation in research, writing, or direct patient services.

4. Attempting to establish that the expert's testimony is essentially for sale. This effort is usually accomplished by trying to establish prior testimony by deposition or trial transcripts where the expert may have stated opinions significantly different than the opinions being stated in the current case, although the injuries may be similar. In such instances, the expert should be relying on their awareness that each case is different and that although we utilize a very consistent methodology of assessing the needs dictated by the onset of a disability, the conclusions that we reach may be quite different by virtue of the patient's age, education, family status, or a thousand other variables which might create different recommendations for similar disabilities.

It's also important in the cross-examination process during *Voir Dire* for the expert to be careful to listen to the questions being asked. Questions such as, "How much are you being paid for your opinions (or testimony) here today?" may be designed to generate a very specific message to the jury. The appropriate response to such a question is that you are not being paid for either your testimony or your opinions. You are being reimbursed for your professional time, but your testimony and your opinions are your own and simply are not for sale.

The Expert's Responsibility in the *Voir Dire* Process

It is important for the rehabilitation professional to listen carefully to the questions being asked before responding. This is particularly true during the cross-examination process. Often, one must listen not just to the words being utilized, but also to the intent behind those words so they can be certain that they are answering in a fashion that fully informs the judge and jury. It is absolutely essential that rehabilitation experts establish through their answers, the clear parameters of expertise, never stretching the truth or manipulating the truth in their responses. Even in preparation for *Voir Dire*, it is essential that the expert clearly educates the attorney, presenting the testimony as to the range of expertise and the qualifying credentials. The development of the resumé or curriculum vitae is the beginning point for such education. For this reason, it should be clear, concise, and accurate with no effort to stretch the professional's area of expertise or manipulate the accuracy of information. One must anticipate that information presented on the resumé can and will be researched by opposing counsel.

When answering questions, it is important to make direct eye-contact with the jury, for their body-posturing and facial expressions will help you understand whether or not you are coming across in a clear and concise fashion. This technique is designed not for purposes of manipulation, but to reinforce the expert's role as an educator or teacher who must pay attention to the class to determine whether or not they understand the information or whether they are being confused or bored by the presentation.

The rehabilitation professional must maintain clear insight into the limits of his or her own expertise and these limits are not set just by the profession but rather by the experience, educational background training, and research with which that particular expert has been involved. Listen carefully for questions which on cross-examination or at times even on direct examination, may just take you slightly out of your area of expertise in what appears to be a relatively harmless area. The lack of caution in maintaining the parameters in which you have set can gradually lead you into greater areas of difficulty and present significant credibility problems before a judge or jury. The expert should never be afraid to indicate in response to a question, that it is either outside their area of expertise or that they simply don't know the answer.

At the same time, the rehabilitation expert should never be afraid to refuse to defer to other types of experts in areas in which they are confident the answer is well within their expertise. Examples of such questions might include the following:

Q. Would you defer to a physician regarding recommendations for the future care and support of this patient?
A. It is within the expertise of a treating physician to provide intervention and care for acute complications or illnesses which arise for the disabled client. It is not typically within the physician's role to be responsible for case management or design of home or facility support systems. It is the role of the rehabilitation professional to act as case manager and team leader in the post-acute stage to organize home or facility care programs and arrange for all the necessary details of durable medical goods, replenishable medical supplies, and formation of the health-related professional team that will be providing rehabilitation and/or maintenance services.

Feel confident in your area of expertise and don't succumb to the suggestion that just by virtue of an M.D. degree, the doctor would necessarily have more appropriate expertise in responding to such questions. It is not uncommon to find this situation even carried over into vocational issues, with questions such as, "Would you defer to a physician in answering questions as to whether or not an individual's disability would qualify them to perform specific vocational tasks?" The answer clearly is that the physician would be helpful in identifying specific anatomical problems and discussing limitations of a functional nature associated with those anatomical findings. On the other hand, the application of limitations to vocational issues is clearly within the expertise of the vocational rehabilitation counselor and well outside the expertise of the average medical doctor. (See Appendix B.)

Presenting the Role of the Rehabilitation Professional

Although the education of the jury reading the general nature and purpose of rehabilitation counseling and how one becomes a rehabilitation counselor begins in the qualifying process, it is insufficient to help them understand fully and appreciate the role, goals, and scope of the rehabilitation counselor's expertise, particularly as it relates to the present litigation. After the attorney qualifies the expert, but before specific questions relating to the client involved in litigation begin, a series of questions should be considered which will help fill in this gap for the members of the jury.

Areas to stress are: an explanation of the nature of the rehabilitation discipline; the general goals of rehabilitation; and the purpose of the rehabilitation expert's involvement in the litigation for which he or she has been engaged as a consultant (the present case).

The following questions may serve as guidelines for the attorney, although quite obviously, a broad range of answers may be proved with respect to these questions.

Q. Would you briefly tell the jury what a vocational rehabilitation counselor is?

A. Certainly. I work with individuals who have incurred either physical or emotional disabilities that result in vocational handicaps. I evaluate the extent to which these handicaps impede educational and vocational development and the specific steps which might be necessary in a rehabilitation plan to enhance this development in the future. It is the responsibility of myself and my staff to provide the specific rehabilitation program outline as well as to coordinate the involvement of any other health-related professionals so that maximum potential can be reached.

Q. What is the general goal of rehabilitation?

A. The goal of rehabilitation is to maximize the individual's post-accident vocational development. Where possible, this goal is an actual return to the labor market with the individual achieving and maintaining the most satisfactory level of work and wage earning capacity possible. In those instances where a return to the labor market is not possible, then the goal must be to enhance quality of life and ensure long-term care that will maximize the individual's developmental potential.

Q. In reference to this present case, could you explain to the ladies and gentlemen of the jury your understanding of the purpose for its referral?

A. It is my understanding that there was basically a twofold purpose for referring this case for rehabilitation services. The first was to assist the attorney in evaluating the extent to which vocational handicaps had been developed and the manner in which those handicaps affected this individual's future vocational potential and earning capacity. The second purpose was to outline an effective rehabilitation plan designed to maximize the remaining potential of the individual. The results of the evaluation, including the testing and the development of the rehabilitation plan, were to be covered with the client and family members so that they have a thorough understanding for the necessary steps as well as the options and alternatives which exist.

Sample Transcripts: Plaintiff and Defense

The following transcript samples are presented from two perspectives. The first is a plaintiff attorney taking video tape deposition testimony for use at trial. In this type of situation, the plaintiff attorney will, even during deposition, be the direct examiner for qualifying the witness and taking all of the direct testimony. The particular case involves a severely head injured individual in his late teens. All names have been changed, despite the fact that these transcripts come from filed lawsuits which are a matter of public record.

The second transcript presented is a deposition by a defense attorney on a case involving a pediatric quadriplegic. The reader certainly can see the significant differences in the approach to qualifying the expert utilized in each instance. Do not be misled into feeling that the difference is simply a matter of the plaintiff versus the defense. Had a defense attorney been presenting the rehabilitation expert in this instance, with a plaintiff attorney doing the cross-examination of qualifications, you would have seen an essential role reversal in the way the information is obtained and the expert is being examined.

Plaintiff Attorney's Presentation and Qualification of the Rehabilitation Expert

PAUL M. DEUTSCH, Ph.D., being by me first duly sworn to testify the whole truth, as hereinafter certified, testified as follows:
EXAMINATION
BY MR. ERIKSEN:
Q. Tell us your name, please.
A. Paul Michael Deutsch.
Q. And your occupation?
A. I'm a rehabilitation counselor.
Q. Can you tell the jury what a rehabilitation counselor is?
A. Certainly. I work with individuals primarily in the catastrophic injury area, individuals who require an evaluation to determine the extent to which they have developed handicapping conditions, and to determine how those handicapping conditions would impede their independent living skills, their activities of daily living, their ability to participate in vocational or educational pursuits.

I design long-term care or life care plans that assess the needs dictated by the onset of a disability, and I develop rehabilitation components of that plan so that the plan brings them to a maximum level of function, as appropriate, based on the disability and how far post-injury the individual is, and I implement those plans, carrying them through not only the rehabilitation phase but also the maintenance phase through the end of life expectancy.

Q. Do you operate a business?
A. Yes, I do.
Q. Tell us about that.
A. Well, it's Paul M. Deutsch and Associates. That is my primary practice. And we are engaged basically in three primary areas. The first is catastrophic case management, which is involving the direct management of catastrophic injury cases, from provision of individual counseling to family counseling and family education programs, to organization of rehabilitation programs, either by making referrals, or bringing in the necessary health-related professionals, and liaising with the physicians.

The second part of my practice involves consultation in program design and development as well as consultation in cases such as this where litigation is involved. And the third part involves research and writing.

Q. Where's your business located?

A. In Orlando, Florida.

Q. Do you have any graduate degrees in your area of specialization?

A. Yes, sir.

Q. Tell us about that.

A. I have a master's degree in rehabilitation counseling with a minor in behavioral psychology from the University of Florida. My Ph.D. is also from the University of Florida, through the College of Health-Related Professions with a major in counseling psychology and counseling education, a minor in rehabilitation counseling, and a sub-specialization in spinal cord injuries.

Q. How long have you been in your present line of work?

A. 18 years.

Q. Can you outline for us your work experience relative to the long-term care of head injury survivors?

A. Well, I've worked on and off with head injury even during the very early years that I began in rehabilitation at the master's level, but the emphasis on catastrophic head injury rehabilitation in this country really began in the mid-1970s, with our primary development of programs being since 1979.

I co-owned and co-directed an outpatient head injury facility in liaison with Orlando Regional Medical Center from about 1983 -- late 1982 until approximately a year and a half ago when I sold it to Orlando Regional Medical Center.

I have been providing case management services to head injured and performing both research and writing to the head injured patient for over ten years and am currently building a long-term supported living facility for head injury patients in the Orlando area, but I have done program consultation and liaison with long-term supported living programs as well as head injured rehabilitation programs extensively over the past decade.

Q. Do you have any experience in actually operating a long-term facility for the care of head injured survivors?

A. I have experience in operating the actual rehabilitation program. My experience with respect to operating a long-term supported living facility at this point has been limited to the past year of designing the programming, the budgeting, hiring an administrator, beginning to train staff, doing the construction, meeting the CARF (Committee on Accreditation of Rehabilitation Facility) standards. I have not and will not be admitting patients into that program for another 60 days.

Q. You said that you have been involved in long-term care planning for head injured people. Is that the same thing as rehabilitation or is there a difference between those two terms?

A. Well, the term itself in terms of long-term care planning or life care planning really makes no distinction. The life care plan considers the needs of the individual from the day I evaluate them through the end of their life expectancy.

So if they are early enough post-injury to warrant rehabilitation, then that's included in the life care plan. If they are not, then we'll move directly into the maintenance stage, but again, if they do require rehabilitation it's outlined and then the plan follows through with the long-term maintenance.

Q. Is there a difference between maintenance and rehabilitation?

A. No question, yes.

Q. What are the differences?

A. Well, rehabilitation is designed to bring the individual up to their maximum potential post-injury. That takes into consideration not only what the average everyday citizen might be thinking of, the ability to speak, think, process information, make decisions, make good judgments, and the ability to move -- those certainly are included; but for us very subtle kinds of considerations are taken under advisement with respect to rehabilitation.

Just improving the ability of the patient to interact more effectively with caregivers, reducing agitation, reducing violent acting-out behavior, can have a big impact on the ease of care without changing the level of care that actually is required.

Maintenance, on the other, hand is designed to keep that patient from regressing to lower levels of functioning. So we know that there's a certain level of range of motion exercises, for example, that we have to maintain to keep spasticity from developing, certain behavioral structures we need to maintain to keep a regression in personality and behavior from being a problem.

Q. You said before you were a rehabilitation counselor. Do you also have work experience and background and training in the maintenance aspects that you just described?

A. Well, basically what the rehabilitation counselor or rehabilitation psychologist does is focus on this long-term. It's not just on the rehabilitation but the maintenance of that individual through life expectancy. My field, which is primarily in rehabilitation psychology, is focused on this area.

Q. Have you written any books concerning the long-term care of head injured survivors?

A. Well, I have written books with respect to head injury and -- or a book and a monograph with respect to head injury, and there are sections within those that deal with the long-term.

My last text, which was *Innovations in Head Injury Rehabilitation* has sections on discharge planning and sections on long-term supported living, even on programming leisure and recreational activities over the long-term for the severe head injured, so it does look at the rehabilitation stage through the long-term living stage.

My monograph on life care planning with spinal cord injuries is a step-by-step guide for the catastrophic case manager on how to plan and implement the plan of care for a head injury patient.

Q. To what extent is the long-term care planning for a head injured survivor within the job description of your kind of specialist as opposed to a medical doctor?

A. Well, medical doctors follow patients for acute care needs -- particularly in head injury, although it's true in most any chronic disability.

Q. What's that?

A. Basically, if our head injury patient develops a complication, a urinary tract infection, an upper respiratory infection, we certainly expect the physician to intervene with respect to that. But a neurologist or neurosurgeon, for example, typically will follow the individual until medically stable.

They don't get involved in the details of providing day-to-day support care, they don't get involved in the details of determining the level of psychological or behavioral intervention, the counseling support. They don't look to meeting family needs as well as patient needs, the details that go into determining wheelchairs and frequency of replacement of wheel chairs and other equipment. Replenishable medical supplies or durable medical goods are just not an issue that they will get into.

They may have comments or be able to answer some questions as it relates to their specialty, but they are not trained in the long-term plan development for the maintenance and care of the chronically impaired.

Q. To what extent is the long-term planning aspect within your specialty?

A. Well, frankly, I was the first to initiate research and publish in the area of life care planning. My first two texts, which came out in the early eighties, dealt exclusively with this issue of the role of the rehabilitation counselor, rehabilitation psychologist and rehabilitation nurse as a case manager. Our role as case manager is something we're trained for in our basic educational background; at the master's level you take courses in the medical aspects of disability and terminology. We, as a profession, represent the team leader that pulls all of these various health-related professionals in the chronic care case together.

But again, I was the first to research and first to publish on the methodology of life care planning.

My third book, *A Guide to Rehabilitation*, provides currently over 1,100 pages of reference material across all disabilities listed in the AMA Guide to

Permanent Impairment specifically with respect to life care planning. I have spent the last twelve to fifteen years of my career exclusively focused on researching and developing the long-term care needs of disabilities.

Q. Are you board certified?

A. Yes, as a rehabilitation counselor by the Commission on Rehabilitation Counselor Certification.

Q. Are you affiliated with any hospitals?

A. With Orlando Regional Medical Center's head injury unit as an allied health professional.

Q. I think you said before that from time to time you get involved in consultation on law cases such as this one, is that correct?

A. Yes.

Q. Have you been asked to consult on cases similar to this by the defense law firm in this case, Peterson and Bernard?

A. Yes.

Q. In the past?

A. Yes.

Q. In fact I understand you are going to give a deposition in their behalf today?

A. That's true.

Q. Just so the jury understands, I have asked you to evaluate the case of Richard Banks, is that not so?

A. Yes.

Q. And we're taking your videotape deposition today because, as I understand it, in the next couple of weeks or so you are going to be out of the country, is that right?

A. That's correct.

Q. Can you tell us where you are going and what the purpose of your trip is?

A. Well, I began working on a research project at the First Moscow Medical Institute in the Soviet Union about five years ago and that developed into a much more extensive relationship where I have extensive publishing interests in the area of Soviet health science research. I have developed a small publishing company that in part works on translating foreign research in the health-related professions.

So I am over there both because of the research project that we have going at the First Moscow Medical Institute and at the Barishtoshvili Research Institute in the Georgian Republic of the Soviet Union. These projects involve the University of Florida and Rollins College. We have a joint research project in studying brain behavior relationship and a new generation of EEG equipment. I was fortunate to be able to organize this between all those parties, and I am going over for that purpose and for the International Book Fair that Moscow runs every other year.

Q. Do you have a resumé that sets out qualifications and background other than that that I have asked you about so far?

A. Yes.

Q. Rather than me go through your remaining background, qualifications, and experience, let me ask you to identify the document you have before you as being the resumé or not.

A. Yes, this is my updated resumé. (Thereupon, the document was marked as Exhibit A for identification.)

BY MR. ERIKSEN:

Q. Does that document set up or set out in an up-to-date fashion the balance of your background, qualifications, and experience?

A. It does. There are a few things that are not on there. I was recently in the past month elected to the Executive Board of the Rehabilitation Psychology Division of the American Psychological Association.

There are also a couple of monographs and book chapters that have been written that I haven't gotten on there yet, but I think for the most part it's up to date.

Defense Attorney's Examination of the Qualification of the Rehabilitation Expert

In reviewing this transcript, take note of how the defense attorney even goes so far as to refuse the title Dr. Deutsch in an effort to avoid reinforcing the expert's credibility to the jury.

The Witness,
PAUL M. DEUTSCH,
having been first duly sworn, testified upon his oath as follows:
EXAMINATION
BY MR. WHITE:

Q. My name is Ted White, and along with Jon Burnett, we are representing Drs. Scott, Sommers, Bukevavich, an East Tennessee OB-GYN in a case that you have been identified by the plaintiffs as a witness. I'd like for you to answer a few questions for me this morning, Dr. Deutsch; but before we get into questions about Sarah Martin specifically, I want to get some background information. If you will, for the court reporter, state your full name.

A. Certainly. It's Paul Michael Deutsch.

Q. Mr. Deutsch, I take it from your accent -- not mine -- but you're the one with the accent here -- are you from the north someplace originally?

A. Well, I was born in the North, but I moved out when I was six-months-old; and I've been in the south ever since. I grew up in North Carolina and Florida.

Q. How old are you?

A. I am thirty-eight years old.

Q. Let me find out a little bit about your educational background. First of all, you are not a medical doctor?

A. No, a Ph.D.

Q. Tell me where you took your undergraduate education.

A. I have a bachelor's in psychology from Rollins College in Winter Park, Florida.

Q. And after Rollins, did you attend another college?

A. Yes. I got my master's in Rehabilitation Counseling, with a minor in Behavioral Psychology, from the College of Health-Related Professions at the University of Florida.

Q. Okay, University of Florida. What year was that?

A. I completed my master's in December, 1972; that's when I completed my internship.

Q. And you actually got your master's in Rehabilitation--

A. -- Counseling.

Q. -- Counseling?

A. That's correct.

Q. What exactly is Rehabilitation Counseling?
A. Well, basically, a rehabilitation counselor works with individuals who have incurred a disabling condition. That disabling condition may impede their vocational or educational development or may impede their ability to demonstrate independent living skills or handle activities of daily living. We evaluate the extent to which handicaps stem from the disability. We develop long-term care plans in the case of catastrophic cases. Or we develop vocational rehabilitation plans in the case of non-catastrophics with the goal of helping people reach a maximum level of post-accident development. Then we, once having developed the plan, will provide services to implement the plan and bring in those additional professionals to make the team that are necessary to achieve the goals we've set out.
Q. So, by training, you're not really able to make the medical recommendations for the care and treatment of any particular patient?
A. I don't make specific medical recommendations, but I think it's important maybe for us at some point to define what's medical and what's not medical in terms of what we can do. For example, I don't prescribe specific physical therapy exercises, but I know with respect to each of the disabilities when we're going to be bringing a physical therapist in and the types of services that we need to include. I know how to set up and do, as a part of my work, the long-term care plans because my responsibility typically is primarily through acute care; and then they prescribe the medications for long-term needs. And if there are other services -- like, a patient who is ventilator-dependent -- then obviously, they are critical as part of the team. But long-term team management in catastrophic cases is what I do; that's how I make a living.
Q. You've drawn the distinction between acute care, which I take it you mean in-hospital mostly for acute care? You mean within short-term after the original trauma or whatever caused the --
A. And/or any onset of acute complications which require medical intervention. So if we have a urological infection, obviously, we need to bring in an appropriate physician to deal with that; and we need a treating physician to follow along with the catastrophically impaired patient. It de-

pends on the type of disability as to just how much physician involvement there is.

Q. You are not a trained physical therapist?

A. I am not a physical therapist.

Q. Or occupational therapist?

A. No.

Q. Or a speech therapist?

A. No. My training is in Rehabilitation and Counseling Psychology.

Q. Does your training encompass, in any large degree, vocational rehabilitation?

A. Well, certainly. I have a master's in Vocational Rehabilitation. I'm on the faculty of the Department of Vocational Rehabilitation at University of Florida as an adjunct. Vocational rehabilitation is certainly a part of what I do, but my research and my primary work over the past ten years has been catastrophic case management. The books I've written have all focused on catastrophic case management. Most of my journal writing and monographs have focused on catastrophic case management. And that's basically what I have been doing intensively for the past ten years.

Q. So a lot of this has been self-training as far as catastrophic case management or recommendations. It's not really the emphasis of the areas of your actual study in school, I take it?

A. I think it depends on what you mean by self-training. Certainly, in rehabilitation counseling, even at the basic master's level, we're all responsible for taking medical aspects, medical terminology, basic physiology courses mostly for the purpose of its application to vocational rehabilitation. But I will admit that even beyond that and beyond my doctoral work, which emphasized catastrophic disabilities, I've taken a great deal of time, not only in personal research, writing, and development and not only in training others, but in taking courses, taking seminars, taking three-day or five-day, ten-day courses in case treatment for the various kinds of disabilities. For example, in the doctoral level, my subspecialization was spinal cord injuries. I had a physiatrist, a physical medicine, and rehabilitation specialist, who was at Shands Teaching Hospital, who sat on my doctoral committee, who wrote my subspecialization exam. So, you know, not everybody in the field of rehabilitation necessarily is going to emphasize a speciality in catastrophic case management, but the opportunity to do so certainly is there if they want the training and they want the skills necessary to accomplish it.

Q. Let me ask you if you won't provide us with a copy of your curriculum vitae as a late-filed exhibit to your deposition, and you can provide that to Mr. Justice.

A. In fact, even before I leave here, I'd be happy to call my office and ask them to mail it up.

(Exhibit Number One to be late-filed.)

Q. Does your CV include what articles and/or texts -- you mentioned earlier texts that you have authored or co-authored?

A. It includes all the texts and most of the updated chapters that I've written for the texts that require annual updating and most articles and monographs. There may be one or two that are relatively recent. I know it doesn't include the latest updates that I've submitted to the publisher. But ninety-eight percent is in there.

Q. Tell me about your doctoral degree. Where did you receive it?

A. University of Florida. I went through the College of Health-Related Professions. Now, in rehabilitation, you don't, with just a few exceptions, get a Ph.D. directly in rehabilitation. It's in a related field with your specialization and minor in rehabilitation.

Q. Let me interrupt you. And yours was in --

A. My Ph.D. was in a joint program between Counseling Psychology and Counselor Education at the time. So my work is in Counseling Psychology. My minor is in Rehabilitation, and my subspecialization was spinal cord injuries.

Q. That wasn't actually instruction you received as an adjunct curriculum from the medical school, was it? Or was it?

A. I'm not sure what you meant by adjunct. I did not take courses on spinal cord injury through the medical school. I had a professor at the medical school who sat on my doctoral committee. And your subspecialization can be done through some course work, but most of it is done through individual study requirements, through reading, through seminars that your professor can require you to go to. I mean, they really are at liberty to do anything with you they want.

Q. Self-direct your own curriculum almost?

A. Well, no, I don't get to self-direct it; the committee, the doctoral committee, gets to direct it, and they can do anything. If you are reasonably diplomatic, and you've got a good relationship with them, you certainly can add things into it. But there's no question that it's the doctoral committee who writes your curriculum, and they have a lot of power within the university setting to do one thing with you and something completely different with another student in terms of courses required, in terms of individual work required, research requirements. That's really up to your doctoral committee once you're at that level.

Q. Okay. So, correct me if I'm wrong, the thrust of your background as far as education is concerned for the services that you provide now would be the vocational rehabilitation background and your psychology rehabilitation or counseling background along with these other areas that you got instruction in while you were at the University Florida and including spinal cord injury and that sort of thing.

A. Well, I think that's the thrust of it as far as the university relationships are concerned. But, you know, I certainly wouldn't want to ignore all that I've done over the past fifteen years of work experience and the last ten years of my own work and research and writing in the field of catastrophic case management because I've, quite frankly, made a substantial contribution to that field and in many instances have initiated new directions, methodologies, et cetera, that have been very successfully adopted by many rehabilitation professionals across the country.

Q. You used the word "catastrophic." That's pretty broad. What do you mean by "catastrophic"?

A. Basically, the definition of catastrophic impairment for purposes of my office are any individuals who require long-term support care or the development of a long-term management plan. For example, a single lower-extremity amputee, a below-knee amputation, may be very catastrophic to the individual that incurs it; but it is a non-catastrophic impairment from our standpoint. The individual can be rehabilitated, stabilized, and does not need long-term services either from my office or from any other health-related professional or physician other than some intermittent monitoring and replacement of the prosthesis; but they can manage that. Spinal cord injuries, to varying degrees, depending upon the level of lesion, severe burns, multiple amputations, severe brain injury, persistent vegetative state patients -- those are catastrophic impairments.

Q. What about disease-related? I notice all those that you mentioned seem to be related to something other than disease or some developmental-type process --

A. From --

Q. -- i.e., CP patients or those patients who might be profoundly neurologically impaired, but you don't trace it to any traumatic event.

A. Well, being brain injured doesn't necessarily have to come from a traumatic event in terms of an automobile accident. We do a great deal of work with cerebral palsy, epilepsy, et cetera. And, in fact, better than half of my caseload is under sixteen years of age; and it's because the majority of them tend to be developmental disabilities. But I don't do a great deal of work with disease processes. Probably the only group that I have had experience with on a consistent basis where disease processes were the primary problem are in pulmonary dysfunction, and most of that is occupational exposure. Usually, with disease processes, number one, it's a secondary category or problem to the primary disability I'm working with. And progressive disorders are not typically something that we usually will get involved with or that we do much work with.

Q. Do you have any other degrees or certifications beyond the Ph.D. that you were just talking about?

A. No other degrees. I'm licensed in the State of Florida under the Psychology Practices Act in the Mental Health Division. I am certified by the Commission on Rehabilitation Counselor Certification. But that's the extent of it.

Q. This last thing you just mentioned, the certification for rehabilitation counseling, is that the CRC abbreviation after your name?

A. That's true.

Q. You do business in the name of Paul M. Deutsch and Associates, Inc., out of Orlando, Florida; is that correct?

A. Actually, it's Paul M. Deutsch and Associates, P.A., now.

Q. Are you the head of that entity?

A. Yes.

Q. How many employees do you have?

A. There are 30 employees. This includes 13 professional staff.

Q. What do you mean by "professional"?

A. Those individuals with B.A.'s, Master, or Doctorate that have professional responsibilities.

Q. I'd like to know beyond the generalities that you used, what you do, you know, for Paul M. Deutsch and Associates.

A. Well, I can split my practice really into three areas: The first is direct services to patient populations, the work I do at the head injury center, or the work I do in catastrophic case management.

Q. What percentage of your time is devoted to that?

A. Currently, because of other projects, I'd say forty to forty-five percent. Specifically, that involves individual counseling, family counseling, family training. We do a lot of work with families to teach them to be disability managers. It's our feeling that our work, basically, with catastrophic case management in any individual case can be ended in about six to twelve months with the ability to train a family member to take over, and then we just act as resource people. We develop life care plans. We will come in, implement the plan, develop the team. We train the team. We develop behavioral modification programs for those patients who require it. For our pediatric cases, particularly head injury or developmental disabilities, we develop --

Q. Now, you are using the pronoun "we." I was asking, specifically, the things that you do.

A. Okay. Well, there's nothing in the office with respect to my practice that I'm not responsible for, but we do it as a team approach. I'm doing those things. I'm the one who is responsible for individual counseling and will perform it. But all of our work, even in developing behavioral programs for toileting, for self-feeding, et cetera, I use various staff members to assist me in implementing the program. So I do have the habit of saying "we." But with respect to my own practice, there's not a bit of work that goes out of that office that I'm not involved in and that I'm not responsible for and that I don't have a direct hand in.

Q. Well, let me interrupt you here. As far as preparing the reports, for instance, like the one that's got Sarah Martin's name on it that I'm holding in front of you here --

A. Yes.

Q. -- is this a collaborative effort of your team? Or is this a singular effort on your behalf?

A. First, there are three parts to that report -- there's a narrative, which is completely dictated by me. There's no collaborative effort there. The life care plan --

Q. That encompasses the first eight pages of the report, which, by the way, we'll mark as Exhibit Number Two in this deposition.

(Exhibit Number Two so marked.)

Q. Have you got a copy of it there?

A. I have a copy.

Q. Is your signature right there?

A. Yes. The next portion that you have would be the life care plan. Now, what I do when I complete an evaluation is map out the basics of the life care plan; this, I put in all of the health-related professional evaluations, all of the therapeutic evaluations, all of the services I want; and then my staff assists me in completing surveys for local pricing information, in pulling catalogs for information. Generally, researching for geographically

Q. Okay. Are you currently affiliated with any particular medical institution?

A. I'm on staff as an allied health professional at Orlando Regional Medical Center, and that's probably the most important affiliation. I'm on staff, also at Florida Hospital, but I have recently basically suspended doing work over there.

Q. At these two facilities, you operate consistent with what you've explained your services to be earlier in this deposition; is that what I'm to understand?

A. Well, with respect to Orlando Regional Medical Center, my primary work is with the neurologist in the neurology department at the brain injury rehab unit there. So my primary focus is head injury at that facility. And we are the outpatient program that's liaisoned with their in-patient program. It's soon to be merged into the ownership of Orlando Regional, and then we'll be contracting back to run it for them. But, currently, I still own it along with my partner. So our focus there is primarily head injury, which is a different set of responsibilities that we didn't get into. We just, at this point, have talked primarily about my private practice and only the first forty to forty-five percent of my professional time.

Q. Well, tell me how you devote the balance of your professional time, the other fifty or sixty percent.

A. Okay. A portion of my time is spent in consultation work, and I split that into two areas: One is consultation in areas such as litigation.

Q. What percentage of your time is devoted to that area?

A. Generally, it ranges from a low of about fifteen percent to a high of about twenty-five percent and included in that would be those instances in which I am consulting directly with a carrier and I'm never going to be used in litigation. It's just for educational purposes and for making certain everybody understands the nature of the disability, even though that's not a litigation case for me. And then the balance of my time is spent in research and writing. And, right now, patient time is down, and litigation time is effected because I'm in the midst of a new book which will be coming out in 1988.

Q. What's the subject of that book? Not in any detail, just --

A. The title of the book is *Innovations in Head Injury Rehabilitation*, and it's being done along with the neuropsychological staff of the First Moscow Medical Institute in the Soviet Union.

Q. As far as the head injury center that you're talking about, I take it that the patients you see there, basically, are seen as a result of some traumatic occurrence that has caused some damages to their neurological function; is that correct?

A. That's true. Eighty percent of them are car accidents; the balance are spread among a number etiologic.

Q. Do the majority of those patients experience mental impairment as well or just neurological --

A. Mental being psychological? Is that what you're --

Q. Psychological.

A. I don't think there's any question that people going through traumatic injuries of that nature experience some degree of psychological impairment, but certainly it's a broad range from very minor to very serious. So, I would say, yes, generally they do.

Q. Beyond those two institutions you told me about, medical institutions, are there any other that you're affiliated with?

A. In terms of providing patient services, no. I'm on the Board of the College of Health-Related Professions at Shands, University of Florida, and I'm on the faculty at the College of Health-Related Professions; but that work has nothing to do with any direct patient services.

Q. How much actual hands-on case management in catastrophic -- to use your word -- type of circumstances -- how much of that is outside the State of Florida?

A. Considerable.

Q. Can you reduce it roughly to an approximate percentage?

A. I'll try for you. I would say that somewhere in the neighborhood of fifty to fifty-five percent of our total work -- forgetting what's litigation, what's direct services, just taking everything -- probably fifty to fifty-five percent of my work is outside the state. Probably five to ten percent is outside the continental United States.

Q. And a percentage of those cases that are outside the State of Florida in which you are actually involved in case management also involve litigation; is that correct?

A. Well, --

Q. For instance, like --

A. -- it's very rare -- okay, it's very rare. Even if I got involved in a case, not from the attorneys, but from whatever resource it was referred, I would say that ninety-five percent of all cases that I ever see -- because we do work primarily with accident victims' that's how they get to us -- are involved in something: Social Security Disability disputes, Worker's Compensation, federal lawsuits, or civil, state lawsuits. Almost everybody gets involved somewhere down the line. And it's very rare that we don't have a case where at least our records are subpoenaed, if not our testimony. So that happens pretty much across the board.

Q. About ninety-five percent of the time, you say, is litigation --

A. I'd say ninety-five percent of all cases have something, whether it's one or the other of the things that I've listed. And in litigation cases, we've had a growing number. But I'd say right now, the best estimate I can give you is about somewhere in the neighborhood of fifteen to twenty percent, maybe at times as much as twenty-five percent of cases that are litigated and when the litigation is over will come back and work with us in terms of follow-through on the life care plan. Others, either we set up with local people and we felt that that's all we needed to be doing, or they just didn't pursue a follow-through with us.

Q. What percentage of the patients with whom you are involved actually are spinal cord injury patients?

A. Right now, roughly sixty-five to seventy percent of my caseload is some type of neurological impairment, and about twenty to twenty-five percent are spinal cord. The remaining five percent are split among a variety of disabilities. But the two largest groups are spinal cord and traumatic brain injury.

Q. What percentage of your patients involve traumatic origin for the spinal cord injury?

A. Well, define --

Q. Virtually all of them --

A. Define -- I mean, any injury to the cord is traumatic. Maybe I'm having a problem with semantics. But I'd say virtually all spinal cord injuries, with the exception of the children that are spina bifida that we work with, I think would be considered traumatic. I only have two spina bifida cases on my caseload, actively, right now. And so I'd say virtually all of them are traumatic.

Q. How many spinal cord injury patients are you seeing? We've got percentages, but how many patients would you say?

A. It's a number I'd be happy to research for you. Off the top of my head, it would literally be a wild guess. And I'd say in one stage or the other of our following them, whether we're actively implementing a plan or whether we've completed it and we're just resource people. We're probably talking up to twenty-five.

Q. Okay.

A. And then the rest, we're resource people for these. And every month a new one comes in. It goes through the pipeline and then becomes, eventually, somebody we follow as resource people.

Q. Of these twenty-five that you estimate you have as active patients with spinal cord injury, how many of those patients are sixteen or older?

A. I'd say my caseload probably follows the statistics fairly closely. The majority of spinal cord injuries are sixteen years of age to twenty-four years of age. And I'd say probably, right now, at least eighty percent are sixteen to twenty-four years; and the rest of the spread -- I've got a couple that are fifty to seventy.

Q. Did they acquire an injury subsequent to a fall or motor vehicle accident or one of the other high-risk areas?

A. I think every one of my elderly spinal cord involves a car accident.

Q. Okay. Motor vehicle accidents, across the board, tend to be the largest cause for spinal cord injury; is that correct?

A. Well, depends on the region. Overall, yes. In Florida, no. In Florida, the vast majority are diving accidents.

Q. That's for those that are sports-related; correct?

A. Well, you know, I guess you could call it sports-related. But we get an awful lot of people just diving into a shallow pool or a shallow spring or a lake; that's just a very, very common problem in Florida. You see that all the time.

Q. So you would say Florida is disproportionate to the national averages, which would --

A. Our statistics are a little different. We do have probably a disproportionately high number of diving accidents. But if you look at the national statistics on spinal cord, diving accidents are not an infrequent problem even nationwide; but auto accidents certainly are the greatest cause.

Q. That's what I was alluding to just a moment ago. I think there are statistics that indicate that about two-thirds of all the sports-related injuries are as a result of diving. So that coalesces with, I think, essentially what you're saying.

A. Okay.

Q. Now, you said eighty percent of your patients were sixteen to twenty-four; and you had a couple of patients that, out of that fifteen or twenty, were in their fifties or older.

A. Speaking specifically about spinal cord, yes, the current caseload.

Q. That's specifically what we're talking about.

A. Okay.

Q. Because in Sarah Martin's case, that's what we're dealing with; correct? A spinal cord injury case?

A. That's correct.

Q. Now, is Sarah Martin included in those numbers of patients that you've enumerated?

A. Well, the only thing we didn't talk about with respect to the breakdown of the caseload was how many are pediatric cases, and she obviously would be involved in the balance that are pediatric cases. We probably have as many early childhood onset of spinal cord injuries as we do geriatric. I mean, it's kind of almost like a bell-shaped curve with the largest share being sixteen to twenty-four and the age group spreading out from there. And I'd say it's pretty even as far as the numbers of peds we see in spinal cord versus the numbers of geriatrics we see in spinal cord.

Q. About even?

A. At least in my caseload, it's been pretty even.

Q. So you have two that are probably in the geriatric category right now. And how many would you have in the pediatrics that are active?

A. In terms of active cases right now --

Q. And I'm including Sarah Martin here.

A. Okay. I would have, too. So -- but in terms of active spinal cord cases now, there may be four or five. I would need to go -- in terms of defining what's active, that might be the only consideration. Some are in the active category, they are beginning to phase down. And so we have a very strong rule about how long we will follow them before we insist that family take over a large share of our responsibility.

Q. You're not connected with any of the spinal cord injury centers in the United States, are you?

A. No, I work with a lot of them, but I'm not connected to any of them. I'm not on staff at any of them.

Q. As far as these, as you referred to them, pediatrics cases, how many of those are neonatal spinal cord injuries? Birth-related?

A. Probably the only one that I've seen in a while is Sarah Martin.

Q. How many have you seen in your entire professional career, that you have actually actively been involved in?

A. I honestly can't answer that. Certainly, it's been a very, very small number.

Q. Fewer than five?

A. That would -- I certainly would suspect that. I mean, I'd have to go back and look over the last fifteen years. But we'd be eliminating anybody that was, for example, spinal cord -- that was spina bifida or anything of that nature. And I doubt I've seen specifically this etiology more than maybe once or twice in fifteen years. The etiology isn't that important to me. The outcome is what I have to deal with. But the specific etiology, I don't' think I've seen more than once or twice. And when I say that, I mean birth-related, not -- I really don't get into exactly the mechanics of an injury, whether it's automobile or anything else. I just don't get involved in reconstructing how it happened.

Q. So Sarah Martin's case, for you, is an unusual case?

A. Only in the nature of its onset. It's not unusual in terms of the fact that she's a spinal cord injury and that certain specific nerves have been enervated and that certain specific results that come from that, certain sequelae. She's perfectly common as a spinal cord injury in terms of the nature of the problems we're having to deal with, but she's unusual in terms of how the onset occurred.

Q. Well, you are not suggesting, are you, that pediatric patients are average as you would compare them, say, with the age group of sixteen to twenty-four --

A. Certainly that depends on what you mean by "average." They are not average in terms of the frequency of occurrence because the larger frequency in spinal cord is sixteen to twenty-four. But it's not unusual to see a pediatric spinal cord injury. They're not average in psychological response because early onset of disability in childhood results in psychological consequences that are in many ways much more dramatic than they are in the sixteen to twenty-four group but also much more easily intervened with and dealt with than they are in the sixteen to twenty-four group. So if you let them go, it's a more serious problem. But if you deal with the pediatric psychological impact, you can usually make better gains than you could in the older population. So there are many things that are different about pediatric onset of any disability, but included in that would be spinal cord injury. But it's the etiology that probably makes this more unique than the injury itself.

Q. How many times in the past -- and just an estimate -- if you can give me an exact figure, fine; but if you can't, just estimate. How many times in the past have you been involved in testifying in cases on behalf of the plaintiff?

A. Now, I can't really give you an estimate of numbers. I can give you --

Q. Percentages?

A. -- percentages.

Q. That would be fine.

A. I can try numbers. It's a little easier for me to talk about, like, the last three or four years.

Q. Percentages are fine. It doesn't really matter.

A. We did, at the request of an attorney, in the past six months -- actually complete an audit ending January 15. It was a thirty-six month audit. And we did it in two ways so that we could give him the information we felt he was asking for: One for catastrophic cases alone, and the other was our total caseload that involved litigation where they were referred because of the litigation as opposed to those who may have ended up in litigation, but we were involved in treating them. Total caseload was fifty-six percent defense, and total catastrophics alone was sixty-one percent defense.

Q. How many times have you personally appeared in court to testify in cases?

A. I can't tell you over my entire career. It's certainly grown over the past fifteen years. The first time I ever appeared in court was with a spinal cord injury when I worked for the State of Florida. It was during the very first year; one of the first things that happened was that I got subpoenaed. I was working for State Health and Rehabilitative Services. In the last three years where I've probably been more active in that area, I would say I've been in court eight to twelve times in a year at a maximum. The vast majority just don't get to court for live testimony.

5

The Presentation of the Evaluation, Data Gathering, and Test Procedures

Having moved the rehabilitation testimony through establishing expert qualifications and educating the jury on the role of the rehabilitation professional, the next step is to make certain that all parties concerned understand the concept of the rehabilitation evaluation, data gathering procedures, and testing procedures. It is not the purpose of this section of testimony to actually review all of the data gathered or interpret the tests which were administered. Instead, the goal here is to make sure that the judge and jury have a thorough understanding of the procedures or steps taken in the evaluation, data gathering, testing, and research process. There is a twofold goal in accomplishing this aspect of jury education. The first is to help the jury understand the thoroughness with which the evaluation was undertaken while the second is to help them appreciate the kinds of data and information which influence rehabilitation conclusions and go far beyond the scope of the basic medical assessments that relate to anatomical dysfunction but not necessarily to functional disability manifested in day-to-day restrictions.

The questions utilized in this portion of the rehabilitation testimony are geared toward helping the jury understand the three primary aspects of the evaluation and data gathering procedures.

The first step in the evaluation is a review of all of the information collected and summarized as part of the overall disability assessment. The jury learns that the rehabilitation professional has reviewed all of the following:

1) Hospital medical reports
2) Physician office notes
3) Pertinent physician/medical depositions
4) Psychological evaluation reports including raw test data
5) Depositions of the psychologists
6) Client and family depositions
7) Pre-morbid as well as post-accident employment records and tax returns
8) Pre-morbid as well as post-accident school records in any instance in which the individual is young enough to make obtaining those records possible and appropriate. School record data should include achievement test results, school psychology reports, teacher comments, and grades. These areas should be considered in that order of priority with achievement tests representing the most objective evidence of pre-morbid function and grades are representing the most subjected.

The questions provided during this section of the rehabilitation testimony will also help the jury understand that data has been collected in the following areas:

1) General identifying information
2) All assistive devices, equipment, or aids for independent function being employed
3) Date of onset of injury and the nature of the injury
4) Initial treatment
5) Work attempts since the onset of disability
6) Rehabilitation program involvement post-accident
7) A review of the disabling problem including the patients subjective description of chief complaints and subjective description of physical limitations
8) The patient's prior medical history including injuries or illnesses resulting in the need for long-term medical care or causing a permanent impairment
9) A review of conservative treatment, surgical procedures, and current medical care

10) Environmental influences and work settings which might exacerbate the individual's disability
11) Activities of daily living
12) Social activities
13) Personal habits
14) Family, social, economic status
15) Income sources including any assistance from state or federal agencies involved in the rehabilitation process
16) Prior history of any criminal activity
17) All past education and training of either an academic, vocational, or apprenticeship nature
18) Military experience
19) Employment history
20) The behavioral observations made of the client during the course of the evaluation process
21) A complete list of all supplies (replenishable medical supplies dictated by the onset of the disability and used on a regular basis)
22) A complete list of all equipment
23) Detailed information regarding any history of complications which have required treatment since the onset of the disability

In addition, specific catastrophic injury cases such as spinal cord injuries, head injuries, or brain damaged infants have a broad range of additional pertinent areas of question and data gathering in the evaluation process that covers items such as the type of bowel program or bladder program being utilized, the level of independence in turning and transfers, the current nursing or attendant care needs, and a complete review in the case of head injury of any cognitive, behavioral social, or motoric dysfunction (sequelae).

The next questions take the rehabilitation expert through any vocational or psychological testing undertaken as a part of the evaluation. Not all rehabilitation professionals will have equal training and background in test administration and interpretation and it is essential that all parties concerned be carefully educated regarding the parameters of the specific professional's expertise before these questions are raised. For those who can handle both vocational and psychological testing, it is important to review the nature of the test, the purpose in their administration, and their value in drawing conclusions in the rehabilitation assessment. At this point, no effort is being made to interpret test results, but only to explain their benefit and why the tests utilized in this particular evaluation were chosen.

Initial Education of the Jury on Rehabilitation Procedures

The process of educating the jury on the role of the rehabilitation professional extends not only to their qualifications, goals, and the scope of the evaluation but also to the specific procedures being used in the case currently in litigation. One of the primary benefits to rehabilitation testimony is that it makes common sense when it is presented to a jury in a clear and concise fashion. The goal is to educate the jury so that they are not just accepting the opinions of the expert but more importantly would be able to reach similar conclusions because of their understanding of the data and how it must be applied in drawing conclusions and in making decisions regarding rehabilitation. This increased effort in jury education demonstrates the extent to which the data has been collected and considered in the development of vocational conclusions and rehabilitation recommendations. Even if the jury comes out with no other conclusion than how thorough the rehabilitation expert has been, it will go a long way toward enhancing credibility and adding weight to the testimony and conclusions drawn.

For this reason, the first questions on rehabilitation testimony presented in the following list focus on enhancing the jury's understanding of the clinical history and interview, the vocational and psychological tests including their make-up, and purpose and the manner in which the medical information is utilized and interpreted in terms of vocational implications. They also focus on the manner in which all of the medical, psychosocial, and vocational data are used in the development of vocational conclusions, conclusions regarding independent living, or the ability to handle activities of daily living, and the scope and purpose of the rehabilitation recommendations.

The sixteen questions presented in Appendix C are restricted to educating the judge and jury in those areas I have outlined in this discussion. The balance of the questions necessary to actually develop the findings and the conclusions drawn from those findings will be presented in Appendix D and Appendix E relative first to the non-catastrophic case presentation and second, to the catastrophic injury case presentation.

Sample Transcripts

There are two sample transcripts being provided for this section of the text. The first involves actual trial testimony involving a pediatric brain injury case with a birth onset. The second involves an adult chronic back/chronic pain syndrome. They are presented to give the reader as broad a concept as possible of the techniques utilized in developing this information.

Transcript #1

Q. Now, how do you go about evaluating somebody to make some determination of what their needs might be?
A. Well, a lot depends certainly on the specific nature of an individual's disability, but generally what occurs first is a review of the medical information. I'm focused primarily, of course, on the current status of the individual, what therapies they've had, and what their current levels of functioning are.
So those are the areas of medicals that I'm primarily focused on. I also look at any materials that may be there from family, from school programs, or educational programs, particularly school programs where they're available, because this is a great deal of data information on a child. Once I've reviewed and summarized that, the next step is to actually evaluate the family and child together.
Q. Why is that important?
A. Well, first of all, I certainly can develop a great deal more insight into the level of functioning of the child by working with them than I can by just reading the materials. I don't care how good the teachers are or how good the physicians are, there's no way a report by itself is going to be as descriptive as my own opportunity to work with the child.
Secondly, I also have some differences of opinion perhaps with the standard, more formal methods of providing psychological or developmental tests. I think most of these

children have a great deal of difficulty demonstrating skills through a formal test setting.

I believe in a lot of child observation during free play to get an idea of the level of function, particularly physically, that the child is showing. So it's important for me to have a chance to do that and to also get to know the family.

Q. Why is getting to know the family important?

A. Well, basically any disability group, I don't care what the age of the individual is, is going to have the best potential to develop and reach their maximum potential if there's a strong family support unit. If the family is comfortable in working with the disability and comfortable in working with the child, even if they may not have all of the answers or all of the information they need at that point, if there's a strong family support unit, that individual is going to go a lot farther in rehabilitation.

So I look to assess the family in part for that and in part to see what the family needs, because frankly, if you're going to maintain a strong family support unit over the long period of time that you will go through rehabilitation or rehabilitation program with an adult, there are certain needs of the family you have to meet, because there's a lot of stress and tension involved in working with the disabilities.

There's a need for the family to receive training and education and support if they're going to be there for the individual who is impaired. So assessing the family becomes as critical in many ways as assessing the child.

Q. Now, when you make this assessment, what areas in your plan are you -- what information are you looking for as far as the plan to prepare for this child?

A. Well, basically it's pretty broad ranges of areas. Once I go through all the medicals and I'm working with the family, the first thing I'm looking at is to develop information about any programs that the individual or the child has gone through since the onset of the disability, whether they've been through a cerebral palsy program or a school sponsored program, whatever it has been, early infant stimulation programs, any training that the parents have received.

I go through general background on any equipment that the child has, any replenishable supplies that the child requires. I go through any medical history in terms of complications or medical treatment or hospitalizations that have been required. I go through with the parents' or family's understanding of the primary programs or disability is, what do they understand the diagnosis to be.

I may add to that through my own observations or through the review of the medicals. I want to get a sense of how much the family understands of the problem before I start soliciting more information through questions. I go through the family's subjective description of limitations that the child has. Basically how are the problems, manifested in terms of daily function, what can the child do in each of the areas and what can't they do.

I go through environmental influences; that is, is there a particular problem that can occur as a result of exposure to heat, cold, wet or humid environments, or stress in the environment, a long list of those.

Q. Once you do come up with the evaluation and these plans, are you and your co-workers involved in actually implementing these plans?

A. Certainly not necessarily in every single case that we develop.

Q. Generally is what we're talking about.

A. Certainly the majority of patients we see, our role and responsibility is to develop life care plans and rehabilitation plans and then to implement them.

Implementing them means, first of all, acting as a team leader to bring together the various therapies, to coordinate liaison with those therapies.

Q. What do you mean by various therapies?

A. It depends on the needs of the child.

Q. Can you give us some examples?

A. Sure. Usually what we're talking about is physical therapy, occupational therapy, speech therapy, the educational program that's provided under the public school system, the special education we wanted to coordinate with them, and actually build a program around that as the central core.

And then we also as staff members, myself and my staff, provide specific services to the family, individual counseling where appropriate or behavioral modification programs where appropriate, family counseling as well as family education.

Q. You threw something in there that lost me. You said behavioral modification programs?

A. Yes.

Q. Would you explain to the jury -- probably I just don't understand. What do you mean by that?

A. Well, basically there are an awful lot of patients to work with that simply will never benefit from the individual counseling. I mean, they're not going to develop insight and understanding and be able to learn and internalize what you're going to need to learn during the counseling session.

But they become behavior problems, and so we teach the family very positive and constructive behavioral modification programs, appropriate ways to shape and train and modify behavior so we stop inappropriate or violent acting out behavior or hyperactivity where possible. We always want to work with hyperactivity behaviorally before we try medications.

Q. Why do you want to try to work with hyperactivity with behavior modification before medication?

A. Well, with any behavior problem, medication masks behavioral problems. They cover them up. They don't solve them. If you cannot change the behavior, then you can look at medication to resolve the problem because it may be the only way you can work with the child.

But if at all possible, in more cases than not, it is possible we can provide a good coordinated program through the family and school system and work with behavioral changes. We can normally get the changes we need without having to resort to long-term medication.

So first of all, it's a healthier approach. Secondly, it's a lot less expensive in the long run because we're not supporting medical and medication regimens throughout the life expectancy of that individual.

Q. Doctor, you mentioned life care plan. Now, this life care plan that you draw up, is that just for your use, or what is the purpose of that?

A. The life care plan started out and continues today primarily to be for family's use. I wanted a system that would allow the family to get to walk away from this lengthy process of evaluation and all the research we do with something that would act as a guideline. Certainly changes can take place. Problems can develop that you can't anticipate.

But this is a basic guideline that says that the very ages we've outlined in the plan, certain things need to be done. You need to seek out certain professionals. You need to make certain changes, what we call phase changes, in the program to meet the needs of the child.

So the basic idea behind the life care plan was to coordinate and provide the family with a master plan. The reason we put the dollars into the life care plan was for budgeting purposes, because frankly, that's a critical part of what has to be done. We have to budget for maintenance of equipment replacement schedules, for new therapies we need to bring in. And so that's basically the idea behind the plan.

Q. Shifting from the general concept to Susan Ann Hartford and her parents before today, have you had an opportunity to meet with the Hartfords in their home?

A. Yes.

Q. Would you please tell the jury when that occurred?

A. Certainly. That was May 9th, 1988.

Q. And how long did that meeting take place?

A. Evaluation runs between three and three and a half hours.

Q. All right. Now, this evaluation, before you did that, had you done any preparation?

A. Yes.

Q. What had you done to prepare yourself to go into the Hartfords' home and evaluate the situation?

A. Well, I had reviewed the records, basic medical records. Should I list them for you?

Q. Well, do you have those record with you today?

A. I have all the records and the notebooks that I've brought up, and I also wrote out a separate list of the records and their dates.

Q. If you would just tell us each record you reviewed before you went into the Hartford home.

A. Well, it was T. C. Thompson Children's Hospital records with the following inclusive dates: 10/4/85 through 10/10/85, and 10/13/85 through 11/8/85; the Team Evaluation Center assessment report, 7/25/86 and 12/16/86; the Emory Clinic ophthalmology report, 11/21/86 to 7/31/87;

Georgia Children's Medical Services notes and the deposition of the mother of February 10, 1988. And those were all the things that were reviewed prior to my going up there.

Q. Would you show the jury what those records look like *in toto*?

A. These are the notebooks in which I have basically put all the medicals and I have labeled them.

Q. Did you go through every one of those before you met them?

A. Yes.

Q. And this meeting took place in May of this year?

A. That's correct.

Q. Now, from that meeting and evaluation, would you tell the jury what you did at that evaluation and working and trying to determine Susan Ann Hartford's exact situation?

A. Well, the first thing I did is basically met in the living room, and we asked the family to be there. So I had the mother there and I had the brother and sister there and Susan Ann was there. I asked that Susan Ann be allowed to remain in the room throughout my interview with the family.

There are no questions that I'm asking during that portion of the interview that I feel will in any way bother the child. But I want the child to have a chance to have free play, to hear my voice, to listen to me, knowing I'm there for an hour before I start working with her so that the child is not afraid, doesn't think I'm a doctor coming in to examine her or hurt her in any way.

So that was the first thing that occurred was an interview with the mother and brother and sister. That probably took close to an hour and 45 minutes, two hours in total.

And then I began working with Susan just after having a chance to observe her. I took notes from the time I was collecting information from the family. I began working with her in terms of the Bayley Scales of Infant Development.

Q. The what? The Bayley Scales of Infant Development?

A. Yes, sir.

Q. What are those?

A. Bayley Scales basically are one of a number of different published infant development scales. You don't give a child at this age or this level an IQ test *per se*. What you do is look for developmental signs, how they've developed mentally or cognitively, how they've developed in terms of behavioral functioning and maturity, how they've developed in terms of physical or motor function.

So I look at each of those three areas within the context of the Bayley Scales. But with Susan Ann, you don't sit her down and start interacting with her as in a more formal situation, as I said --

Q. Why is that?

A. Basically, it's primarily behavioral, number one. She is mildly to moderately hyperactive. She is very close to family members and very resistant to strangers coming in, and the presence of a stranger very much affects Susan's behavior. So it's very difficult to get her to sit down and give any length of attention.

She has a very fleeting attention span. It's very difficult to get her to respond to a formal -- more formal test situation. So what I did was introduce different items in the Bayley Scales just as free play in her environment.

Q. Could you give us some examples of what you did to try to provoke responses from this child to allow you --

A. There are a lot of things. You start out, the very low level, you're looking just to see if you get any response to visual stimuli or auditory stimuli. That was pretty easy to observe just during the course of the family --

Q. Did you get -- what type of response did you get from visual stimulation?

A. Okay. Basically I noted in my report that she did react to the shadow of a hand with eye blink. I could get some coordination -- I believe it was vertical eye coordination to a light. When I used a flash light, I could get her to track. I couldn't get her to continue tracking for any length of time.

I also discussed vision with the family, but apart from that, that's about what I received. It was little question also that just in observing free play, if I put something on the floor, she was able to see it, be attracted to it, would eventually interact with it.

But I was more concerned, quite frankly, with the high levels of function because she was demonstrating higher levels. So even in simple tasks like showing motor skill function in manipulating the blocks or watching me put a block on the floor and a little coffee cup that's in the Bayley Scales inverted on top of the block and watching her figure out how to pick up the cup and get to the block.

There's also other -- there's like a box with almost a hidden top, in essence. We put things into it and close it up and just put her on the floor and let her see if she can get into it. So we're looking at fine motor skills, we're looking at gross motor skills, we're looking at problem solving and judgment on her part.

For example, could she retrieve the red ring that we have in there with the string. We put the ring out of her reach, but the string was in her reach and see if she can figure out that she can retrieve the object by pulling it on the string.

So they sound like very simple tasks, but, of course, when you're dealing with infant development skills, you're talking about simple things. We watch her play, watch her figure out problems, solving them, watch how she interacts with the various items in the Bayley Scales. And a lot also is judgment on my part in terms of assessing muscle tone in the motor section, whether she's basically relaxed, how she is affected by my presence. These are all areas that are critical to assess.

Q. You say this took about three hours?

A. That's correct.

Q. Now, after this meeting and after you reviewed all the records that you told the jury about and then you met with her, what else did you do after that before you came up with this life care plan?

A. Basically, the next step is to go back to my office and begin first mapping out a rough life care plan just based on my evaluation -- what are the items that I need.

Now, I reviewed all of my notes in those areas I've already told you about plus the other areas that I cover. We didn't quite list out all of them, but a lot of family background data, social data was considered as well.

◄ *The Presentation of the Evaluation, Data Gathering, and Test Procedures* ►

Sample Transcript #2

Q. Now, when is the first time that your mission in connection with this case was outlined by Mr. Roper?

A. Well, if you could call it an outline, I'd say March 23rd--or that is his letter of March 23rd, which we received on the 28th. I think it was just fairly assumed that I would look at this file from a rehabilitation standpoint, the way I do any file. So there was no specific request other than -- and I'll read directly from the letter.

"We're interested in your preliminary opinions concerning Marsha Lewis' employability and rehabilitation. And we enclose for your review the following."

And they sent me her deposition and the deposition of Jerry Adato, A-d-a-t-o, and subsequently sent me additional medical information and tax returns, personnel records, et cetera.

Q. When was it that you formed your preliminary opinion?

A. Well, really, my opinion wasn't formed until I had an opportunity to review all of those records, and I typed up, or had typed up -- I didn't personally type it -- a summary of my notes, and I just typed it up on a little appendix -- I called it a vocational worksheet -- and outlined the five basic areas in which I drew any conclusions.

Q. And what is the date of that opinion?

A. Hang on just a moment. I haven't dated the top of the notes, but I think I can get it from other records here in the file, if you give me a moment. September 6, of '88.

Q. Has your opinion changed in any way since that time?

A. No.

Q. So what you are now about to tell us, in response to our question, concerns the opinion you formed back in September, based upon various documents and other material?

A. Yes. And I also have typed a list of the documents I received and had typed up, the notes I made during the review of those documents, so that both of those are available.

Q. Why don't you just tell us now what they were.

A. Okay. I'd by happy to. There is a fairly lengthy list.

It's the deposition -- excuse me, the reports of Carl H. Sadowski, Dr. Sadowski, the neurologist, 2/27/85 and 6/5/86.

Dr. Jordan Greer, 3/3/87, 3/28/86, 1/26/87.

Dr. Jeffrey Penner, P-e-n-n-e-r, on an IME orthopedic evaluation of 9/25/87.

Dr. Albia, A-l-b-i-a, Morariu, M-o-r-a-r-i-u, neurologist, with the following dates: 9/30/87, 10/7/87, 10/9/87, 12/15/87.

Daniel Goldstein, work capacity evaluation of 1/31/88.

The deposition of Daniel Goldstein, 2/10/88.

The deposition of Ms. Lewis, 9/15/87.

The deposition of Jerry Adato, 2/4/88.

The tax records, '81 through '86.

School records.

Good Samaritan Hospital emergency report of 1/22/85.

The ambulance report and the traffic accident report.

And just let me add real quick that just before placing those calls, I walked in here. I left the note -- I have all my notes of those. I left the notebook in the other room, so if I'm going to need it, I'll have to break for two seconds and have it brought in or go grab it.

Q. Why don't you.
A. Okay. Just take a second.

(Whereupon, a break was taken, after which the following proceedings were had:)

THE WITNESS: Okay. I'm back. I'm sorry.
BY MR. BURDICK:

Q. Now, should we understand that in the formation of your opinion to be given in this case on behalf of Hertz Corporation, you took into account all of the material that you have described and gave it such weight as you thought appropriate?

A. I think that's true.

Q. So, therefore, you considered certain material as being true and some material as being untrue, or how did you segregate the value of the various documents?

A. Okay. I honestly don't feel I segregated the value at all. I felt that what was being painted in the medicals and in the rehabilitation reports was a very accurate description of an individual who was having a classic, chronic pain, chronic disability syndrome, secondary to both her accident and, or course, her predisposing personality characteristics.

I mean, we're all inclined to react to a problem in some fashion. It's not something we readily have control over, and I think what we saw here was somebody who was going through a fairly classic chronic pain syndrome, and I felt that the question was one of identifying its severity and identifying what rehabilitation steps would be appropriate in moving ahead with this individual.

So, I didn't discount anything, nor did I specifically segregate out reports saying this one has more value than the next one.

Q. Now, you used the phrase "predisposing". Would you please amplify?

A. Certainly. Well, basically, all I'm saying is, is that we are all the sum total of our experiences in life. I mean, that goes into making up our personality. And it's that personality profile that will give us a predisposition to react to an event in one fashion or another.

If you have an accident tomorrow, you're going to react in a certain fashion. That's pretty such set by the nature of your personality. And I'm talking about your psychological reaction to any injury or disability. And that's what I'm talking about with respect to Ms. Lewis.

Q. From which of the listed material did you obtain that basis for any conclusion you made on her predisposing personality profile?

A. Well, I didn't draw any conclusion with respect to that from any of the medicals, and maybe I'm not making myself clear with respect to the definition I gave.

What I'm saying to you is that we are all predisposed to react in a certain fashion. And all I'm suggesting to you is, is that the reaction she has had in terms of her emotional or psychological reaction to disability is one that was predisposed to occur. I mean, there is no way she could control that aspect.

So, all I've done is assume, basically, that the problems that she has secondary to this accident, both in a physical as well as in a psychological sense, are basically inherent in the problem that I have to now cope with from a rehabilitation standpoint.

Q. How did you conclude that she was the same or different from any of the rest of us who might be confronted with the same experience?

A. Well, that's a very simple conclusion to draw in that nobody is the same. You're going to react your way. I'm going to react mine. Mr. Oxford would react his way. Ms. Lewis would react another way.

Now, there may be a lot of overlapping similarities in the way two people react, but all I'm telling you is, is that she is who she was. She was going to react to an accident in a certain fashion. That's just a part of her personality.

Q. And did you draw any conclusions particularly concerning her personality?

A. Well, I think that there are -- if you wanted to -- well, first of all, the answer to the question is, I don't think I drew any specific conclusions or tried to draw any specific conclusions as regards her personality before this accident.

I mean, you certainly, once having identified someone as a chronic pain or chronic disability patient, as we have here, because she is a chronic back/chronic pain patient, that's the problem she is describing, you can go back to the literature and try and trace back some of the more obvious demographic variables and personality variables that may be associated generally with this population, but that's pretty unimportant in terms of what I'm trying to do here.

All I'm telling you is, is that I have assumed that these are the legitimate problems I have to deal with in rehabilitation.

Q. All right. Tell us what those assumptions are.

A. Well, basically, what I've done is, I've suggested that her complaints, as provided in the deposition, should be accepted on face value and at least in the sense that although they may not in every instance be fully consistent with objective medical findings, they are generally consistent with a classic chronic pain syndrome.

And I have assumed, when I looked at my first conclusion, which was what vocational handicap stemmed from this injury, I basically assumed those problems that stemmed from her complaints as given in her deposition. That is, that she had either restrictions or, in most instances, partial limitations on activities such as lifting, sitting, standing, repetitive bending, stooping, repetitive squatting, prolonged walking, repetitive reaching.

And I noted at the bottom, basically consistent with the history of chronic pain/chronic back disability. And when I say "chronic back", I am including any neck problems.

Q. Now, did you find any, or were you concerned with finding any conflicting medical opinions that you reviewed?

A. Was I concerned with finding any --

Q. Did you find any contradiction in the medical information provided in the reports and depositions of the doctors that you reviewed?

A. I think that may depend on how you define contradiction in the sense that it's not unusual at all for me to see in a chronic back case one doctor focusing primarily on objective medical findings and stating that from the standpoint of X-rays or thermograms or CAT Scans or whatever objective test they use, that they found no evidence of disability; to have another physician then who may focus more on soft tissue aspects, or a chiropractor focusing on soft tissue aspects, that says that they can detect, at least in their subjective evaluation, limitations, and also who give more credence to the patient's subjective complaints.

In that sense, I didn't think it was really a direct contradiction. I mean, nobody said, "I found something on an X-ray that another person said didn't show on that same X-ray". I think that they were evaluating things from a different perspective, and this is a classic chronic pain situation. That's not an unusual situation, nor do I consider that, from my area of expertise, to be a contradiction of concern.

Q. So, therefore, you were not, in the course of forming an opinion, troubled by any contradiction which made it necessary to discount one opinion in favor of another opinion?

A. Quite honestly, no, I didn't do that. I mean, again, I felt that wherein they talked about objective medical findings, it strikes me, as I look back over my notes, that there was no contradiction between the objective findings, contradictions that existed, I think, in a twofold fashion.

One, in which one medical specialist or chiropractor talked about soft tissue, and that may have been a contradiction in terms of some of the objective medical findings.

And, two, where the patient had complaints that weren't objectively substantiated by tests such as an MRI or a CAT Scan, or something of that nature.

I didn't discount the difference between objective versus subjective findings, simply because in the absence of the objective findings, I felt that what we were seeing here was a fairly classic description of a chronic pain patient. And I felt the soft tissue issues that were being brought about were very consistent with that kind of history. That is, the history of a chronic pain patient.

Q. Is it fair to say that you started out with a reasonably clear picture of a lady who, after an automobile collision, was exhibiting residual injuries from that collision?

A. At least by subjective complaint, that's correct.

Q. And that, therefore, your analysis from the area of your specialty, was based upon that picture that you elicited from these sources?

A. I think that's true.

Q. And would you tell us what that picture was?

A. Okay. Well, I've already gone over with you the vocational handicaps that I identified, based on a combination of chiropractic, medical, and subjective patient description.

Q. You haven't done that yet, sir. That's what we're waiting for you to do.

A. No, I did. I just listed the vocational handicaps.

Q. All right. I'm sorry if you did. I missed it entirely.

A. Well, that was the limitations or partial restrictions on lifting, standing, et cetera.

Q. All right. Can you be any more detailed than that general description?

A. Okay. I see. You want to know specifically how much standing, sitting, or walking she said she could do?

Q. Well, you're talking generally about limitations. I want to know what you assumed those limitations to be, from your review of the medical picture.

A. Well, from the standpoint of the medical picture, there weren't any medical doctors who specifically said to her, "You can only sit for so long or stand for so long."

What I did was, I basically accepted her complaints at face value, and as we go through the balance of the conclusions, I think you'll understand why I say that I didn't feel it was necessary for me to write down whether she could sit for two hours right now or stand for two hours right now, because I'm basically accepting that, as of today, the next steps are from a rehabilitation treatment standpoint and not an immediate return to work.

And so I didn't write those down. I'd go back to her deposition and we can start picking them out.

Q. Why don't we just go to our conclusions first, then?

A. Okay. I think that may help solve the question that's coming up.

The next area after vocational handicaps, was to determine whether or not I felt there was any impact on placement.

And I indicated that I felt that there was a moderate to severe impact on placement. And, specifically, what I said in my notes was that this individual's vocational handicaps and physical restrictions present a moderate to severe impact on her ability to be placed in a competitive labor market.

It must be considered that back injuries represent one of the most difficult disabilities to place, due to employer prejudice and hiring practices. And the way to pursue hiring, or course, at the point at which we're saying she is job ready, is to remediate the problem with proper job-seeking skills, training, and selective placement assistance.

So, at the time at which we complete the recommendations, we need to follow through with job-seeking skills, training, and selective placement assistance. That will overcome the placement problem, and it's a process of both educating the employee, that is, Ms. Lewis, as well as a process of educating the employer that she is interviewing with.

After the impact on placement, the next question to be answered is whether or not I feel there is an impact on the range of job alternatives available to her.

Now, I indicated as follows, that I felt there was also a moderate to severe impact on the range of job alternatives.

This individual's past work groups and closely-related alternatives were examined in an occupational analysis.

They included examples such as oral communications, records processing, clerical machine operation, clerical handling, sales technology, and general sales work. And, based on that analysis, I felt that in terms of her ability to maintain employment, she had a moderate to severe impact. That is, there was a reduction in the range of jobs available to her pre-accident, to the range of jobs available post-accident, based on her subjective assessment or her subjective description of limitations.

All right. The next area, which would be the fourth set of conclusions, was the rehabilitation plan itself.

Now, again, I felt that much of what we were seeing in terms of disability was, first of all, subjective in nature, that the description given by Ms. Lewis and when that description was considered in relation to all the available medical information, suggested a patient who is basically a chronic pain patient. And that the first step in rehabilitation was going to have to be assist her in dealing with the chronic pain, chronic disability syndrome, which exists.

So, I indicated, number one, that I recommended a referral for evaluation at a chronic pain management program.

Two, that she participate in a chronic pain management program to include a program of work hardening, and that she could anticipate an eight-week program from 9:00 in the morning to 4:00 in the afternoon, Monday through Fridays.

That, number three, she follow up the chronic pain program with individual counseling to reinforce the pain management techniques, and I anticipate one year of follow-up therapy, and I used a forty-eight-week therapy year, because nobody makes therapy fifty-two weeks a year.

My fourth recommendation was for career counseling and guidance to include career exploration, career decision-making, in an effort to match her interest, job satisfiers, job motivators, and physical abilities to available vocational alternatives and labor market.

Then the job-seeking skills, training, selective placement assistance that we talked about earlier, and, lastly, work adjustment counseling, post-placement.

And I felt that these steps were going to be necessary if we were going to be successful in returning her to gainful employment.

Now, the fifth area of conclusions of the issue of wage loss. I basically looked at wage loss in the following fashion:

Number one, I looked to determine, before I discussed any specific jobs, what her developmental options, her vocational development options were prior to this injury. And I felt there were two.

One was direct placement in the labor market without her completing her training in court reporting that she had expressed an interest in.

And the second was direct placement in the labor market after completion of her court reporting training. I felt that both had to be looked at, because she had not actually completed court reporting at that point in time.

The post-accident developmental options essentially were the same. That is, we could look at direct placement in the labor market without any additional training now, but after her rehabilitation, and take a look at how her problems would affect both placement and wage earning, and we could look at direct placement in the labor market after additional training received in the court reporting area, post-accident.

And, in each instance, what we want to do here is take a look at how her subjective complaints, the medical reports, and the residuals anticipated after rehabilitation, would impact the jobs within each of those two options.

So, going first to pre-accident vocational alternatives, in option one, I indicated that her alternatives were as follows -- and these are examples of jobs that related to areas in which she worked or had expressed an interest.

Number one was sales in the retail area, general merchandise sales, according to the *Florida View*, which is vital information on education and work, which I used as a statistical source, and which I confirmed with the *Florida State Standard Metropolitan Abstracts*.

There is a pay range in that area of $8,320 to $18,720 per year, or an average of $13,520 in the State of Florida.

Data entry, which was the next job classification I used, with a range of $12,000 to $16,000, or an average of $14,000 per year.

Basic secretarial work, $12,480 to $19,760, or an average of $16,120 a year.

And there was even some expression of interest in driving. And I showed a -- I think taxi driving was what had come up -- I showed the average there, based on the Wage Summary Report, employment service job openings, through September 1987, at $15,517.

Now, that was the only one where I used that source, because it was not in Florida View. So, it had an average of $15,517 a year.

When I averaged the entire range of jobs, it came out to $14,789, which was representative of a pre-accident capacity to earn, assuming no additional training had been undertaken.

Now, her second option, pre-accident, was with training. And, of course, what she was expressing an interest in was court reporting.

What I used, again was the Florida View. They gave an average in the State of Florida of $16,000 to $20,000 per year, or an average of that range of $18,000 per year.

Post-accident, I stated the following:

"Given success in the rehabilitation effort, the following assumptions can be made, in the option of direct placement in the labor market, in a clerical field averaging $14,009 on a full-time basis, although full-time work is not within reasonable rehabilitation probability, given this individual's pain complaints."

What I am basically saying is, is that our success with respect to pain clinics has shown us that we have an excellent prognosis for improving an individual's basic quality of life, their enjoyment of life on a day-to-day basis.

And we have a very good prognosis in terms of reasonable rehabilitation probability for a return to at least half-time employment. That we've had sufficient statistics to suggest a good possibility, but not a probability of full-time employment.

If we assume half-time, an average of approximately $7,000 to $8,000 can be anticipated. It's within reasonable probability, but certainly as strong as the half-time that she could make three-quarter placement, which would give her an average earnings of $10,530 post-accident.

Now, if she was successful, post-accident, in completing her court reporting, then direct placement in the labor market, if she were able to handle full-time work, would be $18,000 a year, and there would be no wage loss, although, again, I think we need to look at three-quarter and half-time.

If we assume half-time rate, we can anticipate an average of $9,000 to $10,000 a year. If we assume three-quarter rate, we could anticipate $13,500 to $14,000 a year.

So what I'm stating, basically, is that, number one, I feel she's going to have to be involved in a rehabilitation program to be successful in her return to work, and that is because I'm assuming the accuracy of her subjective complaints, that I'm assuming that she does experience these problems, that although they not be fully objectified by the medical findings, they are not inconsistent with the chronic pain patient, and that if we intervene with appropriate chronic pain treatment, we have again, based on our success rates, I think, a very good chance of -- well within reasonable rehabilitation probability, the opportunity to achieve half or three-quarter time employment, and although possibility of full-time employment exists, it's harder to state that it's within reasonable rehabilitation probability.

And those were my conclusions and notes.

6

Presenting the Non-Catastrophic Case

In reviewing presentation styles of both non-catastrophic and catastrophic injury cases, a likely question for the attorney is whether it leans toward the plaintiff or the defense side by virtue of the questions asked. I would stress to both the attorneys and rehabilitation professionals reading this work that it is essential for them to have a healthy, balanced understanding of the nature of rehabilitation services and their application to forensics. This means that they need to understand a balanced approach and recognize that there should be no difference in either the methodology for evaluating the patient or the manner which conclusions are drawn, despite referral of the case from the plaintiff versus the defense viewpoint. I stress to all rehabilitation professionals that when you enter the courtroom, your role as an advocate for the client ends. Within the courtroom setting, the only advocates are the attorneys representing their individual clients. The role of the rehabilitation professional is restricted to that of teacher or educator and the jury represents the class. This kind of balanced approach which has at its root a consistent methodology for patient evaluation and an insistence on factually-based data from which to draw conclusions will make the role of the rehabilitation professional in an otherwise, stressful courtroom setting, much easier.

Outlined in Appendix A are the nine basic philosophical steps that I believe each rehabilitation professional must adhere to in order to survive successfully in consulting in a litigation setting, while reducing the stress incurred as a result of the courtroom experience.

Open communications, both with the referral source and the patient, as well as the family is essential. In my experience, the courtroom situation has always been made much easier by making a clear and concise statement of the nature of your testimony, opinions, and conclusions in pre-deposition and pre-trial conferencing.

At this point in the non-catastrophic injury case, qualifications of the expert have been reviewed and the role of the rehabilitation professional defined. The rehabilitation professional has been accepted as an expert by the court and the jury has been exposed to an overview of all client evaluation procedures as reviewed in Chapter 5. This section, therefore, is restricted to the research steps taken after the data collection and client evaluation has been completed, followed by a review of the basic conclusions.

Occupational Analysis and Wage Data Research

After the medical, psychological, psychosocial, and vocational rehabilitation data has been gathered, the next step is to complete an occupational analysis and subsequent wage data research. The occupational analysis is designed to assess the vocational handicaps resulting from a disability and the transferable skills remaining after recovery. Transferable skills refer to those areas of job skill remaining and unaffected by the disability. The vocational handicaps are defined simply as impairment of function or skills which are necessary components to the successful completion of the job. In completing the occupational analysis, a variety of resources can be utilized, including the *United States Department of Labor Manpower Division Employment and Earnings* monthly magazine, *The State by State Vital Information on Education and Work* publication supported by federal grant through the State Department of Education, *The Standard Metropolitan Statistical Abstracts* and *Area Employment Surveys* produced by both State and Federal Departments of Commerce and Employment Statistics. Of course, the *Dictionary of Occupational Titles* is a helpful first step in identifying occupational significant characteristics and assessing through a review of worker groups, how the vocational handicaps negatively impact an individual's participation in each of those groups.

The rehabilitation professional should carefully outline the resources utilized in both the occupational analysis and the wage data research and be prepared to enumerate these sources accurately in any questioning.

Conclusions

There are five basic areas of conclusions to be considered in the non-catastrophic injury case. These five areas of conclusions include the following:

1) The extent to which vocational handicaps have resulted from the onset of physical or psychological impairment secondary to an accident.
2) The impact of these vocational handicaps on the ability of the individual to be placed in the labor market. This takes into consideration reduced competitiveness as well as employer prejudice in hiring practices. This area also takes into consideration only the ability of an individual to be placed in the employment market and does not consider their ability to maintain a job.
3) The reduction in the range of jobs for which this individual is capable of competing post-accident as compared to pre-accident. Another way of stating this is the loss of the individual's access to the labor market. Although no individual, prior to an injury, is capable of participating in 100% of the jobs in the open labor market, access to a total population of jobs consistent with interest, work values, job satisfiers, skills and physical abilities, is much greater prior to the onset of a disability. There simply is no injury which an individual can incur that will increase the capacity to work or increase the range of job options. There are certainly times when an injury will cause a change in educational or vocational direction, but if the individual has the capacity to compete in a specific vocational area post-accident then certainly that capacity existed pre-accident whether an individual would have pursued it or not.
4) The next area of conclusion is the steps required in a vocational rehabilitation plan with additional emphasis of the duration of these recommendations and the cost of these

recommendations. Where possible, specific statistical research should be used to document the potential for success. In any instance, this potential should be expressed within degrees of reasonable rehabilitation probability. One must anticipate that there be better than a 51% chance of success for reasonable probability standards to be applied.

5) The final area of conclusion to be drawn in a non-catastrophic case is an individual's diminution of earning capacity. In assessing this, one does not consider only the actual pre-accident earnings but must consider the capacity to earn and develop vocationally, both prior to an injury and subsequent to an injury. This is a particularly important consideration when dealing with youthful clients who may just have begun their career and have had insufficient time to demonstrate the fulfillment of their true capacity. The reader is referred to *A Guide to Rehabilitation* (Matthew Bender & Company, 1985, 1986, 1987, 1988, 1989) which provides extensive detail on the evaluation of diminution of earning capacity among varying age groups. (See Appendix D.)

Sample Transcripts

The first sample transcript presented involves an adult chronic pain/chronic disability syndrome with subjective medical findings but significant psychological involvement. A substantial portion of the transcript is presented because it gives an overview of the correlation between evaluation and data-gathering procedures, their interpretation, and direct application to conclusions.

Sample Transcript #1

Q. What did Mr. Barcus request you to do concerning this case?

A. At the time, he called and spoke with my secretary, and just gave some very general information. He indicated the name of the client and the fact that there was no trial date set at that point. He was requesting a rehabilitation evaluation.

He wasn't anticipating a trial before June of 1990, at that point in time. And that was really all the initial contact contained. Then, subsequently, I received a copy of the medicals and it was my understanding that I was to go ahead and complete a rehabilitation evaluation and to assess the needs of the individual and what my thoughts were regarding the impairment and its impact on employment.

Q. All right. I would like for you to list for me all of the materials that you were provided prior to your interview with Mr. Morris on March 20, excuse me, in March of 1989.

A. Listing out the medicals.

MR. BARCUS: I think that the question concerned the interview in March of '89?

Q. Yes. That's when the report is dated.

A. Yes, the interview was actually earlier than that.

Q. Well, let me ask you that question first. When was your interview with Mr. Morris?

A. December 19th of '88.

Q. Prior to that interview with Mr. Morris, what materials were you provided?

A. Okay, the office notes of Dr. Taylor Griffin from 9/23/87 through 11/9/88. The EMG report dated 9/28/87. The deposition of Dr. John McCormick dated February 8 of 1988. Mr. Morris's notes or letter on his job duties. In addition to Dr. McCormick's depo, attached to it there were his records as well. And that looks like everything that I had up to that point in time.

Q. All right. Do you still have Mr. Morris's letter concerning his job duties?

A. Yes.

MR. ROGERS: I would like to attach a copy of that letter to the deposition as Exhibit 1, Defendant's Exhibit 1.

Q. Dr. Deutsch, were you provided with any written descriptions concerning the factual circumstances of this case?

A. No.

Q. Did you obtain any verbal descriptions of the factual circumstances of this case other than through your interview with Mr. Morris?

A. No.

Q. Did you obtain any other letters or written narratives concerning Mr. Morris's condition or any aspect of this case?

A. No.

Q. Subsequent to your interview of Mr. Morris in December of 1988 and the preparation of your rehabilitation evaluation report in March of 1989, did you receive any other information concerning Mr. Morris?

A. No. Everything else I received, or the next set of medicals I received, were received in June of '89 and then additional deposition of Frank Widgets was received very recently, March the 5th of '90. And I also did an update evaluation with Mr. Morris in February of 1990.

Q. Could you tell me the reason for the delay between Mr. Morris's interview and the preparation of your narrative report?

A. That's just basically common in the office. We're running right now on about a three- to four-week delay from time of evaluation until completion of research to issuance of a report. At that point we were running about two, two and a half months behind.

Q. All right. That's pretty much what I had assumed. Did you interview anyone else concerning Mr. Morris?

A. No, he came to the evaluation alone, he was at the update alone and there is no other participant in the evaluation.

Q. Did anyone besides you, that is, anyone else in your office interview Mr. Morris?

A. I guess actually in both evaluations, the answer is yes.

Q. Besides the narrative report dated March 20, 1989, did your office produce any other documentation concerning Mr. Morris or his rehabilitation evaluation? In other words, were there forms filled out, test reports, and so forth?

A. Well, there is the handwritten notes from the evaluation and the updates, which are on white sheets of paper that are labeled at the top Clinical Interview and History. And then there are the test forms. There are the answer sheets primarily in the file. You'd have to go to the test room itself for me to pull the questions if you wanted those.

MR. ROGERS: Steve, do you have any objection to me getting a copy of the complete file concerning Mr. Morris's evaluation?

MR. BARCUS: No problem.

Q. By the way, Dr. Deutsch, have you ever been provided any information about Gerald Wade Morris, Mr. Morris's son?

A. No.

Q. So you have not been asked to form any opinions concerning Gerald Wade Morris?

A. That's true.

Q. Have you had an opportunity to speak with Mr. Morris's employer or physicians?

A. No.

Q. Former employer I meant to say.

A. I didn't take the opportunity to do so, no.

Q. Have we now discussed the entire data base that you utilized as a basis for the opinions expressed in your narrative report of March 20, 1989?

A. In a general fashion. I think we have covered the reports received, the clinical interview and history, the intake interview and the testing.

Q. Did you also consult any reference sources, that is, sources of statistical information or other types of information in order to form your opinions concerning Mr. Morris?

A. Just with respect to the *Statistics on Wage Data*. No other specific resources were drawn upon for the report beyond that.

Q. You didn't refer to the *Directory of Occupational Titles*?

A. Well, that's all part of the wage data and wage analysis. DOT records, *Florida View, Vocational Information on Education and Work*, the *Standard Metropolitan Statistical Abstracts*, and the *Employment Earnings* are the standard resources for our wage data analysis and wage loss assessing both jobs, job titles and wages associated with them.

Q. Did you also utilize the *Occupational Outlook Handbook*?

A. No. The wage data involved in that is so broad, across country, no distinction between union and non-union and generally so old that it has little real validity as applied to wage earning specifically within this state, which is what I was focused on.

Q. All right. Did you, by any chance, copy any source materials or reference materials in preparing your file concerning Mr. Morris?

A. No.

Q. Did you utilize any computer programs in formulating your rehabilitation evaluation of Mr. Morris?

A. No, I'm afraid I'm well on the record as being generally in opposition to doing that. Although we do have the DOTs on computer to simplify getting into the data base. I don't believe in computer-generated reports or assessments. So I don't have any available in the office and I did not use any with Mr. Morris.

Q. Were any other individuals involved in preparing parts of your report or the appendix to your report?

A. All of my work is done on a team approach. So there were other individuals involved. And the way the system works is that as you go through my handwritten notes, you will see that the clinical interview and history was done by myself. That certain basic intake information like his work history and education was in the initial evaluation taken by Julie Kitchen, and in the subsequent reassessment, I was helped by Stuart Cody. And when the report was originally done, I dictated the report and the conclusions and what my feelings were regarding jobs and then as a memorandum to that, I indicate to whoever is assisting me at that time what records specifically I want them to access and pull for me. Like *Standard Metropolitan Statistical Abstracts* or *Florida View*. And I don't actually go into the library and pull that data, I have it pulled for me. So in the original report it was most likely done by Julie Kitchen. I don't think Stuart was working here at that time. Any subsequent work would most likely be done by him. But there hadn't been any changes or amendment to that.

Q. How many interviews did you personally have with Mr. Morris?

A. Two.

Q. On what dates did those two interviews occur?

A. 12/19/88 for the first interview and March 1st, 1990 for the second. And there is a letter, excuse me, I'm sorry. The letter was dated March 1st, 1990. The actual re-evaluation was on February 9th, 1990. It's a letter that is rather distinctive in its misspelling of Bogin, Munns & Munns. But what can I say? I don't proofread these things.

Q. What occasioned the second interview of Mr. Morris?

A. It's difficult to say what specifically generated it. I assumed that contact was made either indicating that you wanted to set up a deposition and/or that some activity was beginning to re-develop on the case. And any time it's been six months since I have last seen an individual, and I express my concern that it's really difficult to talk much more about that case than what I saw on the day I saw the individual if I haven't done an update or a re-evaluation to determine any changes.

Q. All right. Before we discuss your report, let me ask you whether you have generated any additional reports or documentation as a result of your second interview with Mr. Morris?

A. Right, that was the March 1st, 1990 report in which I indicated we misspelled the referring attorney's law firm.

Q. At this point, I'd like to have your first report dated March 20, 1989 appended as Exhibit 3 to the deposition. And the subsequent report dated March 1, 1990 appended as Defendant's Exhibit 4 to the deposition. By the way, could I have a copy of the second report?

A. Sure.

MR. BARCUS: Did we have a two, Dennis?

Q. I think that number one was, was it the CV?

A. Number one was the CV. Number two was the job duties letter. You never gave a number to the composite file. You asked him if he had any objection to it, but you never had the total file copied.

MR. ROGERS: Let's do this in retrospect. I don't want to make the CV an exhibit. Let's make the letter an exhibit, Defendant's Exhibit No. 1. Let's make the composite file without the two reports, Defendant's Exhibit 2. Then let's make the first report Exhibit 3, the second report Exhibit 4 and that should probably cover it.

MR. BARCUS: I think, Doctor, that when Dennis asked you about who was present on the occasion of the second interview, do you see any reference to Mrs. Morris?

◄ *Presenting the Non-Catastrophic Case* ►

MR. ROGERS: I'm not sure I have asked that yet. I think Dr. Deutsch is probably talking about the first interview. And my question was in addition to Mr. Morris, did he obtain information from other individuals.

Q. (BY MR. ROGERS) But let me go ahead and ask that information. Concerning the second interview of Mr. Morris, Dr. Deutsch, did you interview or obtain information from anyone besides Mr. Morris?

A. His wife was at the second interview and made, I have some notes where at the bottom under comments where it says wife's work hyphen and it goes into a whole set of comments that the wife made at the time.

Q. Are all the comments which Mrs. Morris made contained in your report of March 1, 1990?

A. No, not in their entirety.

Q. Would you please describe for me the information that you obtained from Mrs. Morris?

A. Well, she may well have commented at varying points during here, as the two of them were answering questions and where they both agreed, I didn't make any separate distinction. The only separate note I made from her is her statement that she quit work due to the need to take care of Fred, that Fred could not live alone, that he had problems with short-term memory, noting that at one time he set the kitchen on fire. One time he left grease in the stove. She said Fred needs assistance getting in and out of the tub and shower, occasionally, about as often as two times a week, will need assistance getting up or off the toilet and he is unable to prepare a full meal, only quick items, and that he needs frequent breaks, since he has a problem with duration or how long he can remain on a task. Would need interior/exterior home maintenance assistance, he is not able to do a lot of those chores himself. And that's basically it.

Q. Did you perform a physical examination of Mr. Morris in December of 1988?

A. No. It's all done by interview. I'm a Ph.D., not an M.D., so I don't do an actual physical exam.

Q. In addition to the interview though, you made some observations of Mr. Morris's physical condition?

A. I made some observations, but just in anticipation of the question, so that everything is clarified. The physical limitations section of the report are not my observations but the client's subjective description of his physical restrictions and complaints. Also his chief complaint is his subjective description. I then consider them in relation to the medical reports and objective medical findings. But there are some areas of separate observation by me as well as those. I know that's been confused in other depos, so I wanted to make that clear.

Q. Now in the second paragraph of your March 20, 1989 report, I noticed a reference to some overt posturing. To what were you referring in making that statement?

A. Well, one of the things that I'm concerned about whenever I'm working with an individual either with a back problem, chronic pain and/or major disability is whether or not there is evidence, either through demographics, the direct observation and/or through testing, of the onset of or development of a chronic pain or chronic disability profile or chronic pain behavior pattern. So in observation, one of the things I do take a look at during the course of the interview, is whether or not somebody is showing high verbal complaint rate, and overt physical signs of a chronic pain problem, like exaggerated or overt body posturing, showing a lot of facial grimacing, a lot of posturing in terms of the way they hold the body when they are trying to get up from a chair or into a chair. Any indicators that would suggest that we're dealing with a chronic pain problem.

Q. And at that time you also observed a high verbal complaint rate?

A. That's right.

Q. And what types of complaints did Mr. Morris have at that time?

A. Well, the whole range of complaints that are demonstrated in the subjective physical limitations, that are demonstrated in the chief complaints. The key for me in identifying high verbal complaint rate isn't so much whether the individual is being honest in describing the objective problems that he is having, or even the subjective problems that he is having, but whether or not I feel the individual is showing a lot of underlying anxiety, almost hysterical reaction and is working hard to really make sure I understand the extent of his problems or disability. The extent to which a high verbal complaint rate shows a focus on physical problems, where that really is the central component of his life. And that's what I felt was going on there.

Q.　Is there frequently an unconscious or subconscious motivation or component to the complaints and posturing that you observe?

A.　Well, it certainly can show up. Whether it's in the MMPI results, both sets of his MMPI testing showed significant elevations on what's called the triad profile, the chronic pain, chronic disability profile. And one of the features that certainly is possible to talk about and when we get to those tests, I guess we could get more specific about it, is that there can be an underlying set of factors which might reinforce a focus on physical complaints or physical symptoms and chronic pain. And that can come in a variety of forms, from controlling the social environment to basically using disability as a way of avoiding psychological stress and pressure, to a whole range of other secondary gain considerations. And we can be more specific about that as we go through the testing.

Q.　You use the term secondary gain. Would you define that for us?

A.　Well, secondary gain is nothing more really than a reinforcer for certain behavior patterns. If I can gain something from this behavior, whether it's conscious or unconscious, it reinforces the continued exhibition of that behavior. So secondary gain might be controlling social environment, as I said, for example, getting the wife or family members to attend more closely, to assist, to take care of them. Secondary gain might be where disability becomes a factor in helping you avoid having to deal with a whole range of psychological stresses and pressures. I can't deal with that bill collector today, I just hurt too bad, you're going to have to take care of that for me. There is always of course monetary second gain that can be discussed. But generally speaking, there is a range of factors which may be motivating for some individuals, might not be motivating for others.

Q.　I see. The second paragraph of your first report also mentions that Mr. Morris ambulated with a walker and wore a back brace throughout your evaluation. Did at any point in that evaluation Mr. Morris mention that he was able to ambulate without a walker?

A. Not in the first evaluation. Well, actually he did indicate, just looking over the notes and refreshing my memory with those, he did indicate that -- he's not going around the house, for example, with his walker. If he's going any distance, he was using the walker at that time. If he was just in a single location, not really walking about, but he was just inside his house or just standing, just walking about an immediate work area, for example, he didn't have the walker with him at that point. But for any distance out of the house, he did. And then subsequently he's been off the walker completely.

Q. All right. Did Mr. Morris indicate to you whether he wore the back brace continuously during the day?

A. Well, I made the note that he wore the back brace at the evaluation. Subsequently in the second evaluation, he indicated he does wear it daily, but in neither instance did either myself or Stuart indicate that he wore it 24 hours a day. And if someone indicates that, we specifically note it. And I think the fact that I stated he wore it at the evaluation was just again specific to noting that it was not necessarily a 24-hour-a-day usage.

Q. Did Mr. Morris relate to you why he was utilizing a walker and wearing a back brace at the time of your evaluation of him?

A. Well, he indicated that as far as the back brace was concerned, that he did get some assistance in relief. And I didn't go into a lot of detail because I knew that the back brace had been ordered by the physician or at least that's what I understood from reviewing the medicals. There was no separate conversation about it, I mean to justify it, it seemed clear from his statements and from my review of the medicals that he was requiring it at that time. But we did anticipate that he would improve beyond that point.

Q. As I understand it, you took a history of the automobile accident from Mr. Morris at the time of the initial interview?

A. Well, really maybe a better way of saying it is I took a history that there was an automobile accident. I don't have any notation whatsoever other than next to "how injured", it says "vehicular accident". But the nature of it or the details of it, I did not -- in fact, I specifically asked him not to go into that, because it's totally outside my area and I really wasn't interested in it.

Q. Did Mr. Morris describe at all the circumstances of the accident?

A. No. All I have is notes stating that he retained consciousness at the scene. His head was hurt severely enough that he had to lay back on the seat of the truck. He went home from the scene escorted by a friend and a son. Tried to go back to work on January 3rd, et cetera, but I have no description whatsoever of the accident's circumstances.

Q. Did Mr. Morris by any chance describe to you how his body was thrown inside the truck at the time of the accident?

A. No. Just to be clear, I was very, very specific in how I asked the question regarding how he was injured. I made the statement before I asked it, that I didn't want to know the mechanics, the directions, the basics of how the accident occurred. I had some very, very limited questions, because it is just not an area that I need to get into in all that much detail.

Q. Did Mr. Morris describe for you how soon after the accident he was able to return to work?

A. He said he tried to go back to work on January 3rd. That he was hurting badly and went to see a chiropractor. He feels that it really didn't help and he eventually went on to see a physician about the problems as he became progressively worse.

He said he continued to work until February of 1988. He missed many days due to pain and disability, but "tried to hang on". He has not worked since February of 1988. He terminated his job because he was so severely limited and surgery was scheduled for February 16th of '88. To my knowledge, he has not done any other work, he had not as of the update in February of '90 and I'm assuming he has not through today.

Q. Did Mr. Morris indicate to you that he had been unable to satisfactorily perform his duties at his place of employment subsequent to the accident and prior to his termination of employment?

A. Actually he didn't make the statement that he was unable to perform his duties or that he did perform them but poorly. He simply said that he hurt so badly that he had trouble continuing. I think there is kind of a qualitative difference in there. So it was no clear statement that he couldn't perform it accurately, it's just that he hurt so bad while he was trying to perform it that he couldn't continue his job.

Q. I notice a reference in your report to a medical summary. Is that summary something that you have prepared?

A. Yes, and it's part of the report. You have it in there. It's on page four and five of the report. It starts at the bottom of page four. What you don't have there is the addendum to that, that was dictated on the basis of the additional materials. And all the addendum says is "on 8/25/88 a decompressive lumbar laminectomy at the L4-L5, L5-S1 with bilateral fusion of the right iliac was performed", and the records reviewed were West Volusia Memorial Hospital of 8/24/88 to 9/2/88 and the deposition of Dr. Taylor Wood Griffin of 10/31/89.

Q. When was the addendum prepared?

A. I'll go through the billings in the file.

Q. An approximate date would be fine. I don't mean for you to have to do extensive research to answer any of my questions.

A. It won't take but a second here. Well, I can give you the month and year. And the day, I'd have to research a little bit. The month was June of '89.

Q. That's fine. That's all I need. Did Mr. Morris by any chance describe to you the types of problems, aside from a general complaint of pain, that he was experiencing prior to the termination of his employment?

A. Not at that point. Very quickly thereafter, we got into his chief complaints and his physical limitations. In fact, it was not the very next, but with the exception of one or two questions, it was the next section that we got into. So I kept it fairly limited in his description at that early point. He just indicated that it was just too much pain and disability.

Q. Your report mentions that Mr. Morris was terminated from his employment. Did Mr. Morris describe the circumstances of the termination?

A. Point to that point in the report, because I show in my notes that he terminated, not that he was terminated. Does the report suggest that he was terminated from it by others?

Q. Yes.

A. Where are you looking?

Q. I'm looking at the last sentence in paragraph three of the initial report. Where it says, "having been terminated from his job".

A. Well, I dictated it and you're correct, that's the way it comes out, but as I look at my handwritten notes, what I have written down is specifically this, "terminated job because he was so severely limited and surgery was scheduled for February 16, '88". I do not have terminated from job. So looking at my notes, I would interpret that to mean that he chose to terminate because he simply couldn't physically handle it.

Q. All right. Did Mr. Morris also tell you that another reason for the termination of his employment was his initial back surgery in February of 1988?

A. Yes. He said that was scheduled for February 16th.

Q. Did Mr. Morris provide you any information concerning his educational background?

A. Yes.

Q. Is all of that information contained in this initial vocation rehabilitation report?

A. Yes.

Q. Did Mr. Morris provide you any additional -- did Mr. Morris advise you that he had ever had any courses in computer programming?

A. I don't specifically have computer programming. I have computer electronics, that he had technical training in the field of computer electronics. But I don't use the word programming and he didn't use the word programming.

Q. Did Mr. Morris provide you with any information concerning his vocational training and experience that is not contained in your initial narrative report?

A. No.

Q. Did Mr. Morris discuss with you his desire to return to work?

A. Yes, we discussed that.

Q. What did he tell you about that?

A. Well, he expressed an interest in a desire to do that, while at the same time really expressing his concerns and questions about whether he could achieve it. Actually the conversation that ensued was very typical of the kinds of conversations I have with individuals with significant chronic pain and chronic disability behavior patterns. I think he expresses and has a sincere desire to work, but he also sees disability as interfering with that, and I think that he feels that until something can be done with respect to the disability, it's not going to be something that's going to be easily achievable.

I also felt, based on the conversation, that he was floundering in the labor market, that he didn't really have a clear-cut set of suggestions for himself or ideas as to how to proceed, how to work with his disability, how to identify interests, work values, job satisfiers, and improved tolerance levels and limitations so that he could match all of that to the labor market. So I think there was an expressed desire, but underlying that was, in my opinion, a belief on his part that the disability was going to interfere with it.

Q. To your knowledge, up until today, has Mr. Morris made any attempts to seek gainful employment?

A. I'm unaware of any direct effort to do so. And my own recommendation to him at this point, and I think at the time of the update evaluation, that it might be putting the cart before the horse. I don't want him set up for failure and I think there are steps that need to be taken in rehabilitation if you're going to successfully see him placed back in the labor market.

Q. And would you please describe those steps for me?

A. Certainly. Well, I frankly listed out several recommendations in my report and I feel very strongly that what we're dealing with here is a chronic pain and chronic disability profile. There is clear-cut objective evidence of medical findings, but superimposed on the anatomical pain he is experiencing, he is experiencing a lot in the way of chronic pain and chronic disability behavior, or another way of saying it, is that there is significant psychological reaction to what's happened to him physically. For that reason I think he needs a chronic pain program. I think that the chronic pain program should contain a vocational aspect, and as a part of what goes on in chronic pain treatment, there should be an improvement in his tolerance levels, which is essentially a work hardening concept.

I feel after the participation in the chronic pain management program, he is going to require follow-up supportive counseling. I think that's critical. You might as well not go through with the chronic pain program if you're not going to spend some time transitioning him back into the real world and reinforcing the use of those techniques. I think he is going to have to have career guidance and counseling to assist in that transition back to work. I think work is going to be therapeutic. The longer he stays off work, the longer it is before he can enter into rehabilitation, the more entrenched those disability behaviors will become, and the more difficult it will be for him to deal with those aspects of the pain and disability profile that are a result of psychological reaction versus a result of the objective anatomical problems.

So we have the career guidance and counseling followed up by work adjustment counseling to insure a stable placement in the labor market. Those are the basic sets of recommendations that I gave earlier and that is after the first report, I reinforced them in the second report. I felt that the test results only increased or certainly further reinforced the recommendations for chronic pain treatment and counseling. I still think that that work itself would be therapeutic even on a part-time basis, and so I still very much wish to push for that goal, particularly at his age.

    Q.   Dr. Deutsch, to your knowledge, has Mr. Morris pursued any of those recommended activities?

    A.   He's not directly involved in any of those to my knowledge at this point in time.

    Q.   What physical limitations, if any, did you document during your initial evaluation of Mr. Morris?

    A.   Well, the general areas that I documented limitations in, I'll list first. Now these are physical limitations that represent partial restrictions, not total restrictions. In none of these areas did Mr. Morris indicate to me that he was a hundred percent unable to perform them. But I was asking him capacity levels with the concept of whether or not they were functional for work. That is, whether or not he could do them on a repetitive basis. The areas of limitations, including some restrictions on lifting, sitting, standing, walking, bending, twisting the torso, kneeling repetitively, stooping repetitively or for prolonged periods, repetitive squatting, climbing stairs or climbing ladders, working around scaffolding or unprotected heights, any balance problems that he experienced, and he did indicate intermittent falling when his leg gives out, and a lack of physical stamina and endurance. He has had some improvement in those areas since the first evaluation, but they still all represent areas of restriction for him. They came from a combination of his subjective description of disability, coupled with my review of the objective medical findings.

Q. At the time of the initial examination, did Mr. Morris advise you that he could not do any of those activities, that is, any particular activity?

A. Well, not really, no. I could go down each one individually and quote directly what was discussed.

Q. All right. Please do that.

A. All right, he indicated that he had a normal upper extremity range of motion, but that he had pain on repetitive reaching and stretching. So he had no problem moving his arms through a normal range of motion, it is just that the more he did it, the more it caused pain. He said that, and particularly the notation, the pain was caused by a full reach or stretch as opposed to just moving that arm, or either of the arms, through a range of motion. Lifting, he said he was essentially limited on any repetitive basis to one or two pounds. That he was not able to functionally carry due to the pain and at the early stage, due to the use of the walker. So in other words, he could lift more from a seated position than he could if he was trying to use the walker at the time.

Grip strength and manual dexterity, finger dexterity he reported as normal in his first interview. He did note in his second interview that he will start to get some numbness if he tries to grip something for a sustained period of time. For example, if he is driving and he is tightly gripping the steering wheel for a sustained period.

Sitting, he said he could sit continuously for 15 to 20 minutes, then he needed to shift position, he needed to rise and move about. That at times, if he sat for too long, he would even need some help getting up off the toilet or up out of a chair. Or he would need safety rails to help pull himself up. He does indicate that standing and moving about helps and allows him to resume sitting, although he can't go back and forth for a full workday for that. He said he could stand anywhere from 60 to 90 minutes. The standing and moving about helps if he's been sitting too long, but that also, if he has been standing that long, sitting doesn't really help, he needs to lie down for relief. He says he cannot continually shift position for eight hours and remain out of bed, that he must lie down during the course of the day.

Walking was restricted to basically a block before he had increased levels of pain or he began having problems with his legs giving out. That was at the first evaluation. The second evaluation he said that it increased up to one half mile, if he was taking his pain medication.

Now the next series of areas were not statements that he couldn't perform them, but were questions regarding his functional ability to do these repetitively for work. So I noted that he was not functional for bending repetitively, twisting the torso repetitively, kneeling, stooping, squatting, none of those were comfortable repetitive activities. Climbing, here he notes he avoids even stairs. He was not comfortable with uneven terrain. That was true for both evaluations. He denied blackouts or dizziness. Did report occasionally lightheadedness if he tried to exert himself.

He had shortness of breath, which he attributed to a lack of exercise and to being overweight, so it was an indirect result of the disability. Had headaches occurring daily, described as moderate to severe. Relieved by his pain medications but not by anything else. And in the second evaluation he reported that those were no longer daily but were down to about once or twice a week.

Vision was good with glasses. He felt he needed his hearing evaluated. He reported some problems with his left ear. He felt it was a gradually increasing deficit. And the second evaluation he noted 25 percent loss due to nerve deafness in the left ear. That's 25 percent loss of hearing.

Good command of the English language, he had no problems communicating. He denied any dysfunction in bowel or bladder function. He did note that the pain that he was experiencing interfered with his desire for sexual relations with his wife. He noted easy fatigability. In earlier evaluation, he was lying down three to four times per day, for anywhere from 30 to 90 minutes on the average. He was driving at that time. That hasn't changed. He avoids frequent driving or constant driving or long distances.

So basically those were the statements he made, none of which indicated he was completely unable to perform any single activity, but they weren't functional for work.

Q. All right. In saying that Mr. Morris is unable to do certain things, for example, stooping on a repetitive basis; could you define for us what you mean by repetitive? For example, how many times in an hour would somebody have to do a particular activity for it to be considered repetitive?

A. Well, I think that really is defined first of all by the requirements of a given job. With something like stooping, we are really more concerned with his prolonged ability to do it rather than his repetitive ability to do it because it is usually where an individual is standing and leaning forward or working over a workbench or table. He is not indicating to me that he can't ever get into a stooped or slightly bent position. I have no breakdown or definition by number of times per hour. It's just a recognition that it varies dramatically with jobs.

For example, if you're an air-conditioning mechanic, you can be working for much of the day in a stooped, bent, or awkward position, and you can be required to be doing some lifting from an awkward position. Whereas if you're a secretary, you're going to be sitting much of the day, but stooped working over a typewriter, et cetera. I have no way to define that for you except by describing individual jobs.

But from my standpoint, any concern about whether it's functional is simply whether or not it's something that he can either maintain consistently over at least a half-time work period, that is, 20 hours a week, or maintain consistently for 40 hours a week. And in this instance, based on his current descriptions, that is, current at that time, I didn't feel any of them were functional even for part-time work, but I did feel that later in my conclusions we could make it functional or get to a point where it's functional for at least half-time work.

Q. As a result of your second interview with Mr. Morris, in February of 1990, did you change your conclusions concerning Mr. Morris's physical restrictions or limitations?

A. Well, I felt that there were several areas in which he was describing improvement. There was improved walking, rather substantial if you consider that he went from a block to half a mile and from a walker to a cane. So there were a number of areas where he improved, but there was also no question that he was showing significant chronic disability. The pattern of disability behaviors hadn't changed. And in fact, in testing, seemed worse. The level of pain and disability he was expressing and experiencing seemed relatively unchanged, although how it manifested itself, for example, the walking may have changed. Most everything stayed the same. Just a few areas improved. And in terms of my final conclusions, they really didn't change. I still felt that with proper intervention, we could improve quality of life, improve his tolerance levels, and get to a part-time basis. I did not feel it was reasonable to talk about full time.

Q. In your experience, is it unusual for somebody's activity level to increase, for example, of the distance they're able to walk and yet their level of pain remain the same?

A. Oh, it's not terribly unusual for people to show gradual improvement. I think a number of factors are going on. First of all, even with individuals I have seen whose pain level doesn't really change, they learn various compensation skills for tolerating the pain they're experiencing. I think there is also recognition that when you're dealing with this type of situation, where there is a combined physical or anatomical pain level as well as psychological reaction to disability that acts on that pain, there really are two levels of pain. There is pain that I can't make a direct impact on in the treatment programs I'm talking about because it is anatomically based, but there is pain superimposed on that, that results in the individual's decreased ability to handle stress, with an increase as a result in the physical manifestation of that stress. Increased muscle tension, increased body tension, muscle spasm, increased focus on disability, and so it's not unusual at all to see some relatively small changes, and I think that is a small change, and some improvement without a direct concomitant change in the level of pain. It's just a change in how much they're tolerating.

Q. Have you been able to make any determination as to the percentage or proportion of Mr. Morris's pain that is anatomically based?

A. There is really no way or technique that I know of for drawing that fine line. Frankly, what's going on physically is so significantly influenced by what's going on psychologically, and what's going on psychologically is so significantly influenced by what's going on physically, that it's almost an impossible task to separate the two. I think the key is that if you read the data and the research literature on chronic pain, chronic disability, and a very excellent resource is the *Archives of Physical Medicine and Rehabilitation*, a lot of good articles and recent articles on that. You know, it's pretty clear that one influences the other, that they act on each other and that drawing that fine line is just very difficult to do. We do know we can make some changes in the individual though and that's really what we're focused on wanting to do.

Q. Did you see in reviewing the last deposition of Dr. Taylor Griffin in this case, that he testified that his rating of Mr. Morris's disability was based primarily upon Mr. Morris's complaints of pain?

A. In his deposition, I do recall his talking about that, yes. He didn't specifically state that in his report on the rating, but he did in the deposition. And from what I gathered from reading that, he was basically indicating that the degree to which improvement had occurred as a result of the surgery was in part a judgment on his basis secondary to the level of pain complaints.

Q. In your opinion, are most of the restrictions and limitations which you have noted in your report based upon Mr. Morris's complaints of pain?

A. Well, I think the answer is yes, but I think it definitely requires a qualifier. In that, frankly, if there is no pain, it really doesn't matter how impaired he is, he is going to be able to function because he can tolerate it. I mean, the body is using pain as a way of telling us when we're exceeding tolerances. Now, although I concur that, as I have already said, you can't draw a fine line to tell what's going on physically versus anatomically. You're dealing with an individual who has a history of two surgeries, there are anatomical changes, there is no way for us to determine whether he has a high tolerance or low tolerance for pain. Obviously different people are going to react differently. And it would be very hard for me to suggest, in fact, I think impossible to suggest that his problems were purely psychological in nature when you have got a history of two surgeries and you have my experience base, which says that a history of surgeries in and of itself tends to reinforce the disability and chronic pain profile and also causes anatomical changes that may in fact be generating pain that's only further exacerbating the psychological reaction.

Q. All right. In obtaining medical history from Mr. Morris, did you obtain any statements from Mr. Morris as to whether his initial back surgery in February of 1988 had provided him with any pain relief?

A. While I am looking for specific notes, my recollection is that there may have been some initial post-surgery relief, but nothing that was long lasting. I mean his level of pain and his subsequent discussion of restrictions seemed relatively unchanged. He was still at the time I saw him again in February of 1990, concerned about the Percocet usage and also concerned with making a decision about whether or not electrical implant should be done. And he was discussing that at the time. Neither which I have any further data on.

Q. Do you recall whether Mr. Morris made any comments to you as to whether the February of 1988 surgery may have aggravated his condition in any way?

A. I don't have any notes suggesting that.

Q. Did you reach any conclusions as to the reasons Mr. Morris was unable to return to work following the February of 1988 surgery?

A. Well, I think the answer is yes. When you ask the question, I'll explain what I mean specifically.

Q. Please do.

A. Okay. I think really there are two ways of looking at that. One is just to talk about the clinical interview with the patient, where Mr. Morris is indicating a continuation of severe pain, physical disability, and limitations that prevent a return to work. The second way of looking at that is to look at what's going on in his test results, and to give you insight into what's occurring in that regard. Surgery itself, quite frankly, tends to exacerbate chronic disability profiles. My own feeling, and I think that there is some substantial literature on this, suggests that some caution should be taken in proceeding with back surgeries in instances in which an elevated triad profile exists on a psychological evaluation. Such individuals tend not to have good results from surgery. It's not anything conscious on their part; it's a very real psychological reaction to disability. But frankly, something that needs to be dealt with and treated prior to the undertaking of the surgery because otherwise, the surgery tends to only exacerbate the emotional or psychological reactions, the stress reactions and his body's manifestation of that. Let me give an example if I might. When we talk about psychological reaction and physical manifestations, that's a very real thing, just like peptic ulcers can be a physical manifestation of an individual's psychological reaction to stress, it can perforate, it can hemorrhage, it can kill you. They are very real physical manifestations and for the individual themselves, it's impossible to make a determination over what's going on physically versus what's going on in terms of reaction to stress.

Q. Does that mean that Mr. Morris himself would not have been completely able to fully evaluate all of his motives for undergoing the initial surgery?

A. The only problem I have with the word motives or motivation is that it tends to imply more conscious awareness on an individual's part than I think they have. I think your question implies the same thing, that it really isn't a conscious thing.

Q. I didn't mean to suggest they were conscious.

A. No, I don't think you did. I'm just aware of the term and it sometimes concerns me. And I think it's very true that it would have been very hard for Mr. Morris to evaluate anything or be aware of anything other than the fact that medical treatment recommended by a surgeon had the potential to relieve him from the significant pain of which he was complaining, and I think his, in my own opinion, sole motivation to undertake that, was in anticipation that there would be medical relief.

Q. In your opinion, did Mr. Morris experience significant disappointment as a result of the initial back surgery?

A. Well, although those aren't words he specifically used with me, I feel that there is little question that he was disappointed that he didn't have the kind of relief he was hoping for. I think that he was more than disappointed, depressed over the lack of relief. I think he had an elevation in his tension and anxiety levels. And because I think it was the first time he became confronted, even if it was not on a conscious level, with the possibility that this may be a long-term or permanent situation for him. I mean, there was always in the back of his mind the hope that surgery was going to be a cure. And whenever you're confronted with the fact that it's not, to say the least, it's a disappointment.

Q. You mentioned the term elevated triad profile. Does that triad involve tension anxiety and/or depression?

A. The answer is yes, and if I might, what I think it would be easiest to do is actually show you the profile.

Q. Please do.

A. And talk about it. Now we have two separate profiles in this instance. The first profile is the one I have on top I am showing you. And it begins with the "L", "F", and "K" scales. Those are the validity scales. And you can see that he's clustered right about the mean in his validity scales. He has a slight elevation, one standard deviation above the mean on his "F" scale. That suggests that we have an individual who is focused on some central area of concern or some problem in his life. But it's not elevated to a level that we feel in any way it would invalidate the test results. There is no indication of impression management, no indication that he is trying to give socially acceptable responses or make a better or worse impression of himself than may exist. He was straightforward and in fact, in his "L" scale, he's suggesting here that he is pretty open and nondefensive in answering questions.

Now he has what's called an inverted conversion V in his triad profile. There are three scales on the triad profiles, those are the first three scales of the MMPI. The top scale for him, the highest point of elevation is his depression scale, suggesting here a low energy depression. And we'd anticipate and in fact we see some social introversion, some withdrawal or pulling away from people. And he definitely needs counseling with respect to that, that's had a very significant impact on him.

The second highest point of his inverted conversion V or his elevated triad profile is hysterical reaction. That's his anxiety reaction to disability. So there is no question that he is not only extremely anxious and tense about disability, but he is going to be more likely to react and manifest physically in his reaction to any kind of increases in psychological stress and pressure. The third area, which is the lowest elevation, but still very significantly elevated, is the scale called hypochondriacal reaction. This simply measures the amount of focus on physical disability and that tendency to manifest physically those problems that are secondary to increased levels of stress and pressure. Together they represent a very significant chronic disability, chronic pain profile.

Now scale four on the profile is the psychopathic deviant scale -- now these titles, and I stress that for everybody, sound terrible.

Q. They are categorical.

A. Yes, they are strictly categorical and they mean different things at different levels, we certainly are by no means dealing with a psychopathic deviant. In fact, that is within normal limits for this particular gentleman. But the fact that it is beginning to elevate suggests that he is using disability on a very limited basis at this point in time, probably to help avoid some of the stress and pressure he is dealing with. And he can't handle all of the normal stresses that we all are exposed to in our daily life and he is tending to re-focus attention on the physical and avoiding dealing with that.

Now he has several other elevations that are pretty significant. Most importantly, it's the schizophrenia and psychasthenia elevations. At this level we see a number of things. We are seeing significant levels of underlying anxiety, feelings of inadequacy, poor body concept, poor self concept, he is feeling really a lack of self-confidence.

The psychasthenia, which is the scale seven, to make a simple definition, last time you laid down in bed, you were excited or worried about something, you had a lot of uncontrolled thoughts going through your head, you just couldn't get to sleep, that's a simple definition of psychasthenia. At this level I'd expect that to be bothering Mr. Morris all the time. You know, I mean it's just a situation where he's constantly going to be bombarded with worries, fears, thoughts that he just can't control and handle. And that's only furthering the level of underlying anxiety that he is experiencing and the tension level, the stress level.

The reality is the chicken and egg syndrome. Which comes first, do you have increased tension and anxiety that makes it very difficult for you to control all these thoughts or do you have elevations in these worries and concerns, the thoughts that are going through your head that increase your anxiety levels? In this instance I think it is a reaction to physical disability and a focus and worry about physical complaints that has exacerbated this whole pain cycle.

The last point is a minor elevation on his paranoia scale and frankly, I'd expect any client involved in litigation and any good trial attorney to have an elevation on paranoia to about this level. I think it's a fairly healthy suspicion regarding the motives of others, nothing pathological here, it's just simply one wanting to know the meaning behind a question before one answers it. And I think that's really what's being reflected here.

Now that was his first MMPI. The second MMPI you will note has some fairly significant differences. First of all we are seeing very significant elevations now on that "F" scale to the point now where it's not just a focus on some central problem or concern, but quite frankly, it's representative of an individual who's calling out for help. He is really having, even if it is on a subconscious level, such a significant level of anxiety and stress that he is subconsciously at least recognizing, "I am in trouble. And I need a lot of help".

Interestingly, there is also, at the same time, an increase in defensiveness and guardedness. An individual who's starting to use a lot of denial and repression. You know, the more physically disabled he is, and I think the more perhaps this "F" scale is a reflection of his at least, subconscious awareness, that a lot's going on in terms of stress and anxiety. At the same time, the "L" scale is saying I am going to deny that, I am going to blame this all on physical disability when in fact disability is acting on him psychologically, not just physically.

He has the same elevated triad profile and it still is an inverted conversion V, but you notice that most importantly there is a significant increase in the anxiety or hysterical reaction component. The rest are about the same. We are about the same level on scale four and his paranoia, psychasthenia, and schizophrenia scales are essentially about the same level. So is the social introversion scale. We have a mild, moderate increase in his hypomania scale, which is a measure of psychic energy, psychological stress, and we're seeing that it's even beginning to take shape in his hypomania scale.

Overall, there is no question that we are dealing with not just physical disability, but a very significant psychological reaction to physical disability. And I don't care how hard you try with work hardening programs and work adjustment counseling, you don't make a change in what's going on psychologically, you only deal with this as a physical problem and you're not going to be successful. I think you can be successful. I want to stress that. But we've got to talk about just exactly what the definition of success is.

Q. Dr. Deutsch, will you include in the composite Exhibit 2 copies of all your test data too?

A. Oh, absolutely. Both sides regardless whether there is anything on them, get copied.

Q. From Mr. Morris's scores on the MMPI test and any other psychological profiles or inventories which were administered to him, have you concluded that Mr. Morris shows a definite lack of insight into the nature of his disability and related problems?

A. I think that that's a true statement. I think he is the type of individual who can sit and hear me say it and in fact, we talked a little bit about his MMPI profile at the second evaluation. He doesn't get upset or angry at me by describing it and I think that he's coming to terms with a belief, or at least an understanding, that these psychological problems are occurring. And I think he understands that I'm not trying to suggest that it's strictly psychological and there was never anything physically there; first of all, it wouldn't be appropriate for me to do so, regardless of whether or not I thought it, and I don't think that in this instance, or they wouldn't have done the surgeries. But I do think that he needs a lot of assistance in building personal insight as well as vocational insight. I think he needs a much better understanding of what we call the pain eliciting stimuli in his environment. Much of which is stress related. So the answer to your question is basically a "yes".

Q. If we assume that Mr. Morris was physically no worse off following the first back surgery, would it be fair to assume that the reason Mr. Morris couldn't continue his former employment was primarily related to increases in depression, anxiety, and related psychological factors?

A. Well, I think that is a true statement, as long as we qualify it and realize that the related psychological factors in large part are the physical manifestations of the psychological stress and anxiety and reaction to physical disability.

Q. Part of that reaction though was increased depression as a result of the failure of back surgery to give him the type of pain relief he had anticipated it would?

A. I think that's a fair statement.

Q. Is it also fair for me to state that Mr. Morris's current level of depression and anxiety is related to both of the surgical procedures that he underwent, that is, the results he obtained from those surgical procedures as well as his back injury?

A. Well, I think that's true. I think you have to recognize what's going on with the chronic pain, chronic disability patient. I mean we all are the sum total of our experiences in life. We are all going to react to a disability or an injury in a certain fashion. It's almost predetermined. Because you are who you are and if this occurs, you're going to react one way or another. And so with the onset of disability, it essentially became a catalyst that generated a psychological reaction to physical disability. Then each subsequent event that results from that physical disability has the potential to act on him psychologically one way or another. In this instance, each subsequent surgery would tend to reinforce his image of himself as being disabled and being hurt. Each lack of success from that surgery would tend to reinforce his fear about the future, and his worry and his focus on disability. And so all of it becomes a part of the total physical and psychological syndrome that he is experiencing.

Q. To some extent is the result of the surgery dependent upon the perception of the result on the part of the patient?

A. I think that's a true statement. That's why we, we being the rehabilitation psychologists and the clinical psychologists in our literature have so often stressed to the orthopedic surgeons of the world that these kinds of evaluations ought to be looked at and considered prior to making a final decision on surgical intervention. Certainly it wouldn't and shouldn't influence emergency surgery. But in terms of the point at which to intervene with elective surgery should at least take into consideration the psychological state of the individual and their ability to deal with that surgery. And unfortunately, very little of that's done.

Q. As I understand it, you have trained in the field of psychology?

A. That's true, my Ph.D. is in counseling psychology and counselor education. And my field of specialty is primarily rehabilitation psychology.

Q. Based upon that training, are you able to or in your opinion would anyone with that background be able to make a determination as to how much of Mr. Morris's post-operative, that is following the first surgery, depression and anxiety was related to the back injury as opposed to other events which may have been taking place in Mr. Morris's personal life?

A. There is no way to break it down in terms of percentages. If you read the literature on the accident process and this whole concept of chronic pain, chronic disability, you realize that very often the problem is exacerbated by psychosocial changes of a significant nature that are going on in an individual's life. A divorce can raise anxiety and tension levels, create a lot of psychological problems or firing from a job that you have been on for 19 years, other major psychosocial events. And very often because it's so hard to deal with these events psychologically, when an accident or injury occurs, it becomes a way of dealing with this and using physical disability as a more acceptable excuse for what you're feeling psychologically. Because for a lot of people it's still very hard to accept how difficult it can be to control your psychological or emotional state.

So it's certainly possible that psychosocial events in his life had an impact. Even more probable is again because he is who he is and he is going to react in a certain fashion, the disability played a very significant role as a catalyst in increasing or in developing these kinds of problems. But I don't know of anyone who can draw a fine line and say everything on this side is directly related to the back and everything on this side is either unrelated or only indirectly related to the back. I just don't know how one would do that.

Q. What was Mr. Morris's age at the time of your initial evaluation of him?

A. He was 45 when I reviewed the medicals. I saw him just after his 46th birthday the first time and I believe just after his 47th birthday the second time.

Q. Is it fair to say that it is not unusual for adult males in that particular age range to experience increases in anxiety as a result of transition periods in their lives with respect to vocation realization of lifetime goals and objectives, that sort of thing?

A. That had to be a question coming from a guy in his early to mid-30s. You know, I honestly can't tell you that I am aware of any literature or any personal experience that would suggest that there is a majority or even a large percentage of the male population who at 45 to 50 years of age is uniformly experiencing certain levels of anxiety or concern or worry about their future or the changes in their lives.

I am certainly, although in a somewhat distant future, going to be exposed to that age group myself, and you know frankly, I think it's a very individual thing. I don't think it's a universal rule of thumb across age groups. I think a lot of individuals do experience those things. I think if they tend to be particularly very physically-oriented individuals and that they begin to see a reduction in their physical ability, their body concept, which may have been an important part of their self-concept is now changing, and that can certainly be difficult for some individuals, some males especially, to cope with. But I can't make a statement that it's universal across all 45- to 50-year-old-males.

Q. I understand.

(A short break was taken.)

Q. (BY MR. ROGERS) Could other events in Mr. Morris's life, for example, his son's having difficulty and being suspended from high school and eventually dropping out of high school, could those types of things have also created or contributed to the levels of anxiety and depression which you have documented in your testing of Mr. Morris?

A. I don't think there is any question it contributes to it. I think your changing from creative to contributing was a very effective way and very perceptive way of changing the question. That given no other history, I think he would have dealt with that. And he would have dealt with it fine. But given the history of disability and an increasing set of psychological stressers in his environment, with a decreasing ability that pain causes to handle that stress, each subsequent stress that's superimposed on previous stresses increases anxiety, depression and in the physical manifestation. So I'd say to you there is no question that the stress of being worried about his son, concerned about his son, anxious about that situation would manifest itself physically and it would superimpose itself on the rest of what's going on. And I think the key is that absent all of the other disability problems or the other psychological stressers in his life, he probably would have handled that stress effectively. But superimposed on the rest of the problems, I think that he handled that stress poorly and allowed it to be unconsciously, but nonetheless allowed it to be physically manifested, which has only increased his problems.

Q. Are feelings of guilt a significant psychological stresser?

A. I would say unquestionably any emotional feelings that are of a negative nature can increase his stress levels and the physical manifestations. Just in the same way that positive events, being happy, laughing, et cetera tends to decrease stress. Those are going to increase stress. And so they are going to be manifested as well.

Q. Did any of the tests which you have conducted on Mr. Morris or performed on Mr. Morris allow you to assess the level of the person's guilt feelings?

A. Well, that's a real yes and no kind of response. There is no measure independent of guilt. And the biggest problem you'd have in a case like this is separating out clearly and distinctively something like guilt from other areas of tension, anxiety, because you tend to measure global areas. And guilt is in a global area, it tends to be a sub-part that would manifest itself in increased levels of anxiety or feelings of inadequacy or feelings of inferiority or some of these other problems that are clearly and distinctively shown on the MMPI. So I don't know of any way with this kind of a profile to separate out where guilt is being reflected versus a whole range of other emotions.

Q. Have you been able to make any determinations as to whether Mr. Morris blames himself to some extent for the injuries which he suffered in the automobile accident in December of 1985?

A. He certainly hasn't suggested that verbally. And there is nothing I could point to on the MMPI to suggest that.

I think that it is typical of this type of personality profile to go back and question, "why me?" To be upset and angry about his circumstance, to feel that the circumstance and the disability is unfair and unjust, and a part of that is even to look first at blaming others and second at blaming yourself. Is there something I could have done differently to make a difference? The people go through those emotions, but I don't see anything clinically that would substantiate that, that's a conscious or even subconscious part of this overall disability problem.

Q. Did Mr. Morris provide you with any information as to his current income level and the source of his current income, that is at the time of your initial evaluation of Mr. Morris?

A. Yes. I have it. You want me to go through it?

Q. Yes, please.

A. He indicated that he had a disability policy that continued to age 65. That it was a co-policy with Social Security, so in other words, if Social Security were to increase, then this policy decreases. Social Security disability insurance had just been approved as of, I think, June 20th, 1989, and he did not at the last time we talked have an accurate figure on the monthly amount. I think it had been approved June 20th of '89, but it had just started and so he didn't have an accurate amount. He was getting $1,781 a month off the disability policy, but that would be reduced concomitant with any increase or any income coming from Social Security as I understood it.

Q. To your knowledge, has Mr. Morris ever applied for Social Security disability income?

A. Well, he couldn't have been approved without applying.

Q. All right, well, has he ever applied?

A. Yes, he applied and he has been approved.

Q. Oh, he has been approved?

A. That is what I just said. The Social Security disability income was approved and once he would start receiving checks, that amount would be deducted from the disability policy. So he has applied, he is receiving it, but I don't have an amount for you right now.

Q. To your knowledge, was your assessment of Mr. Morris or were your opinions concerning Mr. Morris's disability one basis on which a determination that he was entitled to disability benefits was made?

A.   I'm sorry. Was my report or my recommendations?

Q.   That's right. Considered.

A.   I have no idea -- I do not have anything in my file where Social Security has asked for my report. Usually they write me directly. If it was submitted by him, it's not anything I am directly aware of.

Q.   Do you have any information as to the conditions upon which Mr. Morris's insurance disability benefits are based? In other words, what requirements he has to meet in order to be entitled to those?

A.   I haven't read the policy. I mean I generally know what those policies say, but I haven't read this policy.

Q.   Generally speaking, does the person have to have a total or near total disability to be entitled to such benefits?

A.   Well, generally there is a two-year period during which the individual must be disabled from performing their usual and customary job. And thereafter, disabled from performing any job for which they are reasonably qualified by virtue of their age, physical condition, and education. Some policies will limit it to just your job, but most do not. And he would need to be totally disabled under that criteria. First, in the first two years totally disabled from his own job and in the subsequent time frame, totally disabled from any other job by which he might reasonably be skilled, trained, or educated. And totally disability certainly would be the key to that.

Q.   Would the fact that Mr. Morris must to some extent be disabled from employment in order to receive disability benefits provide a basis for a secondary gain in this situation?

A.   Well, conceivably, you certainly can't deny the potential for that to exist. Typically the problem is a little more complex than that. It is not that the individual necessarily starts out thinking in terms of monetary gains, but there is a security factor, an awareness that if you give that up, and you fail at the job, you may be in severe financial straits. And so there is a fear of giving that up. That must be dealt with and overcome.

The Social Security tries to help somewhat with that by turning around and providing a trial work period. I don't know whether there is a trial work period though with his disability policy. And if there is not, then it becomes all or nothing. And that leaves the individual feeling extremely insecure in the system, not just because they want to get money, but because of their fear of a total loss of income, that tends to reinforce or at least make very difficult the choice to make a trial work effort. Particularly if you're physically not ready for it or don't believe you're physically ready for it.

Q. In that regard, do you think Mr. Morris believes that he is ready to make a trial effort?

A. Well, I don't believe he feels that he is, but I would advise him not to. Again, I think that you're putting the cart before the horse. If he goes out to work today and he fails and in my opinion, he would, or at least it's more likely than not, then you reinforce the image of disability and you make even my assessment that he should be able to reach part-time work pretty unlikely.

If you start working with him from the chronic pain and psychological support services basis, if you start providing him with the vocational support and work hardening, et cetera, that's built into this set of recommendations, then I think you have the potential to achieve half-time work and I think that he will very much support work along with that program.

So I think the potential is there, but I very much believe that it would be premature to start out with work and then if you fail, go back to talk about rehabilitation.

Q. Over what time frame do you expect with proper training and therapy Mr. Morris could return to a part-time employment?

A. Realistically I think that if we were able to begin this tomorrow, you're talking an eight- to twelve-month period of time to get through a total program. And satisfactory placement where he's consistently handling at least 20 hours.

Q. I'm not suggesting any conscious motivation by this question, but at least on a subconscious level would the expectation of a large damages award in this case also be a source of secondary gain?

A. Well, I think there are a number of things that go on with a lawsuit. The answer to your question is yes, it's certainly possible and in fact, to talk about probabilities, there are a number of things that happen with a lawsuit. One, by being exposed to it, it's a source of stress. And it's unquestionable in my mind that stress is part of what will be acting on him, it is part of the stress in his environment. Two, he has a lot of people like you and I constantly asking him questions about his disability so we are further focusing his attention on disability, and that reinforces it. So there is, and as you said, there is always the possibility that you're going to see secondary gain factors influence it, although I have tried to suggest that, and I think there is at least some acceptance of that. With the level of objective medical findings, the surgeries, et cetera, the best he can do, if he tries his best and he tries to participate, it's not going to negatively influence anybody, because I think there is sufficient objective findings and concerns. I do want to say that there are some positives to the lawsuit as well, although I think they are outweighed by the negatives. I mean lawsuits are catharsis, they are cathartic experiences, a socially acceptable way to go after someone who you feel wronged you. And we certainly don't want to encourage people to do it any other way but that.

On the other hand, the negatives do tend to outweigh the positives in that regard. And so the sooner you can reduce that aspect of their stress, the better. It's one of the reasons why you get some people who suggest that there is a, "green poultice syndrome". It is really not that the individuals with this kind of psychological profile suddenly get better after a lawsuit. I don't buy it and I don't think if you follow for a prolonged period of time, you will see that documented in the literature.

What I do think happens is that for an initial period post-trial, you have removed not only the stress of the trial itself, but given it was a satisfactory result, you remove at least initially some of the financial stress. But unfortunately, when it's all said and done and all the dust settles, the individual is faced with the fact that the psychological and physical problems are still there. And so over, although we may see some initial moderate improvement over the first six months post trial, that tends to dissipate and we are right back where we started from with most of our severe chronic pain, chronic disability patients.

Q. Has Mr. Morris discussed this lawsuit with you?
A. No.

Q. Has Mr. Morris indicated to you whether or not he plans to pursue the interventions which you have recommended to him?

A. He has indicated in our discussions a willingness to be very open-minded and to take a look at these things. We have talked about that. I understand that it's difficult for him to really get a handle at this point on the psychological factors. It takes coming to some terms with that, some acceptance that this has impacted him psychologically as much as it has physically. But I think he's been very open-minded, he's talked to me about it, he's listened, and he hasn't gotten angry and I have had clients get very upset with me in discussing the fact that both of these problems were at issue. So beyond saying that he's been open-minded about it, and seems very willing to consider it, there is no clear-cut statement. Certainly there has been no follow through because there just hasn't been an opportunity to follow through.

Q. Did the MMPI that you have performed on Mr. Morris have validity scales on it?

A. Yes, those were the "L", "F", and "K" scales that we pointed to before.

Q. Did any of the scales indicate that there was, to any extent, a lack of candor in responding to test questions?

A. In the first MMPI, we noted as I went through that with you earlier, that he was very open, responsive to test questions, willing to answer them. In the second MMPI, you saw an increasing amount of repression and denial about psychological versus physical concerns. That he was less open to admitting to common psychological stresses and pressures and more likely to focus on physical disability. So in a sense by being more defensive, more guarded, there is less candor. At least in terms of the psychological components.

Another way of putting it though that I think may be more accurate is that he had more restriction on his personal insight in the subsequent MMPI, much more use of denial as a defense mechanism because that was the only way he could handle the psychological events. Yet at the same time, as you saw an increase in his denial and repression and a decrease in his candor, you also saw the elevated "L" scale where he was clearly calling out for help. And so I think what you were seeing there was an unconscious awareness that "there is a lot going on here, I can't deal with it, so I'm going to deny it and repress it, but I'm asking for help". And I think that's not at all in conflict. And a very real problem that is going on at least on a subconscious level for him.

Q. Is it fair to say that in order to most accurately evaluate Mr. Morris's ability to pursue gainful employment, Mr. Morris would first have to have some psychological counseling to learn to better cope with the stressers in his life?

A. Yes.

Q. Has Mr. Morris indicated to you a willingness to obtain such counseling?

A. Again, very open minded about it, he's not shut me off at all, and I have no reason to assume he wouldn't pursue it.

Q. Did any of the raw data which you obtained from the testing that you performed on Mr. Morris indicate any degree of symptom exaggeration?

A. Well, whenever you're talking about an elevation on scale one of the MMPI, which is the hypochondriacal reaction scale, and whenever you see that kind of elevation on a *Wahler Physical Symptoms Inventory* and a *Whiteley Index*, as we have, you're seeing an exaggerated focus on disability. Somatic or bodily concerns become a central focus of your life, and they're exaggerated at least in the sense that in addition to the actual anatomical problems, there is superimposed on that a tendency to react physically or manifest physically a lot of the stress and psychological and anxiety problems in the individual's environment. So the point being that you have an exaggerated or elevated level of physical complaints in relation to the medicals because some of them occur as a direct result of the anatomical dysfunction, but some of them are occurring as a direct manifestation physically of the stressers in his life that are acting upon him. So it is not a conscious exaggeration, but it very definitely is an increase in somatic focus and complaint rates because of that.

Q. As a rehabilitation counselor, and someone with psychological training, can you make a differentiation as to the extent of conscious symptom exaggeration as opposed to unconscious symptom exaggeration of Mr. Morris's case?

A. The only way is from a testing standpoint, and remember, that even psychological tests are subjective. There is no such thing as an objective psychological test because it isn't like x-rays. In fact, I am not even sure x-rays are objective because you've got to subjectively interpret them. But be that as it may, the answer to your question is that the only way to make that kind of inference is by looking at scales like the elevated scale four in relation to the elevated triad profile, where there is at least a suggestion that the individual is using disability as a way of avoiding psychological stress and pressure.

There is no clear-cut way to say that it's conscious. I tend personally to feel that there is some conscious awareness, that the individual may not be directly aware that they're trying to avoid psychological stresses in their environment by using disability, but they are aware that "gee, I'm going to avoid the bill collector today", or "I'm going to avoid this fight with my wife today, by just saying I am too disabled, I hurt too much", partly because they know it increases their pain, they're aware that when they're arguing or fighting or worrying, that they hurt worse. So I think there is a conscious awareness that we may be avoiding certain things in an effort to feel better. But I am not always sure they understand fully or have full insight as to what may be going on truly behind all of that. You see its manifestation but not its etiology.

Q. I notice on the second page of your initial rehabilitation evaluation report, a section entitled Physical Limitations. Have Mr. Morris's physical limitations changed significantly since this initial report was prepared?

A. I guess it depends on how we define significantly. I don't think it's been a significant change. I mean he is off the walker, using a cane. He's increased the amount of walking he can do, as we talked about earlier. And when I went through in the earlier part of the deposition each of the physical limitations and restrictions he reported, I made a distinction in each instance in which there was a change in the second evaluation from the first, I reported it at that time. So I'd say that there have been some changes, but overall they are not significant.

Q. Is Mr. Morris still essentially lifted, excuse me, limited to one or two pounds in lifting?

A. Again, remember, these are his subjective descriptions and not my statement that he is limited. But I think the answer he would probably give you is that number one, he can carry more now that he is using a cane rather than a walker. The walker has obvious limitations on just being able, forgetting weight, just being able to handle something. So number one, he can carry more. I think he will tell you that he can probably handle on an occasional lift more, but I asked him specifically on a repetitive basis in a work situation, what do you think you could handle? And what we were really talking about at that point was restricted to one or two pounds. And I think he may tell you there is some change, but it is going to be pretty minimal in terms of its impact. Still going to be sedentary work, whether it is one pound or ten pounds, you are still in sedentary work.

Q. At the time of the initial report, did Mr. Morris indicate that he could stand for no more than one hour to 90 minutes at a time?

A. Yes.

Q. Has that changed in any way to your knowledge?

A. It did not as of the second evaluation. Whether or not it's changed obviously since then, I don't know. I haven't talked to him, but that's only been a month. And in fact, it's not even been a whole month I don't think. It has just been a month. And I'm not aware of any other change since then.

Q. As we have discussed, Mr. Morris told you that he was, or indicated to you he was not functional for bending, twisting, kneeling, stooping, or squatting at the time of your initial evaluation of him. Has that changed in any way?

A. No.

Q. Is it your opinion that Mr. Morris should be restricted from ambulating on uneven terrain?

A. Well, I certainly think it makes sense to avoid it. There is no real reason for it, certainly not in the work environment with the problems he has, with the potential for his leg to give out. It's crazy to put him into any kind of work situation in which he might exacerbate his injuries. So it's kind of like the old saying, "You only need your seat belt one time". I could probably put him across uneven terrain multiple times with no problem. But why expose him to the potential for increased disability?

Q. Has Mr. Morris ever mentioned whether or not he was wearing a seat belt in the December of 1985 automobile accident?

A. Never discussed it with him. I didn't mean to bring up that analogy for that reason.

Q. Concerning the problems with Mr. Morris's hearing in his left ear, has Mr. Morris advised you that he believes that those problems were caused by the automobile accident?

A. Well, indirectly he did, because he said number one, he had the problems, and number two, he pointed out that he was struck on the left side of the face and head. And he had no such problems prior. So the implication certainly was that, although he never made a direct statement of that.

Q. Have you obtained information from physicians or other health care providers indicating the nature and basis of that hearing problem?

A. No.

Q. Is that problem to any extent a factor in Mr. Morris's current employment disability?

A. Not at the current level of loss, it's not. In and of itself it certainly isn't going to have an impact as a vocational handicap. On the other hand, in the sense that it is one more symptom, one more physical manifestation, and therefore one more reinforcer for his image of himself as hurt and disabled, it certainly isn't a positive experience or a positive event.

Q. Your report also mentions that Mr. Morris complained at the time of the initial evaluation of situational stress deficits. Could you describe what deficits, stress deficits he was talking about?

A. When we talk about situational stress deficits, first of all, certainly appreciate those are my words, he didn't come in and say, "I have situational stress deficits." Not that he wouldn't necessarily understand it, it is just not likely to be the language that he would use. Situational stress deficits, what we're really talking about here is something that you and I have discussed repeatedly in the evaluation. That's nothing more than noting that he is much less capable of handling stress and pressure in his environment and that as a result, he tends to manifest all of that stress and pressure physically as he gets increased physical tension, et cetera. So that's all it's referencing, is that he just poorly handles stress at this point, and any exposure to increased levels of stress, such as on the job, if we were looking for new job placements today, would be inappropriate. We'd want to locate jobs that were less stressful and less likely to act on him physically.

Q. Dr. Deutsch, is it fair for me to say that you don't have any test data concerning Mr. Morris or data concerning Mr. Morris's psychological profile prior to the automobile accident of December of 1985?

A. That's true.

Q. To that extent, are you somewhat limited in being able to determine how much additional stress and anxiety Mr. Morris suffered as a result of the accident?

A. I think you're somewhat limited, particularly in the way you're asking the question. There is no way really for me to talk about whether he has additional stress or less stress. The question is, is there a difference in the way he handles stress? I suspect that his stress level outside of the events directly associated with the accident and the litigation, most of those things are probably fairly standard for him. Certainly we know he has increased stress, litigation increases stress, financial worries increase stress, the worry about his disability increases stress, so we know for a fact that there is an increase in stress levels. The question is, does he handle it differently?

I think the answer to that is really to rely on the literature. The literature about this whole area certainly suggests to us that there were predisposing personality characteristics that would influence the way he would react to stress and the way he would react to disability. We all have those predisposing characteristics. That is nothing we could have done before or after that would change that. The key is, is that, I think secondary to the accident disability, he is handling stress much less effectively, regardless of whether his means of dealing with stress before was necessarily the best way of dealing with it. He may have just used denial and repression. It doesn't work for him post. And therefore, we're seeing a lot of the physical manifestations. No way for me to tell you more than that though.

Q. Can you tell me what preexisting personality traits have contributed to Mr. Morris's disability?

A. There are a variety of psychological as well as demographic traits that lead into the chronic pain profile. First of all, from a demographic variable, or set of variables, what we often find with these individuals is that they tend to be very hard-working, very focused on their work, they have a strong work ethic. And the absence of work -- well, let me add one more point, that work tends to be a central focus in their life and although they may pursue leisure time activities, they tend to define who they are and their self-concept in response to their work versus their leisure-time activities. The result is the absence of work, because of accident, injury, disability, or whatever, creates undue psychological stress and pressure that influences them.

Secondly, these individuals tend to be, that is, the individuals who develop this profile, often come from backgrounds that are fairly rigid, fairly moralistic, often they will come from very religious backgrounds, but at least backgrounds where as a child they were exposed to a very strong work ethic and that is why work tends to be such a central part of self-concept.

From a psychological standpoint, they tend to be people who have difficulty developing a lot of personal insight. They often use the defense mechanism of denial and repression to avoid dealing with psychological stressors. Often these would be individuals who would have a tendency to think that psychological problems are not as legitimate or not as socially acceptable as physical problems. They would tend to resist going to a psychologist, they would tend to believe that they were capable of handling all these things on their own, they don't need help, and they tend to resist outside help and be fairly rigid in that kind of an attitude.

So these are the kinds of things you're going to see both demographically and in their psychological test profiles before. There may be even be some tendency to have elevations on somatic focus. Even though they're not significant in relation to the disabled population, they would be significant as compared to a non-disabled population. Because they just tend to focus more on physical manifestations rather than admit to any psychological stressers.

Q. With that personality profile, another type of physical injury could have precipitated this same disability, for example, if Mr. Morris had developed severe spinal arthritis with his preexisting personality profile, could he very well have become disabled to the extent he is now?

A. Well, I think the answer to the question is a qualified yes. Now qualified in that I think you would have found a much slower development of the psychological component because again, the literature tends to show the development of the chronic pain profile as a result of a catalyst, which often is a traumatic event. That's not to say that the gradual onset of a physical impairment couldn't result in the same; I think over time it could. I think it would take a little longer, but I do think over time that that's a possibility.

Q. I notice a list at page three of your initial report of various tests that were administered to Mr. Morris. Are those all of the tests that have been administered to date?

A. The answer is they are all of the original tests and then there was a re-administration of the *Minnesota Multiphasic Personality Inventory* in the subsequent evaluation. All of which are contained though together within the file.

Q. Have we already discussed all of the significant findings on those psychological tests, and by significant findings, I mean the findings that entered into your evaluation of Mr. Morris's disability?

A. I think we have really gone into all of that. I'm going to write the dates on the two different MMPI's, but just to further make it clear which one he took, the original MMPI he has was in fact the original MMPI. Then in the last three months we have come out with the MMPI 2, the revision. And that will make a clear distinction between which one he took in which time frame.

Q. Between your two interviews with Mr. Morris, were you provided with any surveillance tapes, videotapes, or surveillance reports concerning Mr. Morris?

A. I have reviewed the surveillance report, but I have not yet had a chance to see the surveillance tape. I have been out of town since, not this past Sunday but the Sunday before. And had it gotten here I wouldn't have been able to see it before this morning's depo. In fact, it hasn't gotten here yet. Only the report has been available.

Q. If we were to assume that the surveillance videotape did show repetitive bending, stooping, and squatting over a period of perhaps an hour at most, at one time that is, while Mr. Morris was fishing at a lake, would that in any way change your opinion as to the types of activity that he could engage in as far as gainful employment is concerned?

A.   I have several comments regarding that. Certainly the possibility of its having an impact on me exists; I'm not going to deny that. On the other hand, I think that we have to be careful in determining the degree of influence based on just exactly what data is being presented. For example, if we have an individual who is intermittently bending or kneeling or stooping or using his upper extremities during that hour, one would first ask how frequently?

The second question I would have is, did he walk away from that -- if it was a highly repetitive rate or a prolonged period, did he walk away from that with absolutely no consequence? Or did he pay for it with increased levels of pain or discomfort in any fashion subsequent to the activity?

The next question is, can he deal with presenting that on more than a one-hour basis? When I talked to him about being functional for work, I was talking about trying to at least maintain consistent behavior for half-time employment. Whether or not he could do it four hours a day. To do it one hour one day out of a week certainly isn't going to influence in a positive fashion his potential for employment.

But the other thing that I think one must consider also is the nature of the events surrounding it. For example, if we have an individual whose tension level is reduced while he's fishing, whose mind is focused on fishing, who takes some leisure and some pleasure out of that and during that course of time, his mind is re-focused away from the constant concerns of disability, then what it does is tell me that he is very consistent with the rest of the behavior pattern involved with the chronic disability, chronic pain profile. That's the very thing we want to teach these individuals, is that we have to re-focus attention, that it is one compensatory skill in dealing with pain, that we know the pain is still there, but if we can draw your attention on to other more pleasurable and less tension-provoking, perhaps even relaxing events, they can have a positive benefit.

So I think it's consistent with the chronic pain patient, but I also think, as I said, that what other influence it might have would really depend on whether or not it had any long-term impact, in other words, at the end of the day, did he hurt worse, was he more fatigued, did he have to increase his breaks, could he maintain it for anything even closely resembling consistency for work, and if that's the case, that is, if he could not do that, then the events you're describing really wouldn't have much of an influence.

Q. As I understand it, when you assessed Mr. Morris, at least initially, he, through posturing and so forth, indicated, readily indicated his feelings of pain and -- is that correct?

A. Yes.

Q. And as I understand, the MMPI's which you performed showed elevations on the hypochondriacal reaction and hysterical reaction scales. Is that also correct?

A. That's true.

Q. Would those elevated scores on the MMPI indicate that Mr. Morris is probably not as able as the healthy person to disguise feelings of physical pain?

A. Interesting question. Well, I guess first of all, it's going to depend a little bit on how we define the healthy person. I mean prior to this injury, we would have looked at Fred Morris and said he would fit in the population of healthy people because no one really knows how the average individual is going to respond. But I'd still like to respond to what is implied in the question, with that restriction. And that is, is he going to react or is he reacting to physical disability and pain and manifesting a lot of symptomatology, including increased pain levels to an extent greater than perhaps the average individual with similar back problems would express it? And I think the answer to that is very probably that he's -- if we have another individual with a similar anatomical set of problems but who's not psychologically impacted by that injury, then they probably -- first of all, they would be dealing only with the anatomical pain and not the increased pain levels over and above those that occur from the stress and the manifestations of that stress.

And secondly, they have an easier time in finding ways to compensate for the pain problem, which he has not been able to do independently. So for that reason, yes, I think that you have a combination of physical and psychological disability which together are greater than either one would be independently.

Q. Is it reasonable to assume then that Mr. Morris is particularly apt to express complaints of pain when he does experience them?

A. I think that's a reasonable assumption as long as you're not restricting it to verbal complaints. He is going to express them, whether it's verbally, whether it's behaviorally, whether it's through posturing, he is more likely to do that, yes.

Q. When Mr. Morris experiences pain walking, is he likely to display that pain through limping or other physical manifestations?

A. Well, whether or not he limps because of the psychological component or whether or not he is limping anatomically, I would really need to talk to the doctors and get a sense --

Q. I didn't mean to differentiate. When Mr. Morris experiences any type of pain as a result of ambulation or walking, is he likely to express that in some manner that's visible?

A. I think that it would probably occur, yes. It would really depend on what was going on. For example, I think if, if I could take it away from Mr. Morris and give you an example for just a minute. One of the things we certainly experience, and I'll give you two quick examples, is the incidence in which we're working with the chronic pain patient and we ask them after two hours of working with them how long they can sit, and they say 20 minutes, and a lot of people want to say oh, they're, you know, they're just not telling the truth. And the truth is that for most of these individuals, when they're focused on disability, it really does restrict their ability to perform activities.

And the result is that now that you have got them focused and involved and working perhaps for the first time since disability on a task, they're able to tolerate more. And a clear example is the old research work that was based on what they called the *Ischemic Pain Test*. You occluded the non-dominant arm with a blood pressure cuff, you simply pumped it up. You handed that individual a hand exercise or asked them to squeeze it and report when they had severe unbearable pain.

Typically, for the non-disabled member of the population, about 12 minutes was the report for severe pain where they could not continue. You did the same thing with the chronic pain population, asking them to report when the pain was equal to their usual and customary pain and when it exceeded it, and the vast majority, they complained of pain exceeding their usual and customary level of pain before you pumped up the blood pressure cuff. And it's not malingering at all, but what you're doing is you're psychologically focusing their anxiety to such a level that they truly experience increase in muscle spasms and a physical pain manifestation because of that focused anxiety.

And so, in answer to your question, a lot of what's going on depends upon what the activity is, whether they are focused on disability versus whether they're focused on a pleasurable or an enjoyable experience. That for a period of time is distracting them. They may pay for it later. But for that period of time, they're very distracted.

Q. Would it be fair for me to say that you do not have sufficient information to completely rule out malingering as playing any part in Mr. Morris's level of disability?

A. Well, I don't know anybody who could rule out malingering as playing no part because we have no real accurate measure of malingering. The best way to assess malingering -- in fact, I just spent three days lecturing out West, and one of the comments I made in this regard was that the only way to define malingering is by behavior. It's very tough to go in and say you are a malingerer. It is easier to go in and say you missed 150 appointments in a row and you failed to do this and you failed to do that.

I think the only close measure we have is the extent to which there is a significant elevation on scale four of the MMPI in relation to the triad profile. And I don't mean just coming up to or approaching clinical significance as we have here, but significant elevations. I don't think that we are seeing that kind of evidence with Mr. Morris. But there is no question that there is no way that you could a hundred percent rule out the concept of malingering on an objective basis. I can only give you my clinical impression.

Q. Does that mean that the most accurate measure of Mr. Morris's ability to perform physical activities is actual observation of him performing those activities?

A. Well, I think that there is little question that observing him in the performance of various activities is going to give you a very good measure, as long as you understand the parameters. For example, again, is he performing an activity that he enjoys, that's pleasurable, that's distracting for him, because remember, we have a psychological as well as a physical component to disability. And even for the individual who doesn't have a severe psychological reaction, the compensatory skill one develops to tolerate increased pain is a refocusing of one's attention on constructive, positive, or pleasurable tasks that distract them from pain. So what the individual is doing will make a very big difference in relation to the measure of pain. And you need to consider this when you're doing what you're describing, which is a process evaluation, an evaluation by assessment, by observation. That gives you some important data as long as you don't lose sight of the influencing confounding variables.

Q. Dr. Deutsch, is computer technology currently opening up new opportunities for people who have severe handicaps?

A. Yes.

Q. Are you aware of programs that Valencia Community College, University of Miami, Florida Community College in Jacksonville and other institutions for severely handicapped individuals to be trained in the field of computer technology and data processing?

A. Absolutely. I have sent several of my severe head injuries as well as several of my spinal cord injuries to those programs.

Q. With the proper interventions and therapy, will Mr. Morris be a reasonably good candidate for that type of program, that is, computer technology or data processing type of program?

A. I think that can be considered. But I think number one, there are other options that are open to him that, as I have already indicated, that don't require his going into that extensive a training program. I would stress that we want to be careful not to compare apples and oranges. To be perfectly frank, I can place a paraplegic who has no pain problem above or below the level of lesion, in a program of that nature and have them functionally working in a program of that nature a lot easier than I can place the chronic pain, chronic disability patient. Because pain is such an influencing factor, psychologically as well as physically, that we just don't have with the non-pain patient, even though they may have a severe disability.

Q. If Mr. Morris did have some training in computer programming and so forth, would that be a reasonable option with the appropriate intermediate interventions as a source of part-time employment for Mr. Morris?

A. Absolutely no question, that the first place you want to look is making use of somebody's past transferable skills. So the answer is certainly that that's the first place we'd look for re-employment.

Q. What description of Mr. Morris's prior job function did you obtain from him?

A. Well, it's written out in a rather lengthy fashion in the material that you're getting a copy of. I have no objection to reading it into the record.

Q. If it's lengthy.

A. Well, you're looking at three pages plus a lot of information on income and benefits.

Q. Did Mr. Morris indicate to you that there were certain aspects of his previous job function that he was currently physically incapable of performing?

A. The answer is yes. I think that what he was physically incapable of handling was just first of all, the amount of time on the job, the physical stamina and endurance were reduced, pain was impacting concentration, and in fact, as I noted in my report, there were a lot of complaints he had that initially, especially when you recognized that he was struck on the head, one might have considered being a head injury, when in fact I don't think that's the case at all.

I think we are dealing with a pain problem that interferes with the focus of his attention and interferes with concentration, attention span, and the first and foremost thing that negatively impacted him on the job was that lack of attention and concentration to tasks. The physical stamina and endurance deficits and his inability to stay on the job because he hurt and he was fatigued. So in that sense, there is no question that it, those represented the primary deficits. It's not a function of lifting, bending alone, although he did notice that he physically was required to bend, crawl under equipment, lift, all of which he was unable to continue doing.

Q. Should Mr. Morris undergo the interventions which you have recommended in order to ready him for part-time employment? Is it realistic to assume that Mr. Morris could eventually work 30 hours a week in a supervisory capacity with respect to data communications, data processing and so forth?

A. Well, you know, I've given the opinion that within reasonable rehabilitation probability, I feel like I can talk about part-time or half-time work up to 20 hours a week. We certainly would want to work toward as high a level of tolerance and functional work on the job as possible. And I'm not going to deny that we're just not going to cut off at 20. We certainly would want to work toward that. I think it's probable we can reach 20. It's possible you could reach 30. I do not think it's probable.

My experience with this level of severe chronic disability and chronic pain patient is that we have a good rate of success in chronic pain programs in improving their day-to-day quality of life, reducing the pain complaints and to some extent, a fairly significant extent, reducing the amount of pain that is superimposed on the physical disability. I think we have a fair to good prognosis for return to up to half-time work, but the statistical data on return to full-time work for those graduating or coming out of chronic pain programs is relatively poor. You're looking at less than 25 percent that are successful in accomplishing that.

A work hardening program, which frankly I think is the basic component of any good chronic pain program, if pulled from the chronic pain and used alone, without any of the other techniques, I just sincerely don't believe would be sufficient to even achieve half-time work, much less full-time. I think it's got to be a package program and in the sense that you're not going to pull out selected parts, you're going to have to deliver the program as a whole.

Q. Have you had patients or clients in the past who have had good pain relief from pain management programs or surgical interventions such as implantation of a nerve stimulator?

A. Well, as to the former, I think we have had fair results from chronic pain programs, in the fashion I just indicated. It's good for improving quality of life, fair for half-time work, and poor for full-time work. As to my experience with patients who have had stimulator implants, I cannot quote the research literature; I think it's a good literature search to do, and I will make a point of trying to accomplish that. But as for my own off-the-cuff experience, I'd have to say to you was that it was certainly no cure-all. And I have not heard of success rates that were any greater than the use of a TENS unit, a transcutaneous stimulator.

      Now I am not, I must stress I'm not an M.D., I'm not this man's treating physician. I'm not a surgeon and I'm not giving him advice by answering the question in that fashion as to what he should or shouldn't do. I'm simply answering based on my experience, that I haven't seen it as a cure-all, I haven't seen it as a miracle surgery. I haven't even seen it as having substantial and significant results, but then again, I also haven't done a research search on it and I think we need to do that to better answer that question.

    Q.   But up to this point in time, Mr. Morris has not pursued any of those interventions in order to increase his ability to deal with his pain, has he?

    A.   Well, with respect to the surgery, I'd have to defer to the docs as to why they have or haven't done it. To my knowledge, it's not been done at this point. As to all the other techniques, no, he hasn't. I think he's been very open-minded about it, but in our discussions, he's also indicated that he doesn't have the money for them. And they are costly interventions.

    Q.   Is it correct for me to say that until Mr. Morris actually has those interventions, you won't be able to accurately assess how much pain relief he has received from those interventions and therefore how successfully he could be assimilated into the job market?

    A.   Well, there is no question that being a Monday morning quarterback is a far more accurate situation and if we want to take my deposition in a couple of years after all this is done, to see whether we were right or wrong, you would be absolutely correct that I would get a much better assessment. I would agree with you, there is no way that foresight is going to beat hindsight. On the other hand, I think we can talk in terms of reasonable rehabilitation probability based on 18 years of hindsight, that is, my work experience. And that's all we really have to go on. We have to talk in terms of reasonable probability based on our knowledge base, our data base, both in terms of the field and in terms of our individual experiences. And that's what I have done here.

Q. Let me ask you one question about the second evaluation of Mr. Morris which you performed. I notice at page two of your report of that evaluation, this statement "increases in these scales," and I think you're talking about scale four and scale six of the MMPI, "Increase in these scales present difficulty when psychological intervention is attempted, as disability has been established as a tool to manipulate his environment and control his stress, accompanied by a suspiciousness of the motives of other creating barriers to the development of a counseling relationship." Is, in your opinion, any of the manipulation which you're discussing in that sentence conscious manipulation on the part of Mr. Morris?

A. Well, first let me stress, or let me correct a typo in that, "other" should be "others." It should be an "s" there. "So suspiciousness of the motives of others, creating barriers to the development of a counseling relationship". And I think that the answer to your question is number one, as we have talked about it a couple of times in the depo, it's extremely difficult to point out whether that's conscious or unconscious. You can really only give a subjective clinical impression. And I think that there may be some awareness on Mr. Morris's part that at least he feels better if he avoids stress situations. He may not even be putting two and two together, it simply may be a behavioral reaction. "I hurt a lot less when I'm not having to deal with a lot of stressful situations." So in that regard there are degrees of conscious awareness.

That's really about all I can say. I think that as far as counseling intervention, his amenability to it, I think that will improve as this suspiciousness improves and I think that will improve as litigation dissipates. So that certainly is something to consider.

Q. As I understand your previous testimony, you believe that it is conceivable that review of the surveillance tape of Mr. Morris could influence your opinions concerning Mr. Morris's assessment. Is that correct?

A. Well, it would certainly be inappropriate on my part to say there is no way it could influence. Any kind of additional data has the potential to influence one's opinions.

From what I understand of it and from what I have read of the surveillance report, I don't have any real change at this stage of the game. I have not seen the tape, but I am not going to say it can't have an impact.

MR. ROGERS: I'd like to just conclude this deposition by obtaining your agreement, Steve, if possible, that if in fact this thing goes to trial eventually and is not settled, that I would have an opportunity to depose Dr. Deutsch in a limited fashion just concerning whether or not he had seen the videotape and whether his opinions had changed as a result of that or as a result of additional data that he's been provided with.

MR. BARCUS: I have no objection to your asking him questions about the videotape.

MR. ROGERS: That's fine. Then I guess we are finished. Of course, you know you have a right to receive a copy and read it over. Would you like to do that?

THE WITNESS: I don't have any desire to do that.

MR. BARCUS: Actually I'd like you to read, Doctor.

THE WITNESS: If you would go ahead and forward a copy to me. (Whereupon, the deposition concluded at 1:05 p.m.)

Sample Transcript #2

The second transcript presented in the non-catastrophic case area again represents an adult chronic pain/chronic disability patient but presented from the viewpoint of a defense referral rather than a plaintiff referral as is the case in the earlier deposition.

PROCEEDINGS
PAUL M. DEUTSCH, Ph.D.,
having been first duly sworn by the Court Reporter, was examined and testified upon his oath as follows:

DIRECT EXAMINATION
BY MR. ROMANI:

Q. Tell us your name, please.

A. Paul Michael Deutsch.

Q. And your address, sir?

A. 2208 Hillcrest Street, Orlando, Florida.

Q. Is that your business address?

A. Yes.

Q. Okay. When were you first contacted in this case, Dr. Deutsch, to evaluate Larry Jones?

A. Right off the bat, that's a question I can't answer without the file in front of me. I don't think it's going to take them more than three or four minutes here to copy that whole thing, so -- if it would help, I can do this. I can grab half the file and we can start on that half and just switch with them or we can wait a minute. Whichever you prefer.

Q. Let's just wait a minute. That way, we won't be jumping back and forth.

(Whereupon, a brief recess was taken, after which the following transpired:)

BY MR. ROMANI:

Q. Now that you have your file back in front of you, when were you first contacted?

A. On May 31st, 1988.

Q. And who contacted you?

A. Joe Taraska.

Q. And what were you asked to do in this particular case?

A. To provide a rehabilitation evaluation and assessment of vocational handicaps.

Q. And I understand you were provided with copies of various medical records and depositions and so forth; is that correct, sir?

A. That's correct.

Q. And are those accurately summarized in your medical summary --

A. Yes.

Q. -- under records reviewed?

A. Yes.

Q. Did you review those matters before Larry came to see you?
A. Yes.
Q. When did he come to see you?
A. On June the 10th, 1988.
Q. And what history did you get from him at that time, sir?
A. Okay. Now the history is contained in approximately nine pages of notes. I don't know if you want the entire nine pages read into the record or --
Q. I really don't want you to just sit there and read them. Is that in the stack of records that were given to me?
A. Right. All of those handwritten notes that you're looking at. The ones where there are no lines or anything, that's where she copied notes that I wrote on the back sides of the page because I ran out of space. I can cover, if you'd like, in the answer, the general areas that I covered and history.
Q. Well, what was pertinent to you in the formation of your opinions in this case?
A. Okay. Well, I think there were a number of areas that were really pertinent. I'm not going to say that all the information wasn't important, but we started out with generally identifying information and, under that, the most important area was his notation that he had continued to use a transcutaneous stimulator, that he uses it three to four times per week on a PRN or as-needed basis.

He said that the TENS unit was not giving him much relief, certainly not as much as it used to give him, he said, but it still helps and it's just that it's less responsive in areas or times of more severe pain.

Under general case information, we cover things like date of accident, the basic nature of the accident, and what occurred and -- not from a standpoint of liability issues, but strictly did he lose consciousness in the initial accident and just a basic history of the injury.

Then we went on to any work he's done since the accident. He said he's not had any work since the accident of 1985. He's done none at all.

Subsequent to the 1982 accident, in approximately 1984, but he wasn't sure what month, he opened Fort Pierce

Motorcycles, Unlimited for the sale and repair of used motorcycles.

He felt the business, "wasn't doing too bad"; thinks the business was open approximately one year prior to the 1985 incident. He sold the business before the 1985 incident and entered business with his brother, Larry.

He said that that was an existing motorcycle business. This was called Fort Pierce Cycle and he said there was an intent also for them to buy a Suzuki shop that was in Okeechobee, Florida. In the end, his brother did buy that shop, but that Mr. Jones was not involved because the incident had occurred and he just basically got out of business with his brother. He's not looked for alternative work since.

I have a brief description of notes on what he said regarding the incident in 1985, but I won't go into all those details other than to note that I asked him if he was unconscious subsequent to that. He said yes, for approximately fifteen to thirty minutes. I asked him questions to establish retrograde amnesia and he basically said he had full recall on awakening, no loss of memory for the incidents leading up to that time, which is retrograde.

Typically, and even in more severe closed head injury, you don't expect retrograde amnesia except in the most severe cases. So I think that was consistent.

No post-traumatic amnesia was described at all. He remembers the details of the crash, in terms of the original accident, also. He said no loss of consciousness, he remembers the details of the crash, he remembered the accident scene fully. So there was no post-traumatic amnesia in either incident.

Q. Let me stop you right there for a moment.
A. Certainly.
Q. In the '82 accident, you had no report of any head injury, did you?
A. No. That's what I was asking him.
Q. Yeah, no loss of consciousness --
A. That's right.
Q. -- as a result of the motorcycle accident?
A. There was nothing associated with the motorcycle accident that represented any kind of head injury and, again, no post-traumatic amnesia and retrograde amnesia, but only

the report of approximately fifteen to thirty minutes of unconsciousness from the 1985 incident.

    Q.   The seizure?

    A.   Correct. Then we went on to past medical history. Wasn't really pertinent. He reported a broken leg and a broken knee as a result of -- in fact, I don't even have an indication of what it was a result of. Just that there was no sequelae. He did fine, recovered from it. No childhood, adolescent, adult illnesses.

    The two areas that were most pertinent here were his chief complaint and his subjective description of limitations.

    Chief complaint included muscle spasms and pain throughout the back from low to the upper back, occasional pain moving into the neck, rarely pain-free, but he states, "Yeah, sometimes." Couldn't put any specifics on it. "Sometimes I'm pain free, but no real estimate".

    He said this may occur -- that is, the onset of pain-free periods -- may occur if he makes a specific effort. That is, if he lies down, changes his position frequently, avoids any activity that would exacerbate his pain. Then he does this for several days. He can work himself to a point where he's pain-free.

    Let's see, he says he sleeps poorly due to pain, does experience headaches on more severe pain. Headaches are moderate to severe. They require bedrest, hot shower, and aspirin. Tension headaches by description, noting he gets worse when excited.

    In other words, when we talked about the precipitators for headaches, it seemed pretty clear that they were very much stress-related. The more stress he had, the more pain he tended to have. The more pain and stress he had, the more likely he was to going to incur a fairly significant headache. And, usually, lying down and relaxing would have a positive impact on headaches.

    Was less positive or less quick to react as far as his back pain was concerned but headaches were much more likely to respond.

    He does say that he's had "a little training", in relaxation techniques from Dr. Hooshmand's office. Apparently, they gave him some tapes. And that that helps his headaches.

He admits to irritability, tension, and depression, made worse by increasing pain. He complained of delayed memory deficits. Remote memory was intact. Immediate recall, he says, is intact. It's just some delayed memory.

He feels he no longer can handle, "taking things apart and rebuilding them".

He has trouble recalling conversations with customers from a previous day. Feels memory problems persist even when his pain level is low. But he also talked about his memory problem being worse sometimes than others.

And the way he described it and the questions he answered suggested that there may definitely be some concentration and retentional aspects to this. In other words, with significant increases in stress, pressure, even depression, psychological factors can play a role in the extent to which somebody has a memory deficit in the delayed memory area. And from his description and from subsequent test results, I really felt it was very psychologically-based.

He reported impotency since his seizure. He said he's been to three or four medical doctors. He's discussed the penile implant. He says that in his recollection, the doctors have noted a clear physiological cause for impotency, but he's not followed through with any other specifics regarding an implant at this point.

He indicates no other head injury sequelae, other than memory, and we went through the whole list of various possible long-term outcomes of a closed head injury, from anoxia, from just diffuse closed head injury and he had none of the sequelae reported.

The next area was physical limitations that he describes subjectively. He notes a surface numbness in the legs, on more severe pain.

A normal upper extremity range of motion with pain on reaching and stretching. Lifting limited to an occasional lift of five to eight pounds, usually less than that. He states, "I can pick up quite a bit, but I end up hurting." Normal prehensile action. Manual finger dexterity was described as normal. Grip strength, normal.

Sitting capacity varied from a few minutes up to an hour. Standing and moving about helps but lying down in bed is best. It's difficult for him to resume sitting if he's had to lie down. Standing was limited to just a few minutes if he was standing still, but he states if he can walk some, then it is "my best position".

And if he can walk about, he can handle two to three hours on a good day; but on a bad day, only up to thirty minutes.

Walking, a quarter to half a mile, although he says, again, if he can walk, that's his best position.

Bending and twisting, he says it hurts to bend to his toes. He can bend to his knees. He can twist the torso with caution. He can kneel, stoop, and squat on occasion. Not repetitively.

He can climb on occasion. Stairs. Certainly, ladders, scaffolding, unprotected heights, these kinds of things would be inappropriate.

No blackouts. Occasional dizziness when he has more severe headaches.

Breathing, he says if he's in severe pain, it hurts him to breathe in and he gets short of breath but otherwise no history of dyspnea.

Headaches, we've gone over.

Vision, good, no complaints.

Hearing, he denied deficits but later noted that on more severe pain, he has trouble. It seemed again to be a concentration problem, but there's also a pattern you see in his complaints of very diffuse kinds of complaints and it's important to note that. We'll come back when we talk about the testing and bring it up.

These are very real complaints to him. No question about it. But when you start seeing diffuse complaints like when I've got more severe pain, I can't hear, I lose my hearing, you begin to recognize a fairly classic kind of chronic pain syndrome pattern in the complaints.

This is a small part of how you try and diagnose chronic pain. But clearly you see it in his verbal complaints, which become very diffuse.

Good command of the English language. He communicated well. And there was just no problem at all in terms of getting him to respond to questions, to be open in talking to me. He was cooperative in that regard.

Bowel and bladder, he described frequency and urgency of urination on occasion, no problems with bowel function, tires easily, limited physical stamina and endurance. He says he lies down intermittently during the day but this varies with his activity level and how much pain he experiences.

He generally tries to lie down every afternoon.

Said valid Florida operator's license was held by him, restricted by his capacity for sitting and his level of pain.

Next, we went over environmental influences and work settings that might exacerbate pain. We covered his current medical care, the fact that he's not taking any medications, except aspirin.

We went over his activities of daily living, his social activities, personal habits, socioeconomic and family background. He's a high school graduate, 1972, with two years training in automobile mechanics as part of his high school program.

No military experience. Most of his work has been in motorcycle mechanics.

He's alert, well-oriented, with clear and rational stream of thought. I felt that remote memory and immediate recall were intact and delayed memory was a function of more of concentration and retentional deficits, that I felt were secondary to a fairly severe depression and what appeared to be a significant chronic pain problem.

Attitudes and insights, I indicated generally fair to good attitude. That is, personal and vocational insights were, at best, fair. He really lacked a lot of insight into what was actually going on. Particularly psychological.

The next thing we did was the testing.

Q. All right. While you were talking with Larry, did you try to delineate what problems he had physically or mentally prior to the seizure, as opposed to after the seizure?

A. No, I really -- well, let me take a look at these notes a little more. I don't think that we really tried to delineate specifically functional levels, like how much sitting, standing, walking he could do before and after.

Now I was aware from talking to him, as well as from the medicals, as to the additional vertebral fractures that occurred. I was aware of his description of the fifteen to thirty minutes of unconsciousness and his complaint of the memory problem.

But I didn't try and delineate capacities for function between the two and I think, at best, that would have been difficult to do for him, to try and remember how well he could sit in 1983 versus how well he can sit today.

Also, realistically, as far as any complaints relative to memory, et cetera, you know, there just were none before. He didn't describe any. He indicated no problems with it and the only thing he's describing after -- from that standpoint is memory. There's no other head injury sequelae he's describing.

Q. Well, I was just trying to determine -- I was looking through your vocational worksheet and I think you have the categories as vocational development options pre-onset, post-onset and then pre-accident vocational alternatives and post-accident vocational alternatives, and I don't know what incident you're referring to.

A. That's fine.

Q. This particular litigation involves the injuries to his thoracic spine and any sequelae from those injuries.

A. I understand that. I did not have any information at the time that I did this evaluation in the medicals that clearly delineated for me that all of his pain came from one incident versus the other.

I don't think I'm the one who can establish etiology of any objective medical findings being responsible for the pain and, from the standpoint of a chronic pain problem, it may well have developed in terms of a progression.

First of all, when you see an individual with a psychological reaction and disability like a chronic pain problem, right off the bat you know that there are always going to be predisposing personality characteristics, even before any accident, that are going to dictate the way an individual reacts to the accident.

That's through no fault of their own. That's just how that person's going to react.

Q. Sure.

A. Then you recognize that events have a cumulative effect. In other words, you can develop a chronic pain syndrome as a result of one accident but the research literature also tends to suggest that you increase focus on disability and tend to exacerbate chronic pain syndromes when multiple incidents occur.

So it would be very difficult to draw a fine line and say the psychological aspects of this, the chronic pain aspects, were exclusively attributable to one versus the other incident.

Q. Yeah, I'm not trying to be critical of you in that regard.

A. No, I wasn't taking it that way. I'm just giving you the best --

Q. All I was interested in is whether, in other words, in order to determine to what extent the seizure and the medical sequelae from that seizure may have had on his earning ability and capacity --

A. Okay.

Q. -- I was just wondering whether or not you had asked him, at least from his standpoint, how he felt that particular medical situation affected his condition?

A. Okay. Beyond what I've already told you. Not in the sense that we tried to break down one set of physical symptoms before versus a set --

Q. All right.

A. -- after. And in all fairness, I looked at, from a report standpoint, at the total person. The individual I was working with.

I certainly could address a hypothetical. If there were doctors or if Mr. Jones, either one, came back and said this is pre-, this is post- or this is attributable to one incident, this is attributable to another, and I was then asked to take that and assume it and how would that affect him, I'd have no problem, given sufficient information, in answering.

But, no, I reached my own conclusions based on the man that was in my office on the day I evaluated him.

Q. All right. So if I'm reading you correctly, the vocational worksheet is based on his physical condition as he presented it to you on the date of your interview, without any attempt to apportion what may have predated the seizure and what came after the seizure?

A. Physical and psychological condition; that's correct.

Q. All right. Why don't you go ahead and tell me what tests you administered?

A. Okay. Well, we started out with the *Slosson Intelligence Test*. He achieved an IQ on that of 104.

Now this deals strictly with verbal IQ, fund of knowledge and his ability to recall and answer questions with fund of knowledge.

He fell in the sixtieth percentile, which, of course, indicating he'd do equally as well as or better than sixty percent of the population.

His reverse digit span was the only area of deficit that was noteworthy. And it's consistent with the other testing that was done. Showed some abstract reasoning and conceptualization problems.

On his *Gilmore* or reading test, he did fairly well. Grade equivalency was 8.2 in accuracy. 3.8 in comprehension and 6.8 in reading rate.

Q. What do those numbers mean?

A. That --

Q. Grade of education or what?

A. Right. That he's reading at a level consistent with second month, eighth grade, in his accuracy. Uses punctuation, sentence structure, et cetera. Eighth month of third grade in terms of comprehension and eighth month of sixth grade in terms of reading speed.

So he's reading above the average for a high school graduate in the State of Florida, in accuracy and in reading rate, and well below the average in comprehension.

Again, even the intelligence test can be very negatively impacted by both concentration and particularly depression and there's no question that we were looking at a lot of depression with this individual.

And I think that's what you're seeing reflected in his comprehension problem.

The next was the *Halstead Booklet Category* test. He had a hundred errors on the test. Upper limits of normal would be fifty errors. So he's showing a lot of problems in abstract reasoning and conceptualization.

Again, the problem seems to focus on concentration and retention. Particularly in light of his own description of where his sequelae is from the seizure incident, it really seems very psychologically-based. Some real problems with depression, focus on disability, chronic pain. Perhaps even beyond chronic pain. Chronic disability syndrome.

That long-term exposure to disability has created some significant psychological reaction that we need to deal with.

I gave him also the *Minnesota Multiphasic Personality Inventory*, but in the interest of avoiding keeping him for an entire afternoon just in the testing portion of this, I knew he was seeing Dr. Edelman and I gave him the option of taking it home and bringing it back the following week and returning it to Dr. Edelman.

Q. All right.

A. He didn't get it done by the following week, but he did get it done and he Fed Ex'ed it to Dr. Edelman's office.

So Dr. Edelman actually is the one who scored that test and I do have the results. They came to me today and I'll need to refer them probably when we start talking about some of the conclusions. But they are from his score, even though it's my test.

Q. Okay. Well, since we're on that, what about the MMPI have you taken into consideration as far as your assessment of Larry?

A. Well, I think that there's some very significant things on the MMPI that we need to attend to in talking about rehabilitation needs of this individual.

First, in the validity scales, he has a very elevated "F" scale and I suspect that the "F" scale is a reflection of the stress that he's under but really a reflection of the degree to which he's focused on disability.

One of two things is occurring with the "F" scale elevated at this level. Either we have an individual who couldn't read or couldn't understand the questions -- that does not seem to be the case, particularly since the consistency of responses is much too great. So that would seem to be inappropriate.

Or we have an individual who's calling out for help. Sometimes what you find is an individual will become really focused on certain areas, like disability, and they utilize their responses in a fashion to let you know they've got a real problem that they perceive and they're calling out for help.

Basically, it's a valid profile with recognition that you may see some extremes of elevation on certain scales that you have to interpret cautiously because those elevations may, in part, be a result of an exaggerated focus on disability, again secondary to this desire to call out for assistance.

And he shows significant elevations on scales -- well, first on scale two, depression. And I'm going to talk first about the triad profiles, which is the first three scales. That's hypochondriacal reaction, depression, and hysterical reaction.

Now he has essentially an inverted conversion V or an inverted triad profile. The highest point is depression. Now it's a fairly classic chronic pain profile, chronic disability profile. With the exception that the most frequently seen profile of this nature has depression elevated but the low point of the V. This has it at the high point. So he has a very severe depression that we're looking at.

Also, he's approaching clinical significance on hysterical reaction, but he hasn't reached clinical significance. He has, though, reached clinical significance on hypochondriacal reaction.

Now most important here -- maybe not most important, but certainly of importance is that he has an elevated scale four in relation to his triad profile.

Now the scale four is called the psychopathic deviate scale. It's partly a reflection of the underlying anxiety that's existing, but in the research it suggests that the individual who has an elevated four in the presence of an elevated triad profile is an individual who tends to use disability in a manipulative or controlling fashion to control social environment.

Now don't misunderstand it or put more words into that than exists. What we are saying here is that, first of all, a lot of individuals like this will use disability as a way of avoiding increased psychological stress and pressure. "I can't deal with that bill problem, I can't deal with this crisis in my life, I'm too disabled, I'll get my wife to do it for me. I control the family and social environment." Maybe on a conscious level; maybe on an unconscious level.

And there's no clear way to delineate that. But the disability tends to be used as a means of avoiding dealing with a lot of those problems and using disability as a controlling mechanism becomes part of the behavior pattern.

It's also the pattern of an individual who, because they can't deal effectively with a lot of stress and pressure, tends to interpret that stress and pressure in a physical realm. So that although there could be -- and I'll leave that up to the doctors -- there certainly could be objective medical findings showing that at least a portion of the pain is resulting from anatomical damage, there is no doubt in my mind, when you look at this profile and the clinical evidence, that he has pain over and above anatomical pain.

Because what he's in is a vicious pain cycle. What happens is that, you know, pain, stress, pressure, psychological problems get interpreted in terms of tension and stress, physically, increased muscle tension, muscle spasm. That tends to increase pain. Increased levels of pain make one less capable of handling stress and pressure.

So they become more irritable, more tense. That tends to make it easier for that tension to become interpreted physiologically. It increases pain and we're in that cycle.

It's in a cycle that we have to break. Now in this case, which is not unusual with chronic pain, chronic disability patients at all, he also shows elevations on three other scales that are significant.

He shows an elevation of -- a fairly significant elevation -- on the schizophrenia scale. And he shows it on the psychasthenia scale. Psychasthenia, I think, is a reflection of a lot of underlying anxiety that he's experiencing. But the eight seven combination that you're seeing there -- that is, those two scales are reflecting relatively long-standing feelings of inadequacy, inferiority, poor body concept, low-self concept. He just doesn't feel good about himself.

Not a lot of self-confidence. And, you know, this is most likely something that's very long-standing, probably not made any better by any means and may well have been increased by his current physical problems, as well as his psychological reaction to those problems.

He's also showing a social introversion, which is very consistent with his depression scale.

So although again we have an elevated "F" scale, the consistency and the fact that there is no indication here of impression management or any effort to manipulate test results -- there's no elevation on the "K" scale, is what basically I'm saying -- would suggest we have a valid profile.

And when you look at that, there's little question -- particularly when you combine it with the clinical side -- that what you're dealing with is a very significant chronic pain, chronic disability syndrome.

MR. TARASKA: Got it?

MR. ROMANI: Yeah.

MR. TARASKA: Okay.

BY MR. ROMANI:

Q. Now, did you dictate the medical summary from the records that were provided to you?

A. Yes. I will say, in the interest of self-defense, that's for my file and my notes, so we don't proof it and correct typing errors or spelling errors, so don't worry about that.

Q. Oh, I didn't know if this was a medical summary which you had gotten in the record --

A. Yeah, that's mine.

Q. -- or if somebody provided it to you?

A. No, that's strictly mine.

Q. All right. Well, after all the testing and your interview with Larry, did you come up with some sort of vocational assessment?

A. Yes. There's basically five areas of conclusions that I have.

Q. Are they set forth on your vocational worksheet?

A. Yes.

Q. Now I'm going to want this attached to the deposition and we'll go through it, but under the vocational handicap area, are these restrictions or limitations that were related to you by Larry?

A. Well, they are but what I do is take a look at the individual's complaints, their subjective description of disability and go back and look at the medical records and the kinds of problems they've been having.

If they're grossly inconsistent, if I have a real, real problem, I'll indicate it. You have to recognize that as long as the areas in which he is complaining are consistent, that's as far as I go.

Q. Yeah. I understand that.

A. If the doctor says, well, I think he can sit for two hours and he says I can sit for only an hour, I'm going to lean towards what he says, not what the doctor says, because I don't know how you would measure that, otherwise.

Q. I understand that. I was going to follow up my question with, are these vocational -- are these restrictions or limitations solely what he told you or handicaps or -- limitations or restrictions which you felt were consistent with the type of injuries described to you?

A. I think they're consistent. I also, though, will tell you that the degree -- that is, the amount of the limitation -- may, in part, be resulting from anatomical problems and, in part, a function of the chronic pain syndrome.

And to the extent that they're part of the chronic pain syndrome, there's something that may be subject to the treatment program that I very strongly feel he needs. We just shouldn't walk away from this kind of problem. He needs to be cared for.

Q. Yes, sir. Let's stop here for a moment so we can make sure the Jury understands that particular aspect of your testimony.

When you talk about separating out pain from an underlying anatomical injury, you're talking about pain which exists because a portion of the body is causing that pain, correct?

A. That's true. That's correct.

Q. Let me just follow up and then you can add or detract.

A. Sure. No. That's correct.

Q. And I assume that you would agree that as long as the underlying anatomical problem exists, that it's more likely than not to continue to cause pain?

MR. TARASKA: I'm going to object to the form because, as you well know, Dr. Deutsch is not a medical doctor.

MR. ROMANI: Oh, I understand that.

MR. TARASKA: I think you need to go to the medical doctor to find out what anatomical problem causes pain and what anatomical problem doesn't cause pain.

MR. ROMANI: I know that, Joe, but what I'm trying to define here a little more clearly, because I think it's important, is that -- that the chronic pain syndrome -- I mean, you've separated those two out, pain caused from an underlying anatomical problem versus a pain -- the chronic pain syndrome.

One, you said, would be subject to possible treatment, to wit, the chronic pain syndrome, leaving out the anatomical pain?

THE WITNESS: That's correct. Well, that's correct but let's make sure we really are clear on this and I'll try and be as simple as possible.

BY MR. ROMANI:

Q. Try to do that just so that some of the Jurors who may not have the level of experience --

A. I understand.

Q. -- that you do in vocational assessment will understand it, Dr. Deutsch.

A. That's a good way of putting it. That's fine.

The bottom line is there is nobody who's going to draw a fine line and say absolutely this is anatomical, this is psychological, because it's so interrelated.

It's quite possible for a chronic pain patient -- we're talking generally now -- it's quite possible for a chronic pain patient to have pain that is exclusively psychologically-based.

Now that's not saying they don't really feel physical pain because, again, we're talking about a situation in which this is interpreted physically. And there are palpable muscle spasms that can occur with these individuals because of increased muscle tension and the fact that they often will pull away from exercise, they tend to have muscle atrophy. These are muscles that become spasmed that much more easily. So it's not to say that in every case of chronic pain, you'll always have something that's anatomical and something that's psychological.

It will vary. So it's up to the doctor to say there are objective medical findings that would cause pain. But what I'm saying to you is that, although you cannot draw a fine line and say absolutely this on this half of the line and this is on this half, there is a recognition that even in the instance in which the chronic pain patient, that individual with a diagnosable chronic pain problem, has some anatomical problem, that patient is also one who's going to have significant increases in pain over and above the anatomical pain because of this psychological reaction.

To the extent that that's true, that's what's most treatable. To the extent to which any anatomical pain is treatable is up to the medical doctors to talk about.

But I will say that the only time you will see success in a chronic pain management program is when the individual who is being treated is satisfied in their own mind that there's no more medical intervention and this is essentially the treatment program they're going to have to undergo.

And the reason for that, in part, is that if there is always this feeling that, well, if this doesn't work, I can always go back to the doctor, we're not going to get their full cooperation and motivation.

The problem is there. When you're being treated anatomically as a patient, that is stimulus-controlled, if you will, for passivity. When you're a patient in a doctor's office or in a hospital, you're a passive participant in care and treatment. Something is done to you, a technique is applied and you, hopefully, will improve.

In rehabilitation, including chronic pain management, you have to be an active participant. You're a rehabilitation client and an active member of the team and you have to give, you have to participate fully, you have to be motivated and you have to learn to internalize and use the techniques that are being taught if you're going to get the benefits of those techniques.

MR. TARASKA: Can we take a minute break?

(Whereupon, a brief recess was taken, after which the following transpired:)

BY MR. ROMANI:

Q. Essentially, in a pain treatment program, such as you've described, we're trying to teach the person how to cope with the pain, how to live with the pain?

A. Okay. No. There are really two aspects to a pain treatment program when you talk about it in that term.

There is pain -- that amount of pain again that we're saying is caused by the psychological reaction where you can literally reduce the amount of pain they're experiencing.

That pain that may be caused anatomically, yes, then you're teaching them to cope more effectively with that.

Q.   And to minimize any psychological overlay caused by the chronic pain syndrome?

A.   Well, you certainly want to minimize. There's no question. But the other thing, of course, you're looking to do is actually give them specific usable techniques designed to reduce or eliminate the problems that have developed because of the chronic pain syndrome.

You know, we talk about the psychological aspects as if they had no physiological basis, but I'll give you a good example of the best analogy I can make, just like I talk to the clients about.

We talk about ulcers. Ulcers are certainly a physical manifestation in many instances of an individual's reaction to stress. An ulcer can perforate, hemorrhage, it could kill an individual. It's a physical reaction to a psychological stress.

But it's treatable. I have seen many chronic pain patients who become very sedentary, they develop extremely poor muscle development, their paraspinal muscles become very atrophied, they get no exercise, they actually have physiological reactions as a result of all of their psychological reactions. It's part of the chronic pain syndrome.

So part of what you're doing in treatment is you're not just giving them techniques for coping or even reducing muscle spasm. You're not just giving them relaxation techniques. You're building back muscle atrophy through appropriately coordinated physical therapy programs and, by that, I mean it's coordinated with the biofeedback and the relaxation techniques. It's coordinated with the therapy.

You're taking them through work hardening and you're building up their tolerances. You're teaching them how to control tolerances.

In other words, if they learn their tolerances, they reach their maximum levels, they learn them and they learn how to work within tolerances so that they don't begin to exacerbate the problems. They learn how to handle consistent approaches to tasks or work so as not to exceed tolerances.

But just as the psychological reaction can result in a physical deficit, the treatment that we're dealing with here, although it may be in many ways psychologically-based, also results in a physical reaction.

Q. Did you reach any opinions or conclusions, Dr. Deutsch, as to what impact Mr. Jones' vocational handicaps that you have delineated in this report have on his placement in the job market?

A. Okay. I did.

Q. All right. And tell us what that opinion is.

A. Well, for him, placement, we're looking at really two aspects because there has been self-employment. I want to address first placement working for others.

Q. Yes, sir.

A. I indicated I felt it was moderate to severe; that is, the impact was moderate to severe. I recognized that many individuals with a history of back problems and chronic pain will have difficulty in placement so they need assistance through job-seeking skills and training.

Q. Why is it that people who have back problems have difficulty finding job placement?

A. Well, there's really two reasons. Two global reasons.

The first is recognizing that most individuals tend to make decisions about jobs and careers in the future based on their sphere of knowledge, so that they don't realize how they can take their interests, work values, job satisfiers, physical limitations and match them to alternatives consistent with their current level of function.

So the construction laborer still looks for jobs in construction labor, even though he's no longer physically able. The result is he's competing for inappropriate jobs and he's competing against individuals who are physically capable, rather than handicapped. And both of those problems are going to keep him from being placed.

That's the first reason. And the first thing we're trying to overcome. We're teaching them that there are alternatives much more consistent, that can make use of their past skills, interests, and work values, but that now are more effective because of limitations.

The second thing is, of course, is that employers -- not all employers or we'd never place them, but certainly many employers have a negative reaction to hiring an individual with a history of back injury and certainly the more signs of physical disability and limitation that the employer perceives in physical posturing or verbalizations by the individual during a job interview, the less likely they're going to get hired.

So what we teach them is to always be honest about the history of disability. That's important and legally required. But to learn how, through job-seeking skills training, to educate the employer. So --

Q. What is --

A. Certainly.

Q. Go ahead. I didn't mean to interrupt you. What were you going to say? Educate the employer?

A. Basically, I was going to say, what you're learning to do is, first of all, make sure the employer understands that you know the nature of the job, that you've chosen to compete for this job because it is within the physical limitations that you have, and to compare negatives with positives. Yes, I have a limitation of my capacity to sit, but I've examined this job and it can be handled sitting or standing, I can shift position, it's well within my capacity, therefore, to accomplish it, all I need is the opportunity to show it.

So you tell your limitation but you tell the positive aspect. You want to focus attention on your abilities and not focus the attention on your disabilities, even though you're being honest about them and that's what you're really learning to accomplish.

Q. So what is Mr. Jones going to require if he wants placement in the private labor market?

A. Well, I think there are a couple of things.

Number one, he's going to require a career counseling and guidance program to help identify appropriate job alternatives.

Two, he's going to need some assistance in job-seeking skills training. We're going to teach him the best methods for handling job interviews and going through the job-seeking process so he's not limiting his options but he's expanding his options.

And, three, I think he could benefit from selective placement assistance. Now this is assuming he's going to go to work for others --

Q. Yeah.

A. -- and not going back with a family member or into his own job or his own company.

But assuming that, then I think he would benefit from selective placement assistance, meaning a professional or rehabilitation counselor, preferably at the master's level rather than the doctoral level. It's economically more feasible.

But he needs somebody then that will assist him in going through that process.

If he's going into self-employment or working for a family member where he can be more in control of his schedule, then there's less of a problem in that regard and he won't need that assistance.

Q. So, one, he's got to adjust his job to something he can handle based on these restrictions and limitations; two, he's got to find an employer who's willing to hire him in whatever position he finds, plus with those limitations and restrictions, right?

A. I think those statements are true.

In the first one, it's not so much that he's adjusting the job. He's adjusting the range of jobs for which he's going to compete. In the sense that he's going to only seek jobs within his capacities.

Q. We're talking the same thing.

A. Right. He doesn't need to adjust the job, itself. I can really simplify this. A disability only becomes a handicap if the job or task you seek to perform calls upon the area of disability.

So if I have my left arm chopped off, but I'm doing a job that only requires the use of my right arm, I don't have a handicap.

Q. I know. But I assume what we're looking for is some vocation or job that would not involve those things which cause him significant restriction or limitation, right?

A. That's correct. Where they don't call upon anything that would exceed his limitations.

Q. All right.

A. But not his limitations as they exist in subjective description today.

Obviously, the rehabilitation plan that we're going to be getting to calls for providing chronic pain management, going thorough all of the process of building work tolerance so that we're talking about the level of capacities he will have after treatment versus the level of subjective description that he's experiencing today, because there's a very different, I think, set of characteristics that you would look at.

Q. All right. Where are those listed in your report? Perhaps I overlooked that.

A. There's no difference in the areas in which he's going to describe limitations. It's the degree to which he's limited in those areas.

Q. Okay.

A. So the vocational handicaps will always remain the same. It's just that if he's saying, "I can only stand for a few minutes now unless I can walk about, and then it will range from thirty minutes to two hours", what we're going to do is work on the pain problem and work to build and make more consistent the level of capacity.

If he can consistently bring an hour to an hour and a half to the job and then needs a five-minute break, I'm not going to have too much difficulty placing him.

If he has to on one day stop after two minutes, on another day get to two hours, on the third day get to thirty minutes, then he's going to have a lot of trouble maintaining employment.

So it's consistency that we're going to be looking for at the highest level of capacity that will be within his tolerance levels.

Q. Okay. And in that regard, Dr. Deutsch, did you form any opinions or conclusions as to the impact of his restrictions or limitations on the range of job alternatives?

A. Yes.

Q. All right. And what were those?

A. Well, basically, right now, based on subjective description, the reduction in range of job alternatives is severe.

Even in terms of treatment in a chronic pain management program, I would tend to avoid his trying to seek a lot of the heavier work occupations that may have existed for him before.

That's not to say that he ever would have tried them before. I mean, he was focused on motorcycle work. I'm not saying that he was going to go out and do heavy construction work. He may have had that capacity. I don't know that he ever would have chosen to do it.

But the point is, in terms of range of choices he had, he's not going to go out and do heavy construction work now.

Q. You have given us some examples in your report.

A. Examples of areas that are impacted by his disability. Okay? These are some of the worker groups that I reviewed and felt were affected, at least in part, if not in whole, by the complaints that he has.

Q. Did you come up with some sort of rehabilitation plan for him?

A. Yes.

Q. Okay. Now these are listed in the report and some of them are pretty self-explanatory.

Essentially, what you've done is listed the rehabilitation plan you would recommend and the cost; is that right, sir?

A. Yes.

Q. And I guess we've already talked about some of these, such as the chronic pain management program and so forth.

Okay. I see under the note, item number four through seven, it would be the cost of each of the items listed under those and the other costs are for -- one, two, three are specified right after them; is that --

A. Right.

Q. Okay. Now, you have a category, vocational development options pre-onset.

What is -- Pre-onset of what?

A. Of any disability. I'm just basically saying -- I didn't separate out, again. We've already talked about that. I'm just simply saying that we're looking at an individual -- this individual in terms of no disability versus the individual that we're seeing today.

Before, he indicates he wanted to be a motorcycle mechanic, he was a motorcycle mechanic. This was his career. This is what he was focused on. And so in terms of developmental options, I would not have assumed that he was going to do anything else pre-onset.

Post-onset, I don't really see him as a strong candidate for academic training or vocational training. I think we need to move him back into the labor market without further training.

The specifics of what he does really depends on him. He still seems very focused on motorcycle mechanics, still very interested in the possibility of working with his brother.

And to the extent that he can work with his brother, he has much greater flexibility in making choices about what he wants to do.

So I've said basically this: if he stayed as a motorcycle mechanic before the accident, you had two options for examining his income potential. One was to look at the average earnings for all motorcycle mechanics in the state of Florida. That ranged from $10,400 to $20,800 or $15,600 average at that range.

The second option was to get an economist to look at his actual business records and tax returns, to see what he was doing. Those are the two ways to examine his pre-accident earnings capacity.

Q. Did you provide any information in that regard to Dr. Raffa? We took his deposition a week or so ago.

A. Yeah, I gave him the information.

Q. On pre-accident?

A. Preliminary information. At the time, I didn't even have, as I recall -- if I remember my chronological dates correctly, and the information I gave him, I didn't even have Dr. Edelman's responses yet and I was being pushed to give him that. And I said, well, here, you know, I'll give you preliminary information until I can get a sense of whether Dr. Edelman concurs that he feels he's a candidate for a chronic pain program. If he's not, that's going to make a difference to me. So pre-accident, I told him the same thing that I've got right here. That didn't change.

These are the only two options for looking at capacity to earn. Because I can't go to a book and find out what somebody would have done in their self-employed business status. All right?

So these are the only two options and the tax returns or the business records will speak for themselves.

Q. What's post-accident?

A. Post-accident, I'm really looking at two options.

One, if we're going to move him into alternative work, that we're basically going to talk about a range of light and sedentary occupations. We're talking about things like automated machine operation. We're talking industrial setting positions, where he's basically able to shift between sitting and standing.

We're talking about a range of four and a quarter to six dollars an hour or five dollars and twelve cents per hour, average, for that range.

So if he's working thirty hours a week, we're looking at $7,987 a year. If he gets to full-time status -- that is, assuming he successfully completes a chronic pain management program -- then you're looking at $10,650 a year.

If he fulfills his own goal of returning to work as a motorcycle mechanic -- I should say if he fulfills his own desire and he gets to stay and is successful in staying in that area, then his wages would return to a similar level as they were pre-; but I still think we'd be looking at needing to give him assistance in lifting.

I mean, he's not going to lift heavy objects even if we're talking post-chronic pain treatment. It's not going to take away the need for him to make sure he stays working within his tolerances.

Q. I was going to ask you that. Are your post-accident vocational alternatives assuming a successful rehabilitation plan, as you have outlined?

A. Yes.

Q. In your overall assessment of Mr. Jones and your vocational assessment, was it significant to you at all that he reported that in the latter part of 1984, he had started getting back into motorcycle repair and that he had, in fact, planned on going into business with his brother, I think sometime in the middle part of 1985?

MR. TARASKA: I'm going to object to the form because I don't think that will be consistent with the facts as they'll develop in the trial. It's an improper hypothetical.

MR. ROMANI: You can go ahead. He's just making words.

MR. TARASKA: We're past that. I get to make a form objection.

THE WITNESS: Okay. I think that, certainly, it's significant. Number one, it reinforces the idea that he was motivated to stay in motorcycle mechanics.

Two, it reinforces the idea that he would have preferred to the extent possible, to stay in self-employment.

It certainly also reinforces the fact that if you're going to look at a pre-accident earning capacity, looking at business records and tax returns and getting a sense of his success when he was self-employed and perhaps bring that current to 1988 dollars with an inflation factor may give you some insight into what his potential to earn was.

The problem is there is no way to go back and say exactly what would have happened in a self-employed status.

BY MR. ROMANI:

Q. That's what I'm trying to determine, Dr. Deutsch, is, based on your experience and training and vocational assessment of Larry, are you able to tell us that -- what his earning capacity or lack of earning capacity would have been had he not had the seizure and subsequent medical sequelae from that in March of 1985?

A. It's -- there's no problem telling you what he could have earned employed by others. The problem that you have is the self-employed status.

Now you have a little more advantage with Larry than you do in most cases when this occurs, in that on one hand you can look at his brother's business, which is the business he was in, and try and get a feel for what is actually occurring now. That can be a partial basis.

But I say partial because, on the other hand, there's no -- still no way to be certain as to what influence Larry's participation in the business would have had in improving or reducing -- but I don't think it would be a reduction --

Q. Yeah.

A. -- but in improving the return.

Now you can't automatically, though, say, well, whatever Larry is doing now is what his income would have been because, of course, they would have been partners, they would have split that, so they would have split profits. I assume paid each other a salary and then split profits.

So you have to take that into consideration, as well. But at least you have a benchmark to start from if you look at the current business records and get a sense of how well the business is doing.

Q. Yeah. In other words, if we wanted to give the Jury some idea of how he would be doing today if he had not had the seizure and subsequent medical sequelae in March, and assuming he had gone into business with his brother, that would be one way to project --

MR. TARASKA: I'll object to the form again, because we're dealing with several different businesses that were bought and sold here and the one we're dealing with now is not the one that the young man was involved in.

MR. ROMANI: Where he was attempting to go into business with his brother in Okeechobee; that's what you're understanding?

THE WITNESS: I understood he did. Again, though, you know, it will be up to the brother and Larry -- certainly not me -- to establish that he would have been, you know, full partner, partial partner, and get a sense of what his wages were.

And one way to do that is to go back and look at how they'd set it up before this occurred because he was already starting there. Was he starting as an equal partner, was he getting a partial income from it and a small percentage versus an equal percentage of the business?

Those are all factors that I don't have any data on.

BY MR. ROMANI:

Q. As you know, I'm here for information --

A. Certainly.

Q. -- and we're starting trial next Tuesday and I'm just trying to determine to date, as of the date of this deposition, you have not, as I understand it, made any attempt to say had he not had the seizure and subsequent medical sequelae in March of '85, he would have nevertheless had loss of earning capacity in the amount of X dollars?

A. I have not made that statement or drawn that conclusion.

Q. Okay.

A. And to go one step further for you, it's not something that I've specifically discussed doing with anyone and the only way I could do that is if either you, Mr. Taraska or -- well, the two of you could provide a hypothetical delineating differences or if a physician comes back and can delineate differences for me, what -- what physical aspects of the 1985 incident may be causing problems now versus what occurred before.

If any of those -- either of those two scenarios occur, then I could more closely analyze that question.

Q. I understand that.

A. But I think there's an absence of data to do it now.

Q. I understand. And all I'm trying to determine, Dr. Deutsch, is I assume you're going to be testifying at the trial and I'm here to try to find out, you know --

A. Sure.

Q. -- what that might be or to get as much information as we have right now. And at least up to this date, which is the Wednesday before the Tuesday of trial, you have not been asked by the defense counsel to determine that particular issue?

A. That's true.

Q. All right. Do you have any other opinions or conclusions regarding this case which we have not discussed henceforth or which is not set forth in your vocational assessment?

A. No.

Q. That's no?

A. No.

CROSS-EXAMINATION
BY MR. TARASKA:

Q. Dr. Deutsch, if Larry Jones was employed -- self-employed prior to his motorcycle/automobile accident in 1982, in the same type of activity that he wanted to pursue over his lifetime, motorcycle repair, am I correct that one good way to try and make at least a beginning estimate of what he would be able to earn would be to look at his tax returns over those years when he was self-employed and working in the type of business he wanted to continue to pursue?

MR. ROMANI: Form.

THE WITNESS: That's -- that's true. Particularly if you can supplement tax returns with business records because sometimes the tax returns don't have sufficient information to let you understand how they were derived from the business.

But no question that that's the best way to approach it.

BY MR. TARASKA:

Q. So if we take an economist and have him evaluate the tax returns and the business records, that is a good way to approach the problem.

A. Sure.

Q. Now with regard to taking a look at Larry's brother at this time, I would guess that we would have to take into account not only the type of business they were performing but whether it was the same business or a different business, whether in fact they would go into business together, what percentages they were going to share in the business, and then we would have to speculate as to whether or not Larry's decision-making process in that business would have led to a successful business or not, because we only have Larry's as it continues on, and I would imagine that we would also have to factor in to account the manner in which each man would have worked in that business and drawn from the business in arriving at any comparison?

MR. ROMANI: Form.

THE WITNESS: All of those are true.

BY MR. TARASKA:

Q. Would we, in fact, then, in looking at Larry's current income and success, really -- as a measure of what Larry would have done, really be speculating as to what Larry would have been doing?

MR. ROMANI: Form.

THE WITNESS: Basically, what I indicated before was not that you could look at Larry and, therefore, conclude what Larry was doing but only that by looking at Larry's business, assuming it was the same business that Larry was going into, that it would give you at least some reference point from which to begin drawing conclusions.

I think what you're saying is true. I can't make an absolute statement that if you look at Larry's business, even assuming it's the same one, that that's what Larry's income would have been. But you could at least have a benchmark.

Then you've got to determine all those other things, what percentage was Larry going to receive, to what extent was he going to be involved in any business decision-making, what impact that would have had.

If he had a significant role in making business decisions, et cetera, then I would tend to assess what's going on with Larry's business, at least in part, by comparing it against a 1988 value for what Larry's business, back in 1982, '83, would have done.

BY MR. TARASKA:

Q. Okay. In essence, by trying to use Larry as a benchmark for Larry, we are, in essence, speculating as to what Larry might have been doing; am I correct?

MR. ROMANI: Form.

THE WITNESS: I think you're correct in the same sense that when there's no brother involvement like this, I've often gone back and said to people, look, I can go to the Bureau of Census Data, I can go to the IRS, there are resources for finding out what self-employed people in specific fields earn, at least in terms of a range.

I can reasonably assume that this person we're talking about, if they were successful, would fall within that range; but the problem is the ranges tend to be very broad.

Looking at Larry doesn't tell me exactly what Larry's going to do. It just gives me an industry benchmark for motorcycle shops and because it's a family member and one he may have gone into, it's a reference point.

But it's certainly -- there's no way to look at what Larry's doing and say, this is within reasonable rehabilitation probability the income he would have earned. It's just a reference point that represents one small piece of the puzzle. In looking at his 1982 business, his tax returns, all these other factors have to be factored in if you're going to get a sense of pre-accident earning capacity.

MR. TARASKA: Thank you. That's all I have.

MR. ROMANI: Dr. Deutsch, always good seeing you.

7

Presenting the Catastrophic Injury Case and Life Care Plan

For purposes of internal administration within the rehabilitation office, it is necessary to make a distinction between the catastrophic and the non-catastrophic case. There is no relationship between this terminology and whether or not the injury is catastrophic to the patients themselves. For example, catastrophic cases tend to reflect those whose injuries are severe enough to require the development of a life care plan which reflects long-term support needs in a wide range of areas. Non-catastrophic cases tend to have more of a vocational involvement with an excellent probability of return to work. Certainly, chronic low back pain patients would not be categorized as catastrophic injuries and yet certainly the individual who is experiencing the injury may well feel that its impact on day-to-day life has been, in fact, catastrophic.

It is critical for definitions such as this to be clearly communicated to the attorneys, insurance carriers, judges, and juries who will be exposed to the terminology. Another good example is the concept of life care planning. Life care plans are not merely a set of charts used to conveniently communicate information. Although they certainly are convenient, the concept of life care planning actually represents a very consistent methodology for analyzing the needs dictated by the onset of the disability. The consistencies from one case to the next are not reflective of any absolute overlap between similar disabilities, but instead reflect that the same methods for analyzing needs have been incorporated. Therefore, you may have very different recommendations for one C6 quadriplegic versus another, but this will occur because your analyses of the various variables have had an impact on the outcome of recommendation.

Life care planning itself, once completed, is utilized as a basis for providing support to the case manager. Case management must also be explained to all third parties involved in forensic situations. The case manager represents the team leader and is actively involved as a liaison between all physicians, health-related professionals, durable medical goods suppliers, replenishable medical goods suppliers, and the patient and family members. Their role is to facilitate a coordination of services, all helping the patient to move in a similar direction rather than pulling the patient into several opposing directions. The case manager may also provide direct services to the patient and family members. Depending upon their background and expertise, this may include individual counseling, family counseling, training family members as disability managers, helping to implement behavioral modification programs, or helping to supervise and augment delivery of nursing support care services.

The implications of life care plans have changed dramatically since their inception in the late 1970s and earlier 1980s. They are by no means restricted for use in the litigation setting but in fact are utilized to aid in management of catastrophic injuries by group health carriers, HMO's, long-term disability carriers, personal injury carriers, Worker's Compensation carriers, rehabilitation facilities, and families. They are an excellent resource for developing an effective structure for settlement purposes so that monies can be made available at those points in time when replacement schedules or other additional expenses dictate their needs.

A question which seems to arise frequently is who is most appropriately qualified for life care planning. This debate has gone on for many years and I'm sure will continue for many years in the future but, in light of my own involvement in the development of life care planning from its inception in the late 1970s, I think it is important for some strong opinions to be expressed. I am not of the opinion that life care planning is a role restricted to the rehabilitation nurse. Although I believe many rehabilitation nurses make excellent life care planners, there is more involved in the planning process than merely an understanding of the medical aspects of disability. There are many rehabilitation psychologists and rehabilitation counselors who have more than sufficient knowledge and work experience in medical aspects to fulfill this role and also bring with them the experience and background in psychological services, counseling services, work with other health-related professionals and the wide range of other variables which must be considered in the development of an appropriate life care plan and case management system. I do not believe that any one speciality area is necessarily, at this point and time, more appropriately qualified for life care planning than another. Much of what we must learn to be effective case managers and life care planners will come from experience. Some of the basic areas which the life care planner must have as part of a knowledge base are:

- the medical aspects of disability;
- the psychological and emotional sequelae of the disability;
- techniques for psychosocial adaptation to disability;
- exposure to durable medical goods and replenishable medical supplies as they relate to each type of disability;
- availability of government collateral source programs for funding;
- an understanding of medical, psychological, rehabilitation, and legal terminology as it relates to the life care planning process;
- an understanding of the impact of disability on the family and not just on the patient so that appropriate services and support can be provided where necessary;
- an understanding of the differences between the pediatric disability cases and adult disability cases.

This is considered a partial list of just some of the knowledge base which is necessary for successful life care planning. It does not include such areas as the extensive knowledge one must have of how to research and develop the data and resources necessary to appropriately complete a geographically specific plan.

I think there is little question that life care planners are going to continue to come from a range of disciplinary backgrounds and the most likely scenario for effective development of life care planning techniques in the future is to bring all such professionals together to promote networking and to help maintain the body of knowledge necessary to make this an effective profession.

Presentation of the Catastrophic Injury Case and Life Care Plan

Whether in deposition or trial, a variety of questions will arise as to the most effective methods for presenting the data which has been gathered in client interview and evaluation and through review of the medical information, psychological reports, and other data resources. The techniques for presentation of basic data gathering procedures are quite similar to those reviewed in the non-catastrophic case but of necessity are somewhat more complicated in the catastrophic injury. I believe it is important for the jury to have a thorough understanding of the steps taken from initial review of medical information through the research done to complete the life care plan and wage data analysis. I do not believe it is always appropriate to go into every detail collected in the data gathering procedure for there is a real fear that you will bore the jury with too much minutia and fail to maintain their attention on otherwise, very important areas. My typical technique is to cover and review all of the areas that have been included in data gathering without necessarily reviewing each individual note collected. It is possible to highlight the most pertinent or important data points, but for the most part, the purpose here is to communicate to the jury your thoroughness and the extensive work-up that has been done in preparation for completing the life care plan and recommendations.

There are a variety of methods for presenting the life care plan to the jury from slides to blow-ups of the charts to overhead projection or simply passing copies out to the jury members for review and return after the testimony. It has been my experience that the later two are the most effective methods. In most instances, judges will allow copies of the life care plan to be passed before the jury with the caution that they not try and read ahead but instead follow along with the testimony. It does speed the process and it provides a visual aid that helps the jury understand both the thoroughness of the life care plan and the factual basis for each of the recommendations. An effective alternative is to use an overhead projector, but I would tend to shy away from blow-ups of each page or from slides because they tend to look like well-prepared "slick" dog and pony shows. It's also an expensive and often unnecessary approach to take.

The most important presentation rests on the interaction between the attorney providing direct questions and the witness providing the testimony. It is essential to listen carefully to the questions and make certain that all parties fully understand the parameters of the individual expert's expertise so as not to exceed these areas. Time must be taken to fully educate the jury, but this must be balanced carefully against the possibility of boring all parties concerned. It must be kept in mind that the primary goal of the witness in rehabilitation is to act as an educator, not as an advocate. Questions from both sides should be answered with equal clarity and forthrightness.

Sample Transcript #1

The following transcript begins during the presentation of the data and after the qualifications have been complete. It is a transcript of actual trial testimony and does not represent a deposition. Both direct and cross-examination questions are included. The case involves pediatric brain damage with a birth onset of disability.

Q. Now, after this meeting and after you reviewed all the records that you told the jury about and then you met with her, what else did you do after that before you came up with this life care plan?
A. Basically the next step is to go back to my office and begin first mapping out a rough life care plan just based on my evaluation, as to what the items are that I need.
Now, I reviewed all of my notes in those areas I've already told you about, plus the other areas that I cover. We didn't quite list out all of them, but a lot of family background and social data were considered as well. And I roughed out a basic life care plan, a plan first to deal with this point through age 21. That's going to be the educational period, the habilitation.

Q. Why do you say 21? What is magic about 21? I know that used to be that's when you became adults back when I was younger. Is there something magical now about the year 21?

A. Well, I guess the only magic is that we're trying to coordinate effectively with the public school program. There are private school and private programs that will provide services to these children, but I find that if you develop a plan to work and coordinate effectively with a public school, you can optimize care and services and minimize costs.

So the public school provides what we call mainstreaming; that is, special education under what is called Public Law 94142. It's the main federal training law for educating handicapped children.

Q. Are you trying to compliment or take away from that, or how are you gearing yourself?

A. No. We're trying to make use of 100 percent of what is provided by the school system and only adding to it those things that concern particularly what the school system can't do or can't be asked to do. And that law allows for a child to continue in special education through to age 21.

Q. Okay. So the law, that explains the 21?

A. That's right. That explains the 21. We coordinate with Public Law 94-142.

Q. In developing, evaluating, and analyzing Susan Ann, you mentioned various aspects of this health care plan service. Does vocational or occupational therapy or rehabilitation enter into your consideration?

A. It does. I only stress, just so we make sure we're staying within fields, that I'm not talking about so much a health care plan, but again, a rehabilitation or life care plan dealing with it from my perspective rather than a health or medical perspective.

There are medical aspects, and recommendations by the medical doctors. Everything I've dealt with are things that are within my area of expertise.

And that's what is provided in the life care plan. It coordinates all the areas including physical and occupational therapy, speech therapy, routine medical evaluations that we know are required. And then if a physician has specific orders or a recommendations or a surgical procedure or something of that nature, we certainly include them, but I don't make recommendations for surgery.

Q. Do you, in coming up with this plan, say you're trying to plan the future out? Do you figure the best case scenario or worst complications? How do you work these future intangibles into this plan?

A. First of all, I have to assume one thing when I'm doing a life care plan, and that is that the child is going to get the life care plan. And I don't make recommendations for things on a life care plan that I truly don't believe are within the probability that a child can partake of. I'm not going to give physical therapy --

Q. You've lost me.

A. Well, for example, if we have a child who is frozen at the sixth month or below of infant development, we're not going to provide speech therapy. You don't intervene with speech therapy until a child reaches at least a six-month infant development.

Prior to that we may have to work on some musculature training like swallowing, behavior sucking and chewing behavior in the infant, but that can be done by an occupational therapist, below the sixth month.

So we only are going to interfere with those therapies that we believe the child, within reasonable probability, can benefit from. If I assume that, then I feel I have to assume that we will achieve success in those therapies and bring up to a maximum level of function the child's abilities, and then we cost out long-term care based on essentially a best case scenario.

Q. But you said to get the child to the maximum level is the intent of this plan?

A. That's the first step, and the next step is maintaining.

Q. Once they get up there, don't they stay there? Why do you have to keep doing --

A. They don't just stay there. Probably these best analogy to use is the physical therapy. Unlike if I break an arm, I have a cast and when it's off, if I need physical therapy to rebuild muscle atrophy, I go to the therapist. After that I'm active, I'm working, I'm using the arm, I'm maintaining it just in my natural every day function.

With a child like Susan Ann, if we suddenly stopped providing services, then she is not going to maintain physical function on her own. Now, we can make a phase change for cost effectiveness.

Q. A what?

A. What we call a phase change. Oh, for example, I don't provide in this plan physical therapy to the end of her life expectancy. I provide it coordinated with the school. At that point I use the attendant care. She is going to need the support of untrained, or rather the lowest level of support care we can provide which is an attendant.

I use the attendant to provide daily range of motion exercises. That's supervised by periodic evaluations medically, but we don't continue to pay a therapist. We make it a part of the responsibility of the attendant, but we still have to make sure that someone works with the child to maintain the level she's achieved because she can't do it on her own.

Q. This attaining and it's maintenance, how does the family fit into that? Are they part of the support system as far as doing this work?

A. Well, I think that they should be. Not every family is capable of that. A large number are -- and wherever we can have the family participate, we certainly want them to. For the children to make the gains, one of the reasons they make the best gains is not only because of the family support, but the fact that we not can actively work with the child not only in terms of the public school program, but in terms of home, home follow-up.

Anybody used to educating and working with the children, knows you can't do it all at the old school. If you don't have support of the family, you don't work with those things at home, whether it's a normal child or a disabled child, she is just not going to achieve the kinds of things at the maximum level you like to achieve.

So there's little question that having family involved is helpful, not only behaviorally and emotionally, but particularly in terms of the levels achieved in motor function and mental development and as well as in social interaction and maturity.

Q. We're going to be talking about some numbers and dollars in a minute. What I'm wondering is when we get into these dollars, you're factoring family support as part of your life plan, as I understand it?

A. That's true.

Q. In factoring a cost for this life plan, are you figuring on Tom and Marge being paid anything for their support system?

A. What I've done is prior to age 21, I've assumed that like any parents, whether it was a disabled child or not a disabled child, there are certain things parents are expected to do and have an obligation to do. I have not provided any monies to reimburse the parents prior to age 21 for those things.

What I have done is recognized that prior to age 21, we're talking about a very intensive effort on the family's part. I've made available respite, meaning a break one weekend a month and one evening a week where we bring someone in to allow the family a break away from the child.

And I provided some assistance for a couple -- I think it was four hours a day during the week to help maintain the program, but I've not provided for Mom separately.

Q. I just want to make sure I understand you. In the factors as far as utilizing Tom and Marge to fulfill their parental obligations, no doubt they will, but your numbers you're going to come up with, do they include a figure to pay these people to give them any money themselves for the hours they are devoting to stimulating Susan Ann?

A. No.

Q. The only thing you are giving is this respite and just basically factoring in some money to let them get out of the house?

A. Prior to age 21, that's correct. After age 21, I've just paid for a recognition that we needed in some fashion to provide 24-hour care, whether it be in a home program with a live-in attendant or whether it be a facility. Although there's no question that the family feels strongly that they don't want to use a facility.

Q. You say a live-in attendant. Have you factored in -- when does this live-in attendant come into play?

A. I've started it at the end of Public Law 94142.

Q. Not for another 17 or 18 years?

A. It's the point where normally the child leaves the home. At that point again, we make a change. If the parents are going to continue to provide for an individual after age 21, then it's certainly my opinion that goes way beyond what you normally expect a parent to do, and that is provide 24-hour care.

So what I've done, I also recognize that I can't guarantee that the parents will be there. I have to make sure that there is a provision for taking care of Susan Ann regardless of who may be around to do it, whether we have to use the attendant program or whether we're using a facility.

So beginning at 21, I provided for coverage to make sure that she's cared for through the balance of her life expectancy.

THE COURT: Will this child ever be left alone?

THE WITNESS: No.

MR. JONES: I'm sorry, what did you ask?

THE COURT: Could the child ever be left alone?

THE WITNESS: I don't believe the child will ever be left alone.

THE COURT: After she's an adult, somebody is going to have to be there to be sure she is looked after?

THE WITNESS: That's correct. Just so I'm not confusing anybody, let's make sure we define what left alone is. I felt that she will reach a level with habilitation that she can use a live-in attendant as opposed to 24-hour awake staff. A live-in attendant does not give direct services, for example, through the night. I felt the child can be in a room asleep as long as someone is in the home during the night.

THE COURT: Somebody has got to be there?

THE WITNESS: Someone is going to have to be there 24 hours a day. I've used a combination of the live-in and what is called an adult developmental program where she goes out each day to a developmental services program. And there are several, both in Georgia and Tennessee, that can be utilized.

So she will get some coverage at the program and the balance from a live-in. When we go through this, you will see why I did that because that became very, very cost-effective over having to use 24-hour awake staff.

BY MR. JONES:

Q. Okay. One other question, and we'll get into real specifics. I look confused. I'm trying to make sure I stay with you. If, God forbid, something should happen to Tom and Marge Hartford or the family support system for Susan Ann was impaired, does your plan factor in some substitute for Tom and Marge before Susan Ann turns 21?

A. No, it does not. It assumes the parents will be there till 21.

Q. So this plan we're getting ready to go into detail factors in or assumes for the next 18 years, these two people are going to provide as much for this child as they possibly can?

A. That's true. If something were to happen or the family wasn't there, I did not provide for 24-hour coverage prior to the end of Public Law 94-142.

Q. Now, when you say a life care plan has been prepared, how many pages is this plan?

A. The life care portion of the plan is 17 pages.

Q. Have you got something that might help the jury understand what we're dealing with here?

A. Well, the simplest way I've always found, regardless of who I'm talking with, is for individuals to follow along with the plan to see what it looks like. So I made copies of the life care plan to follow along with instead of having to go through every detail. I can move more rapidly.

Q. Might it speed things up if the jury were allowed to follow along?

A. No question we can speed it up dramatically if we can do it that way, because it's a good visual representation, and we can move through it much more rapidly.

MR JONES: Your Honor, I ask leave that the copy just of the plan, not of the report, but just of the plan be provided to the jury not as an exhibit, but just for them to follow along in an effort to expedite this and enhance their understanding. And then at the end of Dr. Deutsch's cross-examination, the plan can be retrieved.

MR. SMITH: Your Honor, I'm for speeding it along for the jury.

THE COURT: I've got a copy.

BY MR. JONES:

Q. Okay. Doctor, Judge, the jurors have a copy of this. I guess the best way to do is go to the first page to start it off. The first page says Projected Evaluations. Would you please tell the jury what this means and why this is important?

A. Getting through the first two pages will be the longest, and then it moves very rapidly. We will get the basics down. But I separated evaluations that the child will need, and the reason I do that is because there are instances in which we will do evaluations.

For example, an earlier example I gave you of speech therapy, we will continue to evaluate that child periodically to make certain that they haven't reached the higher level at which point we would institute therapy.

So just as a matter of course, across all cases, we separated evaluations from therapy. The columns here start out with the evaluation that we want to do, the age that we're going to start it, the age and year at which we're going to suspend it, the number of times per year we're going to perform the service, and its cost per year.

The last two columns are the growth trend and who is recommending it. Now, I don't use or discuss growth trends in a litigation kind of situation.

Q. So we can kind of disregard that?

A. I just disregard it because I can only go so far as the budget for next year with families. That's why I have that in here.

Q. Let's stop right there. The figure you've come up with, let's just use physical therapy for example there. Your figures are $60 per year cost for somebody to evaluate how the physical therapy is progressing; is that correct, sir?

A. That's correct.

Q. Now, this $60 figure -- we're going to give the jury a total at the end of this, but do you in coming up with your final figures, sir, does that $60 figure change at all?

A. No. I don't deal with inflation and/or what an economist might normally have to look at in terms of where they think the economy is going to go in the future. That's just not my area of expertise.

These are all 1988 dollars. And when I talk later on about totaling out this plan for you, it's really simply a function of adding it up, because I can't take into account inflation in my area of expertise nor can I take into account any investment strategy or change in those dollars.

Q. The last thing about this number, is this $60 figure working from the physical therapy evaluation yearly, you're saying you think this should continue?

MR. SMITH: Your Honor, I'm going to have to object to the leading. I've been very tolerant.

THE COURT: All right. Just ask him.

Q. Doctor, how long is that figure for this physical therapy evaluation going to have to be conducted?

A. It shows in the third column, its age and the year it's suspended -- I suspended it at age 21 over the year 2006, which is the end of Public Law 94142. The law itself says very clearly that we're required to do what is called a habilitation team evaluation annually, and we develop from that what is called an individual educational plan. The school system does a lot of that.

You'll see later in the plan where I've shown that at no cost. But any time you're working with the school system and providing supplemental therapies, I personally believe that the best way to accomplish that is to have the school system as the core, and we work with the school system in providing a supplement.

So we follow school system guidelines, and that's how this plan is being designed to supplement and work with the school system and the special education personnel rather than to work separately or inadvertently be at odds with them.

Q. Regarding your figures for this physical therapy evaluation, what will you say that's going to cost in the year 2005?

A. I don't show any change in cost.

Q. The same $60?

A. Again, I show the same $60 when I add it up only because I'm not an economist. I don't deal with inflation.

Q. Okay. Now, what is the purpose of the physical therapy evaluation and why is that important?

A. Basically what we're doing is, one time annually the physical therapist is taking a step back from work with the child and going through an evaluation, testing the child for current levels of function to see how they've progressed in the year previous, what the level of progression toward the goals were; that is, what was accomplished, and then setting next year's goals so they can develop their individual education plan or training plan for the following year.

And all of the therapists as well as the teachers are involved in developing their set of goals for this child. Again, that's a function of following the guidelines required by the mainstream of law.

Q. You say started at age three. This child didn't need physical therapy before age three?

A. Well, no. The child needed range of motion exercising and physical therapy from the onset, but my life care plan deals with the child from the time I see them into the future. I does not deal with things in the past that may have already been accomplished or already paid for.

Q. Now, occupational therapy for a three year old?

A. Okay. That's a very common question. Maybe it's an unusual name for occupational therapy. Occupational therapy has nothing to do with work even though it sounds like it does. Occupational therapists do several things. First of all, they're the ones who are going to work with primarily upper extremity development.

Q. The arms?

A. The arms. In the early years they're going to work on upper extremity coordination, they're going to work on balance, they're going to provide tactile stimulation so they may stimulate the child's sense of touch with varying types of textures. And they may also be involved where necessary on working on toileting.

And if the child has a potential to work toward that goal and they're going to work on self-feeding, or if it's more rudimentary, they're maybe the ones who are working on developing the chewing, sucking, swallowing reflexes and behaviors that we need.

So that's what the occupational therapist does. Later when we have an older child, it's the occupational therapist who helps train the child in the activities of daily living. If they can learn how to put on a shirt, for example, or how to do any self-care services at all or even if we're just training the child as to how to better interact with the caregiver in being able to get dressed and cooperate, that's what the occupational therapist is going to do. They call it working on ADL's or activities of daily living. That's what occupational therapy is all about.

Q. Thank you. Speech therapist?

A. Okay. Speech therapy, occupational therapy, and physical therapy all are the same evaluation costs, $60 per year. The speech therapist is going to work with this child, Susan Ann, on verbal development.

Now, we may work with the child who is not talking or not capable of talking on non-verbal items as well, like learning to use gestures to communicate needs or even body posturing to communicate needs. Be here we're also going to work on basic language development, whether it's single word vocabulary or later some limited sentence structure.

Q. What were your findings relative to this child's speech ability when you saw her in May of this year?

A. Well, I had noted in the report that she was -- first of all, she was non-verbal, but she was vocalizing multiple sounds. In other words, instead of just a single consistent monotonal kind of grunt, she does vocalize different sounds. And through vocalization and through body posturing, she indicates pleasure, she indicates displeasure, anger, and temper tantrum.

And she can be very manipulative using those things. So there's no question that we're going to want to work with her first and foremost on taking that ability and making it consistent so it applies to communicating certain things so that she can communicate when she's hungry, communicate when she needs to use the bathroom, even if it's a diaper program that she's on.

Q. Is she toilet trained at all?

A. No.

Q. Does she communicate or verbalize to indicate a soiled diaper, for example?

A. I didn't hear that.

Q. Does she indicate if she's soiled her diaper?

A. No. She is not basically indicating the need to use the bathroom, she is not indicating hunger. And although she is taking food by mouth, she takes a long time to eat, and she's a very picky and difficult eater. So it's a family project to get through a meal with Susan.

Q. Did you see -- actually sit and watch an entire feeding session?
A. Well, not an entire feeding session, no.

So that's basically how it's been set up. I think, quite frankly, this is probably at least in one way the most critical part of the plan. If we can get an improved behavioral program; that is, an improvement in her behavior, we're going to get much more responsiveness and much better interaction with therapists.

I have assumed in this plan that we are going to get that control, and that's the reason we're going to be able to use the lowest level of long-term care.

Q. Not being a math major, but it looks like you're talking about $240 a year for all of these various evaluations?
A. Well --
Q. Three?
A. Well, $240 not including the last one on the page. We have one other, which is the rehabilitation psychological, and that brings it to $340 a year.
Q. These are people basically to see how she's done last year and find out how we got her here and where we're going to get her going this next year?
A. That's correct.
Q. Okay. Let's move then to the next page which is -- I've got a feeling, you say projected therapeutic modalities?
A. Right. This is the therapies, the actual provision of therapy and training that we're going to give her. I avoided specifically using the word education here because that's going to come into the next page where we coordinate very, very closely with the school system and where we basically assume they're going to cover all of that aspect of the cost.
Q. The school system because of this public law is not going to be charged for that?
A. They're not going to be, no.
Q. You factor that in?
A. I factored that in. I've eliminated any cost associated with special education as you'll see when we get to the next page.
Q. Okay. I'm sorry. Physical Therapy.
A. Okay. Physical Therapy here, and the same is going to be true for occupational and speech therapy, what we're

recognizing is we can't put all of the burden on the school system. And, in fact, under Public Law 94-142, the guideline is that the school system is going to provide the minimum services necessary to allow the child to be mainstreamed into the school program.

So they'll provide all of the special education, but they can only provide a limited amount of the physical therapy and occupational therapy and speech therapy. So if a child needs five-day-a-week physical therapy, for example, chances are the school system is rarely going to be able to provide any more than one to two sessions a week.

Q. You've used the term "mainstream," and my sister does counseling so I know what that is, but just for the benefit of any of the jurors that may not know what the term mainstreaming means, would you please explain it?

A. Certainly. When we talk about mainstreaming, we're just talking about trying to bring a handicapped child out of the home or facility environment into as much of the mainstream of the social environment as we can. So we're going to use the public school.

We're not going to use a homebound teacher to go in if we can avoid it. We're going to bring that child to the public school. We're going to bus them in, we're going to get all the advantages of being able to interact with other children. Even the most rudimentary function of the children, even the lowest level of functioning can benefit from interacting in that classroom setting.

So certainly there's no question that at this level of function, that's going to be a benefit. So mainstreaming is basically bringing them into the school system and letting them take advantage of what the school has to offer.

Q. Now, what do you figure this physical therapy is going to cost per unit?

A. We're only providing a supplement to the school system, so instead of providing all that we would normally expect of providing in the plan two times per week, it's based on $60 per session, for a total of $6,240 per year. That's based on following the school year program, and it only goes through again to age 21. It stops at 21.

Q. Does the need for it stop at 21?

A. The need for physical therapy in terms of its global definition doesn't stop. But what happens, we've brought that child certainly by that point to the maximum level we can anticipate, and what we're saying is that from that point forward, whoever is providing the basic attendant care can be taught to go through the maintenance level of range of motion.

So the bulk of the cost as far as long-term care surely occurs after age 21, but in terms of the total cost we're providing because we're on a relatively short time frame, 15 to 18 years, the bulk of the cost actually occurs after age 21 as far as support care is concerned.

Q. But this physical therapy figure blends in with something else you're going to tell the jury?

A. I'm not sure I'm comfortable with the word blend in. The responsibility is given over to another person, but we would be paying that person the same, whether they took over this responsibility along with their others or not. So what we've done, we've completely eliminated the cost of physical therapy after age 21, but we've continued letting the care givers provide the exercise.

Q. Tell us about occupational and speech therapy.

A. We've really gone over occupational therapy, in essence, by telling you what the occupational therapist does. We're going from the very rudimentary kind of things we talked about earlier, tactile stimulation, et cetera, on up through trying to get the child to a point where their interacting with care givers to the maximum level possible, helping them or cooperating with them in everything from the bowel program to their dressing to their feeding.

And we want to just use the occupational therapist to get Susan Ann up to a maximum level of cooperation and interaction.

Q. Okay. When you saw this baby, did she feed herself?

A. No.

Q. Did she dress herself?

A. No. She's not self-dressing.

Q. At three years?

A. At three years she is not.

Q. You've got down here family counseling. What is that all about, Doctor? Why is that necessary?

A. Well, there are two programs we want to provide to the family. First, to family counseling, we recognize that there's a range of the emotions that a family goes through, and different family members have different emotions.

This interacts or impacts on siblings in one fashion and on parents in another fashion. So we're working with the family's range of emotions. We're helping the parents to understand how to give to this child while still paying attention to the needs of the other siblings.

We're helping the other siblings deal with their feelings and with the strain and the pressure or the stress that is placed upon the family in raising handicapped children.

Family counseling is primarily a focus on the needs of the family in terms of maintaining that strong family support unit. But it's very much differentiated from the next area we're going to talk about, which is family or parent education.

Q. Why is it important -- let me back up just a second. Have you worked with many children similar to Susan Ann?

A. Hundreds and hundreds.

Q. You've worked with their families?

A. Yes.

Q. Is resentment or bitterness, does that become a part of the family?

A. Well, I think you sometimes see that particularly among the siblings, but I think the more frequent experience that you see is a range of emotional feelings surrounding guilt.

Q. Guilt? How -- why are they guilty?

A. Well, what happens, they're not. What we have to do is help them overcome that. A lot of times what happens is there's an initial dedication or a period of dedication to the child and then feelings of resentment. I'm angry that I'm having to do this, it takes me away from what I would like to be doing with other children, or maybe the children are feeling resentment and anger over the loss of parent attention.

And then they feel guilty because of the fact that this is a disabled child, it's not the child's fault. And so what we end up seeing is the family is going back and forth through a range of emotions from anger to resentment, to strong feelings of guilt. And these are things that are -- I don't want to say easily resolved, but they're certainly resolvable if you give them support.

Q. That's what this counseling is all about?

A. It's also to reduce stress. They're going to experience it, so we want to teach them how to identify when that stress is occurring and what techniques they can use to reduce stress. We give them good techniques; these are problems we can solve.

Q. Kind of prevention instead of cure?

A. Absolutely. The entire plan is based on the concept of preventive rehabilitation. What we want to avoid doing is reacting to crisis, and that bring us to the next area, which is Parent Education.

Q. I don't want the jury to be shocked at these numbers. Family counseling, you're talking about how much a year or what are the numbers going to be there?

A. One of the things I feel strongly about in terms of family counseling, number one, it's unrealistic to talk about people going to counseling 52 weeks a year. It's not something you're normally going to do -- even if we were talking about one year, we do what we call therapy 48 weeks.

But in this instance, I didn't even provide that. I don't believe in counseling just ad infinitum for years and years into the future. What I do is provide pockets, if you will, of counseling.

I recognize that there are critical ages in the development of the child. There are changes that the child is going to go through that are going to bring about changes in behavior and in the problems that can arise.

So periodically at these critical ages of development, I intervene first with counseling for the family. I gave three months of counseling one time a week for three months.

Q. Is that for all of them at one time, Tom and Marge --

A. That's right. That's the initial counseling, that three month period. Then I follow that with two times per month counseling for three months at age 6, 10, 13, 16, 19, and 21, and I end the family counseling program. The total cost is $774 for the first intervention with counseling and $360 at each of the subsequent ages that we bring in counseling.

So we're not talking about in-depth psychotherapy here. It's very technique-oriented. We're wanting to get the family to get in touch with these emotions and feelings and give them techniques to resolve them.

But we're expecting them to do a lot of homework, and we reduce cost hereby assuming that that homework is going to be accomplished by the family and they're going to be doing a lot of this work on their own, facilitated by the counselor who is going to see them periodically as I've shown you here.

Q. That ties in with the education, which is the next one?

A. That's right. The next step is parent education. The primary difference here is one, the counseling, which I just talked about, but, two, the education is kind of what we call super-parent effectiveness training. How do you be a parent of a disabled child?

What we want the parents to do is understand first of all the basic disability, but understand the changes that are going to take place periodically over time. These children will go through growth and change rhetorically. They will have a range of potential problems, complications, both physically and behaviorally, and the whole idea here is to avoid them.

I can't guarantee that they'll be avoided, but I can tell you that we've had very good success in helping families identify problems very, very early on.

So instead of a crisis in a very involved and costly complication, we resolve the problem very early on. I have no way of costing out complications, but I can say that we can, by developing an effective plan, go a long way toward preventing many of them or at least substantially reducing the cost of treating problems and complications. That's what parent education is all about.

Q. On this page two that the jury has, the first three categories: physical, occupational, and speech, that's for Susan Ann?

A. That's correct.

Q. And the next two are for the family unit?

A. That's correct.

Q. Now, Susan Ann really wouldn't be at these other two?

A. No. She is not going to be able to interact in any type of counseling program.

Q. Go to the next page, page three. Everybody is going to be happy to know there's just one column.

A. That's right. All we've done here, this is the second page of the therapy.

Q. This is still under the category that we've just been talking about?

A. That's correct. What we want to do is identify a team leader, a rehabilitation psychologist or habilitation team leader as close to their geographic areas as possible. This individual is going to coordinate all of this care, provide the annual re-testing, implement the life care plan, and provide the general team leader services, liaison with the school system, for example. We work with them on the implementation of behavioral modification.

So you're looking at this particular aspect continuing through life expectancy. What I've indicated here, though, is that the active part of it will be a cost of $2,000 to $2,500 per year to age 21, to end the Public Law 94-142. Thereafter, I expect the rehabilitation team leader to be a resource person.

Q. What is the difference? What do you mean by resource?

A. Basically the way we conduct this in our office is once we have the child through the developmental years and stabilized in a consistent program, we identify a family member or a care giver as the person who's going to follow through and coordinate and call us if there are problems, problems that usually are resolvable through a consultation over the phone. And my policy is not to charge for that.

And usually we've been able to effectively work out similar systems with other professionals throughout the country as well. You have to charge if you're going to get into actually coming in and providing services in the home, but these are resource services we're going to provide that we don't charge for.

Q. How did you come up with this $2,000, $2,500 a year figure?

A. Basically the only solution in this particular instance as far as a rehabilitation psychologist is to take a look at the amount of hours per year I know it takes to manage a plan. You usually have more hours in the first year, but generally it is a consistent number of hours we take in implementing these plans.

Q. But does this cost -- you said after 21, this rehabilitation psychologist team leader becomes a resource person?
A. That's correct.
Q. Now, when they're a resource person, what is the charge there?
A. As I said, in my office, the policy is no charge for resource services. And we've implemented literally thousands of plans over 17 years, and we've had a very, very effective result as far as designing and developing a local team in getting this kind of resource service made available.
Q. What I'm driving at, Doctor, is are you figuring any in this -- again, we're going to be summarizing this in a few minutes, but are you figuring any additional costs for a rehabilitation psychologist team leader after Susan Ann turns 21?
A. No.
Q. Okay.
A. Again, no. The answer is no, I'm not.
Q. Now, go to page four, if you would.
A. Let me just stress in going to page four and also finishing the answer to the question about costs, all costs have been developed with respect to their local geographic area.
Q. How have you done that? How did you do that?
A. It's all done by developing the life care plan, identifying the suppliers and service providers either in or near Rossville, Georgia or just across into the Tennessee area and making contact with them, doing phone surveys, finding out what the regional costs are.

And, in fact, the regional costs for this area are substantially lower than they are, for example, in Florida and a lot of other areas. As you'll see when we get to 24-hour-a-day care, it's very cost-effective in this particular area.
Q. I'm glad to hear that. Let's go to page four, Diagnostic Testing, Educational Assessment. Now, how is that different from this evaluation on page one?
A. All we're talking about here, first of all, is strictly education-related items. We are costing out the test -- educational testing to determine how she has developed at $250, $350 a year. You'll notice when you look back, for example, of the initial evaluations on page one, from the psychologist and

the rehab, both the rehab psychologist and the child development psychologist, were very lost cost.

I didn't provide any cost for testing. You're basically talking about providing them with an hour of time to interview family and look at the child. And I provided some educational testing under the educational page.

Everything else in terms of education, for example, the pre-school program which goes from age three to five, is not currently available in their area. It is being developed.

I talked to the school system, but it's two years before it will occur, and by that time, she will be too old for it. I've noted we would like to see her have it, it's just not currently available, so we're trying to identify a Head Start Program.

But I do expect, in some fashion, we'll have this provided under Public Law 94-142 if we can identify. After that, starting at age five through age 21, she is eligible for special education. All of those costs are provided under Public Law 94-142.

I stress that well within reasonable rehabilitation probability that 94-142 will continue over this period of time to provide a program. There are no guarantees, but it's a stable program, it's been around a long time, and we're not going far forward into the future. We're only talking over the next 15 to 18 years. So I think it's well within reasonable probability the school system will continue to provide this, and I've assumed all the costs will be covered.

Q.   Let me ask you something, when you say educational testing, $250 to $350 a year, I thought the school system was going to do that?

A.   No. The school system will do that educational testing that they need from their own professionals, but what we've provided here is a supplemental team to do things the school system simply isn't in a position to provide, like a psychologist for the behavioral modification programming and the supplemental therapies.

And so we have our own responsibility as a supplemental team to assess where the child has gone in terms of our areas of expertise. Now, the $250 to $350 is a very low figure. It provides for just a limited amount of testing, and it's testing to supplement what the school system is not going to be doing and to give the supplemental team the information they need to assist in developing the individual education plan.

Q. Okay. Lastly on this page, you've got adult developmental program. Now, when is that supposed to start?

A. When school stops.

Q. When?

A. At 21, a developmental program must begin, so we've taken school through 21 and initiated an adult developmental day program thereafter. Now, frankly, there are several reasons for doing it. Not only is it healthy for the individual, but she will be an adult at that point.

Not only does it help us maintain the child or the young adult much more effectively, but it's a lot cheaper to go through an adult developmental day program to get six hours of care than it is to provide another attendant to cover that period of time.

So by using an adult developmental program, all we had to worry about for attendant care was a live-in. A live-in only provides ten hours a day of direct services, and they sleep in the home, so they're there eight hours at night. And the result is they provide 18 hours of coverage.

They get an hour for each meal and three hours of personal leave time, So there's six hours a day they're not covered. that's the six hours we're going to have this child in an adult developmental program.

Q. What is the purpose of this? What do you mean, what is the intent?

A. Well --

Q. The goal, I guess.

A. Normally with a profoundly-impaired and retarded child, you would look toward higher levels of functioning, you look for their ability to participate in a sheltered workshop.

Q. Tell me what you mean by that.

A. A sheltered workshop would be a work site like Goodwill, for example, where the individual can go and have productive, constructive daily activity, participate in a work setting, have a routine or a structure, and they perform best when their daily routine structure remains consistent and where they're not competing against other people for a job based on maintaining a certain quality, quantity of work like all the rest of us might be.

This child, in fact, I do not believe within reasonable rehabilitation probability, will achieve a level where a sheltered workshop is appropriate. So instead, I move toward an adult developmental program.

What that does is it's the next lowest level below the sheltered workshop. I gives constructed activity. It helps maintain the individuals in therapeutic fashion. It is basically going to save us a lot of cost not just in attendant care, but also to a certain extent in therapists.

I haven't provided for anything to supplement the attendant or the developmental program because between the two of them, it's going to give us all we need.

Q. Okay. Let's move on. You say wheelchair needs.

A. You'll notice there's, first of all, an asterisk next to all three of these items. I'd like to read out loud the note at the bottom.

Q. Okay.

A. "As ambulation improves, a wheelchair will become a backup for mobility over greater distances. It is difficult to judge at this time just how functional her ambulation will be, but Dr. Chien feels it will be limited."

Even if she becomes ambulatory, if she is going to want to be taken for a shopping trip or if there's any lengthy walking, for example, she will need a backup wheelchair.

But the extent to which, for example, we may have a replacement schedule, could be affected by how much she's ambulated. Obviously the less she uses that chair, the more -- or the less frequently then we will have to replace it.

So I'm giving you the best judgment based on current level of functioning and Dr. Chien's assessment of a limited amount of mobility. I've started out with the Ortho-Kinetics Chair II.

Q. That's a wheelchair?

A. That is a wheelchair seating system. It provides for the developing child trunk support, lateral trunk support. It provides what we call abduction and adduction pads, which position the legs. As this child is going through growth, it's important to work on maintaining position so the growth in the skeletal system is normal.

This is on part of what is going to help us avoid contracture deformities and --

Q. What?

A. Contracture deformities. This is one of the complications we worry about where we have weaker muscles, we have spasticity, shortening of tendons and ligaments as a result of the spasticity. And the pressure, for example, in a child with spasticity, you may get knees that cannot be fully extended, toes that are pointed down with the feet hyperextended or hands held in a fisted fashion and curled toward the body in a fetal position.

None of these things are apparent in Susan Ann on a severe level. She has some problems with her ankles. She does use braces. We'll get into that. But she's had very excellent follow-up as far as the family doing range of motion exercises.

And there's been an avoidance of contracture program. As she grows, a continuation of that therapy coupled with a seating system during the early growth years are the most effective ways to avoid skeletal growth problems, and so that's why we've continued the Ortho-Kinetics seating system, and we've placed it through the early developmental years a total of three times.

It's an adaptive wheelchair seating system. The range of cost if $1975 to $2375. Now, the only reason I can't give you more than a range, although that's a fairly narrow type of range, is because the chairs are custom-fitted.

I actually had gone through in 1988 and measured, fitted, and had it assembled to be able to find a final cost. But this is a range that you can expect, and it will fall within that range.

Q. That you anticipate that chair you've got factored in replacement --

A. Three times. The current purchase, age 8 and age 13.

Q. Likewise, you have a replacement for how often this seating system gets replaced?

A. Well, we -- that's the only times we're replacing is three, eight and 13. Then the next replacement after that is going to be with an adult chair, the Everest & Jennings or the E & J, that's the manufacturer.

It's a seating and positioning system for mobility and adaptive seating. Again, you can expect the adult chair to cost $2,000 to $2,400.

Q. So I stay with you, number one, the Ortho-Kinetic care chair, the last one of those that will be necessary to be purchased is at what age?

A. Thirteen.

Q. And then at thirteen that will be the last time the family encounters that expense?

A. That's right.

Q. That particular expense?

A. That's right.

Q. Then they move to another one?

A. They move to an adult chair at age 18, and that's going to be replaced every five to seven years. I can't give a greater, a more definitive range than that. It's going to be replaced in that time frame. We do provide a maintenance schedule you will see on the next page. That's what allows it to go as long as five to seven years.

Q. Let's go to that.

A. One last item on the other page is the rolling shower wheelchair. The most effective way of providing bathing, particularly as an adult or when the child becomes too heavy to conveniently lift, is with a shower chair. We've designed a bathroom that's has a wheel-in shower, we can wheel a child right into it.

It's a $1,000 cost, replaced every three or four years. The maintenance on the chairs is very basic. We're talking on the Ortho-Kinetics one time per year at a cost of $175 to $225, and on the adult chair, once a year at the same cost. And that's just replacing wear and tear on the casters, the heel loops. Believe it or not, on wheelchairs you have to regularly realign the axle and the wheel positions so it reduces wear. All of that is going to be done on an annual basis.

Q. The idea of that is to minimize the cost of the other?

A. That's correct.

Q. It seems like there's a lot of that factored in.

A. That's right. The idea is to do here what we do in the real world situation where we're working with families. And so in every instance, we're trying to maintain these things to avoid replacing it. The next page is one item for thighs or bracing, she wears bilateral --

Q. What do you mean by bilateral?

A. Bilateral means she has them on both legs. And they're called ankle foot orthosis or AFO's. They're replaced two times per year at age 14, then once per year at age 18, and they have to be replaced because of growth.

And we're going to use them through the developmental years. They're $670 each time they're replaced. The cost and replacement schedules I got from Southeastern Brace, which is her brace supplier.

Q. Okay. Moving onward.

A. All right. The orthopaedic equipment on page eight, we just purchased one item. It's a Rollator walker.

That's simply a type of walker that children use that have wheels on the front. If you're familiar with walkers, most of them have the four legs.

Q. The thing like I've seen with elderly people?

A. That's right. This is one for the children, but the front two are replaced with casters, wheels. The back two are as you would normally expect them.

They're taught how to use them. So it's a replacement for her Rollator walker, $300, replaced two to three times throughout her life expectancy. It's a total wheel replacement at $300 each.

Q. Okay.

A. I don't know that we need to go into great detail on the home furnishings and accessories on page nine. I can move through this fairly rapidly. If you have questions on an item, ask.

The bath seat we're using at the early age prior to age twelve, that's to hold and position the child in the tub. It's for safety and for ease of care particularly as she gets heavier.

Once we start age 12, then we're going to use a patient lift. It becomes unrealistic, a child is going to grow to a point where is she is not ambulatory, we're going to need assistance in moving her around.

Now, if you will note the asterisk at the bottom of the page, it says if she does become functional, either in ambulation or independent transfer from a wheelchair, for example, to a bathtub, then I don't need these items, but I cannot tell you within reasonable rehabilitation probability that she will.

Really even the physicians haven't clearly defined that because it's not difficult to assess whether somebody may be functionally ambulatory in terms of walking normally. We know that's going to be limited, but whether or not she is going to be able to assist in patient transfer is a little harder to say. Certainly that's a goal we're going to work for.

If not, the hydraulic patient lift is $933 to $1,000, it's replaced every 10 to 15 years. And the replacement sling is one every three years, $62 to $80. Then we provide an electric home bed. That's not so much for the child, that's for the care givers. That's to be able to more conveniently position the child, particularly if she grows, becomes heavier, is more difficult to work with.

That's to position the child for provision of care. Then we provided a space saver mat and platform for home exercise program, a cost of $894, and it's replaced once every ten years.

The next page, I think, speaks for itself. Susan is at too low a level of function to take advantage of any of the aids for independent function, so I have not provided any.

Q. Let me just clear that up, because I'm not sure I understand what you mean. When you mean independent, are you saying what the judge was asking you about earlier, she is not going to be able to be alone?

A. No. Well, no, that's not the case. It's apart from attendant care. We have many patients who are intellectually intact, the spinal cord patients, for example, or the spinal biffida child who still needs an attendant care person, but you can give them things like an environmental control unit.

It's an electronic unit they can control even just with a mouth stick that will do everything from allow them to make telephone calls independently, to operate the air conditioning and heating system. Or you can even talk about things as simple as using a long-handled reacher, which has a trigger at one end and a pair of grips at the other so you can grab a box out of the upper cabinet if they're wheelchair-bound.

It includes dressing aids, a whole range. The catalog is filled with aids for independent function to allow a disabled person to accomplish --

THE COURT: Let's move on, Doctor.

A. That's just too much. It's too high a level for her to participate in.

Q. Next category is Drug Supply?

A. Okay. This, again, relatively routine. Pharmaceuticals based on what she's been prescribed and the anticipation that she will continue seizure control medication through her life expectancy, $700 to $1,000 a year. I've given you on that page the breakdown of each item that's the cost per month.

Q. Is Phenobarbital, Lanoxin, what is that last one?

A. Slo Phyllin. Okay.

Q. Where did you find out about those?

A. Medications schedule came directly from the family interviewer. It's in many medical prescriptions, and the amounts are -- I got right off the bottles. I talked to the pharmacist for the cost.

Q. Okay.

A. Diapers, now, through age eight are cost at the time at $45 a box, $550 to $625 a year. Then we go to the adult Attends diapers from age nine to life expectancy, $68.90 per case, $1,562 to $1,953 per year.

Q. Okay. Home facility care, what do you mean by this?

A. We've got to make a determination over the long-run as to whether the child will be maintained in the home with an attendant or whether the child will move to a facility. And the family feels very strongly the child will not be moved into a facility.

So I provided between now and age 21 four hours per day, five days per week of attendant care to supplement or to give assistance to the mother, $6.25 to $6.75 per hour. That's $6,450 to $6,966 per year. I've given her a respite care one weekend a month and one evening, indicated here it breaks out to $8,640 to $12,960 based on a 48-hour period during those weekends.

The reason for the broad base is that I get a survey for respite care, the facilities provided that were regionally close enough had range of cost from as low as $1,500 to as high as $2,250. So I've shown you the range in this geographical area for a respite weekend. I've used LPN's in there because of the medications the child is on.

But once the child reaches the live-in attendant; that is, age 21, I've gone to an attendant, not a skilled nurse, $60 to $65 per day. It takes two and one half staff members to staff a live-in attendant position to cover for weekends, sick time, holidays, et cetera.

Q. Takes how many?

A. It takes two and a half staff members. You have to--

Q. How much is each one of those staff going to make a year approximately?

A. Generally speaking, the services are paying about $4.50 to $5.00 an hour for their time. But recognize that they're getting some compensation having a place to sleep at night, et cetera.

Q. You're talking about two, $300 a week?

A. Two is a lot closer. It takes $21,900 to $23,725 in this geographical region that is surrounding this child's home to provide full live-in attendant care throughout 365 days a year. So that coupled with the adult developmental program will give us the 24-hour coverage we need.

Q. Okay. Going on to page 13, Doctor, you've got future medical care. Now, tell the jury what you're basing this on.

A. First of all, there are no aggressive surgical procedures or basic procedures anticipated being suggested, so all I've provided is routine re-evaluations that we need annually to give to any of our children in a preventive plan.

Q. Is this kind of like on the first page, yearly evaluation type deal?

A. Well, some of them are yearlies. Most of these are all twice yearly. We've got her ophthalmology, $45.

Q. Ophthalmologist deals with what?

A. That deals with the visual problems that the child has.

Q. Okay.

A. We've given her the general medical evaluation twice a year, $27 each time. The pediatrician, $30 for each visit, and we took that of course, to age 18.

We've used a neurologist continuing on through life expectancy who is going to monitor the seizure control medications and seizure activity. And because of the heart, she has been given a cardiologist twice a year also at $26 a visit. The neurologist is $88 a visit.

THE COURT: Let me ask you this: The child in the condition as this one is in, do you often find a hysterectomy is performed?

THE WITNESS: I certainly have seen it a number of times. I can't tell you in my experience it happens so frequently I could do it as a routine. I would have to have a medical doctor tell me they wanted to do it.

THE COURT: It's a matter of routine?

THE WITNESS: It's not something we see done as a routine, that's why I couldn't list it out. The next page, 14, I have a note at the top I want to make sure I point out. It says this particular patient is for information only. It is no way to predict complications in terms of a frequency or a date of occurrence, so there is no way to add this up and include it in the figures.

Q. So final figures we're going to talk about in just a second --

A. -- do not include any cost for complications. There's no way to determine, but I put it in here partly because I wanted to show these are the kinds of things we want to work to avoid, parent education and staff training and also to explain that I can't cost it out in the final figures because I don't know how often any problems like this may occur.

Page 15 simply provided transportation. The child is going to reach a point where it's simply not possible to continue to lift her conveniently. Some types, a van with wheelchair tie downs, raised roof and lift, we provide this starting at age 12. We replace --

Q. Age 12?

A. True. We replace it every five to seven years at a cost of $24,000 to $26,000. That's a wheelchair accessible van, a van with a wheelchair tie down to secure the chair so the individual is belted into the chair, the chair is secured to the floor of the van so that they're seat-belted in just like you and I would be in a regular seat.

Up to that point then we see them, their family can get them in and out of a car. Page 16 deals with the architectural renovations. What I've provided for here is a one-time-only cost where the child is old enough that they're in an adult size chair, for example, large enough they can't get around. It's not realistic to renovate a single wide trailer, so I couldn't give you an estimate of exactly what it's going to cost for them, because I don't know where they're going to be living.

So what I've given you is in 1988 dollars the average cost for each of the two different ways we would normally do it. Either you're going to buy an existing home and renovate it to make it accessible, or you're going to build from scratch. And I've shown you the cost for doing renovations for this child, $12,000 to $15,000. If you're adding a room for a live-in attendant, for example, $6,000 to $10,000. If you were building from scratch, generally you save about 50 percent of those dollars.

Q. The last provision --

A. The leisure time provision is Easter Seals Camp through age nine to age 21, two weeks out of the year, the cost of $190 per week, $380 per year for each of those years nine to 21. And the cost we've looked at here, I've noted at the bottom when we use the camp, we suspend the attendant care cost.

Q. Doctor, are these expenses you've been talking about, in your opinion, are they reasonable and necessary expenses?

A. Yes, they are.

Q. Now, do you have a yearly total of what -- the reason I'm saying this, some start and stop and they're interspersed figures, but from this life care plan that you presented to the jury, can you break it down on what the yearly expense factor is going to be?

A. Yes. I can just simply add it up for you.

Q. Your Honor, can I have him come down and write it on the board per year if you would, sir?

A. Okay. I'm going to give a yearly total up through Public Law 94142. After that it basically stabilizes, and I have a single average annual figure.

The start-up cost because of equipment purchases in the first year is $77,631.

Once we've done that, then the next year, age four is $30,142. The next year is $30,142. The next year is $30,862 because of maintenance or a replacement we've done, and we're back to $40,142.

Year eight is $32,317. The next year, again, we've getting back into some equipment replacements or some additional equipment, we're at $56,692.

Q. If you can put an asterisk by year one just to indicate there's some start-up costs -- or age three. Excuse me.

A. Okay.

Q. Likewise down here, is there something out of the ordinary there?

A. Right.

Q. Age 10?

A. We're at $32,412.

Q. Age 11?

A. We're at $31,692.

Q. Age 12?

A. $33,729.

Q. Age 13?

A. We're at $37,953.

Q. Age 14?

A. We're at $31,692.

Q. Age 15, please?

A. Again, we had some replacement costs at $57,428 for everything.

Q. Age 16?

A. $32,077.

Q. Age 17?

A. $31,357.

Q. Age 18?

A. 34,628.

Q. Age 19?

A. We have $31,742.

Q. Age 20?

A. $31,022.

Q. Age 21?

A. We have some replacement cost there, it's $57,813.

Q. And age 22?

A. $31,693. Now, what is happening at this point is we're starting the attendant care. We add in that figure of $22,000 to $23,000 plus the adult developmental services, which were $8,000 to $9,000, but we take out the various therapies and other items that only went to 21. So what happens is we come up with --

Q. What is the total?

A. Life expectancy -- total of this?

Q. Yes.

A. Is $763,166. That's just the total of those figures.

Q. Okay.

A. Now, to life expectancy, then we had with attendant care, et cetera, the average of the range that we came out with annually was $40,000. This provided the $8,000 to $9,000 a year for the adult developmental and the $22,000 to $23,000 of the attendant, so you can see that support care service and programming is the vast bulk of that. The rest is supply, equipment maintenance, and replacement schedules.

Q. What is the grand total of what your life care plan for supporting this child is, sir?

A. If you assume that the child goes through age 77, that is life expectancy --

Q. Where do you get that figure?

A. Basically it's just the normal life expectancy from the tables.

Q. Mortality Tables?

A. From the Mortality Tables. You come out with $40,000 times the remaining years equals $2,200,000.

Q. What is the total?

A. You add the $763,166, and you get two million, nine sixty-three -- well, to round it off, we're basically getting $2,963,000.

Q. Okay. Thank you sir. Now, Doctor, does this factor in any consideration of what this child's injury is going to do to her earning capacity?

A. That does not, no.

Q. This is just straight costs that you have specified?

A. That's correct.

Q. Doctor, from your experience and training, have you developed any skills to determine what, if any, occupational vocational loss this injury will cause this child?

MR. SMITH: Your Honor, I have to interpose an objection. He has already testified he is not an economist, so he hasn't the qualifications to give that kind of testimony.

THE COURT: Well, ask him if he does qualify and see what --

Q. What experience or training do you have in determining vocational or income loss?

A. Well, first of all, the economist cannot determine the impact of an injury on earning capacity. Only once they're given the dollar amount, then they can calculate out inflation and present value from a discount.

Q. Can you --

A. It requires the rehabilitation professional to look at what the individual was capable of doing prior to the injury or what options may have been available to them and the impact of an injury on that.

In this instance because we're dealing with the child, there's a limited range that I've looked at. There's a specific methodology for accomplishing it, which I'll be happy --

Q. Explain that specific methodology for determining that.

A. First of all, there's no way anybody can say what this child would have done. That's certainly, I think, ridiculous.

Q. What makes you to be willing to --

A. You can't say what she would have done. What you can do is take a look at family background data, the educational and vocational history of parents, how siblings are doing in school, background of grandparents, the social environment, and get a sense of the options for development you felt were within reasonable rehabilitation probability.

I can't say that she wouldn't have, for example, gone to college just because the family didn't, but I don't have any data to say she would have. So in this instance, what I felt was we could really deal with just one thing. The average earnings, we had to do it by looking at the average earnings for a female high school graduate in the United States, that was one option, or the other, I felt, within reasonable probability, was based on family background was that she would have had the option to graduate high school and go on for on-the-job training or some vocational school. That's all I looked at. So the average --

Q. Let's assume she would have graduated from high school. Would that information give you, that and your experience and your methodology give you a basis to determine -- what can you determine from that?

MR. SMITH: Your Honor, I feel like --

THE COURT: Sustained.

MR. SMITH: I think it calls for a speculative answer and is leading, too.

THE COURT: Leading question.

Q. Dr. Deutsch, what do you think from the information you have available to you and your knowledge about the family, everything you've previously testified to, about your experience and information, what from that data are you able to, based upon a reasonable degree of certainty, project as to this child's loss of income opportunity?

A. Really you're -- basically the only thing you can say in this instance is that we're looking at a basic wage earner, somebody that would not have been able to go on -- most likely -- would not have gone on for college or extensive technical training.

There's no data to say she would. So the only two options --

MR. SMITH: Excuse me. I'm sorry. Your Honor, I think, based upon his prior testimony, that he has no way of knowing that, it's simply a speculative answer.

THE COURT: What makes it speculation?

THE WITNESS: Well, I think it will be speculation that we're talking about saying she could go on to college, et cetera. But what we do, we take a look at family background and options. We know that certainly one option is to look just at minimum wages, the minimum she would have earned.

But I felt that when I looked at family data, family educational background, assuming a high school education --

THE COURT: What does all this have to do with it, family background?

THE WITNESS: In determining --

THE COURT: Where do you get -- where do you learn that that is reliable criteria --

THE WITNESS: Okay.

THE COURT: -- for making a determination such as you're making?

THE WITNESS: Well, again --

THE COURT: Or trying to make?

THE WITNESS: Okay. First of all, as far as the influence of family and social environment, if you look back in the research that Straum did and many of the other vocational rehabilitation researchers did, we know that role model indicates the child's development in the absence of any other data. For example, we have a child who did not have a school record before, you can't just assume that they would have gone on to college. You're going to have to assume the minimum.

And so minimum wage becomes one factor. In this particular instance, though, because role models, the social environments influence on development, role models influence on education, encouragement for education, I felt it was reasonable to look at minimum wage as one option, to look at graduating from high school is the second option.

That's the only two options that I gave her. And all I did was look at the influence of this injury or this impairment disability on it and indicated that this disability, there's no way she is going to earn on the labor market.

Then I simply went to the *U.S. Department of Labor Statistics in Employment Earnings* and got the average income for a high school graduate and looked, as a second option at the range of jobs, for a high school graduate and the range of salaries in her geographic area for a high school graduate. Those are two ways you can do it.

THE COURT: What kind of education and training qualifies you to make this projection based on --

THE WITNESS: Well, that's what the vocational rehabilitation at the master's level is doing. And I have numerous occasions to determine the impact of a disability on earning capacity for those who either can't work at all or who have an impact, but can return to work.

I give the 1988 figures or whatever year it is to the economist, and the economist simply makes a determination of inflation and discount. But to determine the extent to which the individual has the capacity to earn with an injury, that's something that the vocational rehabilitation counselor is responsible for.

I do that constantly. I've done it in Worker's Comp., and I've done it in many personal injury cases such as this. And I've also written extensively on that. If you look in my text, *Guide to Rehabilitation*, I have three separate chapters, depending on the age of the individual, as to the steps that are taken in identifying and assessing wage loss based on background and how you do the testing or how you do the assessment, even the age of the individual.

THE COURT: I think, counselor, that your objection goes more to the weight the jury should give to his answer than it does to the admissibility. At best, are we not making this opinion based upon an educated guess with some degree of speculation?

THE WITNESS: Well, the only thing we're assuming, first of all, is that she could have worked, not whether she would have or not, but she would have the capacity if not disabled to work.

If she had the capacity to work, she would have earned at least minimum wage, and the second option is that she didn't. I'm indicating the potential to graduate from high school, and she would have earned the average for a high school graduate. That's all that's being done.

So the only real assumption that's an educated guess, if you will, is that she could have had the capacity to work if not disabled. After that, it's published figures right out of the U.S. Tables.

THE COURT: I'll let him testify. Go ahead.
BY MR. JONES:

Q. Doctor, what is your opinion, based upon a reasonable degree of certainty, of the economic loss assuming a high school graduate?

A. Okay. Assuming a high school graduate, again, there were two ways I looked at it. One was the average tables from the United States; that is, the U.S. Department of Labor gives an average earning in 1988 of $13,510 published in *Employment Earnings*, which is the publication of the Department of Labor.

So that's the average annual income for a high school graduate with no further training. I would assume that at most you could look at a work life expectancy to retirement age, age 65.

Q. What does that compute out to be total present day dollars, not --

A. I apologize, but I did not compute out the $13,510. I did compute out the wages in the local region, but not the national figure.

Q. Okay. That's national?

A. That was national based on all high school graduates. And what I did is I looked at --
Q. Localized?
A. In localizing I looked at a specific job range from high school, a secretary, for example, accounting clerk, payroll clerk, and the basic clerical jobs, computer operator, I averaged out to $15,223, so I can --
Q. $15,000 a year?
A. The $15,000 a year came out to over a 45-year work life, $685,485.
Q. $685,000 plus?
A. And if you wanted to go with the thirteen --
Q. No. That's all right.
A. You can simply deduct it or, again, multiply that out by 45.
Q. You say a 45-year work life, what does that mean? Where do you come up with 45 years, from what year to what year?
A. Basically I just assumed that she would retire at 65. She wouldn't work beyond that.
Q. Start at 18?
A. And I gave her some start-up time after high school, so it actually runs from 20 to 65, a total of 45 years.
MR. JONES: Thank you, Doctor. You may sit.
CROSS EXAMINATION
BY MR. SMITH:
Q. Dr. Deutsch, just sitting here and listening to you for the last hour and a half or 45 minutes, I get the feeling that you've been in a courtroom before?
A. Certainly.
Q. Okay. How many times have you come into a courtroom to testify on this subject matter?
A. I've been consulting since I started practice about 17 years ago. I would say in the last four or five years, it averages anywhere from six to ten times a year that I'll show up or become available in a live courtroom testimony.
Q. Six to ten times a year?
A. That's correct.
Q. How many times a year has your testimony been taken by, say, deposition to be shown in court later?

A. Okay. In total probably as many as 40 times, but many of those are not related to cases that were referred for litigation. In other words, I see patients that are involved in accidents, so we see people that are involved in Social Security, Worker's Compensation where my records or my testimony or my deposition is taken after I've seen and worked with the family for a Social Security disability hearing or for Worker's Comp, but they weren't referred for litigation.

But I would say if you total it out, it's around 40 times a year at least that you would see somebody coming back for those reasons.

Q. Now, in this case when you were contacted, you were not contacted by the family of Susan Ann Hartford?

A. That's true. My first contact was with Mr. Shockey.

Q. You knew that you were being contracted by the lawyer?

A. Yes, I did.

Q. And you knew that this was a case of litigation?

A. That's true.

Q. And basically that Mr. Shockey wanted from you is this number that you have provided?

A. Well, I'm not going to testify to what Mr. Shockey wanted, but my understanding was he wanted an evaluation and he wanted all of the information regarding this child and all of the needs detailed by the onset of disability as I outlined them today.

I will certainly assume that this bottom line interest was in finding out what it will cost to provide that.

Q. The 40 times a year that you've testified, do you prepare one of these reports for each one of those times?

A. It depends entirely upon the nature of the case. I have many cases, as I say, for example, in Worker's Comp or others that may not require a life care plan. They're not catastrophically impaired, but they're what we call non-catastrophic.

In that instance, I provide what I call vocational worksheets. I just evaluate and identify the vocational rehabilitation plan. But in every other instance, a catastrophic case, family or litigation, yes, I prepare one.

Q. How much do you charge for the preparation of this?

A. Well, for this one in particular?
Q. Yes.
A. My total bill for everything was, I believe, right around $5,500 to $6,000, not including the travel expense, the plane to come up here.
Q. How many in this price range would you prepare each year for cases in litigation?
A. Strictly for litigation, is that what you said?
Q. Yes, sir.
A. Strictly in this price range, that's pretty difficult to answer.
Q. Well, let me make it simpler. Just plans like this, greater or lesser that you would prepare.
A. About 15 to 20 percent of my time is spent in consulting in litigation-related cases. And that's, I would say, about 80 percent of those are catastrophic in nature, 75 to 80 percent are catastrophic.

And in terms of numbers, it's a little more difficult, but I'd probably say we get consulted 60 to 80 times a year in terms of catastrophic injury cases, and I would say probably at least half of those, the consultation is to go forth as far as litigation.

In other words, on the defense referrals, you're consulting and not necessarily involved in litigation, so I would say about half of those probably end up in reviewing reports for litigation.
Q. All right. Now, how many reports for litigation do you prepare each year?
A. I just indicated I would say roughly 40 to 60 of those.
Q. What would you say is the average charge that you make for these reports?
A. We work with a wide range of injuries, and you can see life care plans ranging anywhere from as low as $1,500 to $2,000 to as high as eight to nine, to even $10,000 depending upon how much follow-through work we've been doing in that time frame.
Q. You've given us a lot of numbers today. Just give me the average cost.
A. Well, if you take a low of $1,500 and a high of $10,000, the average is going to be around $5,000 to $6,000, but

that's unrealistic in the sense that I don't get $5,000 to $6,000 for every single plan. That's the most involved.

And an awful lot of them are done at $1,500. An average doesn't necessarily represent what I get for every plan. You couldn't take the average and multiply it by 40 and say that's my total income.

Q. Well, what could we say was your total income say for last year from the preparations of life care plans to be used in courtrooms in litigation?

A. You know, I've never been asked it in that fashion. I've never calculated it out. Best I can tell you, it's at least 40 to 45, as I said, that we do. And prices can range anywhere from $1,500 to $10,000 depending upon the amount of work that was involved.

Q. All right. If it's $1,500 times 40, that's at least $60,000 a year, and if it's $10,000 times 40, that's at least $400,000. That's $400,000, so somewhere between $60,000 and $400,000 a year of your income is derived from the preparation of these to be used in court?

A. Of the company's income. I don't make $400,000 a year. I certainly would like to, but I have a number of staff members that are involved in all of this, and I have twelve total staff, five professional staff of Paul M. Deutsch & Associates, so I'd say that's probably a reasonable range to talk about in terms of the court income.

Q. What is your total corporate income?

A. My total corporate income includes a wide range of services, research, patient care, and is not something that I feel is appropriate to talk about here.

Q. Well, just the number, please.

A. Again, I'm awfully uncomfortable in releasing information --

MR. JONES: Your Honor, I object. What relevance --

THE COURT: Sustained.

Q. All right. The report that you prepared based upon the Hartford --

A. I couldn't hear you.

Q. The report, this evaluation is based upon one meeting with the family?

A. That's true, yes.

Q. And in terms of the medical records, did you ever talk to any of these physicians who wrote these medical records?

A. No. I did not talk to the physicians. I had all the information I felt I needed from the reports.

Q. You'll notice a number of these physicians here appear to have disagreements about the development of the child, potential for development of the child --

MR. JONES: I object. It's not proper to compare testimony.

THE COURT: Overruled.

Q. Did you notice that a number of these physicians seem to have disagreements about the development of the child, where she is now, what her potential is?

A. Oh, I think in several areas there were disagreements, and I think we dealt with those effectively in laying out the plan.

Q. How many in a plan like this, how many different assumptions do you have to make in a 17-page report, there are multiple categories on each page, sub-categories. Do each one of those -- is there assumption behind each one of those?

A. No. The only assumption we're making -- that I made, is the one I talked about, which was that I assume she would have the availability of proper follow-through as laid out in the plan. And on that basis, that she would reach as high a level of functioning as possible.

That is, we would look at a best case scenario in terms of long-term support care. That's the only assumption. Everything else is based on, I think, very solid data. And any area that I could not base, for example, how much functional or how functional her ambulation would be, I specifically noted in the plan that I couldn't do that.

Q. There's only one assumption in this whole plan, only one educated guess in this whole plan?

A. I think the way you're defining assumption as an educated guess, I think that's quite reasonable to say, because the rest are based on specifics, based on factual data.

I know what therapy she needs based on what I'm observing, what I'm testing, and what I'm reading, and I know what we can anticipate in terms of her ability to take advantage of those therapies. If we're going to talk in terms of reasonable rehabilitation probabilities, there are no absolutes, there are no guarantees. But certainly I think we see this based solidly in rehab probability, and on that basis, I think there is just the one assumption that she is going to get that care and that she will reach a best case scenario.

Q. Let's try some others. You're making an assumption about a certain rate of development for the occupational therapy, speech therapy. You're making assumption about that; aren't you? You're making assumption about how many years it's going to be needed?

A. I'm making assumption only about my belief she can take advantage of those and will reach a maximum level. I'm not making an assumption -- I'm basically designing a program right along with Public Law 94-142 which provides for educational processes for these children through 21, and I give her the advantage of those therapies throughout the developmental years. That's not an assumption. That's standard in the practice of working with these children.

Q. Let's try another word, see if you like this one better. Judgments, how many different judgments would you have to make in putting this report together?

A. I'm not trying to be difficult. I guess maybe semantics is a problem. What I'm saying to you is I have provided in here what I know to be the standard of services. I guess if just concluding that she was a child who can partake of physical therapy would be defined as a judgment, then I made a judgment.

And I made a judgment that she can benefit from and progress in occupational therapy. I made a judgment that she can benefit from speech therapy. If you want to look at it in that fashion, then all of these items are judgments. They're my professional opinion. Most certainly they're based, I think, on solid factual basis, but they are all judgments that I make professionally. So in that instance, every item is a judgment.

Q. This thing basically is you're providing to take care of her -- this child? Is that what it is? That's what the purpose of it is?

A. It does provide for care of the child through life expectancy, but it also provides for her rehabilitation plan up to 21.

Q. This is to take care of all of her needs?

A. That's true.
Q. Okay. Now, you've also provided a number here about lost income. Since her needs are being taken care of by this other, don't you have to make deduction for the cost of living?
A. I probably should have anticipated your question. This as I said earlier, the life care plan which I was asked to define, it provides all of the needs dictated by the onset of the disability. It doesn't provide for things that would routinely come out of wages. It doesn't buy a home, it doesn't provide food, it doesn't provide clothing, it doesn't provide any of those things that would routinely come to an individual through wages.

It only provides those things that are dictated by the onset of the disability. So anything that would come out of wages like a house, for example, I have not included in the plan.

Sample Transcript #2

The second case example represents a late adolescent head injury of a severe nature. It is trial testimony taken by video deposition for presentation at trial. It also begins after the qualifications have been accomplished and includes both direct and cross-examination.

Q. Let's turn to the case of Richard Banks which is what we're here for today. What did I ask you to do with respect to Richard's case?
A. Well, originally it was to travel to Mr. Banks' nursing home, to speak with him and to evaluate him, to evaluate and discuss with the family his current needs and to develop my recommendations with respect to any immediate needs or long-term needs that were dictated by the onset of the disability, basically to develop a life care plan.
Q. Did you travel to the Sparks Nursing Home for purposes of doing what you just said?
A. Yes, I did.

Q. When did you do that?
A. On July 5th, 1988.
Q. As a result of your visit there and reviewing other material that is involved in this case, did you generate a report setting forth specific recommendations about what you feel would be appropriate for the future life care of Richard Banks?
A. Yes, I did.
Q. What is the date of that report?
A. The report is dated August 1st, 1988.
Q. We'll make that Exhibit B to the deposition later on and you are free to refer to it as you go along.
A. Certainly.
(Thereupon, the document was marked as Exhibit B for identification.)
BY MR. ERIKSEN:
Q. Before I get into the specifics of what you did with Richard Banks, did you have any additional information to look at and review before you went up there to see his situation?
A. Yes.
Q. Can you tell us about what you looked at?
A. I had the Doctors Hospital of Lake Worth records, Rebound Incorporated records and the Rebound dates were 10/28/85 to 8/20/86; Brandywood Rebound SIR unit, 8/20/86 to 5/18/87; the Lashley Rehabilitation Service records from 12/87 to 2/26/88. I had that prior to going up to see Mr. Banks, and then I received additional information subsequent to that.
Q. Why don't you tell us the general approach that you take to a case like this, where you are trying to find out about the case and then make some recommendations about what future care you think would be appropriate.
A. Well, the steps are fairly simple and even though there's a lot of detail I think we can make it brief by going over the global steps.
The first is to review the medical information that's available, including any rehabilitation reports, any depositions that were made available regarding the individual, with a focus on just his medical condition or rehabilitation condition subsequent to the accident.

My next step after reading and summarizing that is to evaluate the individual. Now my preference in a case like this, even though he is not able to provide responses to the questions, is to do the evaluation in the presence of the individual, so that even as I'm talking with a family member, for example, it gives me an opportunity to observe him, to observe his reactions, to watch him interacting not only with respect to myself and the family member but any other support caregiver.

For example, it gave me a chance to observe him eating, to observe him being taken up and out of bed, switched out of his wheelchair, ambulated. It gave me an opportunity to watch some of the agitated or more aggressive behavior that had been reported.

I go through a format and interview with the family member, in this case there were two present, the sister Brenda, who is basically the primary person responsible for working with Mr. Banks, and then his sister Gaila.

I go through general case history, basic history of the injury, the description of Gaila and Brenda with respect to his chief complaints or his primary problems as they perceive them, and I also add additional questions after they have a chance to provide that summary to help bring out more information regarding the disability.

I go over his prior medical history, his physical limitations and restrictions, and any environmental influences which might create further problems for him.

His current medical treatment is covered, any activities of daily living, social activities, personal habits, his hobbies previous to the injury and some of his basic activities previous to the injury, his family and social economic background.

I go through any state or federal agency involvement, and there was none in this case. I go through his past education, training, work history, any details that would be pertinent in helping me to have better insight into the level of individual with whom I'm working, getting some idea of both his functioning levels pre- as well as the severity of his functioning levels post-.

After the interview, what normally would be considered would be testing. At this particular level of function it was unrealistic to talk about doing any testing with him so I utilized what data I had from the rehabilitation centers that he had attended, Rebound in particular, and coupled that with the Lashley Rehabilitation reports, and that was the basic interview and evaluation that occurred.

Q. What are the next steps in the process, not necessarily with respect to Richard's case but just in general?

A. Well, the very next step is to come back with all of this data -- usually on the trip home I will briefly dictate an outline of what I expect in terms of rehabilitation needs and maintenance needs.

Now, with respect to this individual, I made the determination at that point that I wasn't going to recommend sending him to an intensive rehabilitation program.

I felt that there was some regression in the behaviors that were being exhibited from the time he left Rebound to the time I observed him, but I felt that by implementing a better program of structure and rehabilitation or structure and behavioral management within the setting that we chose for long-term care was going to be sufficient. That was the first step.

The second step was to determine what the options were as far as long-term supported living. There was no question in my mind that we're dealing with an individual who was far enough post-accident and in this instance he was essentially about three and a half years post-accident when I saw him, about four and a half years post-accident, four years and a couple of months post-accident now, that it was unrealistic to expect that you were going to see any changes in his condition that would warrant his being independent.

So he needed long-term support. I outlined three options I felt existed for long-term support.

And the next step when I returned to my office was to sit down with additional staff members who formed the team, in this instance my associate Julie Kitchen and one of the other social workers or rehabilitation counselors. We all get together in staffing and we go over my basic recommendations.

I outline the total life care plan and I use staff to do two things for me. One is to review our own data base which we're updating on a daily basis in the office, to determine costs and availability of everything from programs to durable medical goods to replenishable medical supplies, with respect to this individual.

The second is then to undertake a specific telephone survey of all of those resources within his geographic area, that is, in Kentucky, to determine those costs, and we'll utilize local costs if they are less expensive, we utilize bulk pharmaceutical suppliers or durable medical goods suppliers that will ship in if they prove to be lower prices and we put together the life care plan in that fashion.

So the only thing not done by me is the direct telephone surveying to individual suppliers. All the rest is my work product.

Q. To what extent is the approach that you just described a standard approach that you use in all cases?

A. Well, it is a standard approach. Certainly I can go into a lot more detail. In fact, I just finished writing a journal article yesterday about developing a philosophical framework for life care planning, but the bottom line is the idea behind a life care plan is relatively simple.

It is simply a consistent method for evaluating the needs dictated by a disability. It is a generic set of plans or a generic methodology in that it can be applied to any disability. There are 18 sub-parts to a life care plan. Each individual is evaluated in terms of each sub-part regardless of their disability with many sub-parts being thrown out because they are not pertinent to the problems that individual has.

But the key here is that the methodology that's utilized to assess the needs of a patient is consistently applied across all patients. That doesn't mean every plan is going to be the same. It means that the method for evaluating needs is going to be the same.

Q. You have generated some information relative to the type of care that you think is appropriate for Richard in the future and the cost of that care. To what extent will a review of your life care plan allow a jury in this case to reach some conclusions about the minimum costing levels that will have to be provided to Richard today in order to allow that care to occur in the future?

A. Well, I think there's two things that the life care plan does. Number one, it satisfies what I think my role is, which is to be an educator, to answer questions regarding the needs and to justify the needs, dictated by the onset of a disability and then to demonstrate the cost.

I think that the plan does both. It answers questions so that everybody involved is going to understand the disability that much better. And it answers questions with respect to my opinion as to how to meet the needs of that disability, and the costs that are associated with it. So everything that I have recommended is outlined in this instance at 1988 costs, because that's when the plan was completed.

Q. Let's talk briefly about your observations concerning Richard when you first saw him at the Sparks Nursing Home in 1988.

A. All right. Well, my immediate observations were that we're dealing with an individual who is grossly impaired, severely head injured, wheelchair-bound with a clear right side hemiparesis, meaning that he was showing extreme weakness and a reduction in voluntary purposeful movement on the right side.

He was not functionally ambulatory. He was awake but semi-alert, with a very severe brain injury. He was basically oriented, I think, as to person, but not as to place or as to time.

He was intermittently combative, agitated, difficult to deal with. He could ambulate only with assistance. And actually that's with two people, one on either side of him and then a third person pushing the wheelchair behind him so that if he fell back he would fall into the wheelchair.

He demonstrated some self-abusive behavior. He was feeding independently, meaning that if he was provided finger food he could pick up food or pick up a cup and take it to his mouth and drink. And eating seemed to be one of the few pleasures that he was still enjoying because he certainly changed in his behavior from agitated, more combative when he wanted something, when he wanted food, to much more relaxed and easier to deal with when he was actually eating or drinking.

Q. What, if anything, did his ability to pick the food up and put it in his mouth tell you about his level of functioning?

A. Well, we have to break level of functioning with the head injured down into three areas. There's the higher level cognitive thought processes; that's one aspect of rehabilitation and maintenance. There's the behavioral and social aspects, and psychological adjustment is lumped under that. And there's the physical or motor function aspects.

Taking those in reverse order for a second, physically it certainly told me that we had an individual who, although demonstrating some pretty significant physical impairment, still had the ability to demonstrate some basic eye-hand coordination, manual and finger dexterity, albeit at a very gross level, and could at least manage to, using finger foods and using a cup, get food to mouth.

It also told me that he, although having some swallowing problems, still is able to chew and swallow food. That's important. It's important in his maintenance because it means we're not having to deal with tube feeding. Tube feeding would take us to another level of nursing care and would be far more expensive.

It tells me from a behavioral standpoint my observations, not just of his feeding but of the whole behavior pattern surrounding feeding, tells me that we're still seeing somebody who's using aggressive, agitated, acting-out behavior and combative behavior as a way of controlling his environment.

Q. What do you mean by that?

A. Well, just like a child will throw a temper tantrum in an effort to get his way, what we're seeing here is an environmental situation in which people in his environment tend to respond to his combativeness and his agitation. He gets attention or he gets food or he gets drink when he demonstrates that combativeness.

That tends to reinforce that behavior and what we need to do is teach these individuals, who are not trained in behavior -- I am not knocking what they are doing, it's just that you need to be trained in a behavioral program that, in a structure for his environment that reinforces less agitated, less combative behavior and reinforces a more positive way of his demonstrating his needs or his interacting with his environment. This is what he uses for communication.

Q. When you say "training these people," you are now referring to his caretakers?

A. His caretakers.

Q. In your report you make the statement that Richard is nonverbal although shows intact receptive speech for simple one- and two-step instructions. Can you explain what that means?

A. Okay. We have to split language also into two areas. One is receptive language skills, the other is expressive language skills.

He does not organize his thoughts and verbalize them. He's not able to communicate in sentences. In fact, it's difficult to get a single word out of him. On the other hand, if you give him a simple one-step instruction, such as, pick up your cup, he will respond and he will do that, or move an arm, he will respond and he will do that.

He cannot handle what we call serial instructions, where you have two, three, four, five steps in an instruction, he will lose that. But if it's a simple one-step command, he generally can accomplish it.

Q. You also indicate that apparently he's able to handle two-step instructions. What's an example of a two-step instruction?

A. Well, two-step instruction might be, pick up the milk, drink it, or, you know, drink your milk, put it back on the table. There are two steps involved in that process.

Q. What does intact receptive speech for simple one- and two-step instructions tell you, if anything, regarding his level of functioning?

A. Well, number one, cognitively we've talked about the three different areas before. Higher level cognitive thought processes are assessed by even rudimentary kinds of behaviors like being able to not only hear the words that are spoken to you but being able to process that and appropriately respond to it.

So for him to appropriately respond to a command to pick up his cup or for him to appropriately respond by seeing the food or being told that the food is in front of him and beginning to eat it, shows that he's aware of his environment, he's interacting with his environment, and albeit it's at a very simple level, that he has intact thought processes, he understands certain basic simple language and can respond to it and he also is monitoring his environment so that he's aware when food is presented or when there's a noxious stimuli presented.

I mean if there's something he doesn't want he makes that very clear in his agitated acting-out behavior.

Q. You say on page two of your report that Richard will show emotion, getting angry, agitated and combative, and even occasionally smiling.

Did you observe that to be true yourself?

A. Yes.

Q. What, if anything, does that tell you about Richard's level of functioning?

A. Well, again, I think, although we're dealing with an individual who's functioning at a lower level, we're certainly not dealing with what we call a persistent vegetative state. I mean he's aware of his environment. His environment and the way he responds to it is changed by the people present in that environment, or by the stimuli present in that environment.

He responds to visual stimuli, he responds to auditory stimuli, he responds to touch, he responds to smells. What it tells me is that we have an individual who's alert and aware of what's going on about him.

Now his whole world is what is going on in his immediate environment. He's not aware of things outside that environment. He's not aware of the news today, he's not aware of who is the president, or what time of day it necessarily is.

Q. What, if any, observations did you make about any physical limitations that Richard might have?

A. Well, there are obvious limitations centered around the fact that he's wheelchair bound, he's non-ambulatory, he has a very restricted upper extremity range of motion primarily in terms of restricted coordination.

He has difficulty making what we would call a lateral bend, where he bends to the side and comes back to mid-line, or forward bend and comes back to mid-line. He's certainly non-functional for repetitive lifting of objects.

He has intact gross motor skills, although they are much poorer on the right, much more intact on the left, because of the right hemiparesis. He is able to tolerate sitting in his wheelchair for up to six to eight hours a day. He needs a wheelchair strap or straps to keep him tied into the wheelchair so he doesn't fall out.

He's in a recliner chair apart from the wheelchair for an additional three to four hours a day. Basically he's tolerating this with appropriate weight shifts which he's making naturally.

He's unlike a spinal cord patient, he can feel what's going on, but still when you are sitting that long you worry about skin breakdowns, and he's not had skin breakdowns, that's not a problem that he has as of the time I evaluated him, so that's being maintained well.

He could only stand with assistance times two and he's non-functional for kneeling, stooping, squatting, climbing, walking. He has a seizure history, poor balance. He didn't indicate and there was no history of shortness of breath, no indication of headaches. His vision seemed intact. Some possible hearing deficits on the right were revealed in testing, but the left side is intact.

His bowel program is strictly by use of an adult diaper and a commode chair, with Dulcolax suppository and Metamucil on a daily basis. The suppository, I should say, is only used every third day if he's not successful with the Metamucil.

He's not on any specific bladder program. He's certainly non-functional for driving. He tires easily. Usually on more fatigue he becomes even more agitated. And that basically is all I have on physical activities.

Q. Tell us what you observed about the Sparks Nursing Home and who's taking care of Richard there.

A. Well, basically the nursing home is providing meals, washing of his clothes, of course, his bedroom, one daily bath and a cable TV. That is it. The diapers are additional, over and above the *per diem*, his clothes are additional. His equipment, wheelchairs, medications are all additional.

So basically the nursing home is providing room and board. All of his support care services are provided by attendants, and these are unskilled nursing attendants. There's no need at this level of function for an LPN or an RN, for example, but the -- at least the majority of care giving and the majority of the case supervision, if you will, currently is being handled by family members.

Q. Are there, in this country today, facilities that cater primarily to the long-term care of head injured survivors?

A. Yes, there's a clear recognition that there are specialty needs of the head injured population that are very different than other disability populations so, you know, we first saw a proliferation of head injury rehabilitation facilities, and now coming after them is a proliferation of what we call long-term supported living and long-term supported work programs for head injury patients.

Q. Is the Sparks Nursing Home that type of facility?

A. No.

Q. What's the difference in what you observed at the Sparks Nursing Home?

A. We have to first of all recognize that even with a nursing home there are different levels of skill care being provided. I believe that the Sparks Nursing Home refers to themselves as a primary level, but they are not a skilled nursing facility for the head injured patient. Without the individual one-on-one kind of assistance being provided this would be a totally inappropriate patient for the Sparks Nursing Home.

Frankly, it was clean, it was a good environment. I am not knocking the Sparks Nursing Home. I am recognizing that nursing homes are not set up to deal with the catastrophic needs of a severe head injury patient, the level of stimulation that they require, the level of maintenance, schedule of programming that they require, the behavioral problems that they present, because that's an ongoing concern with the head injured patient.

So what I found was an effective compromise that had been worked out where at least for a time we're able to see this patient maintained with family members, some support from nonfamily members being added to it, and the nursing home providing the room and board. There are things he still requires and needs and there are concerns with limiting ourselves to relying on family members.

Q. I want to ask you more about that when we get into the specifics of your life care plan but before we do that let me just ask you whether or not, as a result of your review of the material you had and traveling to the Sparks Nursing Home and seeing Richard, whether or not you were able to draw a conclusion as to whether Richard was a type of person who's going to require 24-hour-a-day support in addition to a nursing home-type program.

A. Yes, I did draw that conclusion. There's just no question of it.

Q. Did you endeavor to prepare a life care plan for Richard Banks?

A. Yes.

Q. Is that a part of your report?

A. Yes.

Q. I am looking at something that is captioned Life Care Plan for Richard Banks (Head Injury), and it's got your name on it. Is that the cover sheet for the life care plan?

A. Yes.

Q. Maybe you can just hold that up so the camera can focus in on the first page of it. It looks like that's marked as Defendant's Exhibit 6 in a previous deposition?

A. That's right.

Q. Was your deposition taken by the defense lawyers before today for discovery purposes?

A. Yes.

Q. And your understanding is I am taking your deposition for trial purposes?

A. Correct.

Q. All right. We have taken the liberty, Dr. Deutsch, of having the different pages of your actual life care plan done up in a graphic form on blowups. Will those graphics assist you in going through and demonstrating to the jury the specific components of your life care plan?

A. I believe they will. They will move it faster and I think to everybody's preference, that would make it easier.

Q. Why don't we take a break while we're having those set up on the easel, and then we'll go back and start going through the life care plan that you feel is appropriate for Richard Banks.

A. Sure. (Thereupon, a recess was taken from 10:30 until 10:40 a.m.)

BY MR. ERIKSEN:

Q. Now, Dr. Deutsch, during the break what we've done is we've taken and blown up pages of your life care plan to use as demonstrative evidence and we've set them up on an easel so that you can use those graphics to explain each step in your life care plan, and what I would like you to do is just to go through each step, explain what is being talked about, tell us when you think the item of care ought to start for Richard Banks and then tell us what your opinion is regarding the cost of that item. Can you do that for us?

A. Certainly.

Q. All right. Let's start with the first item which appears to be neuropsychological; what is that?

A. If I could, just to simplify things, I mentioned earlier that there were 18 sub-sections of a life care plan that you analyze for each patient.

The first section is projected evaluations which refers to projected health-related professionals who we would want to bring in either once or periodically during a lifetime.

The first item is a neuropsychological evaluation. You will notice there's an asterisk next to it. I will explain that in a moment.

We're recommending, or I'm recommending, a neuropsychological evaluation being done now and I wanted to have it done at the time that I saw him but that just hasn't been accomplished as yet. It's one time only. You don't do repeated neuropsychs. This is not a deteriorating or degenerative neurological disorder, so there's nothing to be gained by doing them over and over again. There's a cost of $950 to $1,000.

My specific reason for asking for it is noted on the footnote. We're doing neuropsychological evaluation here because we want to use the data as a basis for developing the behavioral protocols.

Specifically what we're interested in accomplishing is identifying what is functional. What are the best ways to stimulate thought processes in this individual? Does he take information in best visually? Does he take it in best auditorily? How does he process it?

We need to understand this if we're going to do an effective job of behavioral protocoling because we can't exclude the patient from the loop. We'd certainly have to train the staff for behavioral protocols but we need to use the patient to determine the most effective protocols to develop.

Q. Is he exhibiting any kind of behavioral problems that you think need to be addressed?

A. Oh, no question. The self-abusive behavior, the combativeness toward others, agitated and acting-out behavior, and a lot of that is done because he has no control over his environment, and this is the only control he can exhibit. Nobody can control his behavior but him.

What we need to do is give him more opportunity to control his environment in a healthy way, and take away or tune out or time out or extinguish the inappropriate acting-out behavior. That agitation can be brought under control.

Q. You referred a minute ago to self-abusive behavior. Does that mean he's hitting himself?

A. Hitting himself, biting himself.

Q. All right.

A. Now basically, because not every clinical psychologist is doing neuropsychological work-ups, I have recognized that we need the neuropsychological testing and we need the clinical psychologist to help us build the behavioral protocols. If they turn out to be the same person, fine. The costs aren't going to be any different.

These are the costs associated with doing this portion of the evaluation, these are the costs associated, that is, $350 to $500, the cost associated with the clinical psychologists doing their eval.

Q. When you say that's to develop behavior modification protocols, protocols is a big word you may need to define.

A. Okay. All we're really saying here is that to modify behavior requires that we understand the individual, we understand the behavior we want to modify. You selectively modify one behavior at a time.

The protocol is nothing more than the structure, the prescription, if you will, for modifying that behavior. It identifies what we're going to use as a reinforcer, what type of reinforcement schedule we're going to use, how we're going to deliver that reinforcement, and who is going to deliver that reinforcement. And how we're going to chart that behavior or count that behavior. How do we judge or set up the criteria for when behavior protocols need to make a phase change to the next level or next behavior. That's all part of setting up the protocol.

Q. Is this behavior modification idea, does that have anything to do with adding brain power or cognitive functions?

A. No, you are not. This has nothing to do with cognition. To be perfectly frank, we're dealing with an individual who is too far post-injury to talk about effective cognitive remediation or rehabilitation and there may be some compensatory skills that he could still learn but I really think it's strictly going to be in the behavioral area.

I don't see further cognitive development but I definitely see the ability to structure his environment to maintain the behavioral protocols that we're developing and to reduce the behavioral problems. But all of the behavioral protocols, the neuropsychological and clinical psychological aspects of behavior -- and we're going to talk about the actual behavior therapy on the next page -- all of those are there to address the behavioral social consequences of this disability. They are not to address the cognitive at all.

Q. You have got a topic of physical therapy there. What does that mean?

A. Yes. Well, we're recognizing that from a physical therapy standpoint we need to evaluate this individual periodically. Anybody who's wheelchair-bound, non-ambulatory, is going to require a monitoring because we worry about things like contracture deformities and spasticity causing further problems.

That's a shortening of the musculature where the legs draw up, the arms can draw up, the hands can become fisted and it can create a lot of physical complications.

We're saying that on a one-time-per-year basis during a reevaluation for $63 we're going to have the physical therapist do a reevaluation. Now as to the actual provision of his physical therapy exercises, that's on the next page.

Q. Why don't we turn to the next page.

A. Certainly.

All right. The next page, while we're getting a change, perhaps I could just explain what the next page is.

The next page is going to deal with the therapeutic modalities as opposed to the evaluations. We separate evaluations from therapy simply because we recognize that they are going to be done on a different schedule and perhaps even by different people, and that's why they are separated in the life care plan.

So this next page, if we can just focus over on this, are the projected therapeutic modalities.

What we see here is physical therapy, being provided at the current age, we want it to go to life expectancy, but we're recognizing something here, that the physical therapists themselves are only going to come in on this plan one time per month for supervision for a period of two years, and that's going to be supplemented by what the nursing staff or the attendant staff are capable of doing, and thereafter the physical therapist is just going to continue seeing the individual one time per year.

What we're saying here is we're using the physical therapist for purposes of monitoring what's being done by the staff, but day-to-day range of motion exercises, a maintenance schedule, which is what this individual is on, does not have to be done by a registered physical therapist at their cost, but instead should be included in the already existing dollars being expended on support care services. The nurse aides.

This is not anything more than range of motion, monitored by a physical therapist to make sure no problems or complications are developing.

Q. Do you have an opinion as to whether or not the type of physical therapy that you have just recommended would be effective to deal with a weight control problem?

A. Well, not in and of itself, but certainly any home exercise program would be important, or in this case, facility-based exercise program would be important to implement because it's going to help reduce weight.

Now you are going to have to with a wheelchair-bound individual talk about a combination of basic exercise and nutritionally-monitored feeding with a calorie limitation. That's just reality. You are in a wheelchair, you are sedentary, you are going to burn fewer calories. You may have the same desire or level for eating, and for this particular gentleman eating is one of the few pleasures he has in life and so weight is a problem.

But we have to maintain that weight lower because if we can't stand him up we're going to lose a lot of side benefits. The more immobile, the more, for example, he remains seated, the more we run the risk of bone demineralization, because he's not weight-bearing, the more problems we run into with decubiti.

Q. What are decubiti?

A. Skin sores and breakdowns. The more problems that we run into with upper respiratory problems, for which he's at risk, all of which has, or is benefitted by his standing, moving, changing position, and being exercised, and all of which can be done by the attendant care staff that are with him anyway.

Q. What is your opinion about the annual cost of that physical therapy service?

A. Well, basically I have indicated $1,512 for each of the first two years, okay? Got to make sure that this isn't confused here. It specifically reads one time per month for supervision for two years to be supplemented by the nursing staff. And thereafter one time per year.

The one time per year is costed out on the earlier page, that's the one time per year reevaluation, but this figure of $1,512 is to cover that two years. And I know that's confusing the way that's written down so that's why I am trying to straighten that out right now.

Q. Okay. How often should Richard actually get the physical therapy from somebody, whether it's a nurse --

A. He's going to get a physical therapy exercise program daily. In fact he's really getting it twice daily, and that's going to continue. I am simply saying that other than the monitoring by the physical therapist the rest is covered under the cost of his support care.

All right. And this figure here just runs for the first two years of the monthly monitoring.

Q. Is the cost of that based on your survey information for that area?

A. That's correct, and based on the physical therapist fees that the current physical therapist who is monitoring him periodically is providing.

This may be appropriate or inappropriate, to bring up at the moment, but I know that one of the questions that came up with one of the other rehabilitation experts, Mr. Woodridge, was his belief that the monitoring needed to be done one time per month to life expectancy. It shouldn't be ended in two years. And if that's the case, this figure would then go to life expectancy instead of dropping every two years.

Q. Is the costing information that you got by means of survey, is that a typical way you do it?

A. Yes, for us, yes. I mean there are two ways that we really collect data. We have responsibility because of other contractual agreements we have to maintain a data base by region of the country on all of the durable medical goods supplies, replenishable supplies, hospital services, physician services, health-related professional services, et cetera, across all disabilities.

So we run a major data base and we have people in the office whose sole job is to survey in writing through research articles and through direct telephone surveys. When there is litigation involved, though, we also direct telephone surveys to confirm our data for that specific geographic region, and that is the way it's done in the office on a daily basis.

Q. Is that type of survey information typically and customarily relied upon by people in your profession to render opinions about the cost of such care?

A. Absolutely. In fact that's what's even published in my textbooks that a lot of people rely on.

Q. All right. The next item you have listed there is family counseling, family education to aid in case management.

A. Right. Now what we're talking about here realistically is an educational process. What I am saying is that as long as Brenda and/or a family member are acting as case manager, and in fact even if we put another case manager in place, you are never going to completely reduce the role of the family member or the guardian as a liaison, and even if we do that we want to provide her with all the skills that we reasonably can provide her or expect her to develop to make her job easier.

This is an educational program basically that two times a month for three months we're going to bring her in, total cost is $540 to $600. And we're going to train her in basic case management techniques. We're going to teach her about things like replenishable medical goods, bulk suppliers, where they exist in the United States, how to get in touch with them, how to negotiate lower monthly supply rates.

(Mr. Methe entered the room and Mr. Warren withdrew.)

We're going to talk to her about all of the various issues in case management, from understanding the life care plan, how do you implement the life care plan, why are you setting up regular repair schedules for wheelchair equipment rather than waiting for the breakdown and then repairing it? Why do you do the regular maintenance and how do you schedule the regular maintenance and what are you looking for?

This is what's being accomplished. We do it for case managers in a two-day seminar. For families we split it up two times a month because it's a little harder for them to learn and internalize all that information in a two-day period when they are not regularly being worked as case managers.

Q. Just for the record, in case somebody looks at the transcript of this deposition as opposed to viewing the videotape, you are continuing now to use your schematics and diagrams as demonstrative evidence in showing not only what the item is, but also when it starts, when it stops, and the cost?

A. That's correct.

Q. Okay. Is case management of a head injured survivor like Richard a skilled occupation or does it require skill and training?

A. Well, there are aspects of it that are skilled and there are aspects of it that are not. In our work, in my personal office we have an agreement with the families we do case management with that somebody will be provided for us to train to take over that portion of our work that doesn't have to be done by the social worker or me or another rehab counselor.

There are portions that are skilled. But, for example, what Brenda is currently doing and what we can facilitate for Brenda through this educational process, there's a lot that we can help her with.

But there's also reality. And that is --

Q. What's that?

A. -- Brenda cannot be the focus in a life care plan of providing case management services to this individual to life expectancy.

Q. Why not?

A. Because I cannot guarantee that Brenda will be there, tomorrow, next year, whether it's personal problems, personal disability, death, burnout, whatever the reason, a life care plan cannot depend on one individual or one nurse service or one nursing home as being the sole provider of service from now to the end of life expectancy, because if they are not costing out at the rate, the predominant rate that it costs to get that service in the area, that is, if they are unusually less expensive and if that service no longer is available or if that family member is no longer available, there's no way the dollars will then be available for the patient or the patient's guardian to replace that service.

So although I applaud what Brenda and the family are doing up to now, there's no way in a life care plan philosophically that I can just assume that that will be sufficient to the end of his life.

We have too many years. We're not talking about four years down the road or five years down the road. We have too many years over which to plan, and for that reason I personally believe the only way to insure the availability of items or services in a life care plan is to provide what the predominant cost of that service is within the geographic region in which the individual is going to live.

Q. You just mentioned something called burnout. To what extent is burnout an occupational hazard for people who are called upon to take care of head injured survivors like Richard Banks?

A. Well, it depends on whether we're talking about staff or family members. I mean, frankly, it's a problem with both. We certainly offer a lot of counseling programs to the staff of head injury centers and other rehabilitation centers because burnout is a problem.

But for family members this has been written about extensively. If you look in my text, *Innovations in Head Injury Rehabilitation*, there's a chapter on family-centered rehabilitation.

And what we do is recognize that those head injury patients who have strong family support units go a lot farther in terms of both their rehabilitation, their maintenance, and their freedom from complications that could become costly. They go a lot farther than those patients who don't have family support.

Yet we also know that the injury itself is as devastating to family members in many ways, at least emotionally and psychologically, as it is to the injured patient. So what we look to do is try and deal with the emotional reaction of the family, and we look to educate them as well, to give them better support. But burnout is a constant problem.

Q. What is burnout in that sense?

A. Well, in that sense what we're talking about is an individual who just cannot cope with the intensity of the schedule, the demands that are placed upon them with respect to the patient.

For those who are parents, who can imagine spending the rest of their lives taking care of a two- or three-year-old, you have the demands, the fact that you cannot leave them unsupervised, that you can't go off for the evening, and just hire the baby sitter from next door. That you can't take any kind of extended time away, just during the course of the normal day, without that constant need to supervise, but that's not just going to happen now when your child is two and it will change gradually through three, four, five, ten, twelve, fifteen, but it's going to be that way for the rest of their lives, and a lot of families just can't face that. It's a burnout issue.

Burnout is only one of our problems. I am not suggesting that that's the only reason by any means that we've got to plan. I can't plan for her life expectancy, I can't plan -- "her" being Brenda -- I can't plan for marriage -- changes in her marital situation, changes in her personal needs, changes in her health. If she's the sole person I depend upon, then we have a serious problem if there are no funds available to replace her if she's no longer available.

Q. Your next topic is rehabilitation psychologist, catastrophic case manager for coordination and services.

A. Correct. What I am suggesting here is the use of a rehabilitation professional to implement the life care plan and act as a resource person and consultant as case manager to the family or to whomever takes over if the family is not available.

Basically it's the total cost of implementing the plan and acting as the first-year case manager, $8,000 to $10,000, and on a yearly basis thereafter $3,500 to $5,000.

But basically we're talking about roughly a $3,500 to $5,000 a year cost for managing all aspects of this case.

Now, you know, to the extent, for example, that a family member continues to be a case manager and can take over from the case manager, the outside consultant, then a portion of those fees should go to pay whatever that family member is providing.

To the extent that that family member becomes unavailable and more has to be taken on by the case manager, then the monies need to be available for the case manager.

The key here is somebody has to manage this case. Regardless of who we're paying the dollars to, that management has to take place. These are not decisions, negotiations, or responsibilities that Mr. Banks can take on.

Q. To what extent is the long-term care of head injury survivors a developing or evolving science worldwide?

A. Okay. Well, there's no question it's evolving now, and we started out recognizing 15, 16 years ago that there was a lot more going on in closed head injury than perhaps we realized, that too many patients were being written off as basically psychiatric patients.

The work of Alexander Luria who was the father of neuropsychology and a Soviet scientist, really began our research into brain function. What has followed is a recognition, a much better diagnostic program for assessing the existence of these injuries, over the past decade an incredible increase, now we have over 600 head injury rehabilitation centers in the United States.

We know that we have over 700,000 head injuries each year. Ten percent of those or about 70,000 to 75,000 require comprehensive head injury rehabilitation. They are now surviving accidents more because of better medical care, are getting better post-acute rehabilitation, and now are leaving the post-acute centers and have no place to live, so the next big area of development is long-term supported-living facilities and they are moving very, very rapidly.

Q. To what extent is it reasonable or not reasonable to expect somebody like Brenda Banks who is in Central City, Kentucky to be able to keep up with those trends in developments without a source of outside information available to her or assistance?

A. It's pretty unrealistic. I mean the only thing she would have conveniently available to her would be the National Head Injury Foundation which is doing the proverbial yeoman's job of trying to keep up with all of that, or she's going to have to have a resource person who's directly tied into what's going on, who's part of the professional organizations and committees that are making these decisions, accrediting these facilities. But that's really something that you are going to get from professionals, not from a family member.

Q. Is that part of what you do for a living, people like you?

A. That's correct.

Q. You can just continue on to the next item then.

A. Okay. Well, the last thing we have on this page are the behavior modification programs, the actual implementation of the protocols. And what we are talking about here is taking the psychologist and covering their time to develop the protocols, work with the patient in the development of the protocols and train the staff to implement them and then be available as a staff resource person, to answer questions, to make phase changes, to guide the protocols.

You cannot do behavior modification dropping the patient from the loop, so the first thing that has to happen is the doctor has to interact with the neuropsychological data, interact with the patient, has to then train staff, actually design the protocols, train staff on the protocols, monitor their initial use, make changes as appropriate and then stay available as a resource person and consultant to the staff who are implementing the plans.

Q. You keep using that word "protocol". Does that basically mean a plan for doing this?

A. It's a plan for doing it. And it's a recognition that with a head injured patient they thrive most effectively in well-structured environments. So the environment itself has built into it the cues, the reinforcements, and the reinforcement schedules for monitoring and maintaining the behavior we're looking to achieve. It's built into that structure.

Q. Let's take his problem with the agitation as being a kind of behavior aspect that you would want to modify. Can you give the jury an example of how behavior modification would address that type of problem?

A. Sure. The first thing you'd have to do is to sit down and evaluate, that is, monitor the patient and do so long enough to get a base line rate of frequency of agitated behavior and types of agitated behavior and what causes or reinforces or stimulates the agitated behavior, because when you do so you are going to find out that different things stimulate it, and you may actually be talking about multiple behaviors to change, and you are only going to change one at a time.

First of all we identify the behavior that we want to change. Second thing we're going to do in monitoring and setting up a base line is determine what it is that's reinforcing for this patient and what kind of controls is he trying to exhibit or what is he trying to get control over through his behaviors.

So we've identified why the behavior exists, what the behavior specifically is, what reinforcers work for this individual, and then we design a program to change that select behavior.

Now we've got base line data to know how frequently that behavior is exhibited and we continue to count or chart that behavior as we're working with it so we can determine whether or not it's being reduced or extinguished over the base line.

Once we've established a change, or a protocol, we-- or a schedule, we teach the staff. We implement it, we monitor it, and when that behavior is changed, we set it up on strictly an intermittent reinforcement schedule built into the environment and we start on the next behavior.

Q. What I want you to do is give the jury an example of a technique of behavior modification that might be applied to his agitation so the jury can understand what we're talking about when we say behavior modification.

A. Well, there is a wide range of ways of doing it. In modern behavior modification the first thing we do is develop what's called a schedule of reinforcement and there are a variety of different schedules.

We usually start the individual on what's called a contiguous or continuous schedule of reinforcement.

A quick, but good example would be if you have a child who's throwing temper tantrums and every time he throws a temper tantrum you give him a lollipop, you are continually reinforcing that behavior.

Now if I tell you to stop doing that, to use time out, not negative reinforcement, but time out, we're going to ignore the child, put him in a time out room and we're going to extinguish that behavior by ignoring it and give him his lollipop when he's behaving well to reinforce it. Then we've got him on again a continuous reinforcement to extinguish the behavior.

Now what happens here is that eventually we want to put the child on an intermittent schedule of reinforcement.

Q. Every so often?

A. So that they don't expect that it's going to happen, every time they are good they get a lollipop. But let's look what happens negatively if you fail to enforce it properly, if the structure is not in the environment.

One day you are getting ready to go to church, your child throws a temper tantrum, you are busy, you have been doing this properly for a year but you are tired, you stuff a lollipop in his mouth; now the child knows it may take one temper tantrum, it may take a hundred temper tantrums, but if he does it long enough he's going to get a lollipop.

Now the child is on an intermittent schedule of reinforcement, it's much tougher to extinguish. What we want to do is turn that around to the positive. The positive behaviors are on an intermittent schedule of enforcement so that they are hard to extinguish.

That's the way we're going to identify reinforcement. Now I am not suggesting lollipops for Mr. Banks. There may be a wide range of reinforcers that we can use and we're going to have to sit down with him in the analysis and determine what's going to be most effective.

Q. Do you have an opinion as to whether or not Richard's agitative behavior is something that can be modified?

A. I do.

Q. What's that opinion?

A. I honestly believe it can be. I have worked with agitated and combative head injury patients for a long, long time, and this has lasted as long as anyone I know, and I think it's lasted because his environment reinforces it, not intentionally, nobody has set out to do that, but I think it's reinforced and I firmly believe you can get control over it.

Q. What value, if any, would there be in modifying Richard's behavior such as the agitation?

A. Well, the first immediate value is that we improve his interaction with his caregivers. We reduce the problems that it creates, and if, by the way, we have no family members left, we're having to use a home health agency, for example, they are not going to put up with agitative, combative behaviors, we're going to have trouble keeping staff.

We certainly improve quality of life by reducing the agitation, the combativeness and the self-abusive behavior. We make him easier to work with in other areas of behavior control. Where we can get him involved in shifting his position, we can train that as a habit pattern with the individual through behavior modification. We don't need to do anything cognitively. We can get him to be a part of his caregiving team through shaping of behavior.

Q. Do you have an opinion as to the frequency with which Richard ought to have the behavioral modification program and then how much that's going to cost?

A. Well, I do. First of all, let's remember behavior modification is for life. Whatever is built into the structure will always stay there.

Now it doesn't cost for life. It costs when we develop the protocols, and once it's being maintained, it's being maintained by the staff, with the consultant being available whenever needed through life. So the cost drops dramatically.

We have 20 to 30 hours initially, and that's at a cost of $1,900 to $2,850. We have a five to eight hour per month cost for the first year, and that's at a cost of $5,700 to $9,120 for the first year.

We have two to four hours per month for the next six months, and that's at a cost of $1,140 to $2,280, and after that we're suggesting that the psychologist should be available as a resource person for monitoring purposes and we haven't put a charge in there for that.

Q. Who would carry out the behavior modification at that point and thereafter?

A. Basically the trained staff, and whoever the case manager is has to be trained so that as there is staff changeover, the case manager trains the new staff coming on board.

Q. We're talking about staff and as it exists right now we're talking about his caretakers?

A. That's right.

Q. Do you have an opinion as to whether or not Richard has regressed from a behavioral standpoint since he got to the Sparks Nursing Home?

A. Yes, I do have an opinion.

Q. What's that opinion?

A. I think he has. I think what we're seeing here is an effort to have installed or instituted behavioral programming within the rehab program at Rebound. I think we see, although we were seeing agitated, combative behavior, it was at a higher level, began to reduce, and I think it's back at a higher level now. It's not as high as it was originally, but I think what's happened is, is that there's an inadvertent reinforcement.

Even during my evaluation I observed some acting out behavior, self-abuse, beating the chair, striking out, and one of the attendants saying, "Well, I know you want food", and running and getting his food, and he calmed down as soon as he had food.

Well, that's good, I am glad he was aware of the food, I am glad that he was aware of his environment, I am glad to see he's trying to exhibit some control over his environment but it's a negative control. And by giving him his food in response to that what we've done is reinforced that behavior. It's going to get worse, not get better, as time goes on.

Q. I want to move from the projected therapeutic modalities we've just been discussing over to what your opinion is about where Richard should be kept or --

A. Certainly.

Q. -- housed, and in what way, over the remainder of his lifetime, which is an area that we've discussed quite a bit in this case and I want to get you on it as quickly as possible.

A. Certainly.

Q. I think that -- we're now on page two of your report and I think that would get us over to page eight of your report, but without skipping directly to page eight just tell the jury what the next few pages of your report generally deal with and we won't get into any specifics of that.

A. Generally the next areas of any report would be whether or not there was any future educational or diagnostic testing needs. There are none for him.

The next page for him would be wheelchairs and we've outlined, or I have outlined his basic wheelchair needs. The next page is his wheelchair's accessories and maintenance. The maintenance schedule on the wheelchairs, what accessories, like wheelchair cushion would be required or lap board would be required and again all the maintenance schedules on the wheelchairs.

Then we have his orthotic needs, that's bracing. Any bracing that would have to be done of the upper and lower extremities.

The next page for him would be any future routine medical care, his drug and supply needs are outlined. So all of these things are issues that surround the basic support care. And support care or what we call home care/facility care sections of the life care plan deal with how we're going to maintain the individual.

Q. All right. Let's bring that up right now -- which is page eight of your report -- and since we've skipped from page two to page eight and you have told us basically what pages three through seven deal with, let me just ask you generally about pages three through seven of your report.

Do those pages contain your opinions, to a reasonable degree of certainty within your profession, about what your recommendations are for Richard concerning such things as wheelchair needs, wheelchair accessories, and maintenance, orthotics, prosthetics, home furnishings and accessories, and drug supply needs?

A. Yes.

Q. And have you made an effort on those pages to set forth when you think those needs will arise in Richard's case and how long those needs will persist?

A. Yes.

Q. And have you also made an effort to render your opinions regarding the cost of those items during the time that they are needed for Richard?

A. Yes.

Q. And are your opinions relative to the items that are needed, the frequency of need, and the cost to a reasonable degree of certainty within your profession?

A. Yes.

Q. All right. I have asked counsel during the break whether or not we can dispense with having you testify about every single item on pages three through seven, and understanding that I am going to be providing, or we've provided this report to an economist to figure out how much money we have to be awarded today to supply those needs, and can I just get on the record that you can cross examine him on whatever you want to, but that I don't need to go into each specific item for the purposes that I have indicated.

MR. DODSON: Sure, as long as you stipulate that we can cross examine on those issues.

MR. ERIKSEN: Absolutely.

MR. DODSON: No objection.

BY MR. ERIKSEN:

Q. We turn now to page eight of your report which has to do with home facility care. Tell us basically what that deals with.

A. Well, we have to concern ourselves here with how we're going to maintain the individual, that is, within what environment we are going to maintain this individual through the balance of his life expectancy.

There's only a few choices with respect to a head injured patient. I mean certainly we can take into consideration returning him home, but that was an unrealistic choice here. The cost of putting somebody in their home when they need this kind of care and this kind of equipment, attention, et cetera, really is no less expensive and it's less stimulating in many instances than using some level of facility care.

So realistically for Mr. Banks I felt that there were two options. One option was to use the nursing home he's currently in and continue the attendant care services on a 24-hour-a-day basis.

The second option was to use what we call a long-term supported living program. I gave as an example here New Medico and I did so because at that time their rates on a daily basis was pretty typical of other long term facilities.

What's happened is a lot of the head injury facilities, recognizing a need to maintain these patients, have just taken some of their post-acute rehabilitation beds and set them aside as long-term care beds. It was a temporary solution until more long-term supported living programs could be purchased.

The cost, for example, here on option two for New Medico was $250 to $300 per day. That has already, in the last 45 days, gone to $384 per day that they are now charging for long-term supported living. But, you know, they will negotiate on individual patients but you can anticipate that the range is going to run somewhere today between $300 to $400.

Q. What does that include? What does the patient get for the $300 to $400?

A. Depends on the facility. At New Medico, for example, at $300 to $400 a day it's a total maintenance. In other words, their routine pharmaceuticals, their routine laboratory testing, their routine physician examinations, their -- any vocational programming that they can participate in, their room, board, nutrition, all of that is going to be included.

An electric wheelchair would not be included. In fact, none of their wheelchair equipment would be included. Now if there was a patient lift required, that would be. Their bed, of course, would be. But specialty equipment, acute medical problems, hospitalizations, none of those would be included.

Q. What about therapeutic interventions like physical therapy and that type of thing?

A. If they are using an actual physical therapist, that would not be included. A PT or an OT would be an additional charge. If it couldn't be handled in the routine way where the-- now if you are using PT like we are in this plan to monitor, that would be included. And we're using the home care staff or the facilities, the care staff to do his range of motion exercises, that would be included. But the use of a physical therapist to do it would not be.

Q. Well, assuming this case, and I think we can, that Richard requires around-the-clock sitters, is that the type of thing that he would have for that $300 to $400 a day at a long-term facility that caters to head injured people?

A. That's correct, although what they would be doing is making him part of a group of similarly disabled individuals and there would be staff on a staff/patient ratio. He wouldn't necessarily have one-on-one 24 hours a day. He probably would have one-on-one for 16 hours a day and have one eight-hour shift during the night in which he had two people in the house that could serve five patients, because not all five are going to be up and needing help during the middle of the night at the same time. So they will have some cost savings.

But now that's New Medico. If you look at Mediplex, for example, who have just opened a group home for long-term supported living here in Tampa, Florida -- actually Bradenton -- that's $390 a day for room, board, and supervision, and they don't provide any of the maintenance therapies, vocational, all of that is extra, and the per diem.

Q. Do you have an opinion as to whether or not there are any advantages associated with having a head injured survivor together with other head-injured survivors in a long-term care facility?

A. No question that there are advantages, and yes, I have an opinion. I guess I just expressed it.

Q. I guess you did. Would you just explain to the jury what you feel about that?

A. Well, first of all, the difference is that instead of going into a home environment or a nursing home environment and trying to train a staff and make a team out of a staff, you have a well-trained team all trained together in head injury rehabilitation, in maintenance of head injury patients. You have a total environment that's already been structured and designed for the behavioral protocols, for the team involvement. It puts them in a social milieu that's much more appropriate. Everything is designed --

Q. Let me interrupt you and ask you why is that more appropriate?

A. Well, because one of the things that we need to do to keep this individual from regressing further is to stimulate him. We need to exercise the brain in much the same way we need to exercise the body.

If I take Mr. Banks and I put him in a room, keep him in bed most of the time, there's no music, there's no TV, the walls are peach, the curtains are peach, there's no pictures on the wall, I make essentially a sensory deprivation situation.

Then I am going to see a regression, severe regression in cognitive functioning because we're not stimulating him.

Now he is getting stimulation but it's on a restricted basis. These facilities are specifically designed to provide -- on a constant basis -- the appropriate level of stimulation tactilely, auditorily, visually, without overstimulating or using too much overlap between methods of stimulation.

The whole structure, the whole program is designed to put him into as near normal a social and behavioral milieu as possible and to maintain him in as good a quality of life as a result.

I am not saying that that makes option two so far superior that we couldn't even consider option one. You have to recognize that either option in this instance becomes a set of compromises.

Q. All right. Let's talk about option one. How do you compare option one with where he is today in the Sparks Nursing Home?

A. Basically this is taking where he is today, without talking about the dollars and cents aspect, this is taking him where he is today, leaving him in the Sparks Nursing Home, and it's providing him with his attendant care, making no commentary on who's going to provide the attendant care.

All of the other therapies we've talked about, the training of staff, the training of case manager, et cetera, are added to it to make this a more effective consideration.

One reason I looked at this as a first option was because it kept him geographically closer to his family and certainly to take him and put him into a facility and reduce family involvement is a compromise, and I am not sure it's a compromise that I am ready to suggest to the family be made.

But I do think that if we leave him in the current situation, we've got to recognize certain basic realities.

Q. Which are?

A. Well, first, it's simply unreasonable to talk about paying at minimum wage, let's say, $3.50 an hour to attendants to continue to provide support.

Q. Why is that?

A. Well, here's what happens. First of all, regardless of the experience of others, in 17 years I have tried numerous different ways to bring about attendant care to long-term catastrophically-impaired individuals.

To hire on their own, there are some basic problems that the family runs into. One, a family member must be identified as the primary person to place the ads, screen individuals, and hire them. They have to be responsible for either paying high enough wages to cost -- for the individual to make their matching Social Security payments as self-employed people or they have to cost in making matching Social Security payments. Do the tax withdrawal, if they are hiring them as employees. Handle all that bookkeeping.

They have got to -- and here's the most critical problem -- they have got to have a family member who is always available as backup because there's no way for a family hiring a team to hire a backup pool of individuals that they are not going to pay, they are not going to utilize until someone calls in sick or someone quits or someone is off for a weekend or some other problem comes up.

So you always have to depend on family to take over in that instance. And it's unrealistic. That puts us back into the position of having to say that we're depending upon one member of the family or one group who are going to continually be involved and available through life expectancy, even if they are reaching age 60, 65, 70, they continue to be the primary caregiver.

The reality is that over the long run the only effective way I have maintained individuals, and I maintain a lot in catastrophic case management now, and all but two currently are through home health agencies. I only have two against my recommendations that are trying to run it on their own and one has been provided a case manager to do it for them. They are still doing their own hiring, they are not doing nurse service, but a case manager does it.

The home health agency then has the responsibility for screening, bonding these individuals, they have the responsibility for all the payroll taxes, all the health care insurance, all the Worker's Comp insurance, and all the other issues that arise. They have the responsibility for maintaining a pool of individuals to replace.

And then there's the one primary comment that I have already made, and that is, if I am hiring somebody at

$3.50 an hour because I currently have somebody who will do it, I am making a statement that I am expecting this to be available through the life expectancy of the patient.

The reality is that if I charge anything less than the prevailing rate for buying that service in this person's home area, I am running a very real risk that at some point during the course of the life care plan there simply will not be the dollars to hire the attendant staff necessary.

So you may go along for a year or two years or three or maybe even five using family members at a lower cost, but you are eventually going to be faced with the reality that you want to make a switch and there are not sufficient dollars to make that switch.

Q. Do you have an opinion as to what the cost would be outside the family of Richard Banks to get people to do the same thing that his family members are doing today for three fifty an hour or whatever it is?

A. If you contact a home health agency in the area, which I have done, that home health agency indicated that they would be charging $9.51 per hour. So our total attendant care cost for 24 hours a day is $83,308 per year. $9.51 an hour is right in the ball park for the southeastern United States. It's low for the Palm Beach area. This happens to be the second highest home health agency cost in the country. Buffalo, New York is the first.

Q. Can you think of any reason why the current sitters are working at the reduced rate other than the fact that they are family members?

A. Well, I mean, number one, they are family members. Number two, you know, I think they have a commitment to Mr. Banks that is going to be difficult to find among individuals who are just generally hired. Three, I don't think anybody has given them the option of earning any more. The funds aren't there to pay any more.

Q. Do you have an opinion as to whether or not it would be reasonable, from your standpoint as a life care planner, to plan Richard Banks' entire life care plan on the assumption that members of his family would continually be available to provide the services that they are providing today?

A. I have an opinion.

Q. At a reduced rate?

A. I certainly have an opinion.
Q. What's that opinion?
A. I have stated it here, I have written extensively about it and in several articles and textbooks. You simply can't do it. That defies or defeats the purpose of the life care plan. You can't use any one nursing service, you can't use any one family member, or any one person.

The way to handle these costs is to determine by surveying the various suppliers what the average or predominant cost in that area is. That's the only way to guarantee that over time, regardless of the direction that, or the increases that occur as a result of inflation, that over time you have a ball park figure, an average figure, that will allow you to keep pace with inflation and purchase those services.

Q. What is minimum wage today?
A. Minimum wage today is $3.35 an hour. It will not stay that way very long, of course. The Congress has already passed a bill, it was vetoed, but we would expect minimum wage to go up to at least between $4.15 and $4.25 an hour in the next year.

Q. Is the type of attendant care services that you feel Richard needs a minimum wage type work?
A. They are usually not paid at minimum wage. Depends on how you define it. I often use a term in my work called the minimum wage range. If you look at minimum wage range today as being $3.25 to $4.50, then let's recognize that if minimum wage goes to $4.25 that minimum wage range is going to be $4.25 to $5.50.

You will find in some areas of the country that the take-home pay of those home health aides may be down around $5.25, $5.50 an hour. That's generally low.

Normally what's happening is out of that $9.51 the actual profit to a nursing home is somewhere in the $1.00 to $2.00 an hour range. The rest is their cost of insurance, paying the individual, providing the other required things that are provided. It's all spelled out, quite frankly, in each state's Nurse Practices Act as to what a home health agency must do in providing care.

Q. Let me ask you a similar question with respect to the Sparks Nursing Home which is where Richard is today. Do you think it's reasonable for you or anybody as a life care planner to plan Richard Banks' entire future life care plan on the assumption that Sparks Nursing Home is going to always be there to provide what he needs?

A.   Well, number one, I think it's unreasonable because we certainly have had many circumstances in which a nursing home has closed. But there are other changes that can take place too. For example, in reading the deposition of the Administrator at Sparks we see her talking about a change in the designation for Sparks Nursing Home coming up in 1990, toward the end of 1990. That's going to change the cost from $70 a day to $110 a day.

Now I have no way of knowing what other changes may take place beyond normal inflation five or ten years down the road. Ten years down the road. So if they make a change in their level of facility and significantly increase their cost I may have to look to another facility to provide the level he requires. I cannot base it on any one facility, even if it's the most expensive, nor can I do it if it's the least expensive. It needs to be the predominant value in that area.

Q.   Let me ask you whether or not as a life care planner you take into account one's life expectancy in order to decide how long care should be provided for in the future.

A.   I don't think a life care planner needs to do that, okay? I mean realistically I can just say whatever the life expectancy we all assume, his service will go to life expectancy.

As a life care planner or as a rehab psychologist, my role has been limited to reviewing and understanding the research in life expectancy. I have done a couple of articles where I have reviewed and discussed the statistical methodologies involved in what we call epidemiological studies, the studies of life expectancy in catastrophic disability, so I can talk to what the statistics say, but I would defer to a physician, a treating physician particularly, on trying to designate the life expectancy of a particular individual based on whatever medical problems that individual may have.

Q.   Well, let's talk about statistics then. Do you have an opinion based on your knowledge of the statistics about life expectancies for head injury survivors as to whether or not there's any literature that supports the concept that someone with Richard's type of injury would have a reduced life expectancy?

A. I have an opinion.
Q. What's that?
A. Well, first of all, I think we need to recognize that generally in the field we consider there to be a dearth of literature out there researching this, although there are a couple of good programs that are developing those statistics.

The research that is out there and the early outcomes from the head injury study that's being done on longevity suggests that we have a reduction in life expectancy in basically only three instances with head injured: One, those who have a progressive neurological condition, a lesion from cancer, or some other progressive degenerative neurological problem. Two, those who have brain stem damage. Neither of those two instances apply here. The only time then that we normally see a reduction in life expectancy is in the third instance in which a head injured individual does not receive sufficient care and dies not from the head injury but from an associated complication. So renal complications --

Q. Is that kidney failure?
A. Kidney problems, repeated kidney infections, or reflux of urine back into the kidneys that cause symptomatology like dysreflexia, severe decubitis that go untreated, the bed sores that can become gangrenous, upper respiratory, pulmonary problems, if they are not caught at very early stages can become life threatening. So otherwise you basically would expect the normal life expectancy.

Taking the decubuti as an example, we have 24-hour care here. Even if he gets a skin breakdown, I would expect that to be discovered at a very early grade one stage. He will never get to a grade two through five. You're never going to have to worry about surgery. This should be, when it's red, massaged and pressure taken off of it, and you should not even get more than maybe a slight breakdown, usually just the redness.

But it's only when these things are allowed to go untreated and uncared for that they become serious enough complications.

So with a good life care plan, although I can't guarantee he won't have complications, in fact I have shown for information purposes only, not for the economist, that the average per incidence cost of complications based on the national statistics, although I can't guarantee it, I can very strongly state that we can avoid them. Even though we can't eliminate all of them, we can reduce the frequency, and you can usually catch them at much earlier stages, and that's what the whole idea behind a proper life care plan is, is to save the dollars from complications.

Q. Well, let me ask this question, assuming that what the jury in this case has to do is to provide a one-time source of funding for the medical care for Richard Banks for the rest of his life. They have to provide that at the end of this case. To what extent is it your opinion as a life care planner that there ought to be some arbitrary cutoff for care at some age in Richard Banks' future, such as age 50 or 60 or whatever?

A. I may be hearing a couple of questions in here. With respect to his routine care, the things we know have to be done, all the things in the life care plan, we know they are designed in part to maintain his quality of life and to maintain him as free from complications as possible.

If you make the decision to cut him off at age 50 rather than at normal life expectancy, you are realistically going to withdraw funding. If you withdraw funding and the life care plan can't be followed, the attendant care can't be there at that level, and he can't be maintained as free from complications, you certainly run the risk -- a much greater risk that he's going to have problems and complications.

So even the patient who's healthy and doing well at that statistical cutoff, whatever reason it was applied by someone, that estimate of life expectancy, even if they are healthy, you now turn them into an individual who has a much higher risk for complications because they are undergoing a much lower amount of care.

But I stress too that there are two things I can't cost out in this plan. I can't cost out frequency of complications, on a date of occurrence. You know, they can occur and there's no way for me to put dollars in here for that. And I can't cost out future technology, changes in equipment, or aids for independent function that might arise five or six years down the road that just don't exist today. So those two things I bring up but I recognize that there's nothing I can do about them.

MR. ERIKSEN: Let's take a break.

(Thereupon, a recess was taken from 11:30 until 11:45 a.m.)

BY MR. ERIKSEN:

Q. Dr. Deutsch, you stated on page six of your report, and I quote, "It's my responsibility in a life care plan to make certain that the necessary funds are available to assure this individual the availability of such services as long as he requires them through his life expectancy. This cannot be done if funding is limited to a specialized program dependent upon a limited number of people."

What does that mean?

A. Basically it's just a summary of what I have been saying for the last, perhaps the last half hour, that it's absolutely necessary if you are going to plan through somebody's life expectancy to take advantage of the predominant cost, predominant value, and predominant availability of those services in the individual's geographic region. If you don't, you run the risk of having to short-change the program at a later date because those people are no longer available.

Q. Let me ask you to assume that Brenda Banks is functioning as a case manager and that the service she's providing is currently being costed at $100 per week.

Given what you feel to be the need for a case manager and the duties of such a case manager, do you have an opinion as to whether or not those type of services could be replaced in the open market for a $100 a week or not?

A. If we went back to page one, and perhaps if you don't mind I will grab that real quickly.

Q. Sure, go right ahead.

A. Have it handed to me here. Let me go back to page two instead of page one.

You are going to find that that's right in the ball park of what we're talking about. If you take case management services through the balance of his life expectancy, I've indicated only in the first year would it be higher, during the implementation. I have indicated $3,500 to $5,000.

If you assume $5,200 or a $100 a week for the rest of his life you are talking about $5,200 for the balance of his life. If an economist were to cost that out I think you would find that the present value of that would be a great deal more than the present value of the $8,000 to $10,000 one time and the average between $3,500 to $5,000 through the rest of his life. So that average is going to be around, you know, $4,200, you would come out with slightly higher dollars.

So it's just really taking the same money and distributing it differently, and I have indicated earlier when I talked about this page, and it doesn't matter who you are paying the case management services to, but the monies need to be available, so if Brenda is doing the bulk of that work, Brenda can receive the bulk of those dollars.

Q. Let's go back to the home care recommendations and let me try to finish up with just a few questions about that, page eight.

Do you have an opinion as to whether or not there ought to be sufficient funding or money made available today so that Richard or his case manager would have the option of utilizing the long-term supported living facility for head injured people which would be option two?

A. I think you are going to find that the answer to that question is really pretty simple. If you look at what's provided in this plan for option one, and all of the secondary costs that might otherwise be included in the slightly higher *per diem* rate of option two, that the dollars are pretty much the same. That if we utilize this set of figures in either option one or two and we utilize the rest of the plan that in fact we've given him the option for either plan.

Q. Have you had a chance to look at your entire plan with a view to answering the question which I am going to ask you now: Do you have an opinion as to a reasonable monthly amount to provide for Richard Banks for the rest of his life expectancy that would, in your opinion, make it reasonably certain that he will have the requisite level or required level of care that you recommend?

A. Yes, I ran a quick calculator, not as an economist, just in terms of present value dollars, the 1988 dollars we're dealing with here, and I came up with a monthly amount.

Q. And what was that?

A. It came out to $11,400 a month.

Q. Are you familiar with how much a monthly amount like that in 1988 will go up in the health care industry or the growth rate, in other words, that you would normally apply to these types of services?

A. Well, I think you have to answer that question in two ways, what the government statistical averages talk about and what my experience is in regards to the technical increase, and then we have to talk about it in terms of the reality of case managers like myself and what we negotiate with programs.

Realistically, programs that have provided long term supported living programs or rehabilitation programs have increased anywhere from between five and 12 percent in a given year. They have some fairly significant jumps.

You can see that when I talked earlier about New Medico going from the $250 to $300 a day in 1988, they are at $384 a day for long-term supported living now for most of their programs. That's a substantial jump.

So the reality is that seven to nine percent, even in nursing homes, is not an outlandish possibility. But when you are talking about the placement of a chronically-impaired individual over a long-term, there's room for negotiations.

I can't say under oath in a courtroom that I can guarantee that a specific growth rate will be accepted by a given facility. But I have had very good success at negotiating long-term agreements where, if it was growing at six percent, for example, if the funds were growing at six percent, that the facility would agree in the years that they went up 12 percent to take the six percent. In the years where they went up three percent, they still get the six percent.

But they never exceed the growth rate, because if they do then I have got a problem with how to pay for it. I start robbing principal, and given the principal is even available, and it creates a problem.

So I think that if we can get a six percent growth rate, I feel very comfortable in saying that I can get a facility to agree to it.

Q. That would depend on the willingness of the facility to agree to that?

A. That's true. Beyond that I would defer to the economist to talk about the consumer price index and what the government says is happening because each of the different things, like home nursing services versus physician services versus nursing homes versus rehab facilities, tend to go up at different rates.

Q. The next page of your plan, and I won't ask you to put it up, is captioned Future Medical Care Routine. I'll just state what you have got listed. You have got dental, general medical, neurological, blood lab work, and you have some pricing for that.

To what extent would you defer to, for example, Dr. Gibbons who is the care provider in Central City to talk about that?

A. First of all, generally on a future routine medical care page, it's fine for the rehabilitation provider to talk about things that are a standard of care. But if a treating physician came in even on a standard of care and gave justification for eliminating it, I certainly would defer to them, in most instances. I have no problem.

If Dr. Gibbons comes in, for example, and says the antibiotics are not necessary any longer, he was not able to tell me that when I talked to his office, then certainly I would defer to him to drop the antibiotics. If he says that he wants to see him once a year instead of twice a year, I have no problem with deferring to that.

That's particularly true for the next page which is any aggressive medical intervention. That's purely physician recommendation, it's not standard of care items.

Q. So that page is captioned Potential Complications, I think it's page 11?

A. Okay. I was referring to any aggressive or surgical intervention that the doctors have talked about and not having it in front of me, I don't recall whether we put that in.

Q. I think we talked about teeth extractions and dental care.

A. Right. The only other thing would be the future complications and that is not something to be costed out by an economist. We simply provide that for information.

Q. The last page in your life care plan has to do with transportation and your recommendation there is for a van with a wheelchair lift, tiedowns, and a raised roof, to be replaced once every five to seven years, for purposes of transportation, with a base cost of $23,000 to $25,000?

A. Yes.

Q. What's the basis for that recommendation?

A. Well, we don't want this individual left sitting inside the nursing home. We don't want him just restricted to the nursing home grounds. This is an opportunity for him to get out with family, to visit family in their homes. It's an opportunity to transfer him back and forth to physicians as he needs to.

Basically, it was something that came up as a request from the attendant care and staff. Brenda also brought it up and I felt it was perfectly appropriate, to get him out, it's part of stimulation, part of socialization, and if we're going to use the nursing home rather than a long-term supported living facility for head injured, then we're going to use that to enhance our ability to keep him out and stimulate him.

I used the five to seven years for a very practical reason, because the last thing we want to do is have a problem with van breakdowns with a disabled client sitting on the side of the road waiting for help. We've had some problems with that in the past, and realistically if you start to stretch them out to eight, nine, ten, eleven, twelve years of usage, you are just significantly increasing the risk of breakdowns and the possibility that it's going to create problems of its own.

Q. I think the last thing that I asked you to look at with regard to Richard Banks is the effect of his injury on his earning capacity.

A. Yes.

Q. Have you basically done that?

A. Yes.

Q. In order to do that, have you in essence arrived at a conclusion about what his pre-injury earning capacity would have been?

A. Yes.

Q. Can you tell us what your opinion is about that very briefly?

A. Okay. Well, one, I took a look at the age of the individual and took that into consideration. We certainly had an individual who from about 19 to 23 years of age was what we would call marginally employed. He's an individual who did not demonstrate at that point a feeling of his capacity to earn. He was vocationally immature and I think socially immature.

I think he had the potential pre-accident strictly for entry level non-skilled kinds of work and his greatest potential or capacity lay within the laboring trades.

What I did was assume that his capacity to earn was equal to a construction laborer, or a basic laborer, based on 48 weeks a year which is the statistic that the U.S. government publishes, saying how many weeks per year we can anticipate a construction laborer working. I am going to have to come forward to my file.

Q. Let me ask you to just resume your seat. I think we're done with those charts there.

A. Based on that --

Q. We need to -- let's take a break here.

(Thereupon, a short recess was taken.)

A. Okay. Basically the general construction laborer within the state of Kentucky earns in the range of $11,520 to $19,200, or an average of $15,360 per year. Now that's based on a 48-week work year.

Q. Let me ask you to assume that Richard Banks' track record up until the time that he was injured at the South Florida Fair was that he didn't work 48 weeks a year, but something less than that. What effect, if any, would that have on your opinion about his pre-accident earning capacity?

A. Well, the reality is that if I was dealing with a 35- or 40-year-old individual who had maintained that track record of being marginally employed, only intermittently employed, had chosen not to work to full capacity, I would feel comfortable in saying that the $5,000 or $6,000 a year they were earning was all they were going to earn.

I am just less comfortable doing that when you are dealing with a 19- or 23-year-old. I fully recognize that he showed poor vocational maturity, or I should say low vocational maturity, that he was socially immature, that he was a marginal employee.

What I can't do is say to you that within reasonable rehab probability that a 19- to 23-year-old individual would never turn themselves around, take on responsibility and fulfill capacity.

So I fully admit that what I am talking about here is that what I felt was his capacity to earn, was not documented by his earnings. And in that regard this represents the maximum he would have earned in 1988 dollars. And I am going to have to leave it up to others, I certainly don't have a crystal ball to say that he definitely would have improved his approach to the labor market, but my experience is that it's wholly inadequate to try and base an individual's future earning capacity on their career development by age 21 or 22.

Q. What is the dollar amount that you assigned in 1988 to his pre-incident earning capacity as a construction worker?

A. The average of that range was $15,360 a year, which is about $1,500 less than the average earnings for a male high school graduate in the U.S.

Q. Do you have an opinion to a reasonable degree of vocational rehabilitation certainty as to whether or not Richard's injury that he suffered at the South Florida Fair has disabled him from gainful employment?

A. I have an opinion.

Q. And what's that opinion?

A. There's no question that he is not gainfully employable in the open labor market, nor is he a candidate for even supported work in a sheltered head injury vocational program.

Q. Do you have an opinion as to whether or not his total loss of earning capacity as you have just described that will continue through the remainder of what would have been his work life expectancy?

A. There's no question it will be permanent.

Q. Same basic question as to the future medical life care needs that you have outlined. Is it your opinion that those needs will persist through the remainder of Richard Banks' life expectancy?

A. All those needs that I have indicated in the life care plan that would go to life expectancy will be needed to life expectancy. Those that are one time only items will only be needed one time.

MR. ERIKSEN: Thank you very much.

THE WITNESS: Certainly.

CROSS EXAMINATION

BY MR. DODSON:

Q. Doctor, I introduced myself before the deposition began. I am Jeff Dodson representing United Shows in this case. I would like to take you back for just a moment. You were talking about the things you had reviewed in preparation for rendering your opinions. Have you reviewed the deposition of Nan Mays?

A. Yes.

Q. And what about--

A. There was an additional forwarding of materials and I can read them off.

Q. If you would, please.

A. There was a deposition of Jan Fransler, 4/11/89; Michael Muscarella, 7/19/89; Emily Neff, 7/21/89, Nan Mays, 7/21/89; Upjohn Health Care Services physical therapy progress reports from May of '87 to May of '89. And an outline of the deposition of Parrot Scheinberg and actually subsequently I have gotten to see the deposition of Parrot Scheinberg.

Q. All right. It's a difficult one. So you have seen Nan Mays' deposition?

A. Yes.

Q. Have you reviewed any other depositions other than the ones you have told us about there since rendering your report?

A. I reviewed the deposition of Frank Woodridge, and just briefly one section of what I think was the economist's deposition. I also reviewed the deposition of the administrator at the nursing home and I can't even recall her name.

Q. Emily Neff?

A. Okay. Emily Neff.

Q. What about Louis Lashley?

A. I do not have Mr. Lashley's deposition, no. I have his notes, but not his deposition.

Q. All right, sir. You have given us your opinions regarding your report. Is it safe to assume that having reviewed those materials since drawing up the report none of those materials changed your opinions?

A. Okay. No, there's really nothing there more than a reinforcement for those opinions and where they would have made any difference, for example, in the administrator's deposition regarding the change in the daily amount, I have mentioned that already.

Q. Okay. Is it safe to say that your primary purpose has been to consult with Mr. Eriksen in the preparation of this litigation?

A. Well, I think it's safe to assume that my primary purpose was to develop my area in preparation for the litigation. I haven't consulted with him in any other aspect of preparing for litigation, but with respect to a life care plan, certainly my primary purpose was to consult and educate regarding future needs.

Q. All right. Along those same lines of consultation, have you consulted with Larry Forman about this case?

A. No, I have not.

Q. Have you reviewed his report?

A. No, I have not.

Q. Do you know from any communications whether or not his report is similar to or very different from yours?

A. The only comments that have been made, there were one or two comments in Dr. Woodridge's deposition, but nothing that really revealed the content. There were a couple of areas where I was presuming that his comments, although directed toward something that was in my life care plan, may have actually been based on an assumption he had gotten out of Mr. Forman, but I have no way of knowing that and he didn't spell it out.

I understand generally that there are not great differences between the two plans as to long-term care but I have not got any indication of what he's recommended in terms of immediate kinds of services.

Q. Is it fair to say that different professionals in your area may have differing opinions, all of which may be valid?

A. Certainly, that occurs.

Q. What about Dr. Raffa, the economist, have you consulted with him?

A. Other than providing copies of my reports to an economist, I don't really consult in any other way, so I haven't really discussed the content. I haven't had any questions to me personally with respect to my report from Dr. Raffa and I haven't had any phone conferences with him regarding it, that I can recall. I can look through my billing to check.

Q. Okay, if you would, please.

A. I don't show any billing for conferencing time with Dr. Raffa. It's possible I may have answered a quick question on the telephone and just not gotten around to charging for it, but I doubt it.

Q. And the same question as to his report, have you reviewed that?

A. No, I don't normally review the economist's report.

Q. All right, sir, thank you. You would agree, wouldn't you, that there are certain factors you look at in determining a person's post-accident developmental potential?

A. Certainly.

Q. Would one of those factors be things such as educational background?

A. Certainly.

Q. And did you look at Richard's educational background?

A. Yes, I did.

Q. And what did you find?

A. Basically we're dealing with an individual with a very limited educational background. He had completed the 8th grade. It was estimated by the family members because, of course, he couldn't give me specifics. They couldn't tell me if he just started and fully completed the 8th grade or not.

Obviously there was no way for me to test for post-accident development academically. So the best we've got is an 8th grade education with no vocational technical school training, no apprenticeship, no on-the-job training, basically someone who would have been limited to marginal entry level work.

Q. Would you agree, then, that he did not have a good academic background?

A. No question, when it comes to applying him to the world of work, or really any other things that would have required good strong academic skills, he didn't have it.

Q. Was there any indication in any of the things you reviewed or any of the interviews you conducted that Richard had intended to return to school?

A. No, and I did not consider that as a possible alternative in establishing pre-accident earnings.

Q. Is one of the other factors you would consider in regard to a post-accident developmental potential things such as a criminal history?

A. Certainly, that's going to be considered.

Q. What information were you provided regarding Richard's criminal history?

A. What I want to do here is try to make a distinction between what I had early on and what I developed later in the case.

I had not shown, in the early stages when I first talked with Brenda, any awareness on her part of felony convictions that he might have had. In fact I don't know what problems he may have had, misdemeanor versus felony, and I am no expert in that area.

Now I do know that he had problems, that he had developed some problems with the law and the extent to which that occurred, I don't know, but it certainly reinforces the fact that we're talking marginal employee. Somebody who would not have been in any jobs requiring bonding. Again, I think that it's still consistent with his being a basic laborer.

Q. All right. What about --

VIDEOTAPE OPERATOR: I am going to have to change tapes.

(Thereupon, a short recess was taken.)

BY MR. DODSON:

Q. Doctor, we had a brief interruption there for an equipment change. We were talking about some of the factors involved in post-accident developmental potential and I want to ask you about another one of those. What about past medical history, does that play a part?

A. Certainly. It depends a lot on what stage post-accident you are talking about. For example, if you are talking about rehabilitation potential and the degree to which the individual is going to improve from not maintenance, but post-acute rehabilitation efforts, then I think it plays a very important role.

His previous medical condition is, unless it's in some way life-threatening or requires certain constant supervision on its own, wouldn't play a part so much in the maintenance of his current situation, but it certainly would have played a role, say, six months post-injury in determining in rehabilitation what potential to develop post-accident he had.

The fact is there has never been a head injury -- in fact there's never been an injury that has improved somebody's capacity to learn or has improved their capacity to work. So it becomes superimposed on any pre-existing conditions and it could affect the potential in the long-run you had to develop in rehabilitation.

Q. And did you make yourself familiar with Richard's medical history?

A. Well, I was aware of his prior medical history but I had already also made the decision that he wasn't a candidate this far post-injury for further active rehabilitation, that there are things we can do within the context of his immediate environment to change behaviors, but in terms of trying to improve cognition, improve functional levels, I have not recommended a long-term facility for that. It could be done in a long-term facility, but I haven't recommended it.

Q. Along those same medical lines, what about his mental, his emotional status, pre-injury, was that a factor?

A. Well, we know in the head injury research that the closed head injury has the unfortunate effect of exacerbating or making worse pre-existing negative personality traits or pre-existing negative psychological problems.

Those individuals, for example, who tend to be addictive personality types before tend to have a much more severe problem -- if they are ambulatory and functional and can get to drugs or liquor, tend to have a much more severe problem post-. Those who are sociopathic personalities before tend to have a more severe problem with that.

So there's little question that the existence of a head injury raises a significant risk for severely elevating negative pre-existing problems.

In this case, your head injury is so severe that, if you will allow a bit of facetiousness, you have solved those problems. I mean there's no way he's going to exhibit an increase in addictive behavior or an increase in sociopathic behavior or an increase in criminal behavior or anything of that nature because he just doesn't have the capacity to perform any of those. It's really a non-issue at his level of injury.

Q. If you have an emotional or a mental predisposition prior to injury for self-destructive behavior such as a suicidal tendency, is that something that can manifest itself post-injury?

A. I think it certainly is. A lot depends on the nature of that behavior. Let me see if I can give you an example.

Typically, first of all, suicidal ideation tends to be a cry for help. Most suicides that are successful are accidents, and they are usually an effort for the individual to indicate I have problems, I need help, and I am asking for it.

Usually you don't see suicidal ideation interpreted as the kind of self-abusive behavior we have now. People don't bite themselves to death, for example, and I don't mean to be humorous, but the biting or the hitting of himself really is not an expression of suicidal ideation. I think it's much more an expression of frustration and a way he's learned to control his environment.

He can't control his environment by asking for things or stating a preference, and if those in his environment do for him -- if, for example, they take him to his exercises and they just start the legs or start with the arms, he has no control.

And a lot of times what you find is he exhibits that control by biting himself or if he could curse he would be cursing, but his verbal behavior or his biting or his hitting behavior is all he can control.

Sometimes we get control over that doing things as simply as saying, with his nodding yes or no or in some way indicating, if you would like to start with your arm exercises first, raise your arm. If you want to start with your legs first, you know, indicate that. Raise your arm twice. Giving him some control.

I think you are talking about two very different kinds of behavioral outcome, so although what you are describing is possible, that prior suicidal ideation and the etiology behind it can get exacerbated by head injury I don't think it's the same as the kind of abusive or self-destructive behavior, self-abusive behavior you are seeing now.

I think that you see behind suicidal ideation, depression, anxiety, and that may well have been exacerbated. It's really very hard for us to judge. And it may be part of his frustration. But I don't think that's where you are getting the abusive behavior.

Q. All right. What about age, is that also another developmental potential factor?

A. Well, age certainly has to be -- you did say age, right?

Q. Age.

A. Age does have to be taken into consideration. I mean pediatric cases respond to head injury and head injury rehab differently. Certainly the age of the individual is a factor in judging a lot of things.

Q. Okay. Let's move into the pre-injury employment history. We've already talked about that briefly, I believe, what you have included on direct. Would you agree that Richard had an inconsistent work history?

A. Yes.

Q. I believe you said in your first deposition he had a type of trial and error approach to work.

A. That was one aspect, certainly, no question that he approached work or career choice on a trial and error basis. Try this, if I don't like it, I will move to something else.

Q. Okay. You also mentioned in that deposition that he had a low career maturity level and you said that again here today.

A. Yes.

Q. What do you mean by that?

A. Basically people with a low career maturity level have difficulty developing insight into what motivates them to work. They have difficulty setting priorities. They generally will see the locus of control for decision making about jobs as being external to themselves.

They don't place blame on themselves, for example, with career problems. They may not be aggressive, or even knowledgeable about how to go about making effective career choices, making a job search, getting employed. Often they rely on family or friends to point them to jobs rather than to go out and seek them themselves.

So what you are talking about with somebody with a low career maturity level, is they tend to have a great deal of difficulty establishing jobs and careers in any other way but falling into them, trial and error.

Q. Would you agree also that in Richard's case as far as what you could determine from his work history, he appeared to just work when he needed money?

A. I am sure there's little question that was one of the primary motivators. I mean money, particularly in that circumstance, generally is a motivator, not in and of itself, but because it buys and satisfies certain basic needs -- we all have to be fed and clothed. So certainly at that time I think that's very true and that's one reason why I mentioned not only the career maturity problem but the social maturity problem.

Q. And all of these are factors that led you to the conclusion that he would not get beyond the status of a laborer?

A. That's true.

Q. Are you familiar with Dr. Robert Sbordone?

A. Yes.

Q. And who is he?

A. Robert Sbordone is a clinical neuropsychologist out in Orange County, California. He's without a doubt, one of the finest neuropsychologists.

Q. And would you agree he's an authority in his field?

A. I think that depends on how you define authority. I don't know how you define it from a legal standpoint. But I would certainly consider him an authority.

Q. All right, sir. In your opinion he is. That's all I'm asking.

A. Certainly.

Q. What about Dr. Michael Howard?

A. Well, Mike is a clinical neuropsychologist who, as of noon tomorrow will be living in New Orleans, Louisiana, rather than in Tampa, Florida. Mike is also a clinical neuropsychologist who I think is extremely knowledgeable, right up there with Bob Sbordone. Both those gentlemen -- I have enough respect for -- that with respect to my publishing efforts, both are under contract with me.

Mike is writing three books for me. Bob Sbordone has been assigned as the editor to the text from Alexander Luria that we're having interpreted and edited. So both are good neuropsychologists, both very knowledgeable.

Q. And you have worked with both of them in the past?

A. Yes.

Q. And in fact anticipate working with both of them in the future?

A. Yes.

Q. Are you familiar with the list of pre-injury predictors of rehabilitation potential and outcome from head trauma that these two gentlemen have put together?

A. Yes.

Q. Have you ever relied on that list in generating your own opinions?

A. I haven't relied on it independently, but I am certainly familiar with it and I certainly use it more in an every day context thinking in terms of that list and similar items when I am thinking in terms of referring an individual to an active rehabilitation program.

And although I can't say I specifically picked up the list and referred to it in relation to my decisions regarding Mr. Banks, certainly knowledge in that area is one of the reasons why I've stated that I wouldn't refer him to an active rehabilitation program, that maintenance is all we really can talk about.

Q. Okay. You would agree with me, then, based on what we've talked about for the past five or ten minutes that it's not possible to divorce a person's pre-injury condition from their post-injury rehabilitation standpoint condition?

A. Oh, no way can you divorce it. Depending upon your question about his needs now, they may have varying degrees of importance, depending on what you pick as a pre-injury factor and what question you tie it to post-injury. But they are never divorced. They have an influence and you are not going to make of this gentleman, regardless of the severity or lack thereof of an injury, you are not going to make of him post-accident something he never had the potential to become pre-accident.

And pre-accident status very much influences what is going to occur post- and what you can expect out of rehabilitation, what your goals would be or whether or not rehab is even an appropriate direction.

Q. All right, sir. As you said before, you can't make somebody better post-injury than they were before, in terms of their ability.

A. All post-injury does is if you have a minor enough injury then the event can change the direction in which somebody moved, but if they have the potential to do it post-, they had the potential to do it pre-. In this case he's too severe to talk about potential post- for anything other than what we've outlined.

Q. In fact you mentioned earlier that if it was earlier post-injury in this case, you would be looking at instituting a rehabilitation program, rather than a maintenance program?

A. Well, if we were six months post-injury there's no question that at that point in time six to twelve months post-injury I would be looking very seriously at it. I think I would be violating professional ethics and responsibilities to say that any predictors of outcome that we have published and on the market today would be stable enough that we can say it's not worth even trying to help this individual.

Besides, it also depends on what you are looking to accomplish. Sometimes our efforts at rehabilitation are merely to get somebody off a feeding tube or off a trach and make them easier to take care of and less expensive to take care of. But six to eight months post-, sure, I would have put him in rehabilitation.

I'm not arguing with the fact that it was done then, but I think that rehabilitation for him probably by the end of ten to twelve months of rehabilitation, we would have had a pretty good idea that what we have is all we could expect to have.

Q. And would you agree that the Rebound program that he was in was in fact a qualified rehabilitation program?

A. I will agree to that.

Q. Okay. You mentioned that you felt that in Rebound, during his time in that program his aggressiveness was reduced. Is that based on the records?

A. Based on my understanding of the records, I think they were making some gains with respect to it. I didn't say it was eliminated. He's always had the abusive behavior, but I did say that I felt that it had reduced and that it has regressed now.

Q. In addition to your involvement in this case with Mr. Eriksen, have you had any recommendations to the family themselves as to Mr. Banks' immediate care?

A. Only what I have done as a report. I mean, I talked at length when I originally was up there for the evaluation about the need for the behavioral protocols, but the reality is that unless you have got somebody who can follow through there's no sense in going into detail because you are not going to teach Brenda and have her turn around and teach everyone else in the space of a couple of hours.

So I would have to say that my recommendations at this point have been limited to what I have stated within the plan and I have not done any portion of the implementation.

Q. All right. Let me take a step back because I moved out of that area of intensive rehab before I meant to.

A. Certainly.

Q. Just so that I understand you, did you say on direct that you would not recommend an intensive rehabilitation program at this point?

A. That's right. You have not seen anywhere on my life care plan where I have returned him to what's called a post-acute rehabilitation center. I am not saying that you can't do that. Certainly, for example, if you wanted to work on behavioral protocols with this individual, you could do that.

And it is true that within a structured laboratory type of environment as you would find in a residential head injury center where everything is controlled, it's easier to gain control of behaviors. But if you don't change the home environment all that is for naught anyway.

So, in my opinion, if the primary problem we're dealing with now is behavioral, then the place to deal with it is within the environment in which he's going to be maintained. So, personally, I wouldn't take him to a head injury rehab program, unless it was specifically for long-term supported living, that that's where he was going to stay, but an active post-acute rehab, no.

Q. All right, sir. And if you had recommended that, it would be in your report?

A. That's true.

Q. Okay. You mentioned before that you saw some -- I don't believe you used the term minor, but you can correct me if I use it -- some minor regression, since Richard's movement to Sparks. Can you describe for me what regression you have seen?

A. Well, what I am talking about is just an increase in the frequency of abusive behaviors, either self-abusive or combative agitated behaviors. It's a daily occurrence with him. He uses it to control his environment and I think he's being inadvertently reinforced for using it to control his environment. People around him respond to that behavior. And that's the change we need to make.

All we're really talking about is the difference in frequency, not a difference in the types of behaviors, or in the intensity of the behaviors, only a difference in the frequency of behaviors.

Q. All right. Anything else?
A. No.
Q. Okay.
A. There's really no other function he really achieved. He was doing, I think, a little bit more, as I understand it from the records, in the way of ambulation with assistance at Rebound, but realistically what's being done now is what's going to be done.

He's not functional for ambulation. The only reason for doing it is because of the positive physical factors, the fact that it promotes blood flow to the surface of the skin and reduces skin problems, it reduces bone demineralization, it breaks up pulmonary congestion, it's good for renal function or kidney function, that's the positive reason for getting him up, changing his position, moving him, trying to get him to walk a little bit. Weight-bearing has a lot of positive physiological value.

Q. What are the negative aspects?
A. Of weight-bearing?
Q. No, sir. Of walking him.
A. Of walking him?
Q. Ambulatory.
A. Well, weight-bearing, walking him, basically we're talking about the same thing. There really are no negatives unless there's something going on medically that would be affected. Behaviorally I don't know of any. It's something that he needs to be doing. It's even good for reducing -- working with his contractures. It's not going to help him alone, but as part of an overall program.

The only negative I could foresee is if he had a physical problem, for example, a heart problem and his heart rate increased on ambulation, then I think a medical doctor would make the judgment that it was inappropriate.

Behaviorally, he gets irritated by it, but frankly, it's more important to proceed with a normal and appropriate program despite his behaviors and work on changing the behaviors than it is to give in to his behaviors and let him control it. I don't know of any negatives medically for him.

Q. What about the possibility of a fall and injury and that type of thing?

A. Well, those things exist, but you know, we don't stop work because we're afraid to cross the street. I mean the reality is, I realize that that may be a lower risk than a fall for him, but you are talking about ambulating him with one person on either side while he wears a physical therapy belt.

The physical therapy belt is specifically designed for the attendants to grab on to so they have something solid to catch him with. The third person is wheeling that wheelchair behind him. The whole thing is just a matter of a few minutes twice a day. I think the risk factor is low unless he gets so heavy that it's unrealistic to do it any more.

Q. Is he being ambulated now, to your knowledge?

A. He was when I last saw him. I do not know whether he is today. I can see on my update notes if that was addressed.

I don't have that addressed in the update notes.

There is one other issue that is addressed in here that I have not brought up but I don't know whether you would want to --

Q. Let's see if we touch on it, and if we don't --

A. Okay.

Q. You did talk about decubitus ulcers or skin breakdown. Did you see any evidence of that in Richard?

A. No.

Q. And have you reviewed his medical history to determine if there has been a history of that?

A. I don't recall any history of decubiti, I will check my notes. For a head injury case like this there's really no good excuse for it but I will check my notes.

I see no prior history.

Q. And have you also been made aware that there have been no muscle contractures or deformity contractures with Richard?

A. There were none when I observed him, I am not aware of any additional since. But he's been maintained well. They have done a good job of range of motioning him. There's no question he was at risk for those if he was left totally unattended but I think that they have done a good job.

Q. Let me hopefully briefly address some of the parts of your report and if you need to refer to it feel free to do so.

You talked about the neuropsychological review, a one-time only review.

A. Right.

Q. Is that something that you feel is essential?

A. Well, as you go through a life care plan you can start carving out those things that would be important to have but you can learn to live without. I mean I would like to see the data that would come out of that because I think it would facilitate the behavioral program and it would stop our need to do some trial and error in the behavioral programming because we would have more effective information on which to develop our protocols, but I am not going to lie and say that, you know, you would have to drop the behavioral if you drop the neuropsych. There are alternative ways of accomplishing it.

Q. Do you have any knowledge as to why that wasn't done, if it wasn't done at Rebound?

A. Why the neuropsych wasn't done? First of all, I think you would have to address Rebound as to when they do their neuropsychs and why. Normally we like to see a neuropsych done at discharge so we have current levels. I don't know that it's Rebound's policy, I have never seen them do a neuropsych at discharge.

Two, even if they had, the truth of the matter is that we're so far post-discharge at this point that to do lesson planning for behavioral protocols today on the basis of a two-year-old neuropsych wouldn't make good sense, so I simply would want to redo it at this point. That would be my recommendation and quite honestly, I do take into consideration the fact that we're dealing with a one-time only charge of a $1,000 or less.

If it were an inordinately expensive concept that didn't have any benefit or limited benefit I would really concur that it would be inappropriate to put it in, but I felt that the costs were low enough and the benefits high enough that updating a neuropsych so we could use it in behavioral protocols was necessary.

Q. Okay. Again, you are talking about updating but do you have any knowledge as to why it wasn't done at Rebound, assuming it wasn't done?

A. Well, early on at Rebound when he first came in he was at too low a level really to do a good neuropsychological evaluation. And why they didn't do any neuropsych eval subsequent to that, I really can't tell you.

Even now his neuropsych is going to be from a time standpoint and a cost standpoint lower than the average that we normally see charged for them, because he isn't going to take that long to do. He doesn't have that many areas in which he can participate.

Q. Okay. The objective of the neuropsychological examination would be the same for you as it would have been had it been done at Rebound to determine what behavior modification programs should focus on?

A. Well, it's a slightly different objective. I know what behaviors I want to focus on. What I need a better handle on is exactly how he's processing information. Does he handle visual cueing and stimuli better than auditory or tactile better than the two of those? What is going to be the most effective way of getting to this individual, of making sure he's getting the information and making sure that we're getting a response? That's really what's going to come out of our neuropsych, to understand how he learns, takes in information and uses it.

Q. All right. As far as the physical therapy, you mentioned, and I got a little confused, I hope the jury didn't, but in case they did, you mentioned at one point on your page two, I believe it was, that physical therapy would be needed, first you said once a year, and then you said once a month. Would you just differentiate about what you are talking about there?

A. Okay. What I was saying was that on an ongoing basis to life expectancy at the very least I expect to monitor the patient one time per year, in a reevaluation for physical therapy.

What I was saying on page one was the fact that we're going later in the plan to talk about monitoring him in a hospital setting for reevaluation periodically, that the physical therapy would be a part of that. That was described on page one.

Page two, what we were talking about was his immediate physical therapy program, it's the actual delivery of the therapies and not a periodic monitoring. What I was saying on page two was that I would monitor once a month and let the staff, the attendant staff actually do the daily exercises.

And I had pointed out one other aspect, which was that Dr. Woodridge had commented that he would go ahead with the monitoring of the physical therapy monthly to life expectancy. You know, you pointed out yourself, we all may have valid reasons for doing it differently. I generally don't feel that a monthly monitoring to life expectancy is necessary.

Q. What's being done now in terms of monitoring the physical therapy?

A. Well, again, when I saw him he was being seen periodically by the physical therapist out of Upjohn Home Health. I will see if and when that's been cut off.

Q. Well, to save your time, Doctor, I don't believe it has.

A. Okay, I don't show any record of it being cut off, and at that point when I first saw him I think he was just being seen one time a month.

Q. Assuming that continues, that once-a-month monitoring, is that sufficient or does he need more?

A. I don't think he needs more monitoring. Because he doesn't need a registered physical therapist to do the daily exercises. These aren't sophisticated. This is a basic range of motion and home exercise or in this case nursing home-based exercise program that the staff can do.

Q. And in fact your plan takes that into consideration, your option one plan?

A. That's right. Well, even option two, I would say to you that if he goes into a long-term supported living facility the amount of physical therapy he needs, I would consider to be a part of the basic *per diem*. I am not going to add anything in.

Now there are certain programs that would differ with that, but I would tend to negotiate with it being part of it because he just needs a very basic program.

Q. All right. The case management, let's move into that briefly. You talked about Brenda being trained a little bit further in her abilities as a case manager?

A. Yes.

Q. And then you talked about your plan assuming that another case manager would have to step in assuming Brenda wasn't there. Did I understand you to say late in your early direct that the costs of a case manager as opposed to the costs of Brenda are about equal?

A. Well, not exactly. What happened was that the question was asked of me if we paid Brenda $100 per week or $5,200 a year for her case management services, what would your response be to that or would that cost additional?

And what I said was, look, I have only allotted $3,500 to $5,000 per year for case management, so if you are paying her, you know, $5,200 a year, then you are actually using those funds that I had allotted.

The difference is going to be the amount of time involved. The per hour cost of the case manager is going to be more, but I think they are also going to be utilizing a more efficient approach to case management.

They are also going to make use of any staff members, family members, or whatever, paid for within the body of the plan to try and implement a lot of the day-to-day stuff that Brenda is going to do on her own.

So the application of the funds may be different, but the concept that Frank Woodridge talked about in his plan of just paying her a $100 a week for case management actually comes out to slightly more dollars on a present value than if you do it my way. I mean I am not going to argue the dollars with him because he's actually a little more expensive his way but in either instance we get the job done.

Q. Okay. Your plan basically assumes that there will come a target date, a day one when your plan will be implemented, is that correct?

A. That's right. I mean it should be implemented, ASAP, as they say.

Q. Okay. And when that point is reached and the plan is implemented, then all those costs are figured from that date?

A. That's true.

Q. So if you have, as you talked about the possibility that the family will continue in their present situation with dealing with Richard's problems on a day-to-day basis for three, four or five years, that's something that's not taken into consideration when you start from target date one paying a case manager, correct?

A. That's true, if they are willing to continue doing it at no cost, or at exceptionally low cost, that's true, I don't take that into consideration. I also don't take into consideration changing minimum wage. For example, if you ask me the $3.51 an hour that's being paid now, how will that be affected, I haven't outlined that in the plan.

What I'm recognizing is that I cannot guarantee, any more than you or the jury or anybody else can, whether it's one day or a thousand days that the family will be available to do these things.

All I can do is, as I said before, is to talk about what the predominant value is of their services, based on similarly trained people or less trained people in some instances, I mean we're talking about going to a home health agency to get people trained at least to the level that his current family members have been shaped up, to take over this, this is what it's going to cost to do it.

Q. Well, the point is that your plan has to take these contingencies into consideration and therefore there are costs in there that may or may not actually be needed? Such as a case manager?

A. Well, every item is needed, but the costs to pay for them is going to be different as long as the current situation continues and everybody is willing to allow that to occur.

Q. Sure, it's going to be contingent upon when the plan in that particular category actually kicks in, is that fair?

A. Yes, the only distinction or qualification I am making -- I mean I give you an unqualified yes, making sure I understand it, though. I mean the plan as far as attendant care has already kicked in. The attendant care is there. The only issue that we're talking about is how long will we be able to get the family to continue doing it at a lower cost than it would cost us to replace it. That's really the only issue.

Q. Okay. And that can differ from category to category as it does in the case management?

A. Yes.

Q. One thing we didn't touch on today. I believe your report recommends a motorized wheelchair. Is that a wheelchair that Mr. Banks himself would have control over?

291

A. No.

Q. And why is that?

A. Basically neither myself nor the family felt that there was sufficient cognitive behavioral and motor function control, particularly behavioral, to give him that kind of control. If he's hitting and being abusive now, he can cause that much more damage running his wheelchair into things.

But because of his size and the inconvenience of getting him around, what they wanted was an electric wheelchair with the control on the back handle where it could be used by the attendant who was taking him around. And for, certainly for anything outside the facility that's perfectly reasonable. Within the facility itself they could continue to manage if they were never taking him out just with a manual chair.

Q. All right, sir.

A. Now if the behavior ever improves sufficiently and appropriately I have no real objection to trying self-control on his part.

Q. That's something that you really can't sit here today and give an opinion on, though, I assume?

A. No, but it wouldn't cost us any more; you just move the control switch.

Q. Okay. You mentioned that at this point you wouldn't be willing to recommend a program that reduces the family involvement. And why is that?

A. Okay. Well, I think that I was addressing this topic on direct when I said that the patients who in the long run do the best and are maintained the best are maintained because they have a strong family support unit.

When I said I didn't want to reduce family involvement I didn't mean that I wouldn't reduce their involvement as far as the number of hours per day of attendant care. You can have other attendants there.

But to remove him geographically from the family so they are not involved in visiting him, not involved in stimulating him, in talking to him, that, I think, would be a disappointment.

It's not that the family wouldn't be willing to consider anything that was really valuable to him. But I can't state that movement to a facility outside the area would be so great a benefit to him that it justifies the compromise of not having the family visiting.

There certainly are advantages to head injury facilities that are designed for these patients, no question about it. But right now I think it becomes a slightly second best choice over what we've talked about as option one simply because it does make it more difficult for the family to be involved.

Q. All right, sir. You would definitely recommend that if at all possible in the future then his family continue to be involved, assuming these catastrophic things we've talked about don't occur?

A. That's right. At least in terms of visiting him, yes. I mean they don't have to be involved in terms of being there to feed, bathe, change diapers, et cetera. What they do need to do is be able to visit, talk with him -- and you are always going to have a family member helping to make some decisions.

One of the family members are most likely to be a guardian, and even if you bring in an outside case manager, it's not the case manager who's going to decide day-to-day changes in programming alone. Maybe that's the wrong way of putting it because programming, they probably will decide contents of programming.

What they are not going to decide is a change in the program or a change in the delivery of services or who the nurse service would be. It's still going to be a guardian who's going to have to make that final choice.

Q. All right, sir. You talked about, a couple of times now, the sitters and the family members being involved as sitters. There are other people other than family members acting as sitters at this point, aren't there?

A. Yes.

Q. Okay. I just wanted to make that clear because I didn't know if it was.

As far as the assumption on the employment, the future statistics or the future costs, loss of earnings, that type of thing, you mentioned that you are basing your figures on a 48-hour work week.

A. No.

Q. And I believe --

A. A 48-week work year.

Q. Excuse me, work year. And I believe you said that was based on the U.S. government statistics?

A. Right, from *Employment and Earnings*, that construction laborers just don't get 52 weeks a year of employment.

Q. Okay. Was there any evidence that Mr. Banks personally had ever worked 48 weeks in a year?

A. No.

Q. Okay. What type of physical activity were you talking about in terms of assisting with controlling Mr. Banks' weight? In terms of physical therapy?

A. Well, the question that was asked was whether or not there was any exercise program that would be instituted for weight control.

And what I said was that the reality is the amount of exercise that Mr. Banks is going to get being wheelchair-bound and physically uncoordinated and not ambulatory is very limited; that what limited range of motion exercise, standing or activity involvement he gets now certainly is a consideration, but the reality is that the only way to control his weight is going to be with the proper nutritional diet and caloric control. You are not going to do it by an exercise program for him. That's just not realistic.

Q. You were asked some questions about Richard's physical condition, his current condition. Do you think Richard is capable of expressing emotions?

A. Yes.

Q. And are there are ways he expresses his dislikes and likes?

A. Yes.

Q. And how does he manifest those?

A. Well, you know, he tends to express his dislikes in his frustration through his acting-out behavior, either biting himself or hitting out at people or pounding on his lap board or in some other fashion getting abusive or acting out. He tends to display his pleasure by smiling.

And I observed the whole range from smiling to anger expression, verbally, not in words, but in grunts, along with his pounding and his biting, so there's certainly a range of emotions being expressed.

He's not always, in my opinion, responding appropriately. In other words, you are not always sure why he's smiling versus why he's getting angry, but inappropriate responses to the environment are not an atypical problem. We have head injury patients who laugh hysterically with no provocation. It's just part of the problem. We have others who cry constantly.

But an inappropriate response to his environment certainly occurs. But for example, smiling with his food was a very appropriate response; it ended his more aggressive acting-out behavior. And his anger and his frustration certainly seemed to be an appropriate -- let me rephrase that. It's not an appropriate response, but it was applied appropriately to what was getting him angry and frustrated.

Q. In your opinion, should Richard's likes and dislikes be taken into consideration in deciding which life care plan should be instituted?

A. To a point. When you say which life care plan, do you mean where he lives?

Q. Sure.

A. Okay. In that respect, I think it has to be considered, and I felt that I lean toward option one in part because he was influenced by the presence of family members, that he seemed to recognize them, even when his child was brought to visit he smiled and calmed down. He seems to recognize the presence of family members, he seems to respond to that. And I took that into consideration when I said that option one may be the more appropriate route to go.

Q. You anticipated my last question. Thank you.

A. Certainly.

MR. METHE: No questions.

MR. DODSON: No further questions.

REDIRECT EXAMINATION

BY MR. ERIKSEN:

Q. Dr. Deutsch, this is Mike Eriksen. I have very few questions to follow up.

You said in response to Mr. Dodson's questions that you would not recommend what you refer to as a post-acute rehab schedule or program for Richard.

A. Right.

Q. What I want to do is make sure that we make a distinction between that term and what we referred to earlier in the deposition as long-term supported living facility that caters to head injured people.

A. Certainly.

Q. Is there a difference between the two?

A. Distinctively different. Let's talk about the phases you go through. You have your injury and you go into your trauma center. You move from there to the acute rehabilitation.

Once you're medically stable, you go to acute rehabilitation. That's within an acute hospital setting. Then you move into what's called post-acute, either residential post-acute or an outpatient post-acute.

Only then, when rehabilitation is complete, do you move into a long-term supported living. Now it may appear to have some rehabilitation aspects, but truly they are maintenance levels, they are not active rehabilitation levels where we expect gains to be made.

Q. And the long-term supported living facility for head-injured survivors, which we've talked about before, that would be the option two that you have set down?

A. That's correct.

Q. Okay. And that would be an option that you could support in reference to Richard's case? As an alternative?

A. Well, there's no question. A lot depends on the family and what the family does in the future. Certainly if one of the facilities decided -- and they are opening all the time -- decided to open one geographically close to him, I have little question that I would prefer that over the effort to make a head injury team out of the individuals we have available and involved in that community.

Q. Let's assume that Richard's family gets out of the picture for some reason, either the death or injury or marriage or geographical relocation, or any number, but the family is not present geographically. What influence, if any, would that have on your decision making or determination about option two?

A. Well, the problem you have if the family is not available is that you don't even have a case manager, in this instance Brenda, who has put this current program together, available to continue managing it. You don't have a lot of availability of in-place case managers there in his own community.

In that instance there's no question I'd move to option two. I mean the main thing that's keeping me in option one is the idea that we have family available that we could take advantage of for all the reasons I have already indicated.

Q. You mentioned a minute ago that within the context of maintaining somebody like Richard there are opportunities for different types of therapy like physical therapy and that type of thing, is that accurate?

A. Yes.

Q. And that's different from physical therapy in a rehabilitation setting?

A. That's right, because what we're doing is maintaining the level of development he has. The fact that he doesn't have contractures shows that there's been a lot of very appropriately applied physical therapy in the past and that's going to solve a lot of problems as far as complications in the future.

If you suddenly ignore that, you stop giving him his daily range of motion exercises, I wouldn't give him six months before he would reach a level of spasticity and hypertonicity, that we would have somebody that may not respond well to physical therapy in terms of reducing those contractures. We might end up having to talk about surgical releases.

And there's no excuse for ever getting to that level. It's relatively simple to maintain him on the range of motion exercises he has and keep him free from that problem.

Q. Your option two, which is the long-term supported living facility for head injured survivors, that's not a Rebound-type facility, is it?

A. No.

Q. Rebound would be the post-acute rehabilitation?

A. That's right.

Q. You have said before, I believe, that you felt that he should receive some types of stimulation --

A. Right.

Q. -- in a maintenance environment. Are there different types of skills that provide such stimulation like speech therapy and occupational therapy?

MR. DODSON: Mike. Excuse me. I just want to object because I think you are moving outside the scope of redirect, but go ahead.

THE WITNESS: Okay. Well, there are different types of skilled areas. For example, you can use a speech and language pathologist to do communication and verbal stimulation, cognitive remediation. You can stimulate the individual on a tactile level. There are visual therapists, there are OT's that do the tactile stimulation, occupational therapists.

The truth is that at his level I don't really feel we need to bring in a licensed or registered speech and language therapist or an OT or a PT, if those are things that we can bring in, using the case manager, if they are knowledgeable about head injury, using the psychologist, to train staff on the level of stimulation that's required.

But it's stimulation right now that he needs that's provided in a more natural environment. He doesn't need to go to occupational therapy. He needs to get out, he needs to be talked to, he needs to be visited, he needs to be touched, he needs to be, you know, held by or hugged by a family member. He needs to be stimulated in terms of his sense of smell, taste-- visually, auditorily, and tactily, because these are exercising those areas of the brain, and we can see a deterioration or a regression in function because of sensory deprivation.

BY MR. ERIKSEN:

Q. I was focusing more on the type of stimulation as opposed to the professional that might provide it.

A. Right.

Q. But do you have an opinion as to whether or not the tactile stimulation, for example, is appropriate in a maintenance type environment?

A. No question it is.

MR. DODSON: Same objection.

BY MR. ERIKSEN:

Q. You were asked some questions on cross examination where you made reference to a Dr. Woodridge.

A. Right.

Q. Did you understand him to be the defense rehabilitation expert in the case?

A. Yes.

Q. I think you gave some indication of where you and Dr. Woodridge agreed on certain aspects of the care plan. Are there points, however, where you and Dr. Woodridge part company on what you feel is appropriate for Richard Banks?

A. Yes.

Q. Would you outline that briefly?

A. Well, in reviewing his deposition, first of all, one of the things that he suggested would be inappropriate was the referral to a rehabilitation program. I'm not quite sure where Frank got that because I haven't made a referral to any kind of rehabilitation program.

Q. He was suggesting that you wanted to refer him to one?

A. That's how I understood it. We don't really differ. I don't disagree with him. I am not going to send this patient to a post-acute rehabilitation program.

We didn't seem to differ on the level of care that's needed; he seemed to support that. The difference was whether or not it could be -- the plan, that is, could be designed to just assume that the family would do this along with whomever they could hire to help at $3.51 an hour for the duration of the life care plan.

Q. Was that his approach?

A. That was his approach, that we would just depend on family for case management and family for attendant care, and again, whomever Brenda was able to hire, to supplement the family, at the $3.51 an hour to life expectancy. And I simply don't believe you can base the life care plan on that. We've talked about that.

Other differences appeared to me to be relatively minor. I mean he applied the physical therapy monitoring over a longer period of time. His case management was a little bit higher and applied differently, but dollar wise it came out essentially the same. I don't really think there were too many other major differences.

Q. You made a response to one of Mr. Dodson's questions that his abusive behavior -- referring to Richard's abusive behavior -- was reduced at Rebound and had regressed now. And I want to make sure that everybody understands what the term regression means here.

Are you saying that the behavior -- abusive behavior got better at Rebound and has gotten worse? Is that basically what you are saying?

A. Basically. What I had said was specifically I think they were beginning to see a reduction in frequency of abusive behavior and possibly a slight reduction in the intensity of it when it did occur, whereas now both the frequency and the intensity seemed to be back to a level that's worse than when he was first discharged.

Q. You were asked some questions about a publication by a Dr. Sbordone and a Dr. Howard entitled, *Pre-injury Predictors of Rehabilitation Potential and Outcome From Head Trauma.*

Given that your opinion is that Richard has gotten essentially past the acute rehabilitative stage and he's now where he ought to have different things to maintain him adequately, in your opinion did any of those pre-injury indicators have anything to do with your evaluation of what he needs today?

A. They really don't, because we're not really trying to predict what his outcome will be. We know what his outcome is. The only thing we're trying to do is change some of the behaviors that we currently have, but beyond that, what we have today is what we have to deal with for the balance of his life.

And in all deference to two highly-skilled neuropsychologists whom I certainly respect, we also have to recognize that this is not the result of extensive research. There are two very qualified neuropsychologists who have sat down and said these are the benchmarks we look at to help us predict outcome.

But it's not the result of a longitudinal study where we have any clear objective data like EEG readings coupled with brain behavior, relationships, being analyzed to determine what's going on day of trauma and using that as a predictor.

That is part of the research project that is now getting ready to gear up between the University of Florida, Rollins, and the Soviets. That's exactly what's being done, and in fact, Mike Howard will be a part of that research.

Q. Can you think of anything that you know about Richard's pre-injury situation, that is, his situation before the injury at the fair in January of 1985 that would have any impact on the success of a behavior modification program?

A. No, I really don't. I don't really see that there is anything pre-accident that's going to influence it. I mean the only thing you could perhaps suggest at all is that because we had some marginal functional individuals vocationally before or that we had some behavioral problems before that maybe it wouldn't be effective now, and I just don't buy that. I don't think he's going to be continually agitated and combative.

If we're going to suggest that, and I firmly believe we can gain control of it, but if we're going to suggest that we're having to deal with the current level of behavior problem on into the future I may have to reassess the cost issue here. Because he becomes a lot more expensive to deal with, particularly in a head injury facility if they have got to start applying one-on-one 24 hours a day because of combativeness.

I have no question in my mind that this level of problem in this level of patient can be controlled.

Q. When you say "reassess the cost", I take it that means you would have to bump it upward?

A. You know, one of the problems you deal with is, let's assume we're using a home health agency, and if I have a problem with a combative patient who is not easily controlled by a home health agency staff, I am liable to lose them. That is, they are going to resign and it's going to increase my cost.

It's a lot easier to work with and provide care to a non-combative patient. So, yes, I think it has the potential to increase costs, but I am also firmly convinced that I can control it, so I didn't even raise it as an issue.

Q. Let me ask you to assume that prior to his injury at the fair, back in his past life that Richard may have expressed suicidal ideation on one occasion or another. In your opinion, does that have anything to do with his present medical or physical or maintenance situation at all?

A. No. I mean the truth is that if depression or anxiety were part of the etiology or the cause for an expressed suicidal ideation before, it may create a problem post-accident at a higher level functioning individual than we currently have. But the severity of his disability would mask any problem we have with that.

I mean he may be extremely depressed and anxiety-ridden now, there's no way for us to really know that. But I don't truly believe that that's the basis for the combative behavior because it's so consistent with his using that acting-out behavior to try and control his environment.

I don't think that he's experiencing the kind or level of depression and anxiety that he may have experienced at the time that event occurred.

MR. ERIKSEN: I think that's all I have.

MR. DODSON: Well, if I know Judge Rapp he wouldn't let me do anything further so I have no further questions.

THE WITNESS: I don't know whether it's appropriate for me to bring something up, but there was one aspect that I had mentioned earlier in the cross examination that came up in the updated information that has not been brought out.

BY MR. ERIKSEN:

Q. Why don't you go ahead and tell us about that.

A. It's from Dr. Gibbons and I have not addressed this, I have not put it in the life care plan and it's going to be up to Dr. Gibbons, but he told me he anticipated moving to a suprapubic catheter program, which is an in-dwelling catheter through the abdomen.

If that occurs, then you have got suprapubic supplies that you are going to have to deal with that I have not put into the plan because no date was set, no specifics were set, and this came after the plan had been developed.

I can give you a rough estimate of what you are looking at in terms of annual cost, but it would be up to Dr. Gibbons to address whether he does intend to follow through with that.

Q. All right. Let's assume that Dr. Gibbons so testifies at some point in the case. Do you have an opinion as to the annual cost of that aspect?

A. You are going to be looking at another, roughly $950 to $1,050 a year in total supplies.

The only other problem we have is that the suprapubic care has to be done by an LPN or an RN. You do not have to bring in an LPN or an RN on a regular shift basis.

You just get a visiting nurse to come in once a week to do the irrigations and once a month to change out the catheter.

So your additional cost from the standpoint of nursing, in reality, it's probably going to cost us a once-a-week visit of about $45 and that would cover it. That would be the technical charge.

If I have got a contract with a home health agency, though, to supply the attendants, I can probably at the very least get that cut in half, if not eliminate it altogether, because it's just one visit a week to deal with it.

Q. Did you have verbal contact with Dr. Gibbons as a part of your evaluation of the case?

A. Yes.

Q. Was that up in Central City?

A. Actually, my social worker had this contact with him. It's her notes that are listed out here.

Q. Did you meet with Dr. Gibbons or talk with him, to your recollection, or review his deposition?

A. I reviewed his deposition. I reviewed his notes. I had specific questions, I had my staff member call and talk with Dr. Gibbons and he spoke directly with her. And all of these notes which were made part of the exhibit from the prior deposition are already in the record.

MR. ERIKSEN: Okay. Thank you very much, Dr. Deutsch. Certainly appreciate it.

THE WITNESS: Certainly.

MR. DODSON: Nothing further.

MR. ERIKSEN: Would you like to waive your signature, reading, and signing, inasmuch as you may be across the way?

THE WITNESS: I will waive the reading and signing and just after this is over give a phone number to the court reporter so if she has any questions she can call me.

MR. ERIKSEN: Good. We have a videotape also.

MR. DODSON: On the record, I will just object to the information that came in about the suprapubic tube, for obvious reasons.

(Thereupon, the foregoing deposition was concluded at 1:05 p.m.)

8

The Role of the Economist: Coordinating with the Rehabilitation Expert

Introduction

Over the past two decades, the presentation of evidence as to the loss or diminution of an individual's earning capacity as well as the cost of future medical and/or rehabilitation care has been increasingly entrusted to the very capable hands of vocational rehabilitation and economics experts. Indeed, it seems likely that we have at long last reached the point where the majority of all personal injury matters now incorporate the professional scientific analysis of both vocational rehabilitation and economics experts. The exact date that this milestone occurred may be open to some debate, however, the reasons for this milestone being reached are quite clear.

Rather curiously, some would argue that the use of vocational rehabilitation and economics experts can be traced to an interesting study by Jury Verdict Research, Inc., which determined that awards in which expert damages testimony was presented were 30 percent higher than the national average in cases involving similar injuries. Although this type of comparison provides a rather tempting explanation for the use of expert damages witnesses, the broader explanation for the emergence of vocational rehabilitation and economics testimony certainly includes additional considerations.

Evolution of Scientific Economic Loss Assessments

A curious evolution has taken place in the personal injury field regarding the proof of economic loss. Initially, testimony on the damages sustained as a result of a personal injury would have been provided by a physician using a physiological impairment rating such as those that can be found in the American Medical Association's *Guides to the Evaluation of Permanent Impairment*. The economic loss calculation was made by first establishing the plaintiff's earnings at the time of the injury and then multiplying this earnings level by the number of remaining years of work-life expectancy (in most cases until age 65). The calculation of the loss or diminution of an individual's earning capacity would then involve the application of the physical impairment rating (or percentage of physical impairment) to the projected future earnings stream.

For example, if a plaintiff had been earning $20,000 a year and had planned to work for another 10 years, the remaining lifetime earnings would be calculated as $200,000 (10 x $20,000). Based on a physician's testimony that the plaintiff had incurred a permanent partial disability equal to 30 percent of the body as a whole, the damages calculation would involve the application of a 30 percent rating to the total earnings stream of $200,000 for a loss of $60,000 (.3 x $200,000). Whether this was deemed to be the present value of the loss or not would typically depend upon the arguments of counsel and/or the jury's subjective impression as to the meaning of present value.

Alternatively, in some cases, the calculation of the plaintiff's economic loss might rest solely on the plaintiff's testimony as to what he or she could no longer do and what (in their opinion) the disability had cost them in terms of lost wages to date and what they expected to happen in the future. As might be expected, the success of this approach tended to vary directly with the closing argument skills of the respective attorneys.

In part, we can explain these early simplistic approaches to calculating damages as being a product of the law. Early statues were sometimes silent on such matters as reduction to present value. In contrast, many statutes now go so far as to include a "fill-in-the-blank" format for a jury to use in reducing future losses to a present value equivalent.

Surely another explanation for these early damages approaches was simply a lack of understanding, appreciation, or awareness of such economic phenomena as earnings growth rates, inflation rates, and the time value of money. The increase in the economics IQ of our population brought on by the post-Vietnam War levels of inflation and government policy experiments (to deal with inflation) no doubt forced a reevaluation of some of these earlier more simplistic approaches to economic loss testimony.

Thus, as statutes became more specific in terms of present value reduction and as juries (often with the help of astute defense attorneys) increasingly questioned the method of projecting the plaintiff's future earnings and reducing that future earnings stream to present value, the economist began to take on a more significant role.

The concept of an earnings growth rate was one of the first modifications provided by the economist. This modification reflects the fact that over the past 100 years, the earnings of workers in the United States have increased. Indeed, since the end of the Great Depression in 1933, when the average non-supervisory manufacturing employee was earning $16.65 per week, earnings have increased in each and every year, reaching a level of $341.59 per week in 1990.

Moreover, questions began to be asked, principally by the defense attorneys, as to just how the projection of damages was being reduced to present value. Indeed, many closing arguments amounted to differing opinions as to the present value of the projected loss. This atmosphere of skepticism and doubt was certainly a principal factor leading to the use of the economist as an expert damages witness.

With the involvement of the economist, economic loss evaluations moved into a new phase. The economist was now called upon to evaluate an individual's pre-accident earnings level, determine a work-life expectancy, and establish an appropriate earnings growth rate in order to project the plaintiff's anticipated lifetime earnings. The techniques used to conduct this part of the analysis involved a review of historical relationships, particularly data on the earnings of individuals over time, so as to establish certain trends or growth rates to be applied to the pre-accident annual earnings level. These same methods had been used frequently by government agencies and the business sector where projections or forecasts from historical data had become an integral part of decision-making.

Once the economist had made the projection of an individual's remaining lifetime earnings stream, the future amounts were reduced to present value using an appropriate interest or discount rate so as to take into account the time value of money. Unfortunately, having established a present value for the plaintiff's remaining lifetime earnings stream, the economic impact of an injury was typically calculated by applying the physician's anatomical impairment rating to the economist's present value lifetime earnings future.

Table 1 provides an example of the "physical impairment" method for calculating the economic loss in a personal injury situation. In this example, the plaintiff is a 55-year-old individual who had worked as an auto mechanic for the last ten years. A review of the plaintiff's income tax returns indicated that the plaintiff was earning $20,000 per year at the time of his injury. Moreover, the historical trend of his earnings over the past ten years reflected a compound average annual growth rate of 5 percent. Assuming that the plaintiff would likely have worked until age 65, the economist would be able to project a base earnings level of $20,000 over a remaining work-life expectancy of ten years, using an annual growth rate of 5 percent per year, to calculate a future value pre-accident remaining lifetime earning capacity of $251,559. In turn, reducing or discounting this stream of future earnings to present value, using an interest or discount rate of 7 percent, the economist calculates that the present value of the pre-accident estimated remaining lifetime earning capacity of the plaintiff would be $177,869. Assuming further that previous testimony from the plaintiff's treating physician reflected an anatomical impairment rating of 30 percent of the body as a whole, plaintiff's counsel would generally ask the economist what diminution of earning capacity had taken place by applying a 30 percent disability rating to the present value of the plaintiff's remaining lifetime earning capacity. Multiplying $177,869 by 30 percent, the economist would calculate a present value loss or diminution of the plaintiff's remaining lifetime earning capacity of $53,361.

TABLE 1

Evaluation of Present Value of Pre-Accident Remaining Lifetime Earning Capacity and Loss or Diminution of Earning Capacity Using Anatomical Impairment Rating

A. Present Value of Pre-Accident Remaining Lifetime Earning Capacity

Base Earnings = $20,000
Time Frame = 10 years
Growth Rate = 5 percent
Discount Rate = 7 percent

Year	Projected Annual Earnings	Present Value of Projected Earnings
1	$ 20,000	$ 19,335
2	$ 21,000	$ 18,973
3	$ 22,050	$ 18,619
4	$ 23,153	$ 18,271
5	$ 24,310	$ 17,929
6	$ 25,526	$ 17,594
7	$ 26,802	$ 17,265
8	$ 28,142	$ 16,942
9	$ 29,549	$ 16,626
10	$ 31,027	$ 16,315
Total	$251,559	$177,869

B.   Present Value of Diminution of Earning Capacity

Present Value of Pre-Accident Remaining Lifetime Earning Capacity	$177,869
Anatomical Impairment Rating	X .30
Present Value of Loss of Earning Capacity	$53,361

This approach represented some improvement over the subjective closing argument approach, but clearly the use of an anatomical rating to measure vocational impairment made this a less than satisfactory evaluation technique. Defense attorneys, judges, and occasionally an astute jury would often question the proposition that there was a one-to-one equivalency between a physiological disability rating and the resultant vocational impairment. Recognizing that this physical impairment method had the distinct potential for either understating or overstating the magnitude of the earning capacity loss, attorneys turned to the vocational rehabilitation counselor to try to provide some much needed expertise in translating physical impairment into vocational impairment.

The Role of the Vocational Rehabilitation and Economics Consultants

Obviously what was missing from this physical impairment rating approach was a means of translating physical disability into vocational impairment. As has been demonstrated in this text, this question lies clearly in the domain of the vocational rehabilitation counselor.

A 30 percent permanent partial physical disability assigned to a school teacher because of an injured right foot has significantly different economic consequences from a 30% disability rating assigned for the same right foot injury sustained by a truck driver. In the former case (school teacher) the vocational/economic impact may well be negligible; whereas the truck driver could conceivably be permanently and totally disabled--only a vocational rehabilitation counselor can make this determination.

With the help of the vocational rehabilitation specialist, the impact of a physiological impairment can be precisely evaluated and a post-accident annual earning capacity established. In turn, the economist can then calculate the present value of the plaintiff's post-accident remaining lifetime earning capacity and by comparing it with a similar estimate of the plaintiff's pre-accident remaining lifetime earning capacity, provide a precise, scientific evaluation of the present economic value of the diminution of an individual's remaining lifetime earning capacity.

NON-CATASTROPHIC PERSONAL INJURY CASES

Loss of Earning Capacity Analysis Using Pre-Accident Earnings History

To illustrate the combined use of vocational rehabilitation and economic testimony, let us assume that the auto mechanic in the previous example has been evaluated by a vocational rehabilitation counselor. Based upon the evaluation, the rehabilitation counselor has offered the opinion that the optimal post-accident employment alternatives for the plaintiff will involve light and sedentary part-time (20 hours per week) employment at or about the federal minimum wage. The rehabilitation counselor's review of the employment opportunities consistent with the plaintiff's post-accident abilities reflects an earnings range of $3.50 to $5.00 per hour.

Thus, the economist, by taking an average of the $3.50 to $5.00 per hour (or $4.25 per hour) multiplied by fifty-two 20 hour weeks, can establish a post-accident base annual earning capacity of $4,420 per year. Projecting this over the plaintiff's remaining work-life expectancy of ten years using a growth rate of 4 percent (reflecting historical annual increases in the federal minimum wage), the economist calculates a post-accident remaining lifetime earning capacity of $53,067. Reducing this to a present value equivalent using again an interest or discount rate of 7 percent, the economist calculates that the plaintiff has a present value post-accident remaining lifetime earning capacity of $37,723. Comparing the present value post-accident remaining lifetime earning capacity with the equivalent pre-accident estimate, the economist calculates that the plaintiff has sustained a present value loss or diminution of earning capacity of $140,146 (see Table 2).

TABLE 2

A. Present Value of Post-Accident Remaining Lifetime Earning Capacity

Base Earnings = $4,420
Time Frame = 10 years
Growth Rate = 4 percent
Discount Rate = 7 percent

Year	Projected Annual Earnings	Present Value of Projected Earnings
1	$ 4,420	$ 4,273
2	$ 4,597	$ 4,153
3	$ 4,781	$ 4,037
4	$ 4,972	$ 3,924
5	$ 5,171	$ 3,814
6	$ 5,378	$ 3,707
7	$ 5,593	$ 3,603
8	$ 5,816	$ 3,502
9	$ 6,049	$ 3,404
10	$ 6,291	$ 3,308
Total	$53,067	$37,723

B. Present Value of Diminution of Earning Capacity

    Present Value of Pre-Accident
    Remaining Lifetime Earning
    Capacity (see Table 1) $177,869

    Present Value of Post-Accident
    Remaining Lifetime Earning Capacity   -37,723

    Present Value of Diminution of Earning $140,146
    Capacity

In this example, the plaintiff's vocational impairment greatly exceeds the 30 percent anatomical rating given by the treating physician, and as such, the failure to use the vocational rehabilitation testimony would have resulted in a significant understatement of the actual loss sustained by the plaintiff. Obviously, in some cases this relationship may well be reversed.

Loss of Earning Capacity Analysis Without Pre-Accident Earnings History

The preceding example reflects an analysis of the loss of an individual's remaining lifetime earning capacity in a situation in which the plaintiff had an established work history. In some cases, the plaintiff will lack a substantial work history, as is the case of a child or young adult who had not established an earnings record prior to an injury. In this type of situation, the vocational rehabilitation counselor is called upon to assess the plaintiff's pre-accident employment alternatives based upon the pre-accident experiences and abilities of the plaintiff. The counselor evaluates the current earnings level for these pre-accident alternatives, such that an estimate of the plaintiff's pre-accident base annual earning capacity can be established. In the case of a young child, this pre-accident estimate may be based upon the specification of an educational attainment and, in turn, the earnings level that would be appropriate for that educational level.

Once a pre-accident annual earnings level has been established by the rehabilitation counselor, the economist is able to project the plaintiff's pre-accident remaining lifetime earning capacity in the same manner as previously outlined. Again, the vocational rehabilitation counselor's assessment of the post-accident base annual earning ability projected over the remaining work life expectancy of the plaintiff and reduced to present value is compared to the pre-accident estimate to establish any loss or diminution of earning capacity that may have taken place as a result of the accident.

Cost of Rehabilitation

Not unexpectedly, an injured party may well require assistance in re-entering the labor market following an injury. In many cases, the rehabilitation plan involves assistance that will be provided with six months or a year. For example, a typical rehabilitation plan might include:

A. participation in an eight-week chronic pain management program at a cost of $10,000; and

B. career guidance and work-adjustment counseling over the next six months at a cost of $500 per month or a total of $3,000.

In the above example, the total cost of the rehabilitation plan is obviously determined by summing the cost of the pain management program and the career guidance counseling to arrive at a total of $13,000. However, in many cases, the rehabilitation plan will include on-going support, such as individual counseling (to reinforce the pain management techniques and provide coping skills) over perhaps a three year period. In this case, the economist must obtain the base annual cost of the counseling from the vocational rehabilitation counselor and, in turn, apply an appropriate inflation (or growth) rate as well as a discount rate to determine the present value of the cost of the individual counseling required by the plaintiff.

For example, let's assume that the rehabilitation plan for our auto mechanic includes the previously detailed chronic pain management and work adjustment counseling, plus three years of one-time individual counseling at a cost of $100 per visit or $1,200 per year. Consulting the U.S. Department of Labor's Consumer Price Index, the economist observes that the cost of counseling (included in the "services of other medical professionals" category of the Consumer Price Index) has increased at a compound average annual rate of 7.46%. Thus, projecting a base annual counseling cost of $1,200 over a three-year period, the economist determines that the future value of the cost of supportive individual counseling is $3,876. Reducing this three-year future projection to a present value equivalent using an interest or discount rate of 7.00%, the economist calculates that the individual counseling program has a present value of $3,495 (see Table 3).

TABLE 3

Present Value Analysis of Cost of Individual Counseling

Year	Projected Cost of Counseling	Present Value of Projected Cost of Counseling
1	$1,200	$1,160
2	1,290	1,165
3	<u>1,386</u>	<u>1,170</u>
	$3,876	$3,495

Combining this present value equivalent of the individual counseling with the one-time cost of the chronic pain management and work adjustment counseling ($13,000) the economist calculates that the rehabilitation program required by the plaintiff has a present value cost of $16,495.

Thus, in the case of the injury to this auto mechanic, the combined vocational rehabilitation and economic testimony would demonstrate that this individual has sustained a total economic loss of $156,641 (see Table 4).

TABLE 4

Summary of Economic Loss Sustained As a Result of Non-Catastrophic Personal Injury

Present Value of Pre-Accident Remaining Lifetime Earning Capacity	$177,869
Present Value of Post-Accident Remaining Lifetime Earning Capacity	-$37,723
Loss of Remaining Lifetime Earning Capacity	$140,146
Present Value of Cost of Rehabilitation Program	+$16,495
Present Value of Total Economic Loss	$156,641

CATASTROPHIC PERSONAL INJURY CASES

In the past several years, there has been a significant increase in the use of the rehabilitation counselor and the economist in the catastrophic personal injury area. In addition to the analysis performed in non-catastrophic cases, these cases require a calculation of the present value or present cost of funding a lifetime program of care required as a result of a catastrophic personal injury. The evaluation performed by the economist involves an assessment of the present value associated with establishing a fund of money today which when invested, earning interest, would permit withdrawals matching the future life care needs of the plaintiff. To conduct this type of present value analysis, the economist relies upon the vocational rehabilitation counselor to establish an appropriate program of care, or life care plan. Specifically, the economist is interested in obtaining an itemized list of the goods and services required by the plaintiff (to maximize his or her functioning in society), the current annual cost of each item, the frequency with which the item will be needed by the plaintiff (i.e., once a year, one time every two years, one time every ten years, etc.), and the future time period over which the item will be required (i.e., is this a lifetime need or a cost incurred over some shorter duration).

Although life care planning varies according to the type of injury sustained by an individual, it is not uncommon to find the following life care need categories in a plan:

1. Evaluations;

2. Therapy and counseling;

3. Wheelchairs and related equipment;

4. Medical care;

5. Drugs and related supplies;

6. Specialized transportation equipment;

7. Leisure time/recreational equipment;

8. Attendant care;

9. Architectural modifications; and

10. Home furnishings.

By applying an inflation rate specific for each category to the base annual costs obtained from the life care plan, and using the time frames and frequencies specified by the vocational rehabilitation counselor, the economist is able to project the future cost of the life care needs of the plaintiff. In turn, adjusting for the interest earning ability of money invested today, the economist can calculate the present value of the life care needs of the plaintiff.

For example, let's assume that the injury to our auto mechanic resulted in a below-knee amputation of his left leg. The vocational rehabilitation counselor has prepared the following life care plan:

LIFE CARE PLAN -- BELOW-KNEE AMPUTATION

I. PROSTHETIC CARE AND RELATED ITEMS

	Annual Cost	Time Frame and Frequency
A. Prosthesis	$4,000	1 X every 4 years to LE
B. Prosthesis repair and maintenance	$ 500	1 X / year to LE
C. Stump socks (12 pr/yr)	$ 216	1 X / year to LE
D. Topical medications	$ 40	1 X / year to LE
E. Orthotic/prosthetic shoes	$ 250	1 X / year to LE
F. Crutches	$ 142	1 X every two years to LE
G. Shower grab bars	$ 150	1 X every five years present to LE
H. Manual wheelchair	$ 680	1 X every 5 years to LE
I. Shower chair	$ 100	1 X every 3 years to LE

II. MEDICAL SERVICES

A. Physicians, including:
- Physiatrist (2 visits/yr) $ 120
- Orthopedist (2 visits/yr) $ 144
- Dermatologist (2 visits/yr) $ 112
    Total $ 376   1 X per year to LE

B. Diagnostics $ 500   1 X per year to LE
   (x-rays, lab tests, etc.)

C. Prescription medications $ 250   1 X per year to LE

III. SUPPORT CARE AND THERAPY

A. Household maintenance assistance ($50 per week) $2,600   1 X per year to LE

B. Occupational therapy (1 X per month) $1,200   1 X per year for 3 years

Consulting the U.S. Department of Labor's Consumer Price Index, the economist establishes the following inflation rates:

Prosthetic Care and Related Items	5.99%
Medical Services:	
Physicians	7.99
Diagnostics	8.04
Prescription medications	6.31
Support Care	
Household maintenance assistance	5.00
Occupational therapy	7.46

Applying these inflation rates to the base costs shown in the Life Care Plan (using the frequencies and time frames specified in the plan) the economist calculates that the future cost of the plaintiff's life care needs is estimated to be $276,297. Reducing these projected future costs to a present value equivalent (using an interest rate of 7.00%) the economist calculates that the present value of the plaintiff's life care needs is estimated to be $122,163.

Thus, if the injury to the auto mechanic results in a below-knee amputation, the total economic loss would be estimated to be $278,804 (see Table 5).

TABLE 5

Summary of Economic Loss Sustained As a Result of Catastrophic Personal Injury

Present value of pre-accident remaining lifetime earning capacity	$177,869
Present value of post-accident remaining lifetime earning capacity	-37,723
Loss of remaining lifetime earning capacity	$140,146
Present value of cost of rehabilitation program	+ 16,495
Present value of cost of Life Care Plan	+ 122,163
Present value of total economic loss	$278,804

SUMMARY

The expertise of the economist and that of the rehabilitation specialist in personal injury litigation are complementary. The rehabilitation specialist serves to establish the impact of an impairment on the individual's immediate earning ability and the initial or base cost of any required rehabilitation or medical care services. In catastrophic personal injury cases, the vocational rehabilitation counselor will establish a listing of the plaintiff's life care needs including medical care, equipment and supplies, attendant care, etc. Based on these findings, the economist can evaluate the diminution of the individual's earning capacity by comparing calculations of the plaintiff's pre-accident and post-accident earning capacities (to arrive at a measure of the loss or diminution of remaining lifetime earning capacity). Where appropriate, the economist will prepare a future cost projection of the vocational rehabilitation counselor's life care plan, adopting base costs, time frames, and frequencies from the plan and applying category-specific inflation rates. Finally, the economist must reduce all future damages to present magnitudes, so as to assess appropriately the current value of the damages to which the plaintiff is entitled.

The use of these experts has become an integral part of an effective assessment of economic loss in personal injury litigation. This combined evaluation technique has proven to be most effective when guided by the following basic objectives:

1. To provide a factual, scientific evaluation of the economic loss sustained by an individual;

2. To properly establish the vocational impact that results from a given physical impairment or disability;

3. To facilitate the jury's understanding of the nature of the economic loss that has been sustained and the present value or present cost of compensating the plaintiff for the damage that has taken place as a result of the accident in question; and

4. To avoid either understatement or overstatement of the damages sustained.

9

Understanding Structured Settlements: The Role of the Rehabilitation Professional in Working with the Annuity Broker

What is a Structured Settlement

The term "structured settlement" refers to the settlement of personal injury or wrongful death litigation through the purchase of an annuity which provides for a series of payments over a specified period of time. It is a situation that exists whenever a monetary award for damages is made in more than one installment.

The annuity program consists of periodic payments and/or lump sum payments. Periodic payments are typically made on either a monthly or annual basis for a specified number of payments. The payment period may be guaranteed, referred to as a "period certain," or may be specified to be life contingent, ceasing upon the death of the annuitant. The payment schedule may also combine each of these time elements specifying guaranteed payments for a period certain and then to continue for the life of the annuitant thereafter.

A lump sum payment is a one-time payment outlined in an annuity program to be made at a pre-determined future date. Lump sum payments may also be guaranteed or contingent on the life on the annuitant. However, it is common that lump sum payments are guaranteed. Lump sum payments are included to compensate for large expenditures expected at a later date such as major surgery, equipment purchases, home modification for disabled persons, or educational expenses.

The parties to a structured settlement agreement include the following:

1. Owner - The defendant or casualty company who purchases the annuity contract from a life insurance company by paying a single premium.

2. Annuitant - The plaintiff or injured party designated to receive the payments outlined in the annuity contract. The age, sex, and physical condition of the annuitant are the basis for determining the premium cost of life contingent benefits.

3. Beneficiary(ies) - The person or persons designated to receive all remaining guaranteed payments upon the death of the annuitant. The beneficiary of an annuity contract may also be the estate of the annuitant, directing distribution of funds according to the will of the annuitant.

A structured settlement annuity package offers a broad range of options as to amount of payments, timing of payments, guarantees, beneficiaries, and inflation offsets. For this reason, a properly designed structured settlement annuity can provide a financially secure means of meeting such needs as:

1. Compensation for the past loss of earnings and medical expenses incurred from the date of accident/death to the date of settlement.

2. Funds for rehabilitation or reeducation programs which may include physical therapy, counseling, or specialized education.

3. Future on-going medical expenses or specialized attendant care, particularly in a catastrophic personal injury situation.

4. The cost of future surgical care.

5. The loss or diminution of future earning capacity.

6. The initial cost and replacement of specified medical equipment.

7. Future educational expenses of the plaintiff's dependents.

8. Attorney fees.

Structured Settlement Advantages

The three primary advantages of a structured settlement are federal taxation, investment, and financial management.

1. Tax Advantage - The tax effect of a structured settlement is the freeing of investment-like income from taxation by treating it as part of the plaintiff's damages. Under Section 104(a)(2) of the Internal Revenue Code of 1954 as amended, damages received for personal injury are tax-free. Whereas a present value lump sum awarded as compensation for future losses sustained by a plaintiff and/or survivors is not taxable, the income earned on the investment of this lump sum in stocks, bonds, certificates of deposit, or other interest-bearing accounts will be taxable.

    Under a structured settlement, the life insurance company invests the premium paid by the defendant and distributes the investment income together with some portion of the principal to the plaintiff as a tax-free payment for damages. It is the tax-free nature of the interest earned on a structured settlement amount that provides the principal advantage to the plaintiff. Revenue Ruling 79-220 (July 23, 1969) states that when an insurance company purchases and retains exclusive ownership of a single premium annuity contract to fund monthly payments stipulated in the settlement of a damage suit, the plaintiff/recipient may exclude the full amount of the payment from gross income. Payments made to the estate after the recipient's death are also fully excludable. To receive this tax exemption, the plaintiff/annuitant may at no time have control of the funds used to purchase the annuity, may not redirect payments subsequent to exercise of the contract, and may not own the annuity contract. Thus, the owner and annuitant of a structured settlement annuity contract is never the same individual. This element of the annuity contract, referred to as constructive receipt, is necessary to exempt the annuity proceeds from federal taxation.

2. Investment Advantage - An additional advantage of a structured settlement results from the fact that the typical life insurance company can realize a higher return on investment than could the plaintiff due to a diversified investment portfolio. In addition, payments are specified at the time the annuity contract is accepted and do not change with future market fluctuations.

A structured annuity is purchased through a structured settlement annuity broker who receives a commission by the life insurance company through which the annuity is placed. Thus, there are no investment costs to the purchaser at the time of settlement nor to the plaintiff at any time in the future.

3. Financial Management Advantage - The third (and often overlooked) advantage to a structured settlement is that the plaintiff and/or decedent's family are relieved from the burden of managing the investment of a cash award. Statistics are available concerning the difficulty of preserving the corpus of a personal injury award in a manner necessary to provide for the plaintiff's and/or survivor's future needs. One recent study indicates that 90 percent of all major cash settlements have been squandered away within five years. Many attorneys have been extremely disheartened to observe the mercenary friends and relatives and unscrupulous financial advisors that a cash settlement normally attracts. Through a structured settlement, the plaintiff and/or decedent's survivors can receive regular payments sufficient for their needs, have protection from misuse or squandering, receive a guarantee of payment, and remain free from the expense and worry of managing the investment portfolio.

The fiduciary responsibilities of the court system in cases involving a minor child is often satisfied through the endorsement of a structured settlement program. The ability to predetermine the direction of funds in a settlement award insures that future proceeds will be received by the minor as intended.

Structured Settlement Program Design

As the final structured settlement annuity contract cannot be later altered or changed by the annuitant, it is important that the pre-determined pay-out schedule closely follow the future financial needs of the annuitant and his or her dependents. In addition, percentage or dollar amount increases can be applied to reflect anticipated inflation or growth rates in the future cost of goods and services.

With regard to catastrophic injuries, the Life Care Plan prepared by a vocational rehabilitation specialist can be analyzed to determine the average on-going monthly costs and duration of medical care and rehabilitation, and the anticipated timing of future one-time expenses for major surgeries, equipment purchases, etc. (see Examples 1 and 2). With this information a structured annuity program can be developed combining periodic monthly or annual payments to provide for recurring expenses, with lump sum payments to provide financial resources for large future expenditures (see Example 2). Severely injured persons are often unable to perform daily household duties. The vocational rehabilitation specialist will generally provide an opinion as to the replacement cost of interior/exterior maintenance and housekeeping services. Household services can also be provided for in a structured annuity program by specified monthly periodic payments for the anticipated duration of the disability.

In addition, an economic evaluation of the plaintiff's damages will provide an appropriate estimated inflation factor for each category of anticipated future on-going expenditure. By calculating a weighted average of these inflation increases, a cost of living adjustment rate can be added to the periodic payments which will provide for payment increases, typically on an annual basis, for the duration of the periodic payments to offset future cost increases.

With regard to damages pertaining to the loss or diminution of future earning capacity, an economist's evaluation can provide an estimate of the annual loss of earning capacity likely to be sustained by the plaintiff over his or her work lifetime. For example, let's assume that a 35-year-old file clerk has been injured such that he or she is no longer able to perform his or her job. As a consequence, the plaintiff has lost a $20,000 per year job. Alternatively, the opinion obtained from a vocational rehabilitation specialist reflects the opinion that the plaintiff, post-accident, would likely work part-time, earning $5.00 per hour or $10,000 per year.

In this type of situation, a structured annuity could provide for the replacement of this loss of earning capacity. Payments would typically be made to the annuitant on a monthly basis for his/her remaining work-life, or for the life of the individual to also compensate for retirement benefits. An inflation factor could also be included to offset anticipated future wage increases.

Premium Cost of Life Contingent Benefits

The cost of an annuity which specifies life contingent benefits, i.e., payments for the duration of the life of the annuitant, is based on the age and sex of the individual. In addition, with regard to severely injured persons, medical summaries are utilized to determine a rated age. The term "rated age" refers to the comparable age of the individual based on his or her shortened life expectancy. For instance, a twenty-year-old individual who, due to physical impairment, is anticipated to have a life expectancy shortened by ten years, would be assigned a rated age of thirty. The life insurance company would then reduce the cost of life contingent benefits, anticipating that fewer payments would be made to the annuitant.

Security of the Structured Settlement Annuity

The payments outlined in a structured Annuity program often extend over a time span of many years. Payments can be made to the annuitant only if the life insurance company from which the contract was purchased is solvent at that time. For this reason, it is important to consider the financial stability of the life insurance company.

The A. M. Best Company provides financial data concerning life insurance companies including a description of the company, its opinion of management, a brief history of the company, and a rating based on its financial size and quality of investments.

A. M. Best provides a class rating from one to fifteen based on the policyholders' surplus. In addition, A. M. Best performs a quantitative and qualitative review of each company to provide an opinion as to the overall financial strength of the company. Life insurance companies receive an A. M. Best rating classification according to the following scale:

A+ Superior
A Excellent
B+ Very Good
B Good
C+ Fairly Good
C Fair

Life Insurance companies involved in the structured annuity business are typically A or A+ rated companies.

Many of the larger life insurance companies offer an assignment of the ownership of the annuity contract, and the obligation to make remaining payments should the company fail, to their parent company or a wholly-owned subsidiary. There is an assignment fee for this service which is typically $500 to $750.

Example 1

Sample Life Care Plan

Date of Birth: December 1, 1975
Current Age: 15
Sex: Female

1. Medical Care/Prescriptions
Start: Age 15
Duration: Life expectancy
Frequency: Monthly
Cost per year: $3,250 - $3,750
Growth rate determined by economist: 3.00%

2. Specialized Equipment
Start: Age 15
Duration: 20 years
Replacement schedule: Once every two years
Cost: $2,000
Growth rate determined by economist: 5.00%

3. Surgical Care
Anticipated date: Age 17
Cost: $ 20, 000 - $ 25, 000

4. Training/Education
Start: Age 18
Duration: 4 years
Cost per year: $15,000 - $17,250

Example 2

Sample Analysis of Life Care Plan

Description	Initial Cost	Annual Cost	Monthly Cost	One-Time Cost
Medical Care/ Prescriptions Duration: Age 15 to life expectancy Growth rate: 3%	$3,500		$3,500	
Specialized Equipment Duration: Age 15 to age 35 Growth Rate: 5%	$2,000	$1,000		
Surgical Care Date: Age 17				$22,500
Training/Education Duration: Age 18 to age 21		$15,000 - $17,250		

Example 3

Sample Structured Settlement Annuity Program

1. Cash at Settlement $5,500

2. Annuity Packages:

A. Payments of $3,500 per month, beginning one month from settlement, increasing at 3% per year, for life.

B. $1,000 per year, beginning one year from settlement, increasing at 5% per year, guaranteed for nineteen payments.

C. Guaranteed Lump sum payments as follows:
    $22,500 to be paid at age 17
    $15,000 to be paid at age 18
    $15,750 to be paid at age 19
    $16,500 to be paid at age 20
    $17,250 to be paid at age 21

10

Glossary of Legal Terms

Abandonment: Improper withdrawal from the care of a patient after the creation of a doctor/patient relationship. Generally, a duty of care continues until the services are no longer required; there is a mutual consent to termination; the patient dismisses the physician; or the physician elects to discontinue care. To avoid abandonment, the physician should provide adequate notice and an adequate opportunity for the patient to obtain substitute care.

Abuse of Discretion: Usually an act or order of court which goes beyond the boundaries of that court as defined by statute, case law, rule, or constitution.

Abuse of Process: A right of action against another who has willfully attempted to use legal process to obtain a result not authorized by law (for example, a suit brought simply to harass).

Actual Damages: The real, substantial, and just damages of the amount awarded in compensation for actual and real losses or injury.

Additur: A court's authority to increase the amount awarded by a jury's verdict. The defendant must agree to the additional amount or submit to a new trial.

Adjudication on the Merits: A determination or judgment based upon a consideration of the facts at issue, as opposed to one based upon procedural matters or legal technicalities.

Administrative Agency: An agency whose sovereign power is charged with administering particular legislation.

Administrative Hearing: Administrative hearings are proceedings held before federal and state agencies, rather than in court for example, workers' compensation proceedings, disputed Social Security disability insurance proceedings before the Bureau of Hearings and Appeals, and determinations to be made under Public Law 94-142 (The Education For All Handicapped Children Act). Such hearings are usually conducted by a hearing examiner or judge who is appointed to the position. Specific hearing rules and rules of evidence vary from state to state and it is the responsibility of the rehabilitation professional to have a full understanding of the procedures that relate to his expert testimony.

Admissible Evidence: Evidence that is of such a character that the court is bound to receive it: that is, allow it to be introduced.

Admissible: Refers to evidence which is received by the trial court to aid the judge or jury in deciding the merits of a case and determining not only liability but also the extent of the damages award. It is the judge's determination, based on applicable state or federal rules of evidence, as to which evidence may be ruled admissible or inadmissible.

Admissions Against Interest: Any statements made by or attributable to a party to an action which constitute admissions against his interests and tend to establish or disprove any material fact of the case.

Adverse Witness: One who gives testimony harmful to the party calling him.

Affidavit: A statement or declaration reduced to writing and sworn to or affirmed before some officer who has authority to administer an oath or affirmation.

Affirmative Defense: A response to allegations in a complaint which, even assuming the alleged facts to be true, would constitute a defense. In effect, an affirmative defense avoids all or part of the liability. Common examples include the statute of limitations and the contributory negligence of the opposing party.

Agency: A relationship whereby one entrusts the performance of an act to another who assumes the duty to so act. It is often characterized by the existence of a right of the principal or master to control over the agency or servant. Such a relationship may be by agreement of the parties or may be implied by law to exist under the circumstances.

Allegation: The assertion, declaration, or statement of a party to an action made in pleading, setting out what he expects to prove.

Anatomical Rating: This is a rating provided by the treating physician and/or independent medical examiners after their examination of the patient. It is usually based on the American Medical Association's Guide to Permanent Impairments. It is not to be interpreted as a functional disability, but is only a level of anatomical dysfunction based on the AMA Guide.

Answer: A document filed with the court which contains the response of the defendant to the allegations set out in the plaintiff's complaint.

Apparent Agency: An agency relationship created not by agreement, but rather due to circumstances created by the parties which indicate that an agency existed. Observors would assume that one party was acting as agent for another. For example, an emergency room physician has, under certain circumstances, been held to be the apparent agent of a hospital even though he was not, in fact, employed by the hospital.

Appeal: The Complaint to a superior court of an injustice done or error committed by an inferior court, whose judgment or decision the court above is called upon to correct or reverse.

Apportionment of Damages: The proration of an award or verdict among those entitled to receive its benefits or against those obligated to pay.

Apportionment of Fault: The proration of responsibility for damages among those whose acts contributed to the injuries or loss. For example, a plaintiff may be partially responsible for his own injury or loss and may be apportioned a percentage of fault which may reduce or bar his recovery. Additionally, where multiple defendants have each contributed to an injury or loss, they may each be assigned a percentage of fault. Depending upon the rules of that jurisdiction, such apportionment may form the basis for determining the amount of the total verdict for which each party is responsible.

Arbitration: In certain instances and by prior agreement of all parties involved in an action, a controversy can be submitted to an arbitration panel. The arbitration panel is made up of impartial persons chosen by the parties to resolve a dispute between them. This panel then becomes vested with the power to determine liability and set a damages award. For the rehabilitation professional, arbitration panels will be seen most frequently in instances in which there is no-fault insurance or in which there is an uninsured motorist claim.

Arrest of Judgment: The court's order, after a verdict has been rendered, staying the entry of a final judgment based in that verdict. It is sought as a post-trial motion where a party believes the entry of the final judgment would be in error or is reversible.

Attorney Work Product: A privilege which allows a party to protect from disclosure to another party documents and other tangible material accumulated in anticipation of, or for, litigation. The privilege is not absolute. If an opposing party can demonstrate that the material is necessary to the preparation of the case and cannot otherwise be obtained without undue hardship, it may be discovered. For example, when the only photographs in existence were taken by one side to help prepare for litigation and the photographs cannot be duplicated, they may be discoverable. Even under hardship circumstances, however, most courts will protect the mental impressions, opinions, and trial strategies of the parties. The rule has been expanded to protect disclosures made to or preparation by insurers and others in anticipation of, and preparation for, litigation.

Battery: A nonconsensual touching. For example, battery occurs where, absent an emergency or other legally justifiable reason, a patient is treated without consent.

Best Evidence: Primary evidence, as distinguished from secondary; the best and highest evidence, of which the nature of the case is susceptible.

Bifurcated Trial: A trial whose issues are tried at separate points in time, and possibly by different juries, such as liability, then damages.

Bifurcation: Refers to the act of dividing into two branches or parts; specifically, to the decision of the judge to split a trial into two separate segments in which the jury first considers the issue of liability and renders a verdict. Only if the jury finds the defendant liable is the damages portion of the case heard and an award returned.

Bodily Injury: A physical or corporeal injury.

Borrowed Servant Doctrine: A legal status which results when an employer or master loans his employee or servant to another. It generally requires that the employee or servant come under the direct supervision and control of the party to whom he is loaned. In certain jurisdictions, this doctrine results in the shifting of responsibility for the acts of the servant to the individual who borrows the servant. For example, a nurse employed by a hospital could, under certain circumstances, become the borrowed servant of a staff physician.

Burden of Proof: The responsibility in a legal proceeding of presenting sufficient evidence to prove a matter.

"But For" Test: A test employed by the fact finder (judge or jury) to determine whether an act is the legal cause of a result. The test requires a determination that, without the act, the result would not have occurred.

Captain of the Ship Doctrine: A legal status imposed in some jurisdictions which holds one responsible for the acts of those under his direct supervision and control. The doctrine is most commonly imposed on a surgeon for the acts of individuals who participate in surgery.

Case Law: Law pronounced by judges which has evolved through court determinations or holdings from given sets of circumstances, which are then applied again to same or similar circumstances.

Cause of Action: Those facts which, taken together, form the basis for seeking a judicial remedy.

Challenge for Cause: A request from a party to the presiding judge that a certain prospective juror not be allowed to become a jury member because of certain specified causes or reasons (See also peremptory challenge.).

Circumstantial Evidence: Facts from which one may infer the existence of other facts which are not within one's personal knowledge. In legal proceedings, it generally consists of testimony or other evidence of facts which would allow the jury to infer the existence of another fact not actually observed by the witness.

Civil Action: A personal action which is instituted to compel payment or the doing of some other thing.

Civil Liability: A responsibility, which is legally enforceable through civil (as opposed to criminal) proceedings, resulting from one's breach or prospective breach of a duty to another.

Clear and Convincing Proof: Proof beyond a reasonable, i.e., well-founded, doubt.

Closing Argument: The summarizing statement of counsel incorporating the facts and law of the case designed to persuade the jury or court to the desired result.

Collateral Source Rule: Under this doctrine, if an injured party is compensated for his injury by a collateral source, for example, insurance benefits such as health care, long-term disability, or personal injury protection, the amount the injured party receives from this collateral source may not be deducted from the award that the wrongdoer must pay the injured party. Further, the existence of collateral sources may not be mentioned in testimony before the jury. A clear distinction should be made between collateral sources and sources of public funding. The existence of the latter is often allowed in evidence. Provisions of the collateral source rule vary from state to state, and this is something which the rehabilitation professional should discuss with attorneys prior to testimony.

Collateral Source: A source of payment for injury or damage which was procured for the benefit of the plaintiff, but without any effort or expenditure by the defendant. Its availability is dependent of the pending litigation.

Common Law: Generally considered to be that body of law comprised of the statutes and cases of England and the American colonies before the American Revolution. However, the term is also used to denote any body of law derived from ancient custom or court decisions.

Community Standard Rule: A test utilized for measuring the required level of care for a patient. It is based upon the level of care provided by similar practitioners in the same locale (See also national standard rule and locality rule.).

Comparative Negligence: A portion of the responsibility for a compensable injury or loss ascribed to the plaintiff due to his own fault. Depending on the rule of the jurisdiction, comparative negligence may reduce the total award for the injury or loss received by the plaintiff.

Compensatory Damages: An award based upon the actual injury or loss sustained. The doctrine is designed to place the injured party in the same position he occupied prior to the injury; damages which will compensate the injured party for the injuries sustained and nothing more.

Complaint: A document filed with the court by the plaintiff which sets out the authority of the court to hear the matter; the allegations of wrongdoing; the nature of the damages; and a request for relief. In civil practice, the first pleading on the part of the Plaintiff. The purpose is to give the Defendant information of all material facts on which Plaintiff relies to support his demand. Also called a declaration or petition.

Conclusive Evidence: That which is incontravertible, either because the law does not permit it to be contradicted, or because it is so strong and convincing as to overbear all proof to the contrary and establish the proposition in question beyond any reasonable doubt.

Confidentiality: This rises out of your relationship with the client. Rules regarding both client confidentiality and right to privacy vary from state to state, and it is essential that the rehabilitation professional understand the law applicable in his state.

Conflict of Interest: A situation wherein someone represents or is the agent for competing or adverse interests, thereby dividing his loyalties among the parties or interests. Serving two or more masters.

Consent: Authorization for an act by one who has the authority to provide it (See also informed consent.).

Consortium: Conjugal fellowship of husband and wife, and the right of each to company, cooperation, affection, and the aid of the other and every conjugal relation.

Contribution: The right of a party required to pay for an injury or loss to then seek reimbursement from others who also caused the injury or loss. It is generally based on an apportionment of fault. For example, a physician against whom an award is sought may join another physician in the same or a later suit, alleging that the other physician is also responsible and should pay a percentage of the award based on his percentage of fault.

Contributory Negligence: A portion of the responsibility for a compensable injury or loss ascribed to the plaintiff due to his own fault. Traditionally, it differs from comparative negligence in that it bars any recovery by the plaintiff (comparative negligence generally only reduces recovery by the plaintiff's percentage of fault). The terms are, however, applied differently throughout the United States.

Counterclaim: A claim brought by the defendant back against the plaintiff in the same suit. The claim may be based on the same transaction or any other occurrence giving rise to a right of recovery in the defendant against the plaintiff. For example, a physician sued for malpractice may counterclaim for payment of his bill.

Court Ordered Examination: Examination of a party to litigation which has been directly ordered or sanctioned by the court and is to be conducted by a professional, such as a medical doctor, psychiatrist, psychologist, psychotherapist, rehabilitation/habilitation expert, or other appropriate expert.

Cross-Examination: This refers to the questioning of a witness by opposing counsel. Questions asked in cross-examination usually must pertain to the matters brought up during direct examination. The goal in cross-examination may be to discredit the expert witness, or to have an expert qualify his previous testimony in an effort to neutralize damaging aspects of that testimony.

Crossclaim: A claim brought by a defendant against another defendant in the same suit. For example, a physician sued for malpractice may crossclaim against another defendant physician, alleging that the other is responsible for all or part of any damages assessed against him (See also indemnity and contribution.).

Damages: Refers to monetary compensation which is awarded under the law to an individual who has been injured by the action of one or more individuals. Testimony given by the rehabilitation expert will usually be addressed to the question of damages.

Defamation: The act of communicating information to a third person which holds another up to ridicule, hatred, shame, or contempt. Defamation generally requires that the information be false and published with malice, although malice may be implied from the words themselves. For example, an erroneous statement that a young, unmarried woman is pregnant may in and of itself be defamatory.

Defendant: Refers to the individual being sued, who is responding to the plaintiff's complaint; the individual from whom the plaintiff seeks relief or recovery.

Dependent: One who derives support from another.

Deponent: One who testifies to the truth of certain facts at his deposition.

Deposition: A procedure utilized in preparing for litigation whereby the witness is placed under oath and either side is afforded the opportunity to question him. Depending on the rules of the jurisdiction, the testimony may be presented as evidence or used to undermine the testimony of the witness during trial.

Diagnosis: A medical term meaning the discovery of the source of a patient's illness or the determination of the nature of its disease by a study of its symptoms.

Direct Examination: Refers to the initial questions of the witness by the attorney who brought the witness into the lawsuit. There are rules which govern the types of questions which can be asked during direct examination. Most importantly, these questions cannot be leading, that is, they may not suggest the answer to the witness. The rehabilitation counselor should be certain to have conferenced with the attorneys who will be taking direct examination prior to the time testimony is given so that all appropriate information can be elicited in a proper fashion.

Directed Verdict: An order of the court which may be issued at the request of either party at the conclusion of the opposing party's presentation of evidence or at the conclusion of the trial. It is a determination by the court that one side or the other is entitled to a judgment as a matter of law, taking the issue out of the hands of the jury. For example, the defendant physician, at the conclusion of the plaintiff's case, may move for a verdict in his favor based on his assertion that the plaintiff has failed to present sufficient evidence upon which a jury could return a verdict for the plaintiff.

Disability: The absence of competent physical, intellectual, or moral powers; impairment of earning capacity; loss of physical function that reduces efficiency; inability to work.

Disclosure: The release of information.

Discovery versus Admissibility: A distinction between the testimony, documents or other tangible items which are capable of being found out during the process of litigation, versus that type or quantity which will be submitted to the jury as governed by the rules of evidence or the evidence code.

Discovery: The formal process of obtaining information in preparation for litigation. It requires notice to all parties and an equal opportunity for all parties to obtain the information. It is distinguishable from the informal investigations conducted by one side or the other in preparing a case in that formal discovery allows the parties to utilize the power of the court to compel discovery. For example, a subpoena may be issued to compel a witness to testify at deposition as a part of the discovery process.

Dismissal With Prejudice: The termination of a lawsuit without the right to reinstitute the proceeding.

Dismissal Without Prejudice: The termination of a lawsuit which preserves the right to reinstitute the proceedings.

◄ Glossary of Legal Terms ►

Docket: The list or calendar of causes set to be tried at a specified term.

Doctor/Patient Privilege: Originally created as a rule of evidence by some jurisdictions to preclude the introduction into evidence of information disclosed or obtained by the physician in the course of the doctor/patient relationship. The concept has been expanded in a number of jurisdictions to preclude such disclosure, whether in or out of court, to any unauthorized person.

Duty: A legally enforceable obligation owed by one to another. For purposes of civil liability, it is distinguishable from a moral obligation which is not generally enforceable at law.

Economic Damages: A term which is used to describe those elements of injury or loss which can be easily and accurately calculated in terms of money damages. These include such items as the cost of medical care and lost wages. Economic damages are distinguishable from non-economic damages (e.g., pain and suffering), which cannot be calculated with the same accuracy.

Emancipation: Freedom from control. Often used to describe minors who have obtained a status apart from their parents or guardians such that they are not dependent upon their parents nor are subject to their control. In some jurisdictions, this status allows minors, as a matter of law, to act as if they were adults (e.g., they have the right to consent to medical care).

Equitable Subrogation: A legal theory used to apportion damages among prior and subsequent tortfeasors. For example, if the driver of a vehicle negligently strikes someone who then receives negligent medical care, the driver may, in some jurisdictions, claim against the physician under the doctrine to apportion the damages between them.

Evidence Code: The codification of certain rules and statutes governing the admission of testimony or documents. It has been requested by a party to the litigation.

Evidence: Any species of proof or probative matter, legally presented at the trial of an issue by the parties and through the medium of witnesses, records, documents, or objects for the purpose of producing belief in the minds of the court or jury as to their contention.

Evidentiary Predicate: The factual basis for the opinions expressed. It must be remembered that the expert's opinion is only as good as the facts and/or assumptions upon which it is based.

Excessive Damages: Damages awarded by a jury which are grossly in excess of the amount warranted by the law upon the facts and circumstances.

Exclusionary Rule: The order of court prohibiting potential witnesses from being present in the courtroom as other witnesses testify.

Exemplary Damages: Punitive damages. A sum of money awarded not to compensate the injured party, but to punish the tortfeasor and deter him and others from similar acts. It generally requires that the defendant act in a willful, wanton, or reckless fashion.

Experiment: A trial or special test or observation made to confirm or disprove something doubtful.

Expert Witness: A person with specialized education, training, or experience who is able to provide information beyond the knowledge of the average person.

Expert: One who, by knowledge, skill, experience, training, or education, is allowed to express an opinion or conclusion which he has drawn from the facts.

Fact Finder: The person or group of persons in a judicial or administrative proceeding that has the responsibility of determining the facts relevant to decide a controversy.

Fact Witness: The fact witness, or lay witness, provides testimony as to actual events, as opposed to the expert witness who provides evidence based on analysis and the opinion formed from that analysis.

Failure to Prosecute: The failure of a plaintiff to take affirmative action (usually such as would be reflected in the documents of the court file) to advance his claim. In some jurisdictions, such a failure for a particular time period is grounds for dismissal of the case.

Fair Market Value: The price at which a willing seller and a willing buyer will trade.

Fair Trial: Hearing by an impartial and disinterested tribunal which hears the evidence before rendering a judgment.

Federal Employers' Liability Act (FELA): Refers to the federal workers' compensation program which protects special groups such as railroad employees.

Federal Tort Claims: The Federal Tort Claims Act is a federal statute establishing that the United States government may be sued in certain cases involving civil injuries. It provides an exception to the doctrine of sovereign immunity, under which the government may not be sued without its consent. FTCA cases are tried in United States District Court, with the United States Attorney General's Office representing the defense (federal government). These are almost always non-jury trials, with liability and award determined by the federal judge.

Fiduciary Relationship: In its strictest sense, a status wherein one manages monetary affairs for another and is therefore obligated to act in absolute good faith in that regard. This same degree of duty has been imposed on others including, in some jurisdictions, a physician with regard to the safekeeping of information obtained concerning his patient.

Foreseeability: A test utilized at law to measure the extent of damages for which one may be responsible. Every act will set a series of events in motion that extend to eternity; however, in most jurisdictions, a tortfeasor is only responsible for those results which would be reasonably foreseeable. For example, it is reasonably foreseeable that a result of negligent surgery will be the patient's pain and suffering.

Functional Disability: This is an area typically determined by the rehabilitation professional as opposed to the physician who has provided an anatomical rating. Functional disability should take into consideration not only the anatomical rating but all objective medical findings as well as the client's subjective description of physical limitations and the results of testing and evaluation by the rehabilitation professional. The functional disability should represent specifically the manner in which the anatomical dysfunction directly impedes the patient's ability to handle activities of daily living and work-related tasks.

Future Damages: That loss or injury expected to occur in the future for which the law allows recovery. In most jurisdictions, with the exception of non-economic damages such as future pain and suffering, the amount awarded is reduced to its present money value (See also present money value.).

General Contract to Treat a Patient: An agreement, either express or implied, between a physician and his patient which forms the basis of the doctor/patient relationship. The contract does not contain any special restriction limiting the doctor's obligation; nor does it have any warranties or agreements expanding the doctor's customary duty to treat the illness.

General Damages: Those compensatory damages which one would reasonably expect to result from an act. For example, pain and suffering and disfigurement could all reasonably be expected to result from unnecessary surgery. General damages are distinguishable from special damages, which do not necessarily result from such an act. Both are recoverable, depending on the law of the jurisdiction. However, where general damages can be alleged in general terms in the original complaint, special damages must be set out with specificity so as to put all parties on notice of the claim (See also special damages.).

Good Faith: A state of mind evidenced by the manner in which one acts. It is generally thought to be the absence of malice or purpose to obtain an unfair advantage over another and is characterized by an honest intention. For example, a physician who seeks to expel another from a hospital staff to gain economic advantage is not acting in good faith with regard to his duty as a staff physician.

Good Samaritan Laws: Statutes enacted in all states which, although varied in their details, generally provide some form of immunity to those who, without a duty to act, nevertheless render aid in an emergency.

Greater Weight of Evidence: The more persuasive and convincing force and effect of the entire evidence.

Gross Negligence: A degree of negligence more aggravated than simply failing to conduct oneself with due regard to the duty owed to others. Although some courts have merged the concept of gross negligence into that of willful, wanton, and reckless acts, others hold that the latter is a higher degree of negligence than gross negligence in that it evidences an express or implied intent to harm.

Guardian Ad Litem: An individual charged by a court with the authority and duty to represent the interests of a minor or incompetent adult in a legal action.

Guardian: A person lawfully invested with the power and charged with the duty of taking care of the person and managing the property and rights of another person, who for some peculiarity or status, or defect of age, understanding, or self-control, is considered incapable of administering his own affairs.

Harmless Error: An error committed in the progress of a trial which was not prejudicial directly to the party, and for which, therefore, the court will not reverse the judgment.

Hearsay: A statement, other than one made by the declarant while testifying at trial or hearing, offered in evidence to prove the truth of the matter asserted. There are many exceptions to this rule.

Hypothetical Question: A question calling for an opinion based on facts not within the personal knowledge of the witness but; rather, those he is asked to assume to be true. When posed to an expert witness, the questioner has the burden of ultimately proving the truth of the facts the witness is asked to assume in order to have the fact finder (judge or jury) consider the expert's opinion in their deliberations.

Immunity from Liability: Freedom from responsibility for damages or loss occasioned by an act which would normally impose such obligations. For example, in some jurisdictions, a health care provider has statutory immunity from liability occasioned by professional negligence in rendering care at the scene of an emergency (See also good Samaritan laws.).

Impeachment of Witness: Producing proof that a witness who has testified in a cause is unworthy of belief.

Impeachment: An attempt to discredit the testimony of a witness. Impeachment is usually accomplished by presenting facts which either contradict the testimony or suggest that the witness is generally not worthy of belief.

Incompetence: An inability to make informed decisions or to discharge one's obligations due to physical or mental impairment, or imposed as a result of one's minority.

Indemnity: The legal duty to reimburse another who has discharged a liability owed by oneself. Such a duty can be created by contract between the parties, as where a person agrees to assume responsibility for the acts of another. It can also, in many jurisdictions, be created by rule of law, as where one's obligation to pay is not due to his own active negligence, but rather his vicarious responsibility for another whose act caused the liability. For example, a physician who himself was not actively negligent may be held liable for the act of his employee who was negligent. The physician may then seek indemnity or total reimbursement from the employee for the sums the physician was obligated to pay.

Inference on Inference: A presumption or inference based upon another.

Informed Consent: A patient's authorization to an act which is based upon sufficient information to allow him to make a knowledgeable decision. The quantum of necessary information to be imparted to a patient will vary according to the jurisdiction. It generally includes the nature of the illness; the nature of the proposed therapy; reasonable alternative therapies; the likelihood of obtaining a desired result; and the substantial risks of the proposed therapy and of failing to undergo therapy.

Intentional Infliction of Emotional Distress: A cause of action recognized in many jurisdictions which allows recovery for damages caused by intentional conduct which results in emotional injury.

Interrogatories: Written questions which are developed by one party and are served on the opposing party to the lawsuit. Interrogatories can be served only on parties to the suit and do not provide for as much latitude as deposition.

Irrebutable Presumption: A legal proposition which allows the fact finder (judge or jury) to accept a fact as true if other underlying facts are proven. The presumption becomes irrebutable when, depending on the jurisdiction, the opposing party is not allowed to offer evidence to contradict the ultimate fact, once the underlying facts are proven.

Issue of Fact: A question regarding the existence of a fact which is generally presented for determination to the fact finder (judge or jury).

Issue of Law: A legal determination made by a judge alone, requiring that the judge apply legal principals to the facts for a resolution of the matter. This may occur in a summary judgment proceeding where one party accepts, for the purpose of argument, all facts asserted by the opposing party, but claims that, in spite of these facts, under the law he is entitled to a judgment in his favor. For example, the statute of limitations may mandate a judgment in one's favor in spite of the underlying fact that negligence occurred.

Joint and Several Liability: A rule of law which allows one who has suffered loss or injury as a result of the acts of more than one person to collect the entire compensation from any one of the wrongdoers without regard to his individual fault or contribution.

Joint Enterprise: An undertaking by two or more parties which is usually characterized by their express or implied agreement to the undertaking; a common purpose or goal; a community of interest in the undertaking; and an equal voice and right to control. In some jurisdictions, the existence of such an arrangement imposes liability on each for the negligent acts of the others.

Joint Tortfeasors: Two or more persons who have acted in concert, each negligently, in producing an injury or loss or whose separate negligent acts, though not in concert, combined to create a single injury or loss. In some jurisdictions, such activity is the basis for the imposition of joint and several liability.

Judgment: The conclusion of the court on the claims of the parties as submitted for determination. In most jurisdictions, a final judgment is the court's documentary ratification of its own decision in a nonjury trial or the jury's verdict in a jury trial.

Judicial Notice: The act by which a court, in conducting a trial, will, without the production of evidence, recognize the existence and truth of certain facts. Usually these are universally regarded as established by common notoriety, e.g., laws of the state, historical events.

Jurisdiction: The authority by which courts and judicial officers take cognizance of and decide cases. The legal right by which judges exercise their authority, over the person, over the subject matter, and to render particular judgments.

Jury Instructions: Instructions given by the court to the jury as to their conduct, the method of their deliberation on the facts, and certain definitions or explanations of the law as applicable to the case.

Jury Interrogatory: A question on the jury verdict form which is answered by the jury and is part of their verdict or determination.

Jury: A certain number of people selected according to the law and sworn to inquire of certain matters of fact and to declare the truth upon evidence to be laid before them.

Last Clear Chance: A doctrine of law in some jurisdictions which provides that a plaintiff who has negligently placed himself in danger, but cannot remedy the situation in time, may still recover if the defendant was, or should have been, aware of the dangerous situation, failed to act with due care and had the last opportunity to avoid the incident.

Leading Question: One which instructs the witness how to answer and puts into his mouth words to be echoed back; a question which suggests to the witness the answer desired.

Legal Causation: Refers to actions that directly result in the injury involved in current litigation, as distinguished for pre-existing conditions.

Liability: Refers in this instance to an individual's responsibility for his won conduct.

Libel: Defamatory information which has been reduced to a written format. This concept has been expanded to include material which has been published in other visual formats such as motion pictures (See also defamation.).

Lien: A charge or security or encumbrance upon property.

Locality Rule: A test utilized for measuring the required level of care for a patient. It is based upon the level of care provided by similar practitioners in the same or a similar community. (Generally, the availability of medical services is used to measure the degree of similarity between communities.)

Long Arm Statute: A statutory rule of law which extends a court's authority over those who are normally beyond its jurisdiction. The rule is generally invoked in circumstances where a non-resident, as a consequence of being allowed to act within a state, must submit to the authority of the state's courts to answer for those acts. For example, an out-of-state manufacturer of medical supplies may be subject to the jurisdiction of a state's courts as a consequence of conducting business there.

Loss of Enjoyment of Life: An element of damages. In essence, it is the allowance of recovery for a state of mind occasioned by a loss or injury which deprives one of the joy associated with everyday living.

Lost Chance of Cure: An element of damages. In essence, it allows recovery if a patient's opportunity to be cured of a disease has been reduced due to another's negligence. Some jurisdictions require proof that a cure was probable prior to the negligent act, but is no longer probable as a result of the negligence.

Lost Chance of Survival: An element of damages. In essence, it allows recovery if a patient's opportunity to survive a disease has been reduced due to another's negligence. Some jurisdictions require proof that survival was probable prior to the negligent act, but is no longer probable as a result of the negligence.

Malice: A state of mind evidenced by an ill motive or willful desire to harm. Malice may be express or implied. Express malice is evident from direct proof of one's intent, while implied malice may be proven by evidence of an act from which the law allows an inference of an ill motive.

Malicious Prosecution: A right of action against another who has maliciously brought a suit without probable cause (the suit has to be terminated in favor of the defendant). For example, a suit for malicious prosecution may be warranted where a plaintiff has filed a malpractice suit without support for his allegations and, as a result, the case was decided against him.

◄ *Glossary of Legal Terms* ►

Malpractice: Any professional misconduct, by error or omission, unreasonable lack of skill or fidelity in professional fiduciary duties, evil practice, or illegal or immoral conduct.

Material Evidence: Such evidence is relevant and goes to the substantial matters of dispute, or has a legitimate and effective influence or bearing on the decision of the case.

Materiality: The concept that evidence is offered to prove a fact which is a matter at issue. Any fact that is of consequence to the termination of the action.

Measure of Damages: The extent of loss or injury for which the law allows recovery.

Mediation: The act of a third person who interferes between two contending parties, with a view toward reconciling them or persuading them to adjust or settle their dispute.

Mental Anguish: An element of damages. In essence, it is the allowance of recovery for a state of mind occasioned by a loss or injury which causes one emotional anxiety, trauma, pain, or suffering.

Mistrial: An erroneous trial and action which cannot stand in law because of a disregard of some fundamental requisite; therefore, the proceedings and result are nullified.

Money Damages: The amount of legal tender determined by the fact finder (judge or jury) to be a sufficient award for the plaintiff's injuries.

Motion for Continuance: Request by a party that the trial or hearing in the matter not be conducted at the scheduled time.

Motion for Protective Order: Motion brought by a party to the court's attention to prohibit some activity, such as discovery, prior to its occurrence.

Motion in Limine: Motion brought before the trial seeking an order to prohibit the disclosure in court of certain testimony, documents, or objects in advance of their mention by other counsel, based primarily upon their prejudicial effect.

Motion to Compel: A request by a party to the court seeking to order another party or a third person to do a stated act, such as to give testimony or to produce a document or thing.

Multiple Defendants: A situation wherein a plaintiff sues more than one defendant in the same cause of action, generally alleging that they are each responsible in whole or in part for the injury or loss.

National Standard Rule: A test utilized for measuring the required level of care for a patient. It is based upon the level of care provided by similar practitioners throughout the country (See also community standard rule and locality rule.).

Negligence: The doing or failing to do something which a reasonable man, guided by those ordinary considerations which ordinarily regulate human fears, would do, or the doing of something which a reasonable and prudent man would not do.

Negligent Infliction of Emotional Distress: Tortious injury occurring where the plaintiff suffers severe emotional distress as the result of the defendant's reckless, outrageous, or extreme conduct. In some jurisdictions, the conduct must cause illness or bodily harm before damages will be awarded.

Nominal Damages: An award which is of insignificant value. However, it reflects the fact that there has been an invasion of a party's rights even though no real damage resulted.

Non-economic Damages: A term which is used to describe those elements of injury or loss which cannot easily and accurately be calculated in terms of money damages. For example, non-economic losses might include pain and suffering, while economic losses would include lost wages.

Notice: Concept that a person who is to be affected by proceedings, whether in court or by administrative or legislative body, must be aware, either actually or constructively, of the proceedings and thus be given the opportunity to be heard on those issues.

Opening Statement: The outline of anticipated proof, the purpose of which is to advise the jury of the facts relied upon and the issues involved and to give the jury a general picture of the facts.

Opinion Evidence: Evidence of what the witness thinks, believes, or infers in regard to facts in dispute, as distinguished from his personal knowledge of the facts themselves; not admissible, except (under certain limitations) in the case of experts.

Pain and Suffering: An element of damages. In essence, it is the allowance of recovery for the physical pain one has had to endure and its subsequent mental sequela. The term may also be used in some jurisdictions to describe mental trauma absent physical pain.

Past Damages: That loss which has accrued up to the time of the court or jury's deliberations on the case and for which the law allows recovery.

Peremptory Challenge: A rule which allows either side the right to eliminate a prospective juror from the final panel without offering a reason or excuse. The number of such challenges is generally limited and equal as to each side. In some jurisdictions, however, the plaintiff will be awarded the same number as all defendants have cumulatively. For example, if each of two defendants has three challenges, the plaintiff will have six (See also challenge for cause.).

Personal Jurisdiction: The court's authority and power over the parties to the action.

Plaintiff: This is the individual who alleges that he has been harmed and brings the lawsuit to seek a remedy for his injury.

Pleadings: The formal written documents filed with the court by the parties which set out the allegations and the answer to those allegations. The term generally includes the complaint, answer, response to affirmative defenses raised in the answer, third party claims, crossclaims, counterclaims, and the answer to each.

Power: Privilege of the court to act unhampered by legal rule, but not in an arbitrary, capricious, or unrestrained manner.

Precedent: A previously decided case which is recognized as authority for the disposition of future cases. This term may also be used in a fashion similar to evidentiary predicate when referring to the rehabilitation expert's testimony. For example, medical testimony preceding the testimony of the rehabilitation expert may set the precedent or basis for the expert's opinions regarding rehabilitation.

Predicate: See evidentiary predicate.

Prejudicial: Evidence which is usually inadmissible if its probative value is substantially outweighed by the danger of unfair prejudice, confusion of issues, misleading the jury, or needless presentation of cumulative evidence.

Preponderance of the Evidence: A test utilized by the fact finder (judge or jury) to determine which side has prevailed on a point in issue. Alternatively described as the greater weight of the evidence, it generally requires that one side prove that the fact is more likely than not. It does not necessarily imply the greater number of witnesses or documents.

Present Damages: That loss or injury which is now occurring and for which the law allows recovery.

Present Value: A mathematical formula designed to reduce a sum of money set aside for future events to a value that, if invested presently and taking into account investment factors such as risk, interest, and inflation, would produce a required amount when needed in the future. It is generally applied to future economic damages such as medical expenses, as opposed to non-economic damages such as pain and suffering. For example, if a plaintiff were to receive an award of one million dollars for future medical expenses, the reduction to present value would be the portion of the one million dollars which, if awarded today and invested, would likely produce the buying power of one million dollars when needed.

Prima Facie Evidence: Evidence good and sufficient on its face, sufficient to establish a given fact, which, if not rebutted or contradicted, will remain sufficient.

Privileged Communication: Certain classes of communications passing between persons who stand in a confidential or fiduciary relationship to each other, which the law will not permit to be divulged or allow to be inquired into for the sake of public policy and the good order of society, absent waiver by the party holding the privilege, i.e., husband and wife, attorney and client, priest and penitent, accountant and client, psychologist/psychotherapist and patient.

Probable Cause: The existence of that degree of reasonable grounds that would persuade a man of ordinary prudence to believe in the truth of the matter.

Procedural Due Process: Those rights which assure a fair and thorough consideration of an issue. This right/standard is generally provided for by the U.S. and state constitutions.

Procedural Law: That law which prescribes the method of enforcing rights or obtaining redress for their invasion; machinery for carrying on a suit.

Process: A means of compelling the defendant in an action to appear in court; or a means whereby a court compels compliance with its demands.

Proffer: Literally, this term means to offer, and usually refers to the offering of proof to the trial judge. It is most frequently encountered by the rehabilitation expert where an attorney objects to a portion or all of the testimony. In that instance, the judge will often excuse the jury from the courtroom and allow testimony to be proffered (offered before the judge for a ruling on admissibility). After the proffer, if the testimony is ruled admissible, the line of questioning and the testimony is then repeated before the jury.

Proximate Cause: An act or omission which naturally and directly produces a consequence. In some jurisdictions, for an act to be considered the proximate cause of a loss or injury, it must be proved that but for the act or omission, the injury or loss would not have occurred.

Proximate Damages: The immediate and direct damages and natural results of the act complained of, and as such are the usual and those which might have been expected.

Punitive Damages: A sum of money awarded not to compensate the injured party, but to punish the tortfeasor and deter him and others from similar acts. It generally requires that the act be of a willful, wanton, or reckless nature.

Qualify: In the initial portion of direct examination, the rehabilitation expert is qualified, that is, he is asked to present a review of his qualifications or curriculum vitae so that the court may determine his status as an expert.

Re-direct Examination: This refers to the questioning of a witness by the attorney who retained that witness after he has gone through cross examination. Questioning is usually limited to matters brought out in cross examination.

Reasonable Person Standard: A test often used by the fact finder (judge or jury) to measure conduct in their determination of negligence. The general level of care expected of individuals under the same or similar circumstances.

Reasonable Probability versus Certainty: Something which is reasonably probable if the mental impressions, conclusions, opinions, or legal theories of an attorney or other representative of a party concerning the litigation.

Reasonable Probability: In most states, the expert witness, whether medical, psychological, or rehabilitation, is often asked to state his final conclusions within a reasonable medical, reasonable psychological, or reasonable rehabilitation probability. Although a wide range of possibilities may occur, it is up to the expert as to whether or not his opinion or conclusion is within reasonable probability within the guidelines of the profession. It is not easy to define "reasonable", and certainly there may be some latitude on the part of the expert. Generally, the conclusion can be considered to meet the criteria of reasonable probability if the expert feels his opinion or conclusion is based on sound fact and evidentiary predicate, is rational, can be well analyzed, and can be fairly and reasonably expected as the outcome. This burden of reasonable probability can be based on the expert's experience in working with similar cases, his training and expertise. Making a determination of reasonable probability should not be taken lightly by the rehabilitation expert; the expert should be prepared to document his conclusion based on all of the data used to formulate his opinion.

Rebuttable Presumptions: A legal presumption is a rule which allows the fact finder (judge or jury) to accept a fact as true if other underlying facts are proven. It is rebuttable when, depending on the jurisdiction, the party opposing the presumed fact is allowed to offer evidence to contradict it.

Rebuttal Evidence: In its most general sense, evidence offered to contradict a matter an opposing party is attempting to establish. In practice, depending on the jurisdiction, it is allowed, after one's initial presentation of evidence, to refute a position taken by an opposing party which was not expected. For example, once a plaintiff completes his case, if the defendant offers evidence to support a defense not previously addressed or contemplated by the plaintiff, the court may allow the plaintiff an opportunity to present rebuttal evidence to the unanticipated defense.

Rebuttal Witness: At the end of a trial, time is allowed for either side to present witnesses designed to refute or oppose conclusions presented by witnesses for the other side.

Record of Case: A history of the proceedings on the trial of the action put in the court file and transcripts of testimony.

Re-hearing: A second consideration of cause for the sole purpose of calling the court's attention to any error, omission, or oversight in the first consideration.

Release: The relinquishment, concession, or giving up of a right, claim, or privilege by the person in whom it exists or to whom it accrues to the person against whom it might have been demanded or enforced.

Relevancy: Relevant evidence must have a logical tendency to prove or disprove a fact which is of consequence to the outcome of the action.

Remittitur: A court's authority to decrease the amount awarded by a jury's verdict. The plaintiff must agree to the reduced award or submit to a new trial.

Request for Admissions: A pleading propounded on a party seeking to establish, by acknowledgment or recognition, the truth of some matter alleged within it, the effect of which is to narrow the area of facts or allegations required to be proved by the evidence.

Request for Production: Formal requests, generally in writing, propounded against other parties to an action, demanding that they produce, for inspection or copying, items or documents in their custody, control, or possession. They are frequently utilized during preparation for trial to allow all parties equal access to relevant items which are not otherwise privileged.

Request for Records: A request for documentary evidence on a particular matter.

Requests for Admission: Formal requests, generally in writing, propounded against other parties to the action, demanding that they either admit or deny certain matters. They are frequently utilized during preparation for litigation to avoid the need to prove matters over which there is no real controversy and to narrow issues for trial.

Res Gestae: Those circumstances which are the automatic and undesigned incidents of a particular litigated act, which may be separated from the act by a lapse of time, more or less appreciable, and which are admissible when illustrative of such act.

Res Ipsa Loquitur: Literally, "the thing speaks for itself." A rule of evidence which allows a fact finder (judge or jury) to assume negligence when the instrument causing the injury was in the control of the defendant, and when the incident does not ordinarily occur without negligence. For example, depending on the jurisdiction, pursuant to the doctrine of res ipsa loquitur, a jury may infer the existence of negligence on the part of a surgeon from the fact that a sponge was left in the patient; no other proof would be required. It is generally a rebuttable presumption which allows the defendant an opportunity to attempt to disprove his presumed negligence.

Respondeat Superior: Literally, "let the master answer." A rule which holds a master liable for the acts of his servant, an employer for the acts of his employee, and a principal for the acts of his agent. It requires that the act for which the master, employer, or principal is held liable be done within the scope of the business. For example, a physician may be liable for the acts of his employed nurse in treating one of his patients.

Responsive Pleading: A formal written answer to allegations set out in a pleading filed by another party.

Right to Read and Sign: Many experts providing testimony do not realize they have the right to read and sign the typed transcript of their deposition before it is submitted to the parties involved in the lawsuit. Although in many instances experts will waive this right, it should not be done lightly. If the expert has reason to believe that the court reporter has had difficulty in transcribing the testimony or is concerned about its accuracy, this right should be exercised. The expert does not have the right to change the content or meaning of passages in the deposition, but does have the right before signing to correct spelling and sentence structure.

Sanctions: A judicial decree or order which inflicts a penalty for the failure to obey a court's requirements.

Service of Process: Delivery pursuant to the procedural rules of the jurisdiction of a document authorized by the law of the jurisdiction which commands the individual or entity to act or refrain from acting in a particular manner. For example, service of process accompanied by a complaint generally requires the individual named in the complaint to respond to the allegations within a set number of days.

Service: The exhibition or delivery of a writ, notice, injunction, summons, or subpoena by authorized person to a person which is thereby officially notified of some action or proceeding in which he is concerned, and is thereby advised or warned of some action or step which he is commanded to take or to forbear.

Settlement: Generally, the compromise of a disputed claim without a decision by a court or jury.

Shall: As used in statutes, contracts of the like, generally imperative or mandatory.

Sham Pleading: One good in form, but false in fact.

Show Cause: Against a rule nisi, an order, degree of execution, is to appear as directed and to present to the court such reasons and consideration as one has to offer why it should not be confirmed, take effect, be executed, or as the case may be.

Show: To make apparent or clear by evidence some goal to prove.

Slander Defamatory: Information which has been published orally (See also defamation and libel.).

Special Contract to Treat Patient: An agreement, either express or implied, between a physician and his patient which forms the basis of the doctor/patient relationship, but contains restrictions limiting the physicians's duty or warranties expanding the physician's duty. For example, a physician may provide that he will not treat hospital in-patients, but rather refer those in need of such care to others.

Special Damages: Those damages which are the natural, but not the necessary, result of the injuries. Special damages must be alleged in the complaint with specificity so as to put all parties on notice of the claim, while general damages can be set out in general terms (See also general damages.).

Special Law: One relating to particular persons or things, one made for individual cases or a particular place or district, one operating in a selective class, rather than for the public generally.

Standard of Care: The level of conduct against which one's acts are measured to determine liability.

Stare Decisis: The abide by or adhere to decided cases. Policy of the court to stand by a precedent and not to disturb settled points. Doctrine that when a court has once laid down a principle, the law is put in a certain state of facts and will adhere to that principle and apply it to all future cases where facts are substantially the same.

State Civil Court: This is the forum in which most personal injury and medical malpractice claims will be heard. Most cases in state civil court are tried before a jury for the purpose of establishing liability and settling damages.

Statute of Limitations: The time within which a claim must be brought. The period is generally established by statute and varies according to the type of claim at issue. For example, the statute of limitations might be different for professional malpractice as opposed to other types of negligence actions.

Statutory Law: Law which is enacted by legislative bodies.

Stipulation: The name given to an agreement by the attorneys engaged on opposite sides of a cause regulating any manner incidental to the proceedings or trial which falls within their jurisdiction, usually in writing.

Structured Settlements: A method of paying an agreed upon amount which generally allows the payments to be made periodically in pre-determined amounts.

Subject Matter Jurisdiction: The authority of the court over the issue or type of case in controversy.

Subpoena Duces Tecum: The additional term "Duces Tecum" on a subpoena simply requires the expert witness to bring with him to the proceeding any and all relevant records produced in connection with the expert's work with the client (plaintiff).

Subpoena/Expert Witness Fee: In most states, subpoenas must be accompanied by a statutory fee for mileage and/or *per diem*. The failure to attach this statutory fee represents an improper service of the subpoena. Courts do not agree, however, as to whether expert witnesses must be paid additional compensation over and above the statutory minimum, or whether the expert may refuse to testify if an additional fee is not paid. It is strongly recommended that the expert establish in writing with the party submitting the subpoena his usual and customary fees for testimony, before the expert testifies at deposition or trial. If an understanding cannot be reached in advance, the expert should not simply ignore the subpoena. If the expert is subpoenaed but it is clear that his customary fee is not going to be paid, many courts hold that the individual cannot be pressed into providing expert testimony, although some have held that the expert may be required to testify without additional compensation. Again, this does not mean that the expert should fail to respond to the subpoena, but it does suggest that the expert can seek a remedy through the court by allowing the judge to determine an appropriate fee and/or whether or not expert testimony should be given in the absence of a fee agreement. Generally expert witness fees include the time necessary to review the file and prepare for testimony; travel time, portal to portal; and the actual time spent testifying at the deposition or at trial.

Subpoena/Proper Service: Rules governing the proper service of a subpoena vary from state to state. It remains the responsibility of the rehabilitation expert to determine the rules that prevail in his area. In most states, the subpoena must be served upon the person, and not left with the secretary or office manager, which is often done to avoid disturbing the expert but does not always represent proper service. It must be stressed that the expert witness does have certain fundamental rights regarding service with a subpoena. Although court rules rarely specify a minimum time period between the time the witness is served and the time he must testify, it is customary for the expert to be given sufficient time to make arrangements in his schedule. If a conflict develops and the expert is unable to work this out with the attorney, then he has the right to seek the assistance of the court in changing the time. It should also be noted that the individual issuing the subpoena does not have the right to force the expert to travel anywhere he so desires to provide testimony. Rules in many states provide that a witness is not compelled to attend a deposition or trial where the witness would be required to travel from out of state, from another county, or from distances greater than 100 miles. Of course, certain common courtesies are usually maintained between attorneys and professionals who are called upon for expert testimony; thus, attorneys often permit depositions to be taken in the expert's own office. But, in the event that you are subpoenaed directly to an attorney's office and don't wish to have the deposition conducted at that location, it may be possible to seek resolution of this problem through the court.

Subpoena: A writ which is issued under the authority of a court and which compels a witness to appear in a judicial proceeding (trial, hearing, or deposition) for the purpose of giving testimony. A subpoena may be issued strictly for records pickup, and is then usually issued to the custodian of records. This type of subpoena is designed to order the custodian of records to produce an original or copy of records which exist in the office. It is strongly recommended that, upon receipt of this type of subpoena, the rehabilitation professional first contact the client or his attorney to determine the appropriateness of producing the record and to ascertain specifically what portions of the record may be covered by the subpoena. To simply produce the records in full without contacting the client or the attorney may violate state laws regarding client confidentiality and right to privacy. Issues involving work product may also come into play. For this reason, consultation with responsible party or referral source is essential.

Subrogation: The right to a claim previously held by another. For example, if an insurer pays a claim on behalf of its insured physician, it may become subrogated to the physician's rights. This may include the right previously held by the physician to sue another person who was also at fault for a pro-rata portion of the damages.

Substantive Due Process: In general, those rights which spring from the U.S. Constitutional guarantees found in the Fifth and Fourteenth Amendments, that no person may be deprived of life, liberty, or property without due process of law. It is distinguishable from procedural due process, which guarantees a fair method for determining whether one's substantive rights have been violated.

Substantive Law: That part of law which creates, defines, and regulates rights, as opposed to a remedial law, which prescribes the method of enforcing the rights or obtaining redress for their invasion.

Summary Judgment: A procedure whereby either party may, if there is no controverted issues of fact, submit a matter to a judge alone for his determination. In essence, the party is asking the judge to apply the law to the facts and render a judgment. It may be sought as to the entire or any part of the dispute. For example, a court may determine by summary judgment that one side is liable to the other, but leave the issue of damages for a later trial. Summary judgment is difficult to obtain in negligence actions.

Summons: A writ directed to the sheriff or other proper officer requiring him to notify the person named that an action has been commenced against him in the court whence the writ issues and requiring him to appear on the day named and to answer the complaint in such action.

Swear: To put an oath; to administer an oath to a person.

Sworn Statement: The sworn oral testimony of a witness obtained under circumstances less formal than a deposition.

Taxable Costs: The allowance made to the successful party and recoverable from the losing party for the expenses in prosecuting or defending a suit.

Testimony: Evidence given by a competent witness, under oath, as distinguished from evidence derived from writings and other sources.

Therapeutic Privilege: An exception to the rule that an informed consent must be obtained prior to therapy. It generally requires that the disclosure of information would likely worsen the patient's condition or render him so emotionally distraught as to hinder effective therapy. It is not an excuse to omit disclosure due to the physician's concern that a competent patient will elect to forego the care. In certain jurisdictions, disclosure to the next of kin is required.

Third Party Claim or Action: A claim filed by a defendant against a person or entity who was not originally named in the suit. For example, in a suit by a patient against a physician, the physician defendant may elect to file a third party claim against the manufacturers of a medical instrument, claiming that it also was at fault and liable for all or a portion of the plaintiff's injuries.

Third Party: Refers to someone other than the plaintiff or defendant whose rights may be affected by the litigation. In personal injury litigation, the third party is generally the insurance company which represents one of the parties.

Tolling: To stay or stop. The term is generally used in issues involving the statute of limitations. For example, depending on the jurisdiction, when a potential defendant leaves the state, the time within which a plaintiff has to file suit may be tolled or stayed, and does not begin to run again until he returns to the court's jurisdiction.

Tort: A wrong or injury. Requires the existence of a legal duty from defendant to plaintiff, break of duty and damage as a proximate result.

Tortfeasor: A person or entity who has committed a civil wrong, other than breach of contract, resulting in loss or injury and for which there is a judicial remedy.

Transcript: An official, certified copy of what has transpired in a deposition or court testimony. A transcript is prepared by a court reporter and may be used for a later appeal of a jury's verdict.

Ultimate Facts: Facts essential to the right of action or matter of defense, usually to be determined by the jury.

Uniform Laws: A considerable number of laws which have been approved by the National Conference of Commissioners on Uniform State Laws and have then been adopted by one or more jurisdictions in the United States and its possessions.

Venire: The panel of individuals summoned to court from which a jury is to be selected.

Venue Jurisdiction: Power of the particular court to function.

Venue: The locale in which a court with authority over the persons and subject matter may hear cases. It is the geographical area within which the action may be brought. For example, jurisdiction (the authority of the court to hear a matter) may lie in several counties. The statute setting out venue, however, may require that in the interest of justice, judicial economy, and/or for the convenience of the parties and witnesses, it may be brought in only one of these counties.

Verdict: The formal decision or finding made by a jury, and reported to the court and accepted by it upon the matters or questions duly submitted to them upon the trial, either in a general or a special form or question.

Vicarious Liability: Often referred to as passive or secondary negligence, this term refers to the responsibility for injury or loss imposed on one for the acts of another with whom he has a requisite relationship. For example, an employer is vicariously liable for the negligent acts of an employee committed in the course of employment.

Vicarious Negligence: See vicarious liability.

Voir Dire: Literally means to speak the truth. Although *voir dire* often refers to the examination of prospective jurors by the court or attorneys, it is also frequently encountered by rehabilitation professionals during the qualification portion of their testimony. The opposing counsel has the right to "*voir dire*" the witness -- that is, to ask specific questions regarding qualifications before the court determines whether the individual will be allowed to testify as an expert in his profession.

Voluntary Dismissal: A termination of a cause of action by the plaintiff, without a court order, before a determination of its merits. If done with prejudice, the action may not be reinstituted. If done without prejudice, the action may be refiled.

Waiver: The intentional voluntary relinquishment of a known right.

Wanton Misconduct: See willful misconduct.

Warrant: This term generally means to guarantee or promise (for example, to warrant a cure).

Warranty: See warrant.

Willful Misconduct: Conduct which is motivated by an intent to accomplish the end result or which is of such a reckless character that the law implies such an intent. For example, rendering medical care when one knows, or should know, that a patient is mentally impaired due to the use of drugs or alcohol may be considered such conduct.

Work Product: Any material prepared by the attorney in preparation for litigation, including material arising out of the retention of expert witness for trial, qualifies as work product. Such material is protected from being obtained by the opposing party during the discovery process. Technically all of your work remains work product unless the court rules otherwise or the lawyers waive the work product provision. It is important for the rehabilitation expert not to confuse work product with material that is protected by state rules involving client confidentiality. It must be left up to your client's lawyer to define what can and cannot be produced under the regulations in each state. The rehabilitation professional should not take it upon himself to settle a dispute over work product by producing the disputed records when the attorneys cannot agree. If the professional is advised by the referral source not to produce certain documents, then it remains the decision of the court and not the rehabilitation professional as to whether or not these should be produced at a later date.

Writ of Certiorari: An order issued by an appeals court upon the application of either party. It is utilized when the parties do not have an automatic right to have the matter considered by the appellate court but, rather, where the appeals court has discretion to hear the matter if they so elect. If granted, it is an order to the lower court in which the matter is pending to forward the record to the appellate court for their consideration.

Wrongful Death Act: Statutory provisions which operate upon the common law rule that the death of a human being may not be complained of as an injury in civil court. The cause of action for wrongful death is for the wrong to the beneficiaries or dependents.

Wrongful Death: A cause of action for the recovery of losses occasioned by the death of an individual caused by civil wrong. Wrongful death actions are ordinarily governed by state statutes.

Appendix A

Philosophical Focus for the Rehabilitation Professional: Nine Steps to Reducing Stress in Testimony

Throughout our training as counselors, psychologists, nurses, social workers, and health-related professionals involved in rehabilitation, it is emphasized that we have a special relationship with the rehabilitation patient. It is the role of all of us involved in rehabilitation to act as advocates for our clients, helping them to reach their greatest potential and to maintain that potential in the future. This advocacy in favor of the client takes many forms and involves many forums, but the courtroom should not be included in this list. When I, as a rehabilitation professional, enter the courtroom, all thoughts of client advocacy are removed from my mind. I have one sole purpose in that courtroom, regardless of whether I have been retained by a plaintiff's attorney, a defense attorney, or an insurance company. My responsibility is to the judicial system and to present fair, professional, and unbiased testimony to the judge and/or jury so that they have adequate data on which to base their conclusions. Anything less than a truly unbiased perspective damages the system and may prove harmful to both the client and the professional.

A few basic guidelines may be helpful in keeping the rehabilitation expert's role clear and making the testimony experience more positive.

1. Maintain intellectual honesty. Never stretch the truth, manipulate facts, or lie. Remember that the testimony can go

on for several hours, and it is much easier to maintain consistency in your testimony if you do not have to remember data or facts which you have manipulated. The truth should be the only basis for your testimony. Even manipulating the truth by simply omitting certain salient points or records is inappropriate and violates your responsibility as an unbiased professional.

2. Maintain consistency from case to case. Don't be influenced by whether you have been hired by the defense attorney or plaintiff's attorney. It is obviously appropriate to express your opinions in a clear and concise fashion to the jury. However, if you present two completely different philosophies regarding a C6-C7 spinal cord injury because you have been influenced by your role as a defense witness in one trial and as a plaintiff's witness in another, then you have prostituted your testimony, damaged your clients, and severely impaired your own professional reputation.

3. Avoid dogmatism. Listen to the questions carefully and recognize your conclusions and opinions may change if different facts are presented either through medical records or through hypothetical questions presented by an attorney. Do not consider the situation to be static; it is not. Changes in basic facts may well lead to changes in your testimony and you must analyze this information carefully before presenting your answer. You are not there to defend a specific position, but rather to present fair and unbiased testimony.

4. Avoid writing statements in your file or presenting oral statements in the testimony which cannot be substantiated by clear fact or observation.

5. If you don't know the answer to a question, do not be afraid to say so. Many professionals seem to feel that they will look bad on the witness stand if they are not able to respond to a question. In fact, the opposite is true. An individual who is able to state clearly that he does not know the answer to a question will most likely improve his credibility before all parties concerned in the trial.

6. Avoid being pulled out of your area of expertise. Nothing will cause more loss of credibility before the jury than for the counselor to present himself as an expert in fields where he or she has no background, experience, or degree. Do not be afraid to respond to a question by indicating that it is outside your area of expertise and that you must defer to the psychiatrist or physician or another health-related professional to respond to questions on that topic.

7. Do not become flustered or angry on the stand. Maintaining a cool, calm, and sincere appearance will enhance the credibility of your testimony. Maintain good eye contact with the jury and respond to questions as though the jury had asked them.

8. Don't let yourself be bogged down in minutia. It is important to hit the salient points without letting them be buried in minute detail. Again, keep good eye contact with the jury and be certain that you are not losing their attention or understanding.

9. Above all be an educator, not an advocate. The courtroom is your classroom while you are on the witness stand. You are there to educate the jury and judge along with all third parties involved in the case as to the nature of the disability and how it affects the patient's future development. You are not there to impress anyone with your vocabulary. If you fail to communicate your thoughts and ideas to the jury in a manner that they can understand, you may as well not have been on the witness stand at all.

Appendix B

Questions for Qualifying the Rehabilitation Expert

It is important to recognize that the list of questions which follow are designed as a generic set of questions to be applied to both non-catastrophic and catastrophic injury cases regardless of disability. Accordingly, there are many more questions in this list than may be appropriate to use in any one case. It is important for the rehabilitation professional and/or attorney reviewing this section, to pick and choose those questions which best represent appropriate techniques for qualification of the expert in the specific type of litigation and disability involved in the case being presented.

Clearly, the extent to which the attorney covers the counselor's background, training, and experience in the qualifying process is dependent in part on the type of case being tried. The severe catastrophic injury may require that more time be spent on qualifications, not so much because the value of the case is greater, but because of the complicated factors involved in the case. It is necessary to demonstrate to the jury that the expert being presented is capable and can provide testimony which is important in the assessment of damages. In the non-catastrophic case it may well be possible to reduce the total number of questions covered or at least reduce the depth to which each question is answered without reducing the overall scope of the inquiry.

The following list of questions presented for qualifying the rehabilitation counselor takes into account the broadest possible application of the counselor's expertise. For that reason, many questions are involved, but it is not necessary that each and every one of these questions be covered in depth. They should be used as a guideline by the attorney to select questions that will meet the needs of the individual case, counselor, and attorney.

1. Would you give us your full name and professional address for the record, please?

2. What is your profession?

3. Will you tell the ladies and gentlemen of the jury what is a rehabilitation counselor?

4. Are you presently employed?

5. Please provide us with a description of what Paul M. Deutsch & Associates is, including how many employees you have, their areas of expertise, and the client population you serve.

6. Are all of the clients that you serve involved with litigation?

7. Would you and your professional staff work with a client (family) such as John Doe if this case were not in litigation?

8. Would you please provide us with your educational background?

9. Would you tell us what fellowships and educational honors you received during your graduate training?

10. Would you share with the jury the requirement for continuing education that your field of specialty has and the specific areas of continuing education that you have pursued?

11. Would you give the ladies and gentlemen of the jury the benefit or your work experience?

12. Are you presently engaged in any research or have you recently completed any research in your field?
13. Have you been involved in publishing any research in your field of specialty or any texts in your field of expertise?

14. In completing the research and publications that you have described, did you merely supervise other professionals in the data collection and research process or were you actually involved in data collection, contact with the patient populations, contact with the professional working with these populations, and contact by phone or in person with the facilities which might be providing medical and rehabilitation services to these patient populations? (If research that has been accomplished is pertinent to a case in which testimony is being provided in more than just a general fashion, specific details and questions can be provided as part of jury education, not only on qualifications, but later with respect to the testimony.)

15. As a part of your work in rehabilitation, do you deal directly with a variety of health-related professionals including physicians, psychiatrists, psychologists, physical therapists, occupational therapists, and other speciality areas?

16. In working directly with these professionals, do you also receive and review their reports and utilize these in the formulation of rehabilitation conclusions and recommendations?

17. Do you have any special training as a part of your educational background or continuing education and experience in utilizing these reports and interpreting them from a vocational standpoint?

18. Is it your practice to actually contact a person's treating doctor or health care team in making your assessments?

19. Could you share with the ladies and gentlemen of the jury the professional organizations to which you belong?

20. Do you currently serve, or have you in the past served on any committees or boards involved in working with the handicapped?

21. Have you been a speaker at any meetings, professional associations, or training seminars with respect to your field of expertise?

22a. Have you taught at the university level in your field of expertise?

22b. Do you now teach seminars or provide guest lectures?

23. At my request, have you gone through and reviewed the files presently on your case load, and involving litigation, with respect to determining what percentage of the cases are for the plaintiff and what percentage of cases were referred by defense counsel?

24. Have you in the past been accepted as an expert witness and provided testimony in other courts?

25. Could you please provide a brief review of the types of courts in which you have been accepted as an expert and provided such testimony?

26a. Earlier you indicated that your case load and that of your staff is made up of not only clients in litigation, but also individuals to whom you provided direct rehabilitation services, is that correct?

26b. In working with these individuals, do you and your staff provide a full range of direct rehabilitation counseling services to these individuals?

27. In providing those services do you actually work with the client through to the point of job placement when that is appropriate in light of the injury?

◄ *Questions for Qualifying the Rehabilitation Expert* ►

28. Do you and your staff members have practical day-to-day experience in working with, not only the disabled, but also employers in the labor market as well as employment data?

29. Could you provide the ladies and gentlemen of the jury with some understanding of how labor market and employment data is collected and processed in your office?

30. Could you summarize the goal of the rehabilitation professional with respect to those clients who may have a capacity to return to work as well as with respect to those who may never have the potential to enter, or re-enter the labor market?

31a. Do you make a distinction between non-catastrophic and catastrophic injury cases within your practice?

31b. Would you please define those terms for the jury and tell us if the current case is catastrophic or non-catastrophic in nature?

Appendix C

Questions for Educating the Judge or Jury on Evaluation Procedures

1. Would you briefly tell the jury how you go about evaluating an individual for the purpose of rehabilitation counseling?

2. You indicate that you review the medical information and other data provided to help formulate your final rehabilitation conclusions and recommendations. What weight do you give to this data versus the information provided by the client in clinical history and interview?

3. Could you provide the jury with a brief understanding of what the clinical history and interview covers?

4. What generally is the purpose of providing the vocational tests which you mentioned as a part of the evaluation process?

5. Could you distinguish for the jury the difference between vocational testing and psychological testing administered to John Doe?

6. Please inform the jury of the purpose of the psychological test administered in your evaluation.

7. Did you, in your professional capacity, have occasion to meet with John Doe?

8. Where did that evaluation take place?

9. What was your understanding of the purpose of that evaluation?

10. The next area of questioning should briefly involve the review of medical information. Depending upon the circumstances in the case, one of two approaches may be taken including the following:

    - Could you briefly state the source of all the medical reports and hospital records you reviewed?

    - Did you review medical reports and hospital records from the following sources? (Attorney lists all medical records as a part of the question.) An attorney should ask the question based on the second question, when in fact not all of the medical information originally provided to the counselor has been admitted into evidence. If it was not possible to share with the counselor, in advance of testimony, that a specific set of medical reports was not admitted and cannot be mentioned, then this can help alert the expert to the change which has occurred. This is not a satisfactory alternative to a pre-testimony conference in light of the fact that the elimination of certain medical reports by the court could result in a change in the counselor's testimony.

11. Was Mr. Doe alone or accompanied by any others during the evaluation itself?

12. Did you complete a rehabilitation evaluation including a clinical history and interview with Mr. Doe?

13. Could you briefly provide the most pertinent data developed from that interview? (As each area is covered and each point of information is provided, the attorney may wish to develop those points further with questions which will appear fairly obvious in relation to the information being provided. Clearly this is done to enhance the jury's understanding.)

14. You have indicated that you provided a series of vocational and psychological tests to Mr. Doe. Could you briefly state the

name of each test, its general purpose and the interpretation of the results as they relate to this client?

15. Were the medical reports you reviewed consistent with the history you were provided by the client?

16. Once all the medical, psychosocial, and vocational rehabilitation data were collected, what were the next steps taken before conclusions could be drawn and a rehabilitation plan outlined?

Appendix D

Questions for the Non-Catastrophic Rehabilitation Case

1. Can you define for the jury what an occupational analysis is and how it is accomplished?

2. Having reviewed all of the medical, psychological, psychosocial, and vocational rehabilitation data collected in your evaluation process, did you then complete an occupational analysis as you have defined it?

3. Could you tell us what resources are utilized in completing your occupational analysis and assessing wage data?

4. Could you briefly outline the areas in which you drew conclusions in this case?

5. You have indicated that the first step is to assess whether or not vocational handicaps exist as a result of the accident which occurred? Would you please list for us the vocational handicaps, in your opinion, Mr. Doe has developed as a result of this accident?

6. As a result of the vocational handicaps and residual physical limitations, has there been an impact on job placement in the competitive labor market for this individual?

7. What impact do these vocational handicaps have on the range of job alternatives for which this individual can compete?

8. Do you feel this individual will require specific vocational rehabilitation recommendations to achieve a return to the labor market?

9. Could you please outline your recommendations including the duration of time involved and the cost of such recommendations?

10. Could you explain to the jury the difference between earnings and capacity to earn? (In the case of young clients with a limited pre-accident work history, several additional questions can be asked.)

11a. Can you explain the concept of career maturity?

11b. Is it reasonable to expect that the vocational development achieved by someone under age 25 is an accurate reflection of their maximum potential to develop either in vocational or financial areas?

11c. Are the earnings achieved by an individual who is under age 25 reflective of their maximum potential to earn as their career develops?

12. As a result of your evaluation, research, and the vocational handicaps described, has there been an impact on this individual's capacity to earn in the labor market post-accident as compared to pre-accident?

13. Could you be specific in indicating the diminution of wage earning capacity which has resulted and how you went about assessing this diminution?

14. Have we covered all of your conclusions as it relates to our client in this case?

Appendix E

Questions for Presentation of the Catastrophic Injury

1. Will you define the concept of life care planning for the jury?

2. In indicating that a critical part of life care planning is consistency of methodology in assessing disability needs are you suggesting that all spinal cord injuries (or head injuries, etc.) have the same needs?

3. Would you and your professional staff customarily be involved in working with clients and their families in the development of long-term care programs?

4. Is the role of the case management and life care planning typically within the purview of the rehabilitation professional or would you defer to the physician for this?

5. Is the physician primarily involved in following the catastrophic patient for acute care of complications rather than involved in day-to-day details of support, durable medical equipment, supplies, maintenance programs, and other areas covered in your plan?

6. Would this service of life care planning and case management be provided to the patient and family even in the absence of litigation?

◄ *Questions for Presentation of the Catastrophic Injury* ►

7. Is it typical for the rehabilitation professional to act as team leader and case manager in catastrophic injury cases after medical stabilization and entry into the post-acute phase of rehabilitation?

8. Does the rehabilitation professional as a routine part of their responsibility work with physicians, medical reports, physical therapists, occupational therapists, speech therapists, and a wide range of other health-related professionals?

9. Is it a part of your daily routine to arrange for services, equipment, supplies, and therapies as part of case management?

10. Do you need to be familiar with the medical aspects of disability in your work?

11. How does the rehabilitation professional develop a knowledge of medical aspects of disability and medical terminology in their training?

12. Did you, in the course of your review of the medical and psychological information on John Doe coupled with your evaluation of the client, work-up a life care plan?

13. I'm handing you a report or life care plan dated ____. Would you identify this for the court?
(At this point, the attorney may request that copies be provided the jury for them to follow along.)

14. Would it be helpful for the jury to have copies to speed the process as we go through this plan?

15. Now before we begin, can you explain the format of the life care plan?

16. Beginning with page one, can you explain your recommendations under Projected Evaluations? (The counselor will explain that this deals with health-related evaluations and should run through each column on the chart.)

◄ *Questions for Presentation of the Catastrophic Injury* ►

17. Moving to the next page, what are your recommendations for Projected Therapeutic Modalities?

18. The next area covers educational needs and testing. Are there recommendations for John Doe here? (Keep in mind that these are generic questions and not all disabilities will use all charts on the life care plan. Choose questions accordingly.)

19. Wheelchair needs are reviewed next. Can you explain the type of chairs and replacement schedules noted on your plan?

20. Please review the maintenance and accessories required for these chairs.

21. Will you explain the Orthopedic Equipment page and your recommendations?

22. Orthotics/prosthetics is the next area. Can you review this for us and explain the function achieved by using this equipment.

23. Please outline all the home furnishings and accessories required to maintain this individual in a home environment.

24. Can you explain what you mean by aids for independent function and give us your recommendations?

25. The next section deals with all drug and supply needs. Please be specific in outlining needs and how you arrived at costs.

26. Your next section is entitled Home Care/Facility Care. Please define these concepts and help us understand your recommended alternatives.

27. Give us your understanding and recommendations for future medical needs of a routine nature and tell us if this is a basic standard of care for this one type of disability.

28. Under Future Medical Care Surgical or Aggressive Treatment you have several procedures listed. Please explain how these were developed and how these costs were developed.

◄ *Questions for Presentation of the Catastrophic Injury* ►

29. Your Potential Complications page says it's for information only. Is it not possible to be specific on costs such as possible complications?

30. Is there any other area you can't cost out? (At this point, the rehabilitation professional must note that future technological advances can't be predicted.)

31. Please explain how you assess transportation needs and how they are costed out.

32. Does this disability require renovations to the house for greater accessibility?

33. If so, could you outline these needs and their costs?

34. Your final section of the life care plan deals with leisure time and recreational activities. Please explain these recommendations.

35. Does this cover all your life care recommendations?

Appendix F - 1

Questions for Attorneys to Use in Deposing the Injured Party

The following narrative information and master list of questions are designed to provide both the defense attorney and the plaintiff attorney an appropriate list of questions of the patient to elicit as much information as possible from a rehabilitation perspective. For the plaintiff's attorney, this is most useful in helping to develop his case with the greatest possible insight into the nature of the injury and its functional impact. For the defense attorney, these questions are critical in the deposition of the client (plaintiff) in order to develop extensive information for use by their own rehabilitation consultant.

These questions are presented in narrative form and followed by Appendices F-2 - F-4 which represent Clinical Interview and History Sheets for different types of disabilities. The initial portion in each of these appendices remain the same, but the latter halves are designed specifically for different types of disability. For example, Appendix F-2 outlines questions for the chronic pain/chronic disability patient while Appendix F-3 outlines questions for spinal cord injury or head injury (see the separate sections), and Appendix F-4 outlines questions for pediatric brain injury cases.

Plaintiff's Deposition

It is important to develop as much information pertinent to the rehabilitation evaluation as is possible and realistic in light of the many other areas of questioning that the attorney will typically pursue. To the extent possible, it is helpful not to skip from one type or section of questions to another, but preferably to keep all of the rehabilitation questions generally within the same area. The attorney should begin relatively simplistically obtaining a current mailing address, marital status, age, and birth date. It is helpful to know where the individual was born and whether or not they received most of their education within that state or from an alternative school system. If the individual speaks any other language besides English, it's appropriate to note this along with such basic information as to whether or not they wear glasses, are right- or left-handed, and what their current height and weight is. Weight at time of accident is also requested. Separate notes should be made by the attorney regarding how the individual presents themselves. This may include noting whether or not there are obvious signs of disability such as scarring, limping, speech deficits, or other overt signs that may be clear even to the lay population. Also making note of the individual's gait can be helpful. It is appropriate to document a list of all of the equipment utilized by the individual including the date of purchase, its current condition, the cost at purchase, and who provided that item. Assistive devices, equipment, and aids for independent function can cover a broad range of categories so this is an important area for the attorney to provide cues. By this, I mean questions which go beyond the obvious, such as wheelchairs, hospital beds, and other household furnishings, but also get into bracing, canes, crutches, transcutaneous stimulation units, or any other devices which can be interpreted as being of assistance to the individual or increasing their independent function and mobility.

General Case Information

In addition to asking general questions as noted above on address and telephone number, it is helpful to ask the client such things as the date the accident or incident occurred, whether or not they were working at time of the accident, and what position they held. Getting a job description can also be helpful. At times, such questions are asked, in part, to see if the client has a memory for names, dates, addresses, and numbers. This is particularly important when dealing with a closed head injury patient. Just the ability of the client to provide an accurate answer, can give you insight into functioning levels. The client's description of initial treatment and any programs they have entered (with respect to rehabilitation) since the date of injury, should be reviewed. A complete list of all work attempts since the accident should also be obtained. This would include as accurate a date of onset of the work experience, as well as termination of the work experiences can be obtained. Details on the type of job, the duties for which the client was responsible, and any problems that they may have had on the job should be outlined.

Disabling Problem

The next step is to obtain a pre-onset of disability medical history from the client. This should not be as detailed as a physician might obtain, but should list out any accidents or injuries prior to the latest accident which resulted in the need for long term medical care or cost of permanent disability. Remember that we are attempting to ascertain the current status of the individual, so even areas of impairment which may have pre-existed the injury for which the current litigation involves, must be considered if an evaluation of the whole person is to be successfully accomplished. After discussing injuries, a review of any childhood, adolescent, or adult illnesses resulting in long-term medical care or permanent disability should be reviewed including whether or not the individual is currently being treated for things such as heart disease, lung disease, diabetes, or other chronic illnesses.

The next step is to review, with the client, their own subjective description of chief complaints. For most types of disabilities, it is simply necessary to ask the individual to describe for you all of the problems they currently have. As they begin the description, you can ask the necessary questions to solicit a complete response allowing you to understand and be able to take notes. For the head injured patient and some psychological disabilities, it may be necessary to be very specific in eliciting questions simply because of the lack of insight or the use of denial and repression. Even in the instance of more complicated disabilities such as paraplegia or quadriplegia, it may be necessary to ask more specific questions simply because the range of problems and complexity of responses may lead the client into a position where they say nothing more than that they are a C6-C7 complete lesion quadriplegic. For this reason, when dealing with specific disabilities, it may be helpful to talk with the rehabilitation professional regarding any specific questions they might have prior to taking the deposition. For purposes of the questions provided within the context of this appendix, I'll simply note that under Chief Complaint, we should get detailed information regarding the client's understanding of their disability and all the problems associated with that disability while still avoiding entering into how that disability manifests itself in interfering with activities of daily living. So, for example, with the quadriplegic we will talk about questions such as the following:

1. The level of lesion.

2. Whether it is a complete or incomplete lesion.

3. Whether there is any pain above the level of lesion.

4. That point at which a complete loss of tactile sensitivity begins.

5. The current bowel program being utilized by the client.

6. The current bladder program being utilized by the client.

7. Whether or not there are any symptoms of or history of dysreflexia.

8. Whether or not there is any history of decubitus ulcers or any skin breakdown problems.

9. Whether or not the client is undergoing any problems with muscle spasms and the degree of the severity of those spasms.

10. Whether there has been any history of thrombophlebitis.

11. Whether the client is maintaining a regular program of home exercise.

The deposition should also cover questions regarding the client's reaction to disability such as admissions of depression, tension, anxiety, stress-related symptomatology, or other psychological deficits. It is helpful to have the client describe their basic conservative treatments since onset of disability, as well as to provide their understanding of surgical procedures which they have undergone.

Physical Limitations

In this section questions regarding how the disability manifests itself to impede specific activities will be covered. In each type of disability it is important to ascertain whether or not there is any loss of tactile sensation in any of the extremities or in the torso. Does the individual have a normal upper extremity range of motion or any pain on reaching or stretching. The individual's capacity for lifting should be reviewed along with any problems in manual dexterity, finger dexterity, or grip strength. Capacities for sitting, standing, walking, bending, twisting, kneeling, stooping, squatting, and climbing should also be reviewed. Does the client have any current problems with seizure activity, dizziness, or loss of balance? Is there any history of shortness of breath, headaches, visual deficits, hearing deficits, speech deficits, or bowel and bladder dysfunction? Does the individual drive and if so, what limitations may be imposed? Is there a normal level of physical stamina and endurance or does the individual have to take periodic bed-rest during the day to such a degree that it would interfere with being able to perform six to eight hours of work on the job?

Environmental Influences

This section will deal with whether or not there are any environmental influences or work settings which would tend to exacerbate the complaints secondary to the disability. Does the individual chill or overheat easily on exposure to air conditioning, heat, cold, wet, rainy, or humid environments, or sudden or marked temperature changes? Do they have problems with working indoors versus working outdoors or are there any upper respiratory problems, sinus conditions, or allergies which would prevent exposure to fumes, dust, odors, or poor ventilation? Do they tend to be tense and bothered by intermittent or constant noise on the job and do they demonstrate any stress-related symptomatology such as low frustration tolerance or difficulty in dealing with the public?

Current Medical Care

Listing the current treating doctors and dates of last appointment and next appointment should be included in this section. Whether or not future surgical procedures are being planned must be outlined along with any conservative management being employed. A complete list of the client's medication, the purpose of that medication, and the frequency of it's administration should be obtained along with the name and phone number of the local retailer supplying those medications. A list of all supplies utilized by the individual, particularly in catastrophic cases such as spinal cord injuries or coma should also be obtained.

Activities of Daily Living

It is helpful to obtain a complete schedule of the individual's daily activities and the extent to which they are independent in accomplishing those. Time up in the morning and to bed at night is helpful, along with notation of any naps. Whether or not the individual has any difficulty sleeping should be noted and the type of difficulty should be reviewed. The total number of hours slept in 24 hours would also be helpful to know. The client's ability to handle personal care needs such as dressing, shaving, bathing, etc. should all be reviewed along with their ability to complete basic household chores such as housework, cooking, laundry, or any yard work. How they spend the majority of their day should also be reviewed.

Social Activities

A review of the individual's pre-accident, as well as post-accident involvement in clubs, social organizations, professional groups, volunteer work, or church should be reviewed. Also, any pre-accident hobbies and post-accident hobbies should be considered and listed because of the potential to add to our list of transferable skills that we can use for vocational placement in the rehabilitation process.

Personal habits should be reviewed including whether or not the individual smokes, drinks alcohol, or has any history of alcohol or drug abuse.

Socioeconomic Status

The individual's marital status along with the name, age, and occupation of the spouse should be reviewed. Whether or not this is a first, second, or third marriage, it should also be noted along with the number of children particularly those living in the home. Total number of people in the residence and their relationship to the plaintiff should be noted. I also like to develop information on any role models for disability in this individual's early childhood years or late adolescent and early adult years. This would involve any family members or close personal friends who were disabled.

Within this same section, a complete list of income sources for this client should be obtained including any information on social security disability insurance, supplemental security income, medicare, medicaid, workers' compensation, or any disability policies providing income. Any state or federal agency involvement in rehabilitation, whether providing direct income or supplemental income sources, should be reviewed along with those that are just providing services such as counseling, nursing, or rehabilitation guidance.

Education and Training

It is important to develop information on the individual's education including determining the last school attended and the highest grade in school (formal academic training) completed. If the individual subsequently received a GED equivalency diploma that should be noted as well as the year and source of that diploma. Any vocational technical school training, apprenticeship training, or formal on-the job training should be reviewed and any licensure or certification for a specific trade should be listed. Whether or not the client is literate should be noted and any history of felony convictions should be listed. Military experience can also be helpful including noting the branch, service dates, type of discharge, and whether or not there was any service-connected disability. The type of training obtained in the military can also be helpful.

Employment History

A complete list of the individual's employment background covering at least the last 15 to 20 years should be obtained. This should include the name of the employer and location of the employer (at least the city or state) along with the position held, rate of pay, date started and left, total length of employment, and the specific job duties. In instances where the client cannot recall all of those details, it is important to at least obtain a list of the types of work within which this individual has been employed over that period of time.

Behavioral Observation

Although not specifically asked as questions, it would be helpful if the individual taking the deposition would make note of whether or not the individual appears alert, well-oriented to person, place, and time, and demonstrates good concentration. Any comments on memory, particularly with respect to remote memory, immediate recall, and delayed memory would be helpful. It would be appropriate to note whether or not the individual seems to demonstrate a clear and rational stream of thought, is able to communicate his own ideas and thoughts, and what his general attitude toward work and rehabilitation seems to be. If it is possible for you to comment on the degree to which the individual demonstrates insight, particularly regarding their psychological reaction to disability, such comments would also be helpful.

Reference to Appendix F-2, F-3, and F-4 may be helpful for use during the deposition.

Appendix F - 2

Clinical Interview & History for Chronic Pain/Chronic Disability

PAUL M. DEUTSCH & ASSOCIATES, P.A.
CLINICAL INTERVIEW & HISTORY FOR CHRONIC PAIN/CHRONIC DISABILITY

Date _____

Location _____

Accompanied By _____

IDENTIFYING INFORMATION

Name_____ Soc. Sec.#_____ Phone_____

Address_____ City/State/Zip_____ Co._____

Citizen: Yes_____ No_____ Married_____ Single_____ Other_____

Sex_____ Race_____ Age_____ Birthdate_____ Birthplace_____

Bilingual_____ Glasses_____ Dominant Hand_____

Height_____ Weight (present)_____ Weight (pre-injury)_____

Appearance _____ Gait _____

Assistive Devices and Equipment _____

_____

_____

CASE INFORMATION

Date of Accident _____ Carrier _____

Defense Attorney _____ Plaintiff Attorney _____

Employer _____ Position _____

How Injured? _____

_____

_____

◄ *Clinical Interview & History for Chronic Pain/Chronic Disability* ►

Initial Treatment _____

_____

Worked Since Accident? _____

_____

_____

DISABLING PROBLEM

Previous Injuries _____

Illnesses: Child _____ Adolescent _____ Adult _____

Chief Complaint(s) _____

_____

_____

_____

_____

_____

Secondary Problem(s) _____

_____

Conservative Treatment _____

Surgical Procedure(s): Type/Date _____

_____ Hospital _____

PHYSICAL LIMITATIONS

Feeling (Loss of Tactile Sensation) _____

_____

Reach _____

_____

Lift _____

_____

Clinical Interview & History for Chronic Pain/Chronic Disability

Prehensile/Grip_____

_____

Sit_____

_____

Stand_____

_____

Walk_____

_____

Bend/Twist_____

_____

Kneel_____

_____

Stoop/Squat_____

_____

Climb_____

_____

Balance_____

_____

Breathing_____

_____

Headaches_____

_____

Vision_____

_____

Hearing_____

_____

◄ *Clinical Interview & History for Chronic Pain/Chronic Disability* ►

Speech_____
_____

Bowel/Bladder_____
_____

Driving_____
_____

Physical Stamina (Average Daily Need for Rest or Reclining)_____
_____

ENVIRONMENTAL INFLUENCE

Air Conditioning	Yes____ No____	_____
Heat	Yes____ No____	_____
Cold	Yes____ No____	_____
Wet/Humid	Yes____ No____	_____
Sudden Changes	Yes____ No____	_____
Inside	Yes____ No____	_____
Outside	Yes____ No____	_____
Fumes/Odors	Yes____ No____	_____
Noise	Yes____ No____	_____
Stress	Yes____ No____	_____

Other(s)_____

PRESENT MEDICAL TREATMENT

Doctor(s)_____

Treatment(s)_____

Date of Last Appointment_____

◄ *Clinical Interview & History for Chronic Pain/Chronic Disability* ►

Medication_____ Purpose_____ Frequency_____

_____ _____ _____

_____ _____ _____

_____ _____ _____

Over-the-Counter Medication(s)_____

_____

ACTIVITIES OF DAILY LIVING

Arises _____ A.M. Retires _____ P.M. Average hours Sleep/24 Hours _____

Sleep Difficulties_____

Dresses Self	Yes___ No___	_____
Housework	Yes___ No___	_____
Cooking	Yes___ No___	_____
Laundry	Yes___ No___	_____
Yard Work	Yes___ No___	_____

Other(s)_____

SOCIAL ACTIVITIES

Organizations_____

Church_____ Volunteer Work_____

Hobbies: Previous_____

Hobbies: Present_____

PERSONAL HABITS

Smoking	Yes___ No___	_____
Alcohol	Yes___ No___	_____
	History of Abuse	_____
Drugs	Yes___ No___	_____

◄ *Clinical Interview & History for Chronic Pain/Chronic Disability* ►

SOCIOECONOMIC STATUS

Spouse_____ Age_____ Occupation_____

First Marriage?_____ Children_____

Number in Residence_____

Parents/Siblings_____

Disability Role Model(s)_____

Income:

Disability Policy	$_____/_____	Total Family Income
V.A.	$_____/_____	$_____
W.C.	$_____/_____	
D.V.R.	$_____/_____	
S.S. Retirement	$_____/_____	Estimated Monthly Expenses
S.S.D.I.	$_____/_____	$_____
Wages	$_____/_____	
Food Stamps	$_____/_____	
Other	$_____/_____	

Current Financial Status_____

OTHER AGENCY INVOLVEMENT

State Vocational Rehab	Yes___ No___	_____
State Employment Services	Yes___ No___	_____
Rehab Nurse(s)	Yes___ No___	_____
Other	Yes___ No___	_____

Previous Felony Conviction?_____

◄ *Clinical Interview & History for Chronic Pain/Chronic Disability* ►

EDUCATION AND TRAINING

1 2 3 4 5 6 7 8 9 10 11 12 F S J SR Grad

Amount_____ Last School Attended_____

Trade/Technical Training_____

Apprenticeship/OJT_____

Other(s)_____

Read/Write_____ Licenses/Certification_____

MILITARY EXPERIENCE

Branch_____ Service Dates_____ Discharge_____

Service Disability: Yes____ No____ _____

Rank/Duties_____

Training_____

EMPLOYMENT HISTORY

Employer_____ City/State_____

Position_____ Rate of Pay_____

Date Start_____ Date Leave_____ Length_____

Duties_____

_____

Employer_____ City/State_____

Position_____ Rate of Pay_____

Date Start_____ Date Leave_____ Length_____

Duties_____

◄ *Clinical Interview & History for Chronic Pain/Chronic Disability* ►

Employer_____ City/State_____
Position_____ Rate of Pay_____
Date Start_____ Date Leave_____ Length_____
Duties_____
_____

Employer_____ City/State_____
Position_____ Rate of Pay_____
Date Start_____ Date Leave_____ Length_____
Duties_____
_____

Employer_____ City/State_____
Position_____ Rate of Pay_____
Date Start_____ Date Leave_____ Length_____
Duties_____
_____

Other Work Experience_____
_____
_____

<u>BEHAVIORAL OBSERVATIONS</u>

Orientation_____ Approach Toward Eval. - ± +
Stream of Thought_____ Concentration_____
Attitudes/Insight_____
Memory: Remote_____ Recent_____

◄ *Clinical Interview & History for Chronic Pain/Chronic Disability* ►

VOCATIONAL TESTS

Check if to be administered:

SIT	_____	WVI	_____
Gilmore/SORT	_____	AVMI	_____
PENN/Crawford	_____	Wahler/Whitely	_____
Other(s)	_____		_____
	_____		_____
	_____		_____
	_____		_____

TENTATIVE REHAB PLAN

_____
_____
_____
_____

COMMENTS

_____
_____
_____
_____
_____
_____
_____
_____
_____
_____

CHRONIC PAIN

Length of Pain Complaint _____

_____

Course of Pain (progressive - consistent - abrupt changes) _____

_____
_____
_____
_____

Quality of Initial/Subsequent Treatments _____

_____
_____
_____
_____
_____

Recent Life Stressors _____

_____
_____
_____
_____

Primary Source of Income _____

_____
_____
_____
_____

Role Reversal_____

_____
_____
_____
_____

Medication Regimen_____

_____
_____
_____
_____
_____

Social Isolation_____

_____
_____
_____
_____
_____
_____
_____
_____
_____
_____
_____
_____
_____

◄ Clinical Interview & History for Chronic Pain/Chronic Disability ►

FAMILY HISTORY

	NAME	AGE	EDUCATION	MAJOR WORK HISTORY
CLIENT:				
FATHER:				
MOTHER:				
SIBLINGS:				
MATERNAL				
GRANDMOTHER:				
GRANDFATHER:				
AUNTS/UNCLES:				

◄ *Clinical Interview & History for Chronic Pain/Chronic Disability* ►

FAMILY HISTORY

	NAME	AGE	EDUCATION	MAJOR WORK HISTORY
PATERNAL				
GRANDMOTHER:				
GRANDFATHER:				
AUNTS/UNCLES:				

Appendix F - 3

Clinical Interview & History for Head and Spinal Cord Injury

PAUL M. DEUTSCH & ASSOCIATES, P.A.

CLINICAL INTERVIEW & HISTORY FOR HEAD AND SPINAL CORD INJURY

Date_____

Location_____

Accompanied By_____

IDENTIFYING INFORMATION

Name_____ Soc. Sec.#_____ Phone_____

Address_____ City/State/Zip_____ Co._____

Citizen: Yes_____ No_____ Married_____ Single_____ Other_____

Sex_____ Race_____ Age_____ Birthdate_____ Birthplace_____

Bilingual_____ Glasses_____ Dominant Hand_____

Height_____ Weight (present)_____ Weight (pre-injury)_____

Appearance_____ Gait_____

Assistive Devices and Equipment_____
_____
_____

CASE INFORMATION

Date of Accident_____ Carrier_____

Defense Attorney_____ Plaintiff Attorney_____

Employer_____ Position_____

How Injured?_____
_____
_____

◄ *Clinical Interview & History for Head and Spinal Cord Injury* ►

Initial Treatment _____

_____

Worked Since Accident? _____

_____

_____

DISABLING PROBLEM

Previous Injuries _____

Illnesses: Child _____ Adolescent _____ Adult _____

Chief Complaints(s) _____

_____

_____

_____

_____

_____

Secondary Problems(s) _____

_____

Conservative Treatment _____

Surgical Procedure (s): Type/Date _____

_____ Hospital _____

PHYSICAL LIMITATIONS

Feeling (Loss of Tactile Sensation) _____

_____

Reach _____

_____

Lift _____

_____

Prehensile/Grip _____

_____

Sit _____

Stand _____

Walk _____

Bend/Twist _____

Kneel _____

Stoop/Squat _____

Climb _____

Balance _____

Breathing _____

Headaches _____

Vision _____

Hearing _____

◄ *Clinical Interview & History for Head and Spinal Cord Injury* ►

Speech_____

Bowel/Bladder_____

Driving_____

Physical Stamina (Average Daily Need for Rest or Reclining)_____

ENVIRONMENTAL INFLUENCE

Air Conditioning	Yes___ No___	_____
Heat	Yes___ No___	_____
Cold	Yes___ No___	_____
Wet/Humid	Yes___ No___	_____
Sudden Changes	Yes___ No___	_____
Inside	Yes___ No___	_____
Outside	Yes___ No___	_____
Fumes/Odors	Yes___ No___	_____
Noise	Yes___ No___	_____
Stress	Yes___ No___	_____

Other(s)_____

PRESENT MEDICAL TREATMENT

Doctor(s)_____

Treatment(s)_____

Date of Last Appointment_____

◄ Clinical Interview & History for Head and Spinal Cord Injury ►

Medication _____ Purpose _____ Frequency _____
　　　　　 _____ 　　　　　_____ 　　　　　　_____
　　　　　 _____ 　　　　　_____ 　　　　　　_____
　　　　　 _____ 　　　　　_____ 　　　　　　_____

Over-the-Counter Medication(s) _____
_____

ACTIVITIES OF DAILY LIVING

Arises _____ A.M. Retires _____ P.M. Average hours Sleep/24 Hours _____
Sleep Difficulties _____

Dresses Self	Yes___ No___	_____
Housework	Yes___ No___	_____
Cooking	Yes___ No___	_____
Laundry	Yes___ No___	_____
Yard Work	Yes___ No___	_____

Other(s) _____
_____

SOCIAL ACTIVITIES

Organizations _____
Church _____ Volunteer Work _____
Hobbies: Previous _____
Hobbies: Present _____

PERSONAL HABITS

Smoking	Yes___ No___	_____
Alcohol	Yes___ No___	_____
	History of Abuse	_____
Drugs	Yes___ No___	_____

◄ *Clinical Interview & History for Head and Spinal Cord Injury* ►

SOCIOECONOMIC STATUS

Spouse_____ Age_____ Occupation_____

First Marriage?_____ Children_____

Number in Residence_____

Parents/Siblings_____

Disability Role Model(s)_____

Income:

Disability Policy	$_____/_____	Total Family Income
V.A.	$_____/_____	$_____
W.C.	$_____/_____	
D.V.R.	$_____/_____	
S.S. Retirement	$_____/_____	Estimated Monthly Expenses
S.S.D.I.	$_____/_____	$_____
Wages	$_____/_____	
Food Stamps	$_____/_____	
Other	$_____/_____	

Current Financial Status_____

OTHER AGENCY INVOLVEMENT

State Vocational Rehab	Yes____ No____	_____
State Employment Services	Yes____ No____	_____
Rehab Nurse(s)	Yes____ No____	_____
Other	Yes____ No____	_____

Previous Felony Conviction?_____

EDUCATION AND TRAINING

1 2 3 4 5 6 7 8 9 10 11 12 F S J SR Grad

Amount_____ Last School Attended_____

Trade/Technical Training_____

Apprenticeship/OJT_____

Other(s)_____

Read/Write_____ Licenses/Certification_____

MILITARY EXPERIENCE

Branch _____ Service Dates _____ Discharge _____

Service Disability: Yes____ No____ _____

Rank/Duties_____

Training_____

EMPLOYMENT HISTORY

Employer_____ City/State_____

Position_____ Rate of Pay_____

Date Start_____ Date Leave_____ Length_____

Duties_____

Employer_____ City/State_____

Position_____ Rate of Pay_____

Date Start_____ Date Leave_____ Length_____

Duties_____

◀ *Clinical Interview & History for Head and Spinal Cord Injury* ▶

Employer_____ City/State_____
Position_____ Rate of Pay_____
Date Start_____ Date Leave_____ Length_____
Duties_____
_____

Employer_____ City/State_____
Position_____ Rate of Pay_____
Date Start_____ Date Leave_____ Length_____
Duties_____
_____

Employer_____ City/State_____
Position_____ Rate of Pay_____
Date Start_____ Date Leave_____ Length_____
Duties_____
_____

Other Work Experience_____
_____
_____

BEHAVIORAL OBSERVATIONS

Orientation_____ Approach Toward Eval. - ± +
Stream of Thought_____ Concentration_____
Attitudes/Insight_____
Memory: Remote_____ Recent_____

VOCATIONAL TESTS

Check if to be administered:

SIT	_____	WVI	_____
Gilmore/SORT	_____	AVMI	_____
PENN/Crawford	_____	Wahler/Whitely	_____
Other(s)	_____		_____
	_____		_____
	_____		_____
	_____		_____

TENTATIVE REHAB PLAN

_____
_____
_____
_____
_____
_____
_____

COMMENTS

_____
_____
_____
_____
_____
_____
_____

SUPPLIES

TYPE/ITEM	SIZE	FREQUENCY OF REPLACEMENT	SUPPLIER	COST

EQUIPMENT

TYPE	DATE OF PURCHASE	PURCHASE PRICE	DEALER	CURRENT CONDITION

◄ *Clinical Interview & History for Head and Spinal Cord Injury* ►

SPINAL CORD INJURIES

Level of Lesion _____

Complete or Incomplete Lesion _____

_____

    Sensory_____ Motor_____

Pain Above or Below Level of Lesion _____

_____

Type of Bowel Program _____

_____

_____

_____

_____

Type of Bladder Program_____

_____

_____

_____

_____

    Urine Check_____

Independence in Turning and Transfers_____

_____

Current Nursing/Attendant Care Needs_____

_____

_____

_____

Transitional Living Program _____

_____

_____

Clinical Interview & History for Head and Spinal Cord Injury

HISTORY OF COMPLICATIONS:

Dysreflexia_____
_____
_____

Spasms_____
_____
_____

Decubiti_____
_____
_____

Thrombophlebitis_____
_____
_____

Respiratory Infections_____
_____
_____

Urinary Tract Infections_____
_____
_____

Other_____
_____
_____

ENVIRONMENTAL COMPLICATIONS (secondary to changed perspiration patterns):

Overheating_____
_____

Chilling_____
_____

◄ *Clinical Interview & History for Head and Spinal Cord Injury* ►

Pattern of Paralysis (where loss of sensation begins) _____
_____

Psycho-social Adaptation to Disability (comment also on any perceived psychological problems)
_____
_____
_____
_____
_____
_____

OTHER:

Architectural Renovations Accomplished _____
_____

Auto Insurance _____
_____

FES/Biofeedback (Neuromuscular Reeducation) _____
_____
_____

◄ Clinical Interview & History for Head and Spinal Cord Injury ►

HEAD INJURY SEQUELA

COGNITIVE:

Attention and Concentration _____

_____

Abstract Reasoning and Conceptualization_____

_____

Immediate Recall_____

_____

Delayed Memory_____

_____

Remote Memory_____

_____

Problem Solving _____

_____

Decision-Making_____

_____

Speed of Thought Processing_____

_____

Thought Organization and Planning_____

_____

Judgment_____

_____

Auditory Processing

    Auditory Discrimination_____

_____

    Auditory Retention_____

_____

Visual Processing

    Visual Discrimination _____

_____

    Visual Retention _____

_____

Insight (awareness of problems) _____

_____

Expressive Speech _____

_____

Receptive Speech _____

_____

BEHAVIORAL/PSYCHOLOGICAL:

Ability to Engage in Purposeful Activity _____

_____

Disinhibition _____

_____

Appropriateness of Response to Environment _____

_____

Socially Inappropriate Behavior _____

_____

Social Skill Deficits _____

_____

Impulsivity _____

_____

Poor Self-Initiation _____

_____

Impaired Capacity for Self-Control/Self-Regulation _____

Social Dependency _____

Emotional/Personality Changes _____

Personality Regression _____

Behavioral Rigidity or Inflexibility _____

Denial _____

Reduced Self-Esteem _____

Exaggeration of Previous Negative Personality Traits _____

Interpersonal Relationship Problems _____

Problems with Family Relationships _____

Issues of Lifestyle _____

Degree of Acceptance _____

MOTOR/PHYSICAL:

Psychomotor Speed _____

Psychomotor Coordination _____

Hemiparesis _____

Gait Changes _____

◄ *Clinical Interview & History for Head and Spinal Cord Injury* ►

FAMILY HISTORY

	NAME	AGE	EDUCATION	MAJOR WORK HISTORY
CLIENT:				
FATHER:				
MOTHER:				
SIBLINGS:				
MATERNAL				
GRANDMOTHER:				
GRANDFATHER:				
AUNTS/UNCLES:				

◀ *Clinical Interview & History for Head and Spinal Cord Injury* ▶

FAMILY HISTORY

	NAME	AGE	EDUCATION	MAJOR WORK HISTORY
PATERNAL				
GRANDMOTHER:				
GRANDFATHER:				
AUNTS/UNCLES:				

Appendix F - 4

Clinical Interview & History for Pediatrics

PAUL M. DEUTSCH & ASSOCIATES, P.A.

CLINICAL INTERVIEW & HISTORY FOR PEDIATRICS

Date _____

Location _____

Accompanied By _____

IDENTIFYING INFORMATION

Name _____ Soc. Sec.# _____ Phone _____

Address _____ City/State/Zip _____ Co. _____

Citizen: Yes _____ No _____ Other _____

Sex _____ Race _____ Age _____ Birthdate _____ Birthplace _____

Bilingual _____ Glasses _____ Dominant Hand _____

Height _____ Weight (present) _____ Weight (pre-injury) _____

Appearance _____ Gait _____

Assistive Devices and Equipment _____

_____

_____

CASE INFORMATION

Date of Accident _____ Carrier _____

Defense Attorney _____ Plaintiff Attorney _____

Employer _____ Position _____

How Injured? _____

_____

_____

◄ *Clinical Interview & History for Pediatrics* ►

Initial Treatment _____
_____
_____

DISABLING PROBLEM

Previous Injuries _____

Illnesses: Child _____ Adolescent _____

Chief Complaint(s) _____
_____
_____
_____
_____
_____

Secondary Problem(s) _____
_____

Conservative Treatment_____

Surgical Procedure(s): Type/Date _____

_____ Hospital _____

PHYSICAL LIMITATIONS

Feeling (Loss of Tactile Sensation)_____
_____

Reach_____
_____

Lift_____
_____

Prehensile/Grip_____
_____

◄ Clinical Interview & History for Pediatrics ►

Sit_____

Stand_____

Walk_____

Bend/Twist_____

Kneel_____

Stoop/Squat_____

Climb_____

Balance_____

Breathing_____

Headaches_____

Vision_____

Hearing_____

Speech_____

◄ *Clinical Interview & History for Pediatrics* ►

Bowel/Bladder _____
_____
Driving _____
_____
Physical Stamina (Average Daily Need for Rest or Reclining) _____
_____

ENVIRONMENTAL INFLUENCE

Air Conditioning	Yes___ No___	_____
Heat	Yes___ No___	_____
Cold	Yes___ No___	_____
Wet/Humid	Yes___ No___	_____
Sudden Changes	Yes___ No___	_____
Inside	Yes___ No___	_____
Outside	Yes___ No___	_____
Fumes/Odors	Yes___ No___	_____
Noise	Yes___ No___	_____
Stress	Yes___ No___	_____

Other(s) _____

PRESENT MEDICAL TREATMENT

Doctor(s) _____
_____
_____
_____
_____

Treatment(s) _____

Date of Last Appointment _____

◄ *Clinical Interview & History for Pediatrics* ►

Medication _____ Purpose _____ Frequency _____

_____ _____ _____

_____ _____ _____

_____ _____ _____

Over-the-Counter Medication(s) _____

_____

ACTIVITIES OF DAILY LIVING

Arises _____ A.M. Retires _____ P.M. Average hours Sleep/24 Hours _____

Sleep Difficulties _____

Dresses Self	Yes___ No___	_____
Housework	Yes___ No___	_____
Cooking	Yes___ No___	_____
Laundry	Yes___ No___	_____
Yard Work	Yes___ No___	_____

Other(s) _____

_____

SOCIAL ACTIVITIES

Organizations _____

Church _____ Volunteer Work _____

Hobbies: Previous _____

Hobbies: Present _____

SOCIOECONOMIC STATUS

Number in Residence_____

Smoking in Environment?_____

Parents/Siblings_____

Disability Role Model(s)_____

Income:

Total Family Income: $_____

Estimated Monthly Expenses: $_____

S.S.D.I.	$_____	/_____
SSI	$_____	/_____
Other	$_____	/_____

◄ Clinical Interview & History for Pediatrics ►

OTHER AGENCY INVOLVEMENT

State Vocational Rehab	Yes____ No____	_____
State Employment Services	Yes____ No____	_____
Rehab Nurse(s)	Yes____ No____	_____
Other	Yes____ No____	_____

EDUCATION AND TRAINING

1 2 3 4 5 6 7 8 9 10 11 12 F S J SR Grad

Amount_____ Last School Attended_____

Trade/Technical Training_____

Apprenticeship/OJT_____

Other(s)_____

Read/Write_____ Licenses/Certification_____

BEHAVIORAL OBSERVATIONS

Orientation_____ Approach Toward Eval. - ± +

Stream of Thought_____ Concentration_____

Attitudes/Insight_____

Memory: Remote_____ Recent_____

VOCATIONAL TESTS

Check if to be administered:

SIT	_____	Others	_____
Gilmore/SORT	_____		_____
PENN/Crawford	_____		_____
Bayley	_____		_____
Vineland	_____		_____
Slosson Drawing	_____		_____
Adaptive Behavior	_____		

TENTATIVE REHAB PLAN

_____
_____
_____
_____
_____
_____

COMMENTS

_____
_____
_____
_____
_____
_____
_____
_____

◄ *Clinical Interview & History for Pediatrics* ►

SUPPLIES

TYPE/ITEM	SIZE	FREQUENCY OF REPLACEMENT	SUPPLIER	COST

◄ *Clinical Interview & History for Pediatrics* ►

EQUIPMENT

TYPE	DATE OF PURCHASE	PURCHASE PRICE	DEALER	CURRENT CONDITION

◄ *Clinical Interview & History for Pediatrics* ►

DEVELOPMENTAL DELAY

Seizure Disorder _____
_____
_____
_____
_____
_____
_____

Surgeries (Performed/Anticipated) _____
_____
_____
_____
_____
_____

Therapeutic/Educational Programs Since Onset _____
_____
_____
_____
_____
_____

Daily Care Needs & Level of Care Required: Skilled/Unskilled _____
_____
_____
_____
_____
_____
_____

◄ *Clinical Interview & History for Pediatrics* ►

I. MOTOR SKILLS

ABILITY TO:

_____ Bring Hands to Mid-Line _____

_____ Grasp: Left _____ Right _____ _____

_____ Grasp with Thumb and Forefinger _____

_____ Make Voluntary Purposeful Movements of Upper & Lower Extremities _____

_____

_____ Sit Unassisted _____

_____ Hold Head Erect _____ How Long? _____

_____ Roll Over _____

      Front to Back _____ Back to Front _____

_____ Pull Self-Upright _____

_____ Drink from Cup _____ Bottle _____ Tube Fed _____

_____ Stand _____

_____ Ambulate _____

_____ Assist in Dressing _____

_____ Perform Household Chores _____

_____ Perform Personal Hygiene _____

_____ Crawl _____

_____ Ascend/Descend Stairs _____

_____ Balance _____

◄ Clinical Interview & History for Pediatrics ►

II. SOCIAL SKILLS

ABILITY TO:

_____ Smile _____

_____ Laugh Out Loud _____

_____ Distinguish Family from Strangers _____

_____ Demand Personal Attention _____

III. COGNITIVE SKILLS

ABILITY TO:

_____ Imitate Sounds _____

_____ Talk in 1- or 2-Word Sentences _____

_____ Follow Simple 1- or 2-Step Instructions _____

_____ Avoid Hazards _____

_____ Communicate Wants and/or Needs _____

_____ Attention to Task _____

LONG-TERM CARE OPTIONS

Facitlity/Home Care _____

_____
_____
_____
_____
_____
_____
_____
_____

◄ Clinical Interview & History for Pediatrics ►

FAMILY HISTORY

	NAME	AGE	EDUCATION	MAJOR WORK HISTORY
CLIENT:				
FATHER:				
MOTHER:				
SIBLINGS:				
MATERNAL				
GRANDMOTHER:				
GRANDFATHER:				
AUNTS/UNCLES:				

◄ *Clinical Interview & History for Pediatrics* ►

FAMILY HISTORY

	NAME	AGE	EDUCATION	MAJOR WORK HISTORY
PATERNAL				
GRANDMOTHER:				
GRANDFATHER:				
AUNTS/UNCLES:				

Appendix G

File Check List for Testimony

A critical part of being prepared for any pre-deposition or pre-testimony conference, deposition testimony, or trial testimony is proper development of your file and medical information. The most effective approach is to create an in-office check list so that support staff can properly prepare files and you do not find yourself fumbling around during the course of conferencing or testimony appearing unprepared or as if you lacked knowledge and understanding of the case. Consistency of file organization is essential in resolving this problem.

The system recommended here provides for an administrative file separate from a three-ring notebook binder of all medical information. Each administrative file has four sections and consistency is maintained between administrative files as to how each section is organized so that the professional utilizing the file can always move quickly to the information necessary.

All medical, psychological, and rehabilitation reports from other sources are contained within three-ring notebook binders. They are separated with all duplicates pulled out and everything put in alphabetical order. Within each set of medicals (i.e., hospital records or physician reports) all information is put in chronological order. All records are separated by tabs appropriately identifying the source of the information.

Finally, an itinerary check list is completed usually by the secretary. This contains the client's name, the attorney's home phone number for any conferencing the night before testimony, the courtroom location including the room number and judge's name as well as case stylist, the attorney's address and telephone number, the information regarding appropriate arrangements that have been made for rental car, taxi cab, or air transportation.

The following file/testimony check list is recommended so that the support staff can make certain that all files are in proper order before conferencing their testimony:

Administrative File:

Section #1

___ Referral letter
___ Fee schedule
___ Referral sheet
___ Bills (all)
___ Reports & Vocational Worksheets
___ Medicals received sheet
___ Our correspondence

Section #2

___ Final medical summary
___ Intake forms
___ Equipment lists
___ Family history
___ Tests (make sure they belong to proper client)

Section #3

___ Source list
___ Progress notes
___ Release of information forms

◄ *File Checklist for Testimony Preparation* ►

Section #4

___ Attorney correspondence (in dated order)
___ Medicals (if no notebook)

Loose in File:

___ Life Care Plans (need to assess # of copies of Life Care Plans needed for trial)
___ Resumés
___ Other rehabilitation expert report/Life Care Plan
___ Any brochures on facilities and/or equipment

Notebooks:

___ Medicals in alphabetical order
___ All medicals checked against medical summary, medicals reviewed, and log-in sheet

Itinerary for Testimony:

___ Client's name
___ Attorney's home phone #
___ Courthouse location, room #, & judge's name
___ Attorney's address & telephone #
___ Rental car or cab
___ Airport location

Appendix H

Life Care Plan Shell

◄ *Life Care Plan Shell* ►

LIFE CARE PLAN

FOR

<u>NAME</u>

(Type of disability)

Paul M. Deutsch & Associates, P.A.

P. O. Box 6933

Orlando, Florida 32853

407/898-7710

◂ *Life Care Plan Shell* ▸

LIFE CARE PLAN
Projected Evaluations

Paul M. Deutsch & Associates, P.A.
P. O. Box 6933
Orlando, Florida 32853

Client Name _____
Date of Birth _____
Date of Accident _____
Date Prepared _____

Evaluation	Age/Year at Which Initiated	Age/Year at Which Suspended	Frequency	Base Cost Per Year	Growth Trend	Recommended By

◀ *Life Care Plan Shell* ▶

LIFE CARE PLAN
Projected Therapeutic Modalities

Client Name _____
Date of Birth _____
Date of Accident _____
Date Prepared _____
Growth Trend _____ Recommended By

Paul M. Deutsch & Associates, P.A.
P. O. Box 6933
Orlando, Florida 32853

Therapy	Age/Year at Which Initiated	Age/Year at Which Suspended	Treatment Frequency	Base Cost Per Year	

Paul M. Deutsch & Associates, P.A.
P. O. Box 6933
Orlando, Florida 32853

LIFE CARE PLAN
Diagnostic Testing/Educational Assessment

Client Name _____
Date of Birth _____
Date of Accident _____
Date Prepared _____

Diagnostic Recommendation	Age/Year at Which Initiated	Age/Year at Which Suspended	Per Year Frequency	Base Cost Per Year	Growth Trend	Recommended By

◄ Life Care Plan Shell ►

◄ *Life Care Plan Shell* ►

LIFE CARE PLAN
Wheelchair Needs

Wheelchair Type	Age/Year at Which Purchased	Replacement Schedule	Purpose of Equipment	Base Cost	Growth Trend	Catalog or Supplier Reference

Client Name _____
Date of Birth _____
Date of Accident _____
Date Prepared _____

Paul M. Deutsch & Associates, P.A.
P. O. Box 6933
Orlando, Florida 32853

LIFE CARE PLAN
Wheelchair Accessories and Maintenance

Paul M. Deutsch & Associates, P.A.
P. O. Box 6933
Orlando, Florida 32853

Client Name _____
Date of Birth _____
Date of Accident _____
Date Prepared _____

Wheelchair Accessory	Age/Year at Which Purchased	Replacement Schedule	Purpose	Base Cost	Growth Trend	Catalog or Supplier Reference

◀ *Life Care Plan Shell* ▶

LIFE CARE PLAN
Orthotics/Prosthetics

Paul M. Deutsch & Associates, P.A.

P. O. Box 6933

Orlando, Florida 32853

Client Name _____
Date of Birth _____
Date of Accident _____
Date Prepared _____
Recommended By _____

Equipment Description	Age/Year at Which Purchased	Replacement Schedule	Base Cost	Growth Trend	Other

LIFE CARE PLAN
Orthopedic Equipment Needs

Paul M. Deutsch & Associates, P.A.
P. O. Box 6933
Orlando, Florida 32853

Client Name _____
Date of Birth _____
Date of Accident _____
Date Prepared _____

Equipment Description	Age/Year at Which Purchased	Replacement Schedule	Equipment Purpose	Base Cost	Growth Trend	Catalog or Supplier Reference

◄ *Life Care Plan Shell* ►

LIFE CARE PLAN
Home Furnishings and Accessories

Paul M. Deutsch & Associates, P.A.
P. O. Box 6933
Orlando, Florida 32853

Client Name _____
Date of Birth _____
Date of Accident _____
Date Prepared _____

Equipment Description	Age/Year at Which Purchased	Replacement Schedule	Equipment Purpose	Base Cost	Growth Trend	Catalog or Supplier Reference

◄ *Life Care Plan Shell* ►

LIFE CARE PLAN
Aids for Independent Function

Client Name _____
Date of Birth _____
Date of Accident _____
Date Prepared _____

Equipment	Age/Year at Which Purchased	Replacement Schedule	Equipment Purpose	Base Cost	Growth Trend	Catalog or Supplier Reference

Paul M. Deutsch & Associates, P.A.
P. O. Box 6933
Orlando, Florida 32853

◄ *Life Care Plan Shell* ►

LIFE CARE PLAN
Drug/Supply Needs

Paul M. Deutsch & Associates, P.A.
P. O. Box 6933
Orlando, Florida 32853

Supply Description / Drug (Prescription)	Purpose	Per Unit Cost	Per Year Cost	Growth Trend

Client Name _____
Date of Birth _____
Date of Accident _____
Date Prepared _____
Recommended By _____

Life Care Plan Shell

LIFE CARE PLAN
Home/Facility Care

Paul M. Deutsch & Associates, P.A.
P. O. Box 6933
Orlando, Florida 32853

Client Name _____
Date of Birth _____
Date of Accident _____
Date Prepared _____
Base Cost Per Year _____

Facility Recommendation	Home Care/Service Recommendations	Age/Year at Which Initiated	Age/Year at Which Suspended	Hours/Shifts/Days of Attendance or Care	Growth Trends

469

LIFE CARE PLAN
Future Medical Care - Routine

Paul M. Deutsch & Associates, P.A.
P. O. Box 6933
Orlando, Florida 32853

Client Name _____
Date of Birth _____
Date of Accident _____
Date Prepared _____

Routine Medical Care Description	Frequency Of Visits	Purpose	Cost Per Visit	Cost Per Year	Growth Trends	Recommended By

◀ *Life Care Plan Shell* ▶

LIFE CARE PLAN
Future Medical Care
Surgical Intervention or
Aggressive Treatment Plan

Paul M. Deutsch & Associates, P.A.

P.O Box 6933

Orlando, Florida 32853

Client Name _____

Date of Birth _____

Date of Accident _____

Date Prepared _____

Recommendation (Description)	Age/Year Initiated	Frequency of Procedure	Per Procedure Cost	Per Year Cost	Growth Trend	Recommended By

◀ *Life Care Plan Shell* ▶

LIFE CARE PLAN
Potential Complications

Client Name _____
Date of Birth _____
Date of Accident _____
Date Prepared _____

FOR INFORMATION ONLY. NO PREDICTION OF FREQUENCY OF OCCURRENCE AVAILABLE.

Complication						Estimated Costs			Growth Trend

Paul M. Deutsch & Associates, P.A.
P. O. Box 6933
Orlando, Florida 32853

◄ *Life Care Plan Shell* ►

LIFE CARE PLAN
Transportation

Client Name _____
Date of Birth _____
Date of Accident _____
Date Prepared _____

Equipment Description	Age/Year at Which Purchased	Replacement Schedule	Equipment Purpose	Base Cost	Growth Trend	Catalog or Supplier Reference

Paul M. Deutsch & Associates, P.A.
P. O. Box 6933
Orlando, Florida 32853

◄ *Life Care Plan Shell* ►

Paul M. Deutsch & Associates, P.A.
P. O. Box 6933
Orlando, Florida 32853

LIFE CARE PLAN
Architectural Renovations

Client Name _____
Date of Birth _____
Date of Accident _____
Date Prepared _____

Accessibility Needs	Accessibility Needs	Costs
Ramping	Bathroom	
Light/Environmental Controls	Sink	
Floor Coverings	Cabinets	
Hallways	Roll-in Shower	
Doorways	Temperature Control Guards	
Covered Parking	Heater	
Kitchen	Fixtures	
Sinks/Fixtures	Door Handles	
Cabinets	Additional Electrical Outlets	
Appliances	Central Heat/Air	
Windows	Therapy/Equipment Storage	
Electric Safety Doors	Attendant Bedroom	
Fire Alarm	Other	
Smoke Detectors		
Intercom System		

◀ *Life Care Plan Shell* ▶

Paul M. Deutsch & Associates, P.A.
P. O. Box 6933
Orlando, Florida 32853

LIFE CARE PLAN
Leisure Time and/or Recreational Equipment

Client Name _____
Date of Birth _____
Date of Accident _____
Date Prepared _____

Equipment Description	Special Camps or Programs	Age/Year of Purchase or Attendance	Replacement or Attendance Schedule	Base Cost	Growth Trend	Catalog or Supplier Reference

Index

A

Activities of Daily Living, questions on, for deposing injured party, 398
Adult development program in life care plan for pediatric brain injury, 207-208
Annuity program in personal injury settlement, 323-332. *See also* Structured settlement
Appearance, personal, for presentation by defense RHE, 23-24
Attorneys, deposing injured party by, questions for, 393-401

B

Back, chronic, syndrome of, trial testimony on, 85-95
Bayley Scales of Infant Development in pediatric brain injury evaluation, 82-84
Behavior modification in life care plan for late adolescent head injury, 241-243, 300-302
  protocols for, 251-255
Behavioral observation, questions on, for deposing injured party, 400-401
Brain injury
  clinical interview and history for, 417-436
  late adolescent, testimony on, 229-303
  pediatric, from birth, trial testimony on, 77-84, 187-229
Burnout in care of head injured client, 248-249

C

Case management, 184
  family education for, in life care plan for late adolescent head injury, 246-247
Case manager in life care plan for late adolescent head injury, 249-250, 289-291
Catastrophic injury
  case of
    economic loss assessment in, 316-320
    presentation of, 183-303
      for late adolescent head injury, transcript of, 229-303
      for pediatric brain damage from birth, transcript of, 187-229
    questions for, 389-392
  definition of, 61-62, 183

Catastrophic -- *continued*
   early consultation with rehabilitation expert for, 27, 28
Chronic back/chronic pain syndrome, trial testimony on, 85-95
Chronic pain/chronic disability syndrome
   clinical interview and history for, 403-416
   trial testimony on
     from defense referral, 151-181
         conclusions in, 170-181
         data gathering in, 153-155
         evaluation in, 155-166
         interpretation in, 161-165
         test procedures in, 161-162
     from plaintiff referral, 100-151
         conclusions in, 132-151
         evaluation in, 102-120
         interpretation in, 120-132
         test procedures in, 122-125, 134-135
Chronic pain syndrome, early consultation with rehabilitation expert for, 27-28
Client
   discouraged, early consultation with rehabilitation expert for, 27-28
   evaluation of, by defense RHE, 14, 16
   explanation of rehabilitation expert's role to
     in courtroom, 5-6
     in litigation, 3-5
     outside courtroom, 7-8
   introduction of rehabilitation expert to, 2
   living with, in trial preparation, 35
Collateral source, ethical situation involving, 12-13
Conclusions
   in chronic pain/chronic disability presentation, 132-151, 170-181
   for non-catastrophic case, 99-100
Consultant in litigation, rehabilitation professional as, 4
Costs in life care plan for pediatric brain injury, 216-218
Courtroom
   role of rehabilitation professional in, 5-6
   role of rehabilitation professional outside, 7-8
Credibility of defense RHE during presentation, 19-20
Cross-examination
   goals of, 44-45
   of plaintiff attorney, surprise, avoiding, 39-40

D

Data gathering
   in chronic pain/chronic disability presentation, 101-102, 153-155

Data gathering -- *continued*
  in late adolescent brain injury, testimony on, 230
  presentation of, transcript of, 78, 81-82, 86
  representation of, 74-75
Defense attorney
  examination of qualifications of rehabilitation expert by, transcripts of, 56-72
  rehabilitation expert utilization by, 9-24. *See also* Rehabilitation expert, defense's
Demeanor for presentation by defense RHE, 23-24
Deposition
  of defense RHE by plaintiff's counsel, 17
  of injured party, questions for attorneys to use in, 393-401
Disability, chronic, syndrome of, trial testimony on
  from defense referral, 151-181
  from plaintiff referral, 100-151
Disabling problem, questions on, for deposing injured party, 395-397
Discovery, defense utilization of rehabilitation expert in, 14-18

E

Earning capacity, diminution of
  calculation of, evolution of, 306-307
  conclusions on, in non-catastrophic case, 100
  in late adolescent brain injury, 271-273, 293-294
  in non-catastrophic injury case, analysis of
    using pre-accident earnings history, 311-313
    without pre-accident earnings history, 313-314
  in pediatric brain injury, 218-223
Earnings growth rate in economic loss assessment, 307-308
Economic analysis and vocational rehabilitation to assess economic losses in personal injury situations, 305-321
Economic losses in personal injury situations. *See also* Earning capacity, diminution of
  assessment of
    in catastrophic injury cases, 316-320
    in non-catastrophic injury cases, 311-316
    scientific, evolution of, 306-310
    vocational rehabilitation and economic analysis in, 305-321
Economics consultant in economic loss assessment, 310-311
Education
  of family in case management in life care plan for late adolescent head injury, 246 247
  of judge on evaluation procedures, questions for, 383-385
  of jury
    on evaluation procedures, questions for, 383-385
    on rehabilitation procedures, 76-95
    rehabilitation professional in, 6

Education -- *continued*
   of parent in life care plan for pediatric brain injury, 203
   questions on, for deposing injured party, 400
Educational testing in life care plan for pediatric brain injury, 205-206
Educator of jury, rehabilitation professional as, 6
Employment history, questions on, for deposing injured party, 400
Environmental influences, questions on, for deposing injured party, 397-398
Evaluation
   in chronic pain/chronic disability presentation, 102-120, 155-166
   defense utilization of rehabilitation expert in, 18-19
   in late adolescent brain injury, testimony on, 231-232, 234-238
   presentation of, 73-74
      transcript of, 77-79, 81-84, 85-91
   procedures for, educating judge/jury on, questions for, 383-385
Expenses for rehabilitation expert's services, 38-39
Expertise, limits of, presenting, 46-47

F

Family counseling in life care plan for pediatric brain injury, 200-203
Family education in case management in life care plan for late adolescent head injury, 246-247
Family support in life care plan
   for late adolescent brain injury, 248-249, 260-263, 292-293, 296
   for pediatric brain injury, 190-193
Fees for rehabilitation expert's services, 38-39
File, reviewing, working with rehabilitation expert in, 33-37

G

Gain, secondary, in chronic pain/chronic disability presentation, 108, 131-132
Gilmore reading test in chronic pain/chronic disability presentation, 161

H

Halstead Booklet Category test in chronic pain/chronic disability presentation, 161
Handicaps, vocational, conclusions on, in non-catastrophic case, 99
Head injury. *See* Brain injury

Home facility care in life care plan
   for late adolescent head injury, options on, 257-264, 292-293, 296-298
   for pediatric brain injury, 213

◄ *Index* ►

Hypothetical questions, defense RHE and, 18

I

Income opportunity, loss of. *See also* Earning capacity, diminution of
   in late adolescent head injury, 271-273, 293-294
   in pediatric brain injury, 218-223
Interpretation in chronic pain/chronic disability presentation, 120-132, 161-165
Investigation, defense utilization of rehabilitation expert in, 10-14
Investigative rehabilitation/habilitation expert, 10-14
Ischemic Pain Test in chronic pain/chronic disability presentation, 144-145

J

Judge, education of, on evaluation procedures, questions for, 383-385
Jury, education of
   on evaluation procedures, questions for, 383-385
   on rehabilitation procedures, 76-95
   rehabilitation professional in, 6

L

Labor market
   loss of access to
      conclusions on, in non-catastrophic case, 99
      in late adolescent brain injury, 271-273, 293-294
      in pediatric brain injury, 218-223
   placement potential in, conclusions on, in non-catastrophic case, 99
Life care plan
   concept of, 183-184
   cross examination on, 223-229
   development of, 33-34
      in late adolescent brain injury, testimony on, 232-234
      in pediatric brain injury, testimony on, 187-195
      qualifications for, 184-186
   form for, 457-474
   implications of, 184
   presentation of, 37, 186-187
      in late adolescent brain injury
         cross examination on, 273-295
         redirect examination on, 295-303
         testimony on, 240-303
      in pediatric brain injury, testimony on, 193-216

Life care plan -- *continued*
  purpose of, 80-81
  sample, 330
  sample analysis of, 331
Life expectancy in life care plan for late adolescent head injury, 264-266
Litigation, role of rehabilitation professional in, 3-5

M

Maintenance, rehabilitation versus, 52-53
Malingering in chronic pain/chronic disability presentation, 145
Medical care, current, questions on, for deposing injured party, 398
Minnesota Multiphasic Personality Inventory (MMPI) in chronic pain/chronic
    disability presentation, 108, 122-125, 129-130, 134-135, 141, 143, 145, 150, 162

N

Neuropsychological evaluation in life care plan for late adolescent head injury, 241-
    242, 287-288
Non-catastrophic injury case
  economic loss assessment in, 311-316
    rehabilitation cost in, 314-316
    using pre-accident earnings history, 311-313
    without pre-accident earnings history, 313-314
  occupational analysis for, 98-99
  presentation of, 97-181
    conclusions for, 99-100
    transcript of
      from defense referral, 151-181
      from plaintiff referral, 100-151
    wage data research for, 98-99
  questions for, 387-388

O

Occupational analysis for non-catastrophic case, 98-99
Occupational therapist, role of, 196-197

P

Pain, chronic, syndrome of, trial testimony on, 85-95
  from defense referral, 151-181

Pain, chronic, syndrome of, trial testimony on -- *continued*
    from plaintiff referral, 100-151
Parent education in life care plan for pediatric brain injury, 203
Pediatric brain injury from birth, trial testimony on, 77-84, 187-229
Pediatric injury, clinical interview and history for, 437-452
Phase change in life care plan for pediatric brain injury, 190
Philosophical focus for rehabilitation professional, 373-375
Physical limitations, questions on, for deposing injured party, 397
Physical therapy in life care plan for late adolescent head injury, 244-246, 288-289
Plaintiff attorney, rehabilitation expert of. *See also* Rehabilitation expert, plaintiff's
Presentation, defense utilization of rehabilitation expert in, 19-24
Professional, rehabilitation. *See* Rehabilitation expert
Psychological reaction, early consultation with rehabilitation expert for, 27-28
Public Law 94-142 in life care plan for pediatric brain injury, 188, 199, 206

Q

Qualification
    goals of, 43-44
    of rehabilitation expert
        plaintiff attorney's, 50-56
        questions for, 377-381

R

Rehabilitation, maintenance versus, 52-53
Rehabilitation expert
    in catastrophic cases, 30
    defense's
        in discovery, 14-18
        in evaluation, 18-19
        in investigation, 10-14
        in presentation, 19-24
        purpose of, 9-10
        in settlement, 18-19
        testimony of, on adult chronic pain/chronic disability case, 151-181
    examination of qualifications of, by defense attorney, transcripts of, 56-72
    introduction of, 2
    investigative, 10-14
    in life care plan for pediatric brain injury, 204
    philosophical focus for, 373-375
    plaintiff's
        background of, to avoid surprise cross-examination, 39-40
        identification of, by defense investigative RHE, 12, 15

Rehabilitation expert -- *continued*
    in non-catastrophic cases, 29-30
    presentation and qualification of, transcripts of, 50-56
    selection criteria for, 26-27
    testimony of, on adult chronic pain/chronic disability case, 100-151
    utilization of, pros and cons of, 38-41
    working with, in reviewing file and preparing for trial, 33-37
  presentation of, by plaintiff attorney, transcripts of, 56-72
  qualification of
    by plaintiff attorney, transcripts of, 56-72
    questions for, 377-381
  responsibility of, in Voir Dire process, 45-47
  role of
    in courtroom, 5-6
    dual, 1-8
    in litigation, 3-5
    outside courtroom, 7-8
    presenting, 47-49
  utilizing of
    defense attorney's perspective on, 9-24
    plaintiff attorney's perspective on, 25-42
  as witness, timing of, 27-29
Rehabilitation plan, implementation of, evaluation of, 40-41
Rehabilitation program(s)
  local, evaluation of, by defense investigative RHE, 13
  selection of, plaintiff's rehabilitation expert in, 30-33
Rehearsal for presentation by defense RHE, 22
Report on plaintiff evaluation by defense RHE, 16-17
Resource person, rehabilitation professional as, 7

S

Secondary gain in chronic pain/chronic disability presentation, 108, 131-132
Settlement
  defense utilization of rehabilitation expert in, 18-19
  structured, 323-332. *See also* Structured settlement
Situational stress deficits in chronic pain/chronic disability presentation, 138-139
Slosson Intelligence Test in chronic pain/chronic disability presentation, 161
Social activities, questions on, for deposing injured party, 399
Socioeconomic status, questions on, for deposing injured party, 399
Spinal cord injury, clinical interview and history for, 417-436
Stress
  situational, deficits from, in chronic pain/chronic disability presentation, 138-139
  in testimony, reducing, steps to, 373-375
Structured settlement, 323-332

Structured settlement -- *continued*
  advantages of, 325-327
  definition of, 323-325
  parties to, 324
  premium costs of life contingent benefits in, 328
  program design for, 327-328
  sample, 332
  security of, 328-329

T

Test procedures
  in chronic pain/chronic disability presentation, 122-125, 134-135, 161-162
  presentation of, 75-76
    transcript of, 77-78, 82-84
Testimony
  file check list for, 453-455
  sequence of, 36
  stress in, reducing, steps to, 373-375
Time value of money in economic loss assessment, 308
Training, questions on, for deposing injured party, 400
Trial, preparing for, working with rehabilitation expert in, 33-37

V

Verbal skills for presentation by defense RHE, 23
Vocational handicaps, conclusions on, in non-catastrophic case, 99
Vocational loss, cost of. *See also* Earning capacity, diminution of; Economic losses in personal injury situations
  in late adolescent head injury, 271-273, 293-294
  in pediatric brain injury, 218-223
Vocational rehabilitation and economic analysis to assess economic losses in personal injury situations, 305-321
Vocational rehabilitation consultant in economic loss assessment, 310-311
Vocational rehabilitation plan, conclusions on, in non-catastrophic case, 99-100
Voir Dire
  expert's responsibility in, 45-47
  goals of, 43-44
    opposing counsel's, 44-45

W

Wage data research for non-catastrophic case, 98-99

◄ *Index* ►

Wahler Physical Symptoms Inventory in chronic pain/chronic disability presentation, 135
Whiteley Index in chronic pain/chronic disability presentation, 135
Witness, plaintiff's rehabilitation expert as, timing of selection of, 27-29